BRIDGING MULTIPLE WORLDS

BRIDGING MULTIPLE WORLDS

Case Studies of Diverse Educational Communities

LORRAINE S. TAYLOR

State University of New York at New Paltz

CATHARINE R. WHITTAKER

State University of New York at New Paltz

Boston ■ New York ■ San Francisco
Mexico City ■ Montreal ■ Toronto ■ London ■ Madrid ■ Munich ■ Paris
Hong Kong ■ Singapore ■ Tokyo ■ Cape Town ■ Sydney

Vice President: *Paul A. Smith*
Series Editor: *Traci Mueller*
Marketing Manager: *Elizabeth Fogarty*
Editorial Production Service: *Whitney Acres Editorial*
Manufacturing Buyer: *Andrew Turso*
Cover Administrator: *Kristina Mose-Libon*
Electronic Composition: *Omegatype Typography, Inc.*

For related titles and support materials, visit our online catalog at
www.ablongman.com

Between the time Website information is gathered and published, some sites may
have closed. Also, the transcription of URLs can result in typographical errors. The
publisher would appreciate notification where these occur so that they may be
corrected in subsequent editions.

Library of Congress Cataloging-in-Publication Data

Data not available at the time of publication.
ISBN: 0-321-08669-4

Printed in the United States of America

10   9   8   7   6   5   08   07   06   05

For my grandparents, George and Mary Louise Wesley,
and for my mother, Ida Mae Young

L. S. T.

For my husband, William S. Whittaker

C. R. W.

CONTENTS

■ ■ ■ ■ ■

THE PURPOSE AND CONTENT OF THE BOOK

Our major purpose in writing this book is to help to prepare preservice and in-service teachers to successfully teach students from diverse backgrounds. We are interested, first, in helping teachers to understand the critical issues related to diversity in the society and briefly introducing them to relevant research. However, we expect that instructors will use other sources in multicultural education to supplement our overview. Additionally, we hope to help teachers to become skilled decision makers who reflect on their practices and approach problems from a comprehensive perspective in order to arrive at long-term solutions. We have found that using case studies is an effective vehicle for bridging the gap between the real world of students in classrooms and the university setting. We believe that cases taken from schools and classrooms, involving authentic teachers, students, and their families, provide the most honest and effective learning experiences. Cases that present the complex, multiple worlds of children give preservice and in-service teachers the opportunity to appreciate the complexity of issues that arise and to apply a decision-making approach that ensures long-term solutions. Finally, our third objective is to assist teacher educators in their crucial role in preparing teachers who will commit themselves to equity and equality in their services to students.

We have developed a series of authentic case studies for this textbook that involves real students, teachers, families, and community members from different backgrounds as an effective approach to understanding the issues involved in educating an increasingly diverse student population. The cases raise some of the most urgent issues in diversity that challenge every school system across the country. They will stimulate the processes of reflection and decision making that are central for those who will successfully teach our school-aged children and adolescents. Although we do not provide solutions to the problems or issues in the cases, we believe that they reflect guiding principles that lead to comprehensive, long-term solutions to the complex situations.

In addition to the cases, we have included background information on important aspects of the issues involved in each case. Chapter 1 discusses immigration trends, our meaning of diversity, and the new metaphors for the American society. Chapter 2 outlines the current state of education as it relates to diverse student populations, discusses various approaches to multicultural education, and describes the preparation of teachers for diverse students. Chapter 3 discusses the multiple worlds of school, home, and community that students must negotiate and offers suggestions for helping students and teachers to bridge these worlds in the classroom. Chapter 4 details the benefits of using cases in teacher education programs and presents a decision-making scaffold that can be used as a guide when reading and discussing the cases in class, and Chapter 5 presents a model case and the process for using the decision-making scaffold. Twelve individual cases then follow in Chapters 6 through 11, each preceded by essential background information.

The cases that we present represent difficult and complex issues that educators, families, and community members have had to confront in the educational arena. Our purpose in sharing these cases is to offer specific situations in which attitudes, understandings, approaches, and policies must be radically altered in order for the students involved to have positive educational experiences. In reviewing these cases, you should not in any way infer that because we present problematic cases we sanction the attitudes and actions of those we describe. Rather, we hope that by carefully moving through the decision-making process described in Chapter 4 you will learn how to identify alternative values and actions in working with students and their families. Such alternative values and actions are clearly delineated in a comprehensive view of multicultural education. Sleeter and Grant (1999) and Banks and Banks (1995), among other researchers, have contributed immensely to our understanding of multicultural education by synthesizing the research and theory related to diversity and schooling and delineating the various approaches to multicultural education. We will address these approaches in Chapter 2.

ACKNOWLEDGMENTS

Writing a book of authentic case studies is a process that involves the expertise, cooperation, good will, patience, and time of many individuals. First, we want to acknowledge the kindness of many colleagues who offered their professional wisdom. Lee Bell, Joyce Bickerstaff, Sue Books, Margaret Gutierrez, Elaine Hofstetter, Spencer Salend, and Barbara Simmons who were generous in offering resources and support. Second, we are deeply indebted to the many individual teachers, administrators, staff, and families who welcomed us into their schools, communities, and lives so that we could tell their stories. In particular, we want to acknowledge Denise Bernstein, Maureen DeHaan, Aida DeQuarto, Jane Eakins, Cecily S. Frazier, Rosibel Gonzalez, Francis Gorleski, Raka Gulati, Liaquat Ali Khan, Cyndy Knapp, Erin McGurgen, Ted W. Petersen, Linda Stevens, Lyn Umble, Mana Watsky, and Dennis Yerry. In addition, it is important to recognize the many students in the SUNY New Paltz School of Education who have taught us the value of using teaching cases in teacher preparation and who have given us the opportunity to refine the process of writing and discussing cases. Furthermore, we are extremely grateful for the encouragement and expertise of our reviewers: Dr. Blidi Stemm, Northeastern University; Pamela Taylor, University of Southern Indiana; and Michelle Vandervelde Woodfork, University of Washington, Seattle, and our editor, Traci Mueller. Finally, we would like to thank our families for their continual support, encouragement, and sustenance throughout the writing of this book.

FOREWORD

We write the final pages of this book in the weeks immediately following the suicide plane crashes of September 11, 2001, in New York City, Washington, D.C., and southwestern Pennsylvania. The victims of this horrific tragedy came from more than 40 nations, included members of every social class and economic status, represented all major religious groups, and encompassed both genders and all age categories. When confronted with such a reality, we are reminded of John Donne's somber words, "Do not ask for whom the bell tolls. It tolls for thee."

The State University of New York at New Paltz is located within a 100-mile radius of Ground Zero. Each conversation with students, faculty, staff, family, and friends yields new stories of life and death, heroism and tragedy, horror and hope. As we struggle for sanity and understanding in the midst of destruction and confusion, there seem to be many unanswered questions, but the following seem to be on everyone's mind. People repeatedly ask, "How did this happen?" "How could they hate us so much?" "What should we do?" To date, the answers that we have to these questions are far from satisfying. One statement that all seem to agree on is that "this changes everything."

The degree to which the world will change is, at this time, hard to imagine. Yet already major alterations of policy are occurring in governmental and economic arenas, with equally dramatic changes predicted in other fields such as health and education. We hope that we will not experience increasing intolerance of the "other." We believe that the focus of this casebook, understanding diversity, will only become more important as we all seek to make wise decisions for ourselves and for future generations on Earth.

In times like these we cling to the hope that we have learned from the past, that we value high moral principles, and that we have the wisdom to make good decisions for the future of the United States and the world. This book suggests a decision-making process that includes understanding, tolerance, clarification, and deliberation and that ultimately leads to social action. As we listen to the questions that permeate our society and declarations about what should be done, it seems that we no longer have the luxury of talking about what *they* should do to address the political, racial, educational, medical, religious, and economic problems of this century. We must ask ourselves what *we* are willing to do or, if we lack the ability, what we can in good conscience ask those we love and respect to do. Our commitment to a just, peaceful, and inclusive society and world will determine the direction, degree, and extent to which "this changes everything."

One of the greatest challenges facing American schools today is the ability of educators to successfully teach students from a wider variety of backgrounds that differ from their own. The knowledge, attitudes, and skills required of teachers as we enter the 21st century will include understanding the important issues associated with diversity in race and ethnicity, culture and language, religion, gender, and ability. Although the United States has always been a diverse nation in which immigrants from many different origins have settled, the character of this diversity has changed. In addition to new patterns of immigration, changes in society's values and customs have intensified the presence of previously oppressed groups who, inspired by the civil rights movement, also demand inclusion in the mainstream. These groups include persons of different sexual orientation, persons with disabilities, and females. Although the country was founded by those fleeing religious persecution, the increasing diversity of religious groups is also challenging organizational norms in the society.

THE MEANING OF DIVERSITY

A standard dictionary defines the term *diversity* as "the state or fact of being diverse; difference; unlikeness; variety " (*Webster's New Universal Unabridged Dictionary*, 1994). However, researchers in the area of multicultural education have chosen to focus on areas of diversity depending on their views of the importance of each area. In this text, we discuss diversity in race and ethnicity or skin color, socioeconomic level, culture and language, exceptionalities, gender, sexual orientation, and religion since these areas are associated with important issues for students and their teachers in the public schools. These issues are involved in the case studies that follow. Knowledgeable teachers with appropriate skills and attitudes can help all students to bridge their multiple worlds of home, school, and community and successfully engage in essential learning experiences (Phelan & Davidson, 1995).

The New Metaphor

Immigrants to the United States have historically assimilated into the mainstream society, replacing their language and culture of origin with the English language and Eurocentric culture of white America (Novak, 1972). According to Spindler and Spindler (1990), this culture has been characterized by fluency in English with a nativelike oral skill and internalization of the values traditionally viewed as American. Thus, fluency in English and the adoption of values such as equality, honesty, and the work ethic, coupled with clear goals and meaningful participation in American society, have been assumed by immigrants who wish to assimilate (Novak, 1972).

However, changes in the national rhetoric as well as more recent emphasis by educators on intercultural and multicultural education have resulted in "a context ostensibly more accommodating of cultural diversity than the contexts of the past" (Fuchs, 1995, p. 313). Certainly, this view is far from universal in U.S. society. Nevertheless, the encouragement of ethnic consciousness and diversity has contributed to the rise of cultural pluralism, and new metaphors are replacing the "melting pot." *Salad bowl, mosaic,* and *tapestry* are examples of new terms to describe a population in which one's culture and language of origin are maintained and valued, adding to the overall richness of the society, while the individual also participates in the mainstream culture. Ideally, the immigrant becomes bicultural and is able to enjoy both the culture of origin and the mainstream culture of the United States.

We prefer the metaphor of a *kaleidoscope,* an image that is enduring, yet constantly changing. Each piece is self-contained, colorful, and unique, yet contributes to the overall beauty and richness of the whole. Pieces are not permanently placed as in a mosaic, but are constantly reconstituting themselves. A kaleidoscope changes its configuration each time it is moved, just as individuals can change their attitudes and beliefs as they come in contact with new cultural groups. Thus, we view the many diverse cultures that make up the society like a kaleidoscope.

AUTHORS' STATEMENT OF PHILOSOPHY

It is important to understand the authors' belief system regarding the approach that teachers and the broader society should take regarding educating students from diverse backgrounds. First, we oppose any thinking that assumes that various groups must be assimilated into the mainstream of society and forced to abandon cultural and linguistic or other core values and practices. The mainstream of society, whether it is represented in an individual classroom or school or a national social organization, must be redesigned to meet the diversity of the children and adults within this society. This is an ongoing process. Although resources are presently inadequate, teachers must receive an education that provides the necessary knowledge about issues of diversity, challenges attitudes that support the status quo, and offers the skills that are crucial for change.

Second, we believe that both teachers and students need to discuss issues involving interpersonal relations and to come to an awareness of their own identity and an understanding of their commonality with one another, regardless of personal characteristics. Racism, classism, homophobia, and other prejudices threaten the very fabric of our society and must be decried. However, many prejudices remain at the unconscious level. Educators must help students to know and experience the dissonance inherent in becoming aware of the privileges that some groups enjoy, often at the expense of other groups. Because of age and background, some people are much further along in this process than others, so we must be patient with one another while promoting such awareness.

Third, we believe there is a need to continually examine the school curriculum so that all racial and ethnic, gender, language, socioeconomic, ability, and religious groups in our pluralistic society are included and affirmed. Authentic voices of representatives of these groups must be heard. Such a curriculum should allow students to recognize that, at times, intragroup differences can be greater than intergroup differences.

Fourth, we believe that instruction should be designed with multiple learning styles and multiple intelligences in mind, with high and equitable expectations for all students and with consideration of students' prior knowledge and the development of cooperative and social skills as well as academic skills.

Fifth, we firmly believe that positive school–home–community relationships are critical to all successful educational programs. An understanding of the multiple worlds of students' homes, school, and community and the possible dissonance that occurs as they move among these worlds is necessary for all educators. Families must be welcomed, listened to, and involved in the schools.

Sixth, we believe that the underrepresentation of teachers of color in the teaching profession is a serious problem that must be corrected. Likewise, both genders should be equitably represented on the elementary and secondary levels and in administrative positions. Students need role models from their own groups who will understand their particular backgrounds. This is a complex problem that will involve the joint efforts of government, teacher education institutions, public schools, and community groups.

Finally, we believe that schools should prepare citizens to work toward social justice, equity, and equal opportunity. Teachers can accomplish this by organizing curricula around issues such as the meaning of democracy, justice, compassion, and community. Furthermore, teaching critical and reflective thinking and social action skills must be accomplished in collaboration with parents and the community.

In many schools, teachers will need to assume leadership in school-wide reform where major changes are needed in curriculum and school organization. They will need to "speak up about conditions that limit their effectiveness and policies that restrain positive momentum. This means engaging in continuous professional developmental [and] comporting themselves as professional educators who know what is best for students" (Baumgartner, 2000, p. 24). Other researchers support this view: "School wide reform requires a new vision of professionalism, where teachers assume a major role and responsibility for the schools"(Bodilly cited in Desimone, 2000, p. 24). And, in the words of Muncey and McQuillan (1996), "professional development is at the heart of school change efforts" (p. 1).

There is agreement among many educators that "it is no longer viable for one person to act as the school-level authority" (Vasquez-Levy & Timmerman, 2000, p. 363). Teachers are a vital agent in school-wide reform and can provide important leadership in the identification and solution of school-wide problems. Others have noted that teachers can "navigate the structure of schools, nurture relationships, model professional growth, help others with change and challenge the status quo by raising students' voices as well" (Silva, Gimbert, & Nolan, 2000, p. 78).

However, principals must play a major role in developing teacher leadership. They must identify, develop, and support the teacher leaders in their schools, define teacher leadership, be comfortable with teachers as leaders, and encourage teachers to become leaders and develop their leadership skills (Buckner & McDowelle, 2000). In addition, principals will need to provide feedback that is constructive and limited. In other words, principals must "create the infrastructure to support teacher-leadership roles" (Childs-Bowen, Moller, & Scrivner, 2000, p. 28). Principals need to create opportunities for teacher leadership, build professional learning communities, and celebrate innovation and teacher expertise (Childs-Bowen et al., 2000).

For social actions to be successful, there must be a consensus among those involved regarding values held in common. Stakeholders involved in schools must take the time to clearly establish which goals are possible, given mutually shared values. Working for justice is a long and arduous path, and many have faltered along the way once they understood the implications for their own lives of the values that they claim to espouse. Furthermore, even when values are held in common, the time, resources, and emotional skills that each person brings are limited. Given the immensity of the task, there is a need to develop and nurture patience, perseverance, personal responsibility, understanding, forgiveness, and caring as educators thoughtfully make decisions about individuals and the collective action to be undertaken.

Finally, we must recognize that teaching is a moral endeavor. Educators must learn to identify their own spiritual values and ethics before they can understand or guide others. While it may not be possible to agree as a society on one rigid and extended set of values, it is worthwhile to try to agree on an essential set of values to which we can ascribe. The culture of the United States espouses a commitment to the development of a life of justice, freedom, and equality based on a democratic process. Such a society can only be established and sustained through love, compassion, and unselfishness based on an understanding that these qualities refer more to actions performed on the basis of what is right than to feelings of the moment. This essential set of values will be the foundation on which we can build as we undertake the difficult decisions involving multiple worlds and diverse backgrounds.

USE OF TERMINOLOGY RELATED TO DIVERSITY

As Nieto (2000) points out, language is always changing because it mirrors social, economic, and political events. Consequently, the terms used to refer to various individuals in this book will inevitably change over time and represent different meanings to our readers, depending on their own experience. Our attempt has been to use terminology that the individuals themselves use in the case studies. However, much of our discussion in the opening chapters relates to the U.S. Census and, therefore, it seems most accurate to use those terms.

Census 2000 defined race categories as follows:

- *White* refers to people having origins in any of the original peoples of Europe, the Middle East, or North Africa. It includes people who indicated their race or races as "white" or wrote in entries such as Irish, German, Italian, Lebanese, Near Easterner, Arab, or Polish.
- *Black or African American* refers to people having origins in any of the black racial groups of Africa. It includes people who indicated their race or races as "Black, African Am., or Negro" or wrote in entries such as African American, Afro American, Nigerian, or Haitian.
- *American Indian and Alaska Native* refers to people having origins in any of the original peoples of North and South America (including Central America) and who maintain tribal affiliation of community attachment. It includes people who indicated their race or races by marking this category or writing in their principal or enrolled tribe, such as Rosebud Sioux, Chippewa, or Navajo.
- *Asian* refers to people having origins in any of the original peoples of the Far East, Southeast Asia, or the Indian subcontinent. It includes people who indicated their race or races as "Asian Indian," "Chinese," "Filipino," "Korean," "Japanese," "Vietnamese," or "Other Asian," or wrote in entries such as Burmese, Hmong, Pakistani, or Thai.
- *Native Hawaiian and Other Pacific Islander* refers to people having origins in any of the original peoples of Hawaii, Guam, Samoa, or other Pacific islands. It includes people who indicated their race or races as "Native Hawaiian," "Guamanian or Chamorro," "Samoan," or "Other Pacific Islander," or wrote in entries such as Tahitian, Mariana Islander, or Chuukese.
- *Some other race* was included in Census 2000 for respondents who were unable to identify with the five Office of Management and Budget (OMB) race categories. Respondents who provided write-in entries such as Moroccan, South African, Belizean, or a Hispanic origin (for example, Mexican, Puerto Rican, or Cuban) are included in the "some other race" category.

The federal government considers race and Hispanic origin to be two separate and distinct concepts, and Census 2000 asks respondents a separate question about whether they are Spanish, Hispanic, or Latino. Hispanic or Latino is defined as a person of Cuban, Mexican, Puerto Rican, South or Central American, or other Spanish culture or origin regardless of race (Grieco & Cassidy, 2001).

Given the above parameters, we also recognize that there are personal and political reasons that individuals and groups may resist these terms and prefer others. For example, many people who fit the above definition of Hispanic prefer not to use that term, believing that Hispanics–Latinos are not a race, but a heterogeneous group in terms of ethnicity, language, national origin, religious beliefs, and cultural assimilation (Davila, 1997). *Latino* is more acceptable to many who reject bureaucratic and colonial imposition on the part of the U.S. government. The term includes all Latin Americans, especially those born in the United States, without regard to language, nationality, or ethnic affiliation. Similarly, some individuals prefer the terms *Indigenous Peoples* and *First Nations People* to *American Indian, Indian,* and *Native American,* seeing the use of the former terms as an act of intellectual liberation and a rejection of the "discovery and progress" narrative maintained by European Americans (Pewewardy, 1999).

The terms *minority* and *people of color* are often used synonymously. However, these terms, too, have been somewhat politicized. In general, we have tried to remain true to the terms used by people in the case studies, the literature cited, and current general usage, such as African American to designate people of African ancestry. We have attempted to use the most appropriate word given the context. For example, the case study about the Onteora Indian in Chapter 7 uses the term Indian because of the name given to the team mascot and the term Native American because it is used locally in the setting of the case. Nevertheless, we affirm the need to dispute the dominant mindset that Indigenous Peoples obtained status only in relation to their "discovery" by "explorers." We also try to use a more specific term when appropriate, such as Mexican American, rather than Hispanic, or Hmong, rather than Asian.

Finally, we support the idea that individuals with disabilities are people who happen to have a disability and thus have tried to use "people first" language.

REFERENCES

Banks, J., & Banks, C. A. McGee (Eds.). (1995). *Handbook of research on multicultural education.* New York: Macmillan.

Baumgartner, A. (2000). Teachers as leaders: Notes from a leader who never planned to become one. *NASSP Bulletin, 84*(616), 23–26.

Buckner, K., & McDowelle, J. (2000). Developing teacher leaders: Providing encouragement, opportunities, and support. *NASSP Bulletin, 84*(616), 35–41.

Childs-Bowen, D., Moller, G., & Scrivner, J. (2000). Principals: Leader of leaders. *NASSP Bulletin, 84*(616), 27–34.

Davila, E. (1997, Spring). Hispanic/Latino: What is in the name? *Diversity.* New Paltz, NY: Academic Senate Task Force on Cultural Diversity.

Desimone, L. (2000). *The role of teachers in urban school reform.* New York: ERIC Clearinghouse on Urban Education (ERIC Document Reproduction No. ED 442 912).

Fuchs, L. (1995). The American civic culture and an inclusivist immigration policy. In James A. Banks & Cherry A. McGee Banks. (Eds.). *Handbook of research in multicultural education* (pp. 293–309). New York: Macmillan.

Grieco, E. M., & Cassidy, R. C. (2001). *Overview of race and Hispanic origin: Census 2000 brief.* Washington, DC: U.S. Census Bureau.

Muncey, D. E., & McQuillan, P. J. (1996). *Reform and resistance in schools and classrooms: An ethnographic view of the Coalition of Essential Schools.* New Haven, CT: Yale University Press (ERIC Document Reproduction No. ED 399 345).

Nieto, S. (2000). *Affirming diversity: The sociopolitical context of multicultural education* (3rd ed.). New York: Longman.

Novak, M. (1972). *The rise of the unmeltable ethnics.* New York: Macmillan.

Pewewardy, C. (1999). From enemy to mascot: The deculturation of Indian mascots in sports culture. *Canadian Journal of Native Education, 23*(2), 176–189.

Phelan, P., & Davidson, A. (Eds.). (1995). *Renegotiating cultural diversity in American schools.* New York: Teachers College Press.

Silva, D. Y, Gimbert, B., & Nolan, J. (2000). Sliding the doors: Locking and unlocking possibilities for teacher leadership. *Teachers College Record, 102*(4), 779–804.

Sleeter, C. E., & Grant, C. A. (1999). *Making choices for multicultural education: Five approaches to race, class, and gender* (3rd ed.). Upper Saddle River, NJ: Prentice Hall.

Spindler, G., & Spindler, L. with Trueba, H. & Williams, M. D. (1990). *The American cultural dialogue and its transmission.* London: Falmer Press.

Vasquez-Levy, D., & Timmerman, M. (2000). Beyond the classroom: Connecting and empowering teachers as leaders. *Teaching and Change, 7*(4), 363–371.

Webster's New Universal Unabridged Dictionary. (1994). New York: Barnes and Noble.

BRIDGING MULTIPLE WORLDS

CHAPTER 1

THE CHANGING PATTERN OF IMMIGRATION

The increasing diversity of our population is primarily due to dramatic changes in immigration patterns to the United States. Immigrants from Asia, Africa, and Central and South America have largely replaced those of Western Europe. As we continue to receive large numbers of immigrants whose culture, language, and race and ethnicity differ from those of the dominant American mainstream, it will be essential to help all children to acquire the knowledge, understanding, attitudes, and skills to live and work together for the common good. We hope that the content of this text will aid teachers in achieving these goals.

HISTORICAL OVERVIEW

Although Mexico has been one of the major sources of immigrants to the United States since 1920, in every decade between 1880 and 1924, 13 million immigrants from Southern Europe, on average, came to the United States (Figure 1.1). This massive, predominantly European immigration ended in the mid-1920s during an isolationist period of anti-Jewish, anti-Catholic sentiment when laws restricting immigration were passed (Jacobson, 1996). Quotas restricted the numbers and were lowest for those from countries labeled "undesirable," a category in which the countries change periodically depending on American attitudes regarding race and social class. For example, the Chinese Exclusion Act of 1882 reduced the number of Chinese immigrants to the United States. Chinese laborers had been imported to build the transcontinental railroad that would connect San Francisco to the Atlantic states and cultivate the rich soil of California (Takaki, 1989). Palmer in 1848 commented, "No people in all the East are so well adapted for clearing wild lands and raising every species of agricultural products as the Chinese" (cited in Takaki, 1989, p. 22). Although the Chinese constituted only 0.002 percent of the U.S. population in 1880, the passage of the act was a response

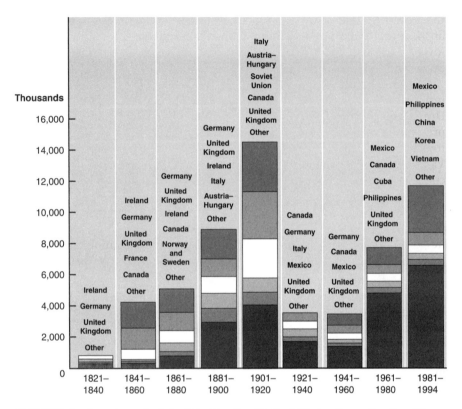

FIGURE 1.1   Immigrants Admitted to the United States from the Top Five Countries of Last Residence: 1821–1994

Source: U.S. Department of Justice (1994). *Statistical yearbook of the Immigration and Naturalization Service.*

to the class tensions and conflict within white society during a time of economic crisis (Takaki, 1989). Thus, "Congress voted to make it unlawful for Chinese laborers to enter the United States for the next ten years and denied naturalized citizenship to the Chinese already here" (Takaki, 1989, p. 111). The prohibition that was initially directed at Chinese laborers was broadened to include all Chinese in 1888 (Takaki, 1989).

Changes in the immigrant population also occurred from 1841 to 1861 when France, Canada, Norway, and Sweden were added to the list of dominant sending countries (Figure 1.1) and from 1901 to 1920 when Italy moved to the top of the list followed by Austria–Hungary, the Soviet Union, Canada, and England (Figure 1.1). Important changes were seen again from 1921 to 1940 when Mexico became one of the top sending countries. In fact, during the 1920s, immigration from Mexico increased significantly when both families and single men crossed the border in search of work and in 1942 when an emergency wartime agreement between the United States and Mexico allowed the legal entry of temporary agricultural workers known as the braceros. This arrangement lasted for 22 years until 1964.

Amendments to the U.S. immigration laws in 1965 resulted in higher immigration rates than at any time since the early 1920s (Jacobson, 1996). During the 1960s, Asia, Central and South America, and Mexico became the predominant countries of origin for the majority of immigrants. By 1994 the top five sending countries were Mexico, the Philippines, China, Korea, and Vietnam (Figure 1.1), and from 1995 to 1998 Mexico continued to lead all countries in the number of immigrants to the United States, followed by China, India, and the Philippines (Figure 1.1).

The dominance of Asians and Latin Americans in the recent immigrant population is due to family unity-based selection priorities, which favor newer immigrant groups, and a shift in the demand for immigration to the less developed regions of the world (Meissner, Hormats, Walker, & Ogata, 1993). As Pastor (1983) noted, people of the Caribbean Basin, for example, pull up their roots for a new land for two "of the elemental human instincts, hope or fear, and in some cases, both" (p. 98).

The 1990s revealed an economic gap between "relatively few, but mostly very rich, developed countries of Europe, North America, Australia and Japan on the one hand, and on the other, the very many countries, mostly, but by no means all, poor, developing countries of the Third World, where more than three quarters of the world's population live" (Gould & Findlay, 1994, p. 23). Large, economic disparities among countries are the root cause of most international migration (United Nations, 1999). However, migration is also driven by (1) internal and international conflicts, (2) the failure of governments to respect the rights of minorities, (3) the lack of good governance, which includes the collapse of the state, and (4) the lack of security in terms of basic necessities, the environment, or human rights (United Nations, 1999). To some extent, the interaction of race and the push to emigrate is another factor. Citizens of Cuba and Haiti, for example, who have attempted to flee poverty and persecution have not received equal treatment in their pleas. The "asylum" explanation has apparently worked for Cubans fleeing Castro's communist regime, while it has not worked for Haitians.

Other incentives for migration have arisen from the advent of global media and multinational corporations that initiate international transfers of employees, as well as from the collapse of internal controls in former Eastern Bloc countries, more accessible means for migration, and "brain drain" migration from countries where young, well-educated persons cannot find suitable employment. Calls for temporary labor in agriculture have also contributed to the intense pressure for migration in developing countries in the 1990s (Gould & Findlay, 1994).

The United Nations has been very involved in human rights and other issues regarding international migration. Thus, international protection for those who emigrate from one country to another is embodied in certain agreements and conventions of the United Nations. For example, the 1975 Helsinki Accords required countries to lower the barriers to free movement of people and ideas, and the Refugee Act of 1980 made countries more open to the claims of refugees (Sassen, 1996). Secondly, The International Convention, adopted by the United Nations in December 1990, protects the rights of all migrant workers and members of their families. Courts have blocked the attempts by several countries to limit family reunification based upon that Convention (Sassen, 1996). The Programme of Action of the International Conference on Population and Development in 1999 called for cooperation between governments of origin and countries of destination. In response, the governments of Canada, Mexico, the United States, and each of the Central American countries have set up a consultation mechanism known as the Puebla Process (United Nations, 1999). This process involves a multilateral mechanism to coordinate the policies, actions, and objectives agreed to by participating countries. This process, also known as the Regional Conference on Migration, is important, because it provides a focus on effective responses to problems arising in the area of migration (International Organization for Migration, 1999). Countries participating in the process include Belize, Canada, Costa Rica, Dominican Republic, El Salvador, Guatemala, Honduras, Mexico, Nicaragua, Panama, and the United States.

Finally, the 1999 United Nations Conference on Population and Development focused on the need to ensure protection against racism, ethnocentrism, xenophobia, and physical harm for both documented, or legal, immigrants and undocumented, or illegal, immigrants (United Nations, 1999, p. 56). In fact, Sassen (1996) has noted that "there is a shift to the rights of the individual regardless of nationality, and respect for international human rights codes" (p. 95).

LEGISLATION

Important national legislation has also affected the flow of immigrants to the United States. Immigration law in the United States began with World War I when fears regarding the arrival of enemy spies encouraged Congress to pass a law in 1917 that introduced literacy requirements, banned "Asiatic" immigrants, and required all arrivals to have a passport (Harris, 1995). This law was superseded by legislation in 1921 and 1924, which introduced immigrant quotas in proportion to the national origins of the U.S. population (Harris, 1995).

After World War II, the U.S. Congress conducted a review of the country's immigration policies and passed new legislation, the Immigration and

Nationality Act, also known as the McCarran–Walter Act. This legislation, in effect since 1952, continues as the basic immigration law (United Nations, 1998). The McCarran–Walter Act eliminated previous racial exclusions, but retained the national origins formula of the Quota Act of 1924 (United Nations, 1998). It allocated visas according to nationalities already represented in the U.S. population. The McCarran–Walter Act also gave preference to relatives of American citizens and skilled workers.

As mentioned earlier, in 1965, during the Kennedy administration, Amendments to the Quota Act abolished quotas based on national origins, fixed a ceiling on Western Hemisphere immigration, and devised a preference system favoring close relatives of U.S. residents and citizens; those with needed occupational skills, abilities, or training; and refugees (Fuchs, 2000). Other aspects of the amendments allocated visas on a first-come, first-served basis and placed no numerical limit on immediate relatives of U.S. citizens (Fuchs, 2000). The 1965 legislation resulted in a great shift in the nationality of immigrants and, by 1985, 46.4 percent of immigrants to the United States came from Asia (United Nations, 1998).

The Refugee Act of 1980 provided that refugee admissions would be a permanent component of immigration. In addition, the Immigration Reform and Control Act (IRCA) of 1986 legalized the status of many illegal aliens, most of whom were from Mexico and had lived in the United States continuously since 1982. In the amendments of the IRCA, family reunification is a high priority, which has led to a tremendous increase in immigration and a change in the ethnic composition of the immigrant population. Nevertheless, the number of illegal immigrants has continued to increase due to both regional and global changes (Jacobson, 1996).

Subsequently, the Immigration Act of 1990, which provided the first major change in immigration legislation in 25 years, changed the quota preference system to allow an increase in skilled workers, reduce the delay in the admission of immigration-eligible family members, and provide greater diversity in the sending countries (Meissner et al., 1993; United Nations, 1998). The IMMACT (Immigration Act of 1990), in fact, "established annual overall limits on total legal immigration; created a guaranteed minimum number of visas for close family members; increased the number of persons admitted for employment reasons, with higher priority for professionals and highly-skilled persons; and created a diversity class of admissions for persons from nations that had not recently sent many immigrants to the United States" (U.S. Commission on Immigration Reform, 1997). Diversity admissions refers to provisions in the IMMACT to "increase national diversity in the immigrant population by widening access for immigrants from underrepresented countries whose citizens have neither strong family nor job ties to the United States" (U.S. Commission on Immigration Reform, 1997).

Thus, in recent years the percentage of foreign-born persons in the general U.S. population increased from a total of 5.4 percent in 1960 to 8.6 percent in 1993 (Jacobson, 1996). About 68 percent of immigrants in 1993 came from only 15 countries (Jacobson, 1996), and recent immigrants are most concentrated in five states: California, New York, Texas, Florida, and Illinois (Jacobson, 1996).

The Illegal Immigration Reform and Immigrant Responsibility Act of 1996 is the most recent U.S. legislation. This act was designed to provide increased funds to apprehend, detain, and deport illegal aliens. Rules were severely tightened for those claiming asylum and for illegal aliens who tried to prevent their deportation to avoid severe hardship (Fuchs, 2000).

ASSIMILATION AND ACCULTURATION

Both documented and undocumented immigrants may come for employment, to be reunited with their families, as refugees, or, in the case of documented immigrants only, through special agreements. Castles and Miller (1993) have described the four stages experienced by migrants who come initially to find work or attend school. In stage 1, they send money home to the family and maintain orientation to their homeland. Stage 2 involves prolonging their stay and developing social networks based on kinship or common areas of origin and the need for mutual assistance. Stage 3 brings about a growing sense of long-term settlement, increased orientation toward the new country, and the emergence of ethnic communities with their own institutions. Stage 4 involves permanent settlement. In this final stage the outcomes may vary. In some countries, the immigrants may become an integral part of a society that is "willing to reshape its culture and identity," while in other societies the immigrants may be excluded and marginalized, "living on the fringes of a society determined to preserve myths of a static culture and homogeneous identity" (Castles & Miller, 1993, p. 26). Immigrants who are excluded and marginalized may face impenetrable barriers to participation in the mainstream society. Race and color have contributed to the exclusion and marginalization of some immigrant groups. African Americans, who have been described as involuntary immigrants (Ogbu, 1995), provide a striking example. Their assimilation has been prevented through segregation, discrimination, and racism.

Assimilation

Nevertheless, immigrants to the United States have historically assimilated, adopting the new customs and language as their own. A standard definition of the term *assimilation* is quite descriptive. To assimilate is to "take in and incorporate as one's own" (*Webster's New Universal Unabridged Dictionary*, 1994). Assimilation occurs when an individual or group does not maintain its own culture when in contact with other cultures or social environments (Castles & Miller, 1993). Mrs. Lee, for example, emigrated from Taiwan 40 years ago. She commented to one of the authors that she was so eager to "fit in" and to have her children "fit in" the United States mainstream that she never taught them much about Taiwan, the culture, or the language. She wanted them only to learn English. Recently, her daughter, who is 18 years old, complained bitterly that she "really didn't know who she was and that she wanted to go to Taiwan to learn about her background and language" (S. Tung, personal communication, 1995).

Acculturation

In contrast, *acculturation* has been defined as "the product of cultural learning that occurs as a result of contact between the members of two or more culturally distinct groups" (Castles & Miller, 1993, p. 155). Acculturation may be influenced by the individual's characteristics, the intensity and importance attached to the contact between groups, and the numerical balance between the groups (Castles & Miller, 1993). Both behavioral and attitudinal changes occur in the acculturation process, which may be superficial, intermediate, or significant (Casas & Pytluk, 1995; Marin, 1992). Whereas superficial changes may only involve learning and forgetting cultural facts and traditions, significant changes involve alterations in one's beliefs, values, and norms (Marin, 1992).

Another term used less frequently in reference to the settlement of immigrants in a new country is *accommodation,* which refers to the mutual consideration and adjustments made by groups in order to live together harmoniously. This may be contrasted with the process of *marginalization,* which can occur when an individual loses contact with her own culture and does not or cannot establish contact with other cultures. This results in a feeling of being left out or marginalized, without a sense of belonging anywhere (Kerwin & Ponterotto, 1995). In a discussion of Southeast Asian children who are torn from their culture of origin through wars and other trauma, Trueba, Jacobs, and Kirton (1990) provide an example of marginalization. These children enter the United States without the language and other means of participating in the U.S. culture, and they are also without experiences in their own culture and thus unable to share in those cultural experiences with older members of their culture who have usually retained sufficient knowledge of the culture that they left.

However, marginalization can also occur when barriers to participation in the new culture are erected. Royce (1982), for example, points out the difference between the treatment of groups considered inferior versus those viewed more positively by the receiving society. Immigrants fleeing religious or political persecution are often met with feelings of generosity by the receiving country, while groups that have been viewed as inferior are more likely to be treated with hostility (Royce, 1982). Or, when the receiving country is experiencing labor shortages, the availability of foreign workers allows for the productive use of capital, and immigrant workers are positively received (United Nations, 1997). On the other hand, when unemployment is high, the reception of foreign workers in various sectors of the country may be very negative, and they may be viewed by citizens according to the stereotype that "They're all dependent on welfare" (United Nations, 1997). In fact, such concern about the impact of immigration on the society prompted a 1997 report by the U.S. National Academy of Sciences, which concluded that "the impact of migration on most of the population, as well as on the total gross domestic product of the country, is probably modest" (United Nations, 1997, p. 2).

Assimilation requires an individual to give up the culture and language of origin, whereas acculturation allows for the acquisition of a new culture and language while maintaining one's native culture and language. Cultural pluralism recognizes the plurality of cultures in the U.S. population as equally valued and respected. This philosophy is embodied in multicultural education, which we will discuss in Chapter 2. As we reflect on the diverse students in our schools who are in the process of acculturation, it will be important to understand the process, remain empathetic to the challenges, and employ the skills needed to engage the students in learning.

DEMOGRAPHIC CHANGES

The changing patterns of immigration have resulted in a school-aged population in the United States in which the enrollment of children from diverse cultural and linguistic groups increased to almost 25 percent by 1994 (U.S. Department of Education, 1999). The greatest increases have been among Hispanic and Asian children. Children from Central America and the Caribbean have also increased significantly over the past 20 years; however, immigrants from Central and South America have been primarily adults, while those from Mexico, Puerto Rico, and Cuba have involved younger populations.

The increased number of ethnically and linguistically diverse immigrants in the central cities, which are densely populated centers of a metropolitan area with a concentration of cultural and commercial facilities and a disproportionately high population of disadvantaged persons, and metropolitan areas of major cities in the United States has also affected the school population. Between 1972 and 1993, African American and Hispanic students in public schools of central cities increased from 42 percent in 1972 to 53.8 in 1993 (Gordon, 1998) (see Table 1.1). It is important to add

TABLE 1.1   Percentage of Public School Students Who Are Black or Latino by Metropolitan Status: 1972–1993

YEAR	TOTAL	CENTRAL CITIES	OTHER METROPOLITAN	NON-METROPOLITAN
1972	20.5	42.0	10.6	14.9
1973	20.3	41.8	10.1	14.6
1974	21.5	44.0	10.9	16.2
1975	22.0	44.5	12.0	15.9
1976	22.4	44.9	13.4	15.3
1977	21.9	47.0	12.6	15.5
1978	22.3	47.4	13.3	15.3
1979	22.7	49.5	14.1	14.4
1980	—	—	—	—
1981	24.6	51.4	15.6	16.0
1982	24.7	51.0	15.5	16.1
1983	25.2	51.5	16.6	15.6
1984	—	—	—	—
1985	26.8	56.7	18.1	16.8
1986	27.1	52.4	16.5	18.3
1987	27.1	51.7	17.5	16.7
1988	27.4	51.1	18.6	16.9
1989	27.8	51.8	20.0	15.3
1990	27.8	52.1	19.5	16.4
1991	28.1	52.9	19.6	15.9
1992	28.3	52.6	20.4	15.5
1993	28.4	53.8	20.2	16.0

Note: Figures for 1980 and 1984 are unavailable.

Source: National Center for Education Statistics, *1995 Condition of Education.*

that in many central cities and metropolitan regions the population of African American and Hispanic students may be close to 100 percent due to hyper-segregation (excessive segregation) or resegregation by which a school previously desegregated becomes segregated again through tracking of these students.

The disproportionate number of disadvantaged persons and Hispanic and African American residents of central cities and metropolitan areas has also resulted, at least in part, from *white flight* in response to school desegregation (McDonald, 1997). However, McDonald concluded, in her study of the Boston public school system, that trends in population changes were more complex than could be explained by white flight. Fairlie and Resch (2000) also investigated white flight to private schools using data from the

National Educational Survey and the National Center for Educational Statistics to determine whether whites are more likely to flee public schools with larger concentrations of minority children, all else being equal. They also questioned whether white flight was from all minorities or only certain groups based on race or income. Fairlie and Resch (2000) found that the clearest flight was from poor, black schoolchildren. Their results were less clear for Asian and Hispanic students. However, based on their study, racism did contribute to white flight. In contrast, Goodman and Streitweiser (1983) found that low outmovement by blacks better explained the higher outmovement by whites than did white flight or socioeconomic differences.

The population changes of central cities are further complicated by the more recent outmovement of young families and college graduates from urban to rural areas of the country (Fulton, Fugitt, & Gibson, 1997; Nord & Cromartie, 1999) and the gentrification phenomenon, which brings young professionals and families back to neighborhoods of the central city (Sites, 1998).

Interestingly, regions of the country are also differentially affected by population changes involving the new immigrants (and aging baby boomers). For example, in *The State of the South, A Report to the Region and Its Leadership* (1998), striking changes were noted. The report concluded that: "The historically black/white, mostly Protestant, and native-born South is fast becoming a multiethnic society. After a century of black out-migration, African Americans are now headed South from every corner of the United States, and they are joined by millions of other newcomers from this country and abroad. A region once distinguished by small towns and farms, the South is now far more urban and especially suburban than rural" (1998, p. 15).

Contributing to the changing South are the migration and settlement patterns of Latinos. Torres (2000) points out the trends, noting that "the rural South's healthy economy will continue to attract Latinos looking for economic opportunities and a chance at the American dream" (p. 5). By 2025, Torres concludes that the proposed changes will at least double the Hispanic population in the South and most in-migrants will seek permanent rather than seasonal employment (Torres, 2000). Interestingly, he notes that the Latino population will constitute a relatively low proportion of the population in most of the Southern states for the next 25 years, with the exception of Texas (approximately 38 percent) and Florida (almost 24 percent) where significant proportions exist.

In an interesting discussion, Frey and DeVol (2000) have projected that "America's demography in the 21st century will be affected by two major players—baby boomers and new immigrants" (p. 6). They note that the aging boomers and new immigrants are "creating regional divisions that will be just as important as old distinctions such as city versus suburb or rural versus urban. The new divisions will encompass entire metropolitan areas and states becoming "melting pot regions" and "heartland regions" (p. 6). Frey and DeVol (2000) identified 21 multiple melting pot metropolitan areas in which they note that "interracial marriage should be most prominent" (p. 9). These regions, according to the report, will "become increasingly younger, multi-ethnic and culturally vibrant" (p. 6). They include California, Texas, southern Florida, the eastern seaboard, and Chicago. In contrast, heartland regions will become "older, more staid, and less ethnically diverse, including growing parts of the sunbelt as well as declining areas of the farmbelt and rust belt. The aging boomer population will grow fastest in regions of the heartland (p. 7).

Statistics show that foreign-born immigrants continue to cluster into a handful of metropolitan areas. According to Frey and DeVol (2000), "just 10 metropolitan areas house fully 58% of the U.S. Hispanic population. Ten metro areas, led by Los Angeles, New York and San Francisco, house 61% of all U.S. Asians. Gains in the White population in the 1990s were greatest in Atlanta and Phoenix while African Americans are moving back to the South, increasing their concentration in that region" (pp. 22–23).

DEMOGRAPHIC CHANGES IN THE SCHOOLS

Thus, the most recent data on the school-aged population reflects the national, regional, and local changes in the general population. Cities will have degrees and types of diversity among their residents that will be reflected in the school-aged children. Current demographics of the school-aged population show the following breakdown (National Center for Education Statistics, 2000):

533,000 or 1.1%	American Indian–Alaskan Natives
1,828,000 or 3.9%	Asian–Pacific Islanders
6,939,000 or 14.9%	Hispanics
7,923,000 or 17.0%	Black–non-Hispanics
29,142,000 or 62.6%	White–non-Hispanics

Geographic variations exist in the diversity of the school-aged population among states, as well as among urban, suburban, and rural areas of the country. For example, comparisons between California and South Dakota show that California has many students in each of the racial or ethnic groups identified, while South Dakota has relatively few (Table 1.2). This means that teachers can expect differences in the population of their schools and classrooms. They will need to learn about the cultures of students in the community served by a specific school and classroom. Language diversity may also be a challenge because in some locations there will be more English

TABLE 1.2   Public School Membership by Race and Ethnicity and State: School Year 1998–1999

STATE	AMERICAN INDIAN– ALASKAN NATIVE	ASIAN– PACIFIC ISLANDER	HISPANIC	BLACK NON- HISPANIC	WHITE NON- HISPANIC
United States	532,526	1,828,467	6,938,813	7,922,953	29,142,074
Alabama	5,246	5,024	6,879	266,225	452,154
Alaska	33,597	6,839	4,103	6,211	84,623
Arizona	58,469	16,171	268,038	38,358	465,370
Arkansas	2,000	3,530	11,449	106,211	329,066
California	50,029	648,511	2,412,059	507,506	2,210,494
Colorado	8,054	18,876	139,451	39,402	493,352
Connecticut	1,502	14,063	67,318	74,215	387,600
Delaware	234	2,278	5,597	34,422	70,731
District of Columbia	31	1,126	5,956	61,717	3,059
Florida	6,037	42,970	401,254	595,238	1,292,134
Georgia	1,898	27,693	47,157	533,736	790,807
Hawaii	734	134,844	8,700	4,584	39,207
Idaho	3,050	2,953	23,835	1,651	213,134
Illinois	3,054	63,990	279,717	429,736	1,235,033
Indiana	1,936	8,733	27,904	112,197	837,324
Iowa	2,372	8,332	14,059	18,115	455,336
Kansas	5,500	9,722	35,356	40,519	378,020
Kentucky	631	2,775	4,102	65,519	556,981
Louisiana	5,188	9,831	9,819	362,031	381,865
Maine*	982	1,980	1,002	2,375	204,214
Maryland	2,840	34,065	33,580	307,906	463,280
Massachusetts	2,187	40,080	95,843	82,522	741,685
Michigan	17,684	28,550	51,859	334,654	1,279,203
Minnesota	17,152	39,993	22,607	49,914	725,434
Mississippi*	744	3,094	2,525	256,210	239,806
Missouri	2,561	9,883	12,903	155,464	731,623
Montana	16,349	1,353	2,528	819	138,939
Nebraska	4,359	4,114	17,186	18,474	247,007
Nevada	5,635	15,806	68,475	30,691	190,454
New Hampshire	497	2,390	2,947	2,018	196,861

* BIA data subtracted from state totals.

—Data missing or not applicable.

Note: Race–ethnicity categories may not sum to total membership (the 50 states and D.C.) if data are reported at different times and/or race–ethnicity was not reported for some students.

Source: U.S. Department of Education, National Center for Education Statistics, Common Core of Data, State Nonfiscal Survey.

STATE	AMERICAN INDIAN– ALASKAN NATIVE	ASIAN– PACIFIC ISLANDER	HISPANIC	BLACK NON- HISPANIC	WHITE NON- HISPANIC
New Jersey	2,319	74,138	181,618	229,507	781,414
New Mexico	35,359	3,181	160,398	7,659	122,156
New York	11,283	161,304	519,538	585,622	1,599,396
North Carolina	18,827	21,171	38,806	391,393	784,624
North Dakota*	8,324	830	1,354	1,103	102,986
Ohio	2,130	19,561	28,002	291,666	1,501,200
Oklahoma	100,734	8,558	30,795	67,123	421,282
Oregon	11,134	19,831	47,027	14,754	450,063
Pennsylvania	2,018	34,006	72,933	265,899	1,441,558
Rhode Island	728	5,089	18,972	11,780	118,216
South Carolina	1,384	5,574	7,476	271,327	359,889
South Dakota*	12,682	1,148	1,327	1,391	115,947
Tennessee	1,302	9,570	11,065	216,344	665,493
Texas	11,904	100,006	1,523,769	567,998	1,741,690
Utah	7,319	12,252	34,482	3,941	423,182
Vermont	539	1,094	449	976	102,062
Virginia	2,608	41,965	44,275	305,859	729,315
Washington*	26,123	70,450	90,827	50,662	759,991
West Virginia	289	972	1,446	12,416	282,407
Wisconsin	12,208	27,425	33,729	85,900	720,280
Wyoming*	2,760	773	6,317	993	84,127

Outlying Areas, DOD Dependents Schools, and Bureau of Indian Affairs

Bureau of Indian Affairs	50,125	—	—	—	—
DOD Dependents Schools	571	6,875	5,220	13,027	36,194
American Samoa	—	15,372	—	—	—
Guam	22	31,285	70	140	705
Northern Marianas	—	9,420	—	—	78
Puerto Rico	—	—	613,862	—	—
Virgin Islands	17	80	2,925	17,766	188

language learners than in others. The need for interpreters and translators will vary accordingly.

While the population of culturally diverse students in the schools is changing dramatically, the characteristics of the teachers and administrators remain stable and largely homogeneous. From 1971 to 1991, 88.3 to 88.8 percent of the public school teachers were white (National Education Association, 1993). The slight decline of minority teachers has been attributed to "the overall decline of the numbers of college bound students from ethnic groups, the widening of professional opportunities for people of color, the increased prevalence of competency examinations, the lack of prestige for teaching as a profession, low salaries, and less than optimal working conditions" (Delpit, 1995, pp. 105–106). School principals are also predominately white, approximately 84 percent in the 1993–1994 school year (National Center for Education Statistics, 1996).

The implications for teachers are obvious. Even in areas of the country that remain predominantly white, it is essential that teachers learn about the cultures and languages of many children who are entering our schools for the first time and others who are arriving in greater numbers. Furthermore, many of the jobs available in the next decade will be in urban areas where the population is likely to be more diverse. In addition, all children will need to learn to work and live harmoniously with members of many diverse groups in the society. Teachers will need to develop the knowledge, skills, and attitudes essential to prepare a diverse population of students for success in mainstream America, while respecting their cultures and languages of origin. The preparation of teachers for diverse students will be discussed in Chapter 2.

REFERENCES

Casas, M. J., & Pytluk, S. D. (1995). Hispanic identity development: Implications for research and practice. In J. G. Ponterotto, J. Manuel Casas, L. A. Suzuki, & C. M. Alexander (Eds.), *Handbook of multicultural counseling* (pp. 155–180). Thousand Oaks, CA: Sage Publications.

Castles, S., & Miller, M. J. (1993). *The age of migration.* New York: Guilford Press.

Delpit, L. (1995). *Other people's children: Cultural conflict in the classroom.* New York: The New Press.

Fairlie, R. W., & Resch, A. (2000). *Is there white flight into private schools? Evidence from the National Educational Longitudinal Survey* (Working paper, 211). Washington, DC: Joint Center for Poverty Research. (ERIC Document Reproduction Number: ED 450 208).

Frey, W., & DeVol, R. (2000). *America's demography in the new century: Aging baby boomers and new immigrants as major players. Milken Institute Policy Brief.* Santa Monica, CA: Milken Institute.

Fuchs, L. (2000). Immigration. In Grolier Multimedia Encyclopedia, http://gme.grolier.com/cgi-bin/gme.

Fulton, J., Fugitt, G., & Gibson, R. (1997). Recent changes in metropolitan–nonmetropolitan migration streams. *Rural Sociology, 62*(3), 363–384.

Goodman, J., & Streitweiser, M. L. (1983). Explaining racial differences: A study of city-to-suburb residential mobility. *Urban Affairs Quarterly, 18*(3), 301–325.

Gordon, R. (1998). *Education and race.* Oakland, CA: Applied Research Center.

Gould, W. T. S., & Findlay, A. M. (1994). *Population and the changing world order.* New York: Wiley.

Harris, N. (1995). *The new untouchables: Immigration and the new world order.* London: J. B. Tauris Publishers.

International Organization for Migration. (1999). Retrieved December, 2001, from http://www.iom.int/

Jacobson, D. (1996). *Rights across the borders: Immigration and the decline of citizenship.* Baltimore, MD: Johns Hopkins University Press.

Kerwin, C., & Ponterotto, J. G. (1995). Biracial children. In J. G. Ponterotto, J. M. Casas, L. A. Suzuki, & C. M. Alexander (Eds.), *Handbook of multicultural counseling* (pp. 199–217). Thousand Oaks, CA: Sage Publications.

Marin, G. (1992). Extreme response style and acquiescence among Hispanics: The role of acculturation and education. *Journal of Cross-cultural Psychology, 23*(4), 498–509.

McDonald, L. E. (1997). Boston Public School white enrollment decline: White flight or demographic factors? *Equity and Excellence in Education, 30*(3), 21–30.

Meissner, D., Hormats, R., Walker, A. G., & Ogata, S. (1993). *International migration challenges in a new era.* New York: The Trilateral Commission.

National Center for Education Statistics. (1996). *Report.* Washington, DC: Department of Education.

National Center for Education Statistics. (2000). *Report.* Washington, DC: Department of Education.

National Education Association. (1993). *The status of the American public school teacher 1961–1991.* Washington, DC: Author.

Nord, M., & Cromartie, J. (1999). Rural areas attract young families and college graduates. *Rural Conditions and Trends, 9*(2), 28–34.

Ogbu, J. (1995). Understanding cultural diversity and learning. In J. A. Banks & C. A. McGee Banks (Eds.), *Handbook of research on multicultural education* (pp. 582–593). New York: Macmillan.

Pastor, R. (1983). Migration in the Caribbean Basin: The need for an approach as dynamic as the phenomenon. In M. M. Kritz (Ed.), *U.S. immigration and refugee policy: Global and domestic issues* (pp. 95–112). Lexington, MA: D.C. Heath.

Royce, A. P. (1982). *Ethnic identity: Strategies of diversity.* Bloomington, IN: Indiana University Press.

Sassen, S. (1996). *Losing control: Sovereignty in an age of globalization.* New York: Columbia University Press.

Sites, W. (1998). Communitarian theory and community development in the United States. *Community Development Journal, 33*(1), 57–65.

The State of the South. (1998). *A report to the region and its leadership.* Chapel Hill, NC: MDC Inc. (ERIC Document Reproduction No. 425882).

Takaki, R. (1989). *Strangers from a different shore.* Boston: Little, Brown & Company.

Torres, C. (2000). Emerging Latino communities: A new challenge for the rural South. *Rural South: Preparing for Challenges of the 21st Century,* no. 12, Aug. 2000 (ERIC Document Reproduction No. ED444806).

Trueba, W. T., Jacobs, L., & Kirton, E. (1990). *Cultural conflict and adaptation: The case of Hmong children in American society.* Bristol, PA: Falmer Press.

United Nations. (1997). *International migration and development: The concise report.* New York: Author.

United Nations. (1998). *International Migration Policies*. New York: United Nations, Department of Economic and Social Affairs Population Division.

United Nations. (1999). *Review and appraisal of the progress made in achieving the goals and objectives of the Programme of Action of the International Conference on Population and Development*. New York: Author.

U.S. Commission on Immigration Reform. (1997). Washington, DC: General Accounting Office.

U.S. Department of Education. (1999). *Challenging the status quo: The education record 1993–2000*. Washington, DC: Government Printing Office.

Webster's New Universal Unabridged Dictionary. (1994). New York: Barnes and Noble.

CHAPTER 2

THE CURRENT STATE OF EDUCATION FOR DIVERSE STUDENTS IN THE UNITED STATES

The increasing diversity among school-aged children in the United States raises several important questions. First, how is the education establishment responding to the diversity? What is the current progress of diverse students in our public schools? Second, how can multicultural education help us to address the needs of culturally diverse students and their peers and teachers? What have we learned from research in multicultural education about approaches to curriculum reform and effective pedagogy for diverse students? Finally, how can teachers be prepared to ensure the success of the diverse population?

THE EDUCATIONAL PROGRESS OF DIVERSE LEARNERS

The progress of diverse students in our schools can be determined from assessment data provided by the National Assessment of Educational Progress (NAEP). The NAEP, which is conducted by the National Center for Education Statistics, regularly reports on the educational progress of students in grades 4, 8, and 12 in public and private schools. Both short-term data and long-term trends are included in the report. Data include average scale scores and achievement levels. Basic, proficient, and advanced levels of students' achievement have been developed by the National Assessment Governing Board in consultation with experts in the respective academic areas. Although eight academic areas are assessed—mathematics, science, reading, writing, U.S. history, geography, civics, and the arts—we will consider only four areas: reading, writing, mathematics, and science. The summaries and interpretations have been provided by the NAEP.

Reading

Scores available in reading are shown in Table 2.1 Average scale scores in reading increased only for Asian–Pacific Islander students between 1992 and 2000. Scores for black, Hispanic, and American Indian students (which are not shown) remained unchanged during this period. At the same time, scores in 2000 for white and Asian–Pacific Islander students were higher than scores of black and Hispanic students. In addition, the gap in performance between whites and blacks and the gap between whites and Hispanics did not change between 1992 and 2000.

With respect to achievement levels, only Asian–Pacific Islander levels showed any changes, with an increase in the percentage at or about the proficient level, from 25 percent in 1992 to 46 percent in 2000. The percent at

TABLE 2.1   Overall Performance in Reading

		GRADE 4			
Year	Total	White	Black	Hispanic	Asian/Pacific Islander
2000	5880	224 65% (0.5)	191 15% (0.4)	198 12% (0.4)	227 3%
1998	6242	225 66% (0.7)	192 17% (0.4)	198 10% (0.5)	216 3%
1992	4982	223 69% (0.5)	191 17% (0.4)	200 7% (0.3)	212 3%

		GRADE 8			
Year	Total	White	Black	Hispanic	Asian/Pacific Islander
1998	9079	270 65%	241 15% (0.4)	244 13% (0.4)	266 4% (0.4)
1992	7601	265 69%	236 16% (0.3)	240 9% (0.3)	267 3% (0.2)

		GRADE 12			
Year	Total	White	Black	Hispanic	Asian/Pacific Islander
1998	10,607	297 67%	269 14%	275 (1.4) 12%	286 (4.4) 4%
1992	7,738	296 70%	272 16%	277 (2.6) 8%	288 (3.5) 4%

Standard errors are given in parentheses.

Source: National Center for Education Statistics, National Assessment of Educational Progress (NAEP).

TABLE 2.2   Average Performance in Writing (Scale Scores)

	GRADE 4				
Year	White	Black	Hispanic	Asian/Pacific Islander	American Indian
1998	157	131	134	164	138

	GRADE 8				
Year	White	Black	Hispanic	Asian/Pacific Islander	American Indian
1998	158	131	131	159	132

	GRADE 12				
Year	White	Black	Hispanic	Asian/Pacific Islander	American Indian
1998	156	134	135	152	129

Source: National Center for Education Statistics, National Assessment of Educational Progress. The Nation's Report Card: Writing. Retrieved July, 2002 from http://nces.ed.gov/nationsreportcard/

or above the proficient level for whites (4) and Asian–Pacific Islander (46) were higher than for blacks (12) and Hispanics (16). Only 17 percent of American Indian students were at the proficient level.

Writing

Average scale scores for 1998 are shown in Table 2.2. At grade 4, the average writing scale scores for Asian–Pacific Islander students were higher than those for white, black, Hispanic and American Indian students. At grades 8 and 12, the average writing scores for Asian–Pacific Islander and white students were similar and were higher than those for black, Hispanic, and American Indian students.

Mathematics

At grade 4, white, black, and Hispanic students' average scores in 2000 were higher than in 1990 or 1992. At grade 8, the average scores for white students

TABLE 2.3   Average Performance in Mathematics (Scale Scores)

	GRADE 4			
Year	White	Black	Hispanic	Asian/Pacific Islander
2000	234	204	213	****
1996	232	200	206	232
1992	228	193	202	232
1990	220	189	198	228

	GRADE 8			
Year	White	Black	Hispanic	Asian/Pacific Islander
2000	285	245	253	288
1996	282	243	251	274
1992	278	238	247	282
1990	270	238	244	279

	GRADE 12			
Year	White	Black	Hispanic	Asian/Pacific Islander
2000	308	273	282	317
1996	311	280	287	319
1992	306	276	284	316
1990	301	268	276	311

****Insufficient sample size to permit a reliable estimate

Source: National Center for Education Statistics, National Assessment of Educational Progress. *The Nation's Report Card, Mathematics 2000.* Retrieved June 2002 from http://nces.ed.gov/nations reportcard/

were higher in 2000 than in the three previous assessment years, while the average scores for black and Hispanic students were higher in 2000 than in 1990 or 1992. At grade 12, all students had a higher average score in 2000 than in 1990.

Science

The average scores in science for Black, Hispanic, Asian–Pacific Islander and American Indian students were lower than those for white students in grades 4, 8, and 12. Scores were not significantly different between 1996 and 2000 for most

TABLE 2.4   Average Performance in Science (Scale Scores)

			GRADE 4		
Year	White	Black	Hispanic	Asian/Pacific Islander	American Indian
2000	160	124	129	****	140
1996	160	124	128	151	144

			GRADE 8		
Year	White	Black	Hispanic	Asian/Pacific Islander	American Indian
2000	162	122	128	156	134
1996	159	121	129	152	148

			GRADE 12		
Year	White	Black	Hispanic	Asian/Pacific Islander	American Indian
2000	154	123	128	153	139
1996	159	124	130	149	145

****Result omitted due to special concerns

Source: National Center for Education Statistics, National Assessment of Educational Progress. *The Nation's Report Card, Science 2000.* Retrieved June, 2002 from http://nces.ed.gov/nationsreportcard/

subgroups. However, scores declined for American Indian students at grade 8. At grade 12 white and Asian/Pacific Islander students had higher average scores than Balck, Hispanic, and American Indian students. American Indian students had higher average scores than either Black or Hispanic students (Table 2.4).

Achievement Levels for Diverse Groups

Although closing the gaps between the performances of diverse racial and ethic groups and those of white students is a major focus of the annual reports by the U.S. Education Department, it is more important, in our view, to determine the extent to which diverse students are meeting expected levels of achievement in the schools. Thus, the "proficient levels" established by the National Assessment Governing Board provide more valuable and objective information by avoiding a comparison with white students as the informal "standard for achievement." It is possible to determine how close a group's average scores are to the level for proficiency in each academic area.

As established by the National Assessment Governing Board the proficient level in reading represents scores of 238 at grade 4, 281 at grade 8, and 302 at grade 12 (Table 2.1). Therefore, all diverse groups need improvement in reading.

In writing, the scores for black students in 1998 correspond to levels at which writing is described as "disjointed, unclear" at grade 4, "incomplete, vague writing" at grade 8, and "beginning, focused, clear writing" at grade 11 (National Center for Education Statistics, 1996). The scores for Hispanic students are equally problematic, indicating a need for improvement. Scores in writing for other groups are not available at this time (Table 2.2).

In mathematics, scores of 249 at grade 4, 299 at grade 8, and 336 at grade 12 represent the proficient level. None of the scores for diverse groups in 2000 reached the proficient level at grade 4, 8, or 12 (Table 2.3).

Scores of 170 at grade 4, 170 at grade 8, and 178 at grade 12 have been established as representative of the proficient level in science. Again, none of the scores has reached the designated level of proficiency (Table 2.4).

Based on the NAEP assessment data, diverse students are performing below a level of proficiency in reading, writing, mathematics, and science. It is obvious that new knowledge, skills, and dispositions in teachers of diverse students are needed to assure satisfactory progress. The contributions of researchers in multicultural education can contribute to this aim.

Although the NAEP data presented here are discouraging, the 1999 report, *Challenging the Status Quo,* offers a more positive picture. For example, reading scores of 9-year-olds in the highest-poverty schools, where over 75 percent of students qualify for a free or reduced-price lunch, rose by nearly one grade level on the NAEP between 1992 and 1996, reversing a downward trend (Education Record, May, 2000). In nine states, achievement of students in the highest-poverty schools met or exceeded the national average for all public school students in 1996 (Education Record, May, 2000).

Another indicator of progress is the enrollment of diverse students in advanced placement courses. For every 1,000 high school seniors, the number of girls taking the advanced placement exams rose from 111 to 145 between 1992 and 1997, the number of African American students who took the exams rose from 26 to 37, and Hispanic students grew from 68 to 85, the highest minority and female participation rates in history (U.S. Department of Education, 2000). Overall, minority students comprised 30 percent of all students who took advanced placement exams between 1992 and 1997.

High-Poverty Schools

Conditions in high-poverty schools affect the achievement of many diverse and low-income students. High-poverty urban schools are most likely to suffer from unqualified teachers. Many Title 1 schools are hiring teacher aides at twice the rate of qualified teachers and increasing the numbers of teacher aides who are providing direct instruction without supervision (U.S. Department of Education, 1999). Title 1 served over 11 million students in 1996–1997. Thirty-six percent of these students were white, 30 percent Hispanic, and 28 percent African American. Seventeen percent of children served were English language learners. In addition, many high-poverty schools include old, dilapidated facilities with few of the resources required for satisfactory educational activities (Kozol, 1991). Unequal funding practices contribute to the deplorable conditions in many central city and urban public schools (Darling-Hammond, 1995; Kozol, 1991).

Tracking

Practices such as tracking also affect the achievement of diverse students. Tracking or ability grouping has been justified by proponents as allowing the separation of students so that teachers can more easily manage the spread of ability within a group. Five types of grouping have been used: (1) age grouping, (2) heterogeneous grouping within grades, (3) homogeneous grouping within grades, (4) homogeneous grouping across grades, and (5) homogeneous grouping within classes (Mosteller, Light, & Sachs, 1996). In some communities, ability grouping has also been used as a strategy to avoid school desegregation (Welner & Oakes, 1996). Despite considerable research that finds that tracking or ability grouping is not pedagogically effective, the practice continues (Darling-Hammond, 1995; Mosteller, Light & Sachs, 1996).

Educators have assumed various positions on tracking based on changing political climates. The belief that grouping led to better outcomes when materials and methods were geared to students' aptitudes was followed by the view, during the 1930s under John Dewey's influence, that grouping was undemocratic, encouraged bland teaching, and resulted in lower self-concepts and less learning and leadership skills for students. Grouping gained favor again in the 1950s when students with higher aptitudes became the focus of attention after *Sputnik* was launched by Soviet Russia. However, the civil rights movement brought about a renewed rejection of ability grouping during the 1960s and 1970s.

When tracking is implemented, all students are deprived of learning opportunities available only from their peers. In addition, students in the lower tracks are likely to be stigmatized and unprepared for postsecondary educational opportunities (Oakes, 1990). While many schools are engaged in declarations of antitracking positions, the practice continues to result in students grouped according to race, socioeconomic level, or ethnic group (Welner & Oakes, 1996).

Mosteller, Light, & Sachs (1996) have noted that the lack of rigorous evaluation is an important drawback in determining the benefits of skill grouping, and they conclude that more exploration and evaluation are needed. Nevertheless, they found that approximately 85 percent of public school students in U.S. middle and high schools are currently placed in skill-grouped classes for mathematics instruction.

Mathematics and science are important areas of the curriculum since these subjects act as gatekeepers to courses required in preparation for careers that are more highly compensated in salary and status. The short supply of culturally diverse students available for careers such as astronauts, astrophysicists, engineers, mathematicians, and geneticists, for example, is due, in part, to their lack of preparation in higher levels of mathematics and science courses (Carmichael & Sevenair, 1991; Fouad & Spreda, 1995).

High School Completion

The rate of high school completion based on enrollment in postsecondary institutions is also an indicator of diverse students' educational progress. Accordingly, high school completion rates between 1967 and 1995 have increased for black as well as Hispanic and Asian–Pacific Islander students (U.S. Department of Education, 1999a). The slower rate of increase for Hispanic students has been attributed, in part, to the continuing influx of immigrants into the Hispanic population (U.S. Department of Education, 1999a). The decrease in high school dropout rates for African American and Hispanic students during this period was encouraging. For African American students the dropout rate decreased from 28.6 to 6.1 percent between 1967 and 1995; the rate for Hispanic students fell from 34.3 percent in 1972 to 11.6 percent in 1995 (U.S. Department of Education, 1996). However, it is important to note that, despite the decrease, the dropout rate for Hispanic students is twice the national average (U.S. Department of Education, 1996).

Bilingual Education

In addition to tracking practices, segregation of students within a school may also occur through programs for students with limited proficiency in English or for non-English speakers. In some cases, such classes are stigmatized within the school, and diverse students remain segregated from others for extended periods. In the case of Malee Vang, to be introduced later, her exit from bilingual classes into the mainstream was for her a cause for celebration and expectations for a more positive school experience.

The Bilingual Education Act of 1968 provided financial assistance to local education agencies for the purpose of developing and maintaining new and innovative programs to meet the needs of limited English proficient students (Miller-Lachman & Taylor, 1995). The law was later expanded to include languages other than Spanish. In addition, the 1974 Supreme Court case *Lau* v. *Nichols* asserted that school districts had to provide special language programs, either English as a second language or bilingual education.

Models of bilingual education include (1) the bilingual transition program in which students receive instruction in English as a second language while keeping up with their academic subjects in the native language, (2) bilingual maintenance programs that allow students to maintain proficiency in their native language at the same time that they are learning English, (3) the total immersion model in which all subjects are immediately taught in English with no special instruction in the native language, and (4) English as a second language (ESL), in which students are in self-contained classrooms until they learn enough English to keep up in regular classes (Miller-Lachman & Taylor, 1995). ESL can also mean several periods of instruction a day in English and spending the rest of the day in the regular classes.

Bilingual education has been a battleground since its beginning in 1968 (Ovando, 1990; Steinberg, 2000). According to Ovando, "language enables members of society to transmit and exchange values, attitudes, skills and aspirations as culture-bearers and culture-makers" (p. 34), and many people look to the acquisition of English as a requisite for the rapid assimilation of immigrants into American society (Ovando, 1990). Others view bilingual education as essential for true learning and achievement. However, Spener (1988) argues that bilingual education programs prepare people to fill undesirable jobs, and transitional bilingual education offers a very limited period of native-language instruction and does not ensure mastery of English.

Furthermore, immigrant parents are not united in their views of bilingual education (Navarro, 2001). Families that expect to maintain ties with their country of origin, traveling frequently back and forth, may prefer maintenance of the native language for their children, while families without such ties may choose total immersion in English. Controversy continues as we begin the 21st century.

In an effort to address some of the issues involved in bilingual education, California recently adopted the UNZ Initiative (named after Ron K. Unz), which specifies the English language options available to immigrant children. Under this legislation, all children in California public schools must be taught English as rapidly and effectively as possible. However, sheltered English immersion can be provided to children who are English learners during a transition period not normally intended to exceed one year. Waivers are available to parents with their informed consent. Other aspects of English instruction are also included in the UNZ legislation.

MULTICULTURAL EDUCATION

The lagging educational achievement of diverse students in the United States has been a major concern of researchers in multicultural education. As noted by Banks (1997), "Multicultural education incorporates the idea that all students regardless of their gender and social class and their ethnic, racial, or cultural characteristics, should have an equal opportunity to learn in school" (p. 3). The fact that multicultural education is a reform movement as well as a concept and a process (Banks, 1997) means that it provides a comprehensive approach to assuring the educational progress of diverse students. As defined by Banks (1997), it is "a total school reform effort designed to increase educational equity for a range of cultural, ethnic, and economic groups" (p. 7).

In fact, the dimensions of multicultural education encompass content integration, the knowledge construction process, prejudice reduction, an equity pedagogy, an empowering school culture, and a view of the school as a social system (Banks, 1997). Thus, researchers in the field seek to address important issues involved in curriculum reform, teacher education and pedagogy, and changes in the schools as a system. For proponents, the ultimate purpose is a more just and equitable society (Banks, 1995).

For example, Nieto (1996), has defined multicultural education in a sociopolitical context. In her words,

> Multicultural education is a process of comprehensive school reform and basic education for all students. It challenges and rejects racism and other forms of discrimination in schools and society and accepts and affirms the pluralism (ethnic, racial, linguistic, religious, economic, and gender, among others) that students, their communities, and teachers represent. Multicultural education permeates the curriculum and instructional strategies used in schools, as well as the interactions among teachers, students, and parents and the very way that schools conceptualize teaching and learning. (p. 307)

The underachievement of diverse students has been attributed, in part, to a traditional school curriculum that has failed to meet the needs of too many students from culturally and linguistically diverse groups. Historically, the traditional curriculum has neglected the participation and contributions of minorities to the history of the United States. American history and social studies, in particular, have been criticized; however, the exclusion of minority groups has occurred, until recently, in all content areas, thereby contributing to the incongruity between the worlds of home–community and school for many students (Phelan, Davidson, & Cao Yu, 1996).

The multiple worlds of students' home, school, and community and the extent to which these worlds are congruent can facilitate the transition among them and students' engagement in school learning (Phelan, Davidson, & Cao Yu, 1996) (see Figure 2.1). A curriculum that integrates the worlds of diverse students becomes relevant to their lives and enables them to engage successfully in the world of the school. As Delpit (1995) has pointed out, "When a significant difference exists between the student's culture and the school's culture, teachers can easily misread students' aptitudes, intent, or abilities as a result of differences in styles of language use and interactional patterns" (p. 167).

Related to the issue of inappropriate curriculum as a barrier to learning for diverse students is the question of preferred learning styles. Nieto (2000) defines learning style as "the way in which individuals receive and process information" (p. 142). Teachers of students from different cultures may use instructional approaches that confuse both teacher and students concerning the students' ability to comprehend and learn. However, despite intuitive appeal for many educators, little support has been found for matching learning styles according to one's culture, and past attempts to match a culture with a particular learning style have been strongly criticized (Irvine & York, 1995; McDermott & Glutting, 1997). As Irvine and York (1995) in their review of the

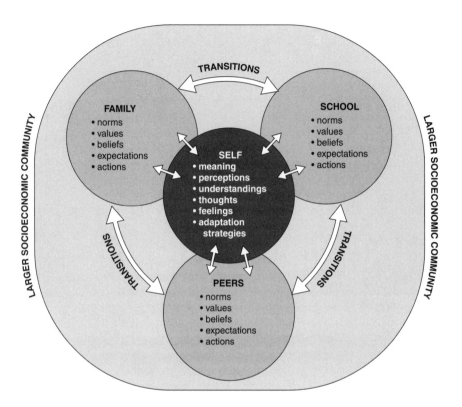

FIGURE 2.1   The Multiple Worlds Model

Reprinted by permission of the publisher from Phelan and Davidson, *Renegotiating Cultural Diversity in American Schools,* (New York: Teachers College Press, © 1993 by Teachers College, Columbia University. All rights reserved.), p. 56.

literature on learning styles and culturally diverse students have indicated, "The assumption that diverse students can learn only if they use their preferred style also ignores what developmental psychologists call the malleability and plasticity of children" (p. 493). In other words, children can master various learning styles with the appropriate instructional and psychological support. Furthermore, differences in the content to be learned often require different approaches to learning.

Rather than assume that a particular cultural group learns best in a particular way, it is helpful to all students when the teacher employs various approaches that require different learning styles and observes how individual students respond. Although there is limited support for matching learning styles with cultures as a basis for planning instruction, the approach does consider the cultural background of students, and different students may certainly have different approaches to learning that the teacher must recognize.

Closely related to issues involving learning style is the concept of multiple intelligences. Howard Gardner's (1993) work on multiple intelligences has important implications for learning and teaching diverse students. Gardner has helped educators to understand the narrow focus of most assessments of intelligence and the fact that we shortchange students when we address only verbal–linguistic or logical–mathematical intelligence. He had originally identified seven types of intelligence: linguistic, logical–mathematical, spatial, musical, bodily-kinesthetic, interpersonal, and intrapersonal. According to Gardner, "the purpose of school should be to develop intelligences and to help people reach vocational and avocational goals that are appropriate to their particular spectrum of intelligences" (p. 9). These intelligences are related to particular styles of learning, and teachers need to recognize the multiple ways in which students learn in planning and implementing instruction. Traditionally, schools have focused on linguistic and logical–mathematical learning to the exclusion of all others. Gardner's work has broadened our understanding of intelligence and the need for more comprehensive assessment of students' abilities, interests, and approaches to learning.

Alternative Viewpoints

Educational anthropologists have made extensive contributions to the research literature in multicultural education through their studies on the influence of culture on educational progress and the underachievement of diverse students in the schools. In a very enlightening discussion, Erickson (1996) notes that "as educational anthropology became a distinct field in the mid-60s, its members were generally appalled by the ethnocentrism of the cultural deficit explanation" (p. 27).

Sociolinguistically oriented anthropologists identified cultural differences in communication style between teachers and students as the explanation for underachievement, while others pointed to the inequity in access to employment over many generations as the basic explanation (Erickson, 1996). Erickson (1996) labels these two major positions of anthropologists as the "communication process explanation" and the "perceived labor market explanation" (p. 28).

Thus, the culturally learned patterns of verbal and nonverbal communication can explain, for some, the high rates of school failure among some minority students. When the teacher and students have different styles of speaking and listening, miscommunication in the classroom can result (Au and Mason, 1981; Barnhardt, 1982; Erickson & Mohatt, 1982; Heath, 1983; Michaels & Collins, 1984; Phillips, 1983).

John Ogbu (1995), the main proponent of the labor market explanation described by Erickson (1996), has pointed out that it is important to recognize that all culturally diverse students do not underachieve in school. In fact, he notes the difference in achievement between domestic minority students and immigrant minorities, labeling the former "castelike" minorities. Castelike minorities are involuntary immigrant groups characterized by secondary cultural differences developed largely in opposition to the dominant culture. In addition, the phenomenon of cultural inversion exists, which involves the identification of certain forms of behavior, events, symbols, and meanings as inappropriate for the group because they are white American characteristics. Therefore, according to Ogbu, some minority students resist engagement in school learning activities because that means "acting White" (Ogbu, 1995). One example of Ogbu's theory is seen in the positive school engagement among refugees from Southeast Asia when compared with that of African Americans as "domestic or castelike minorities."

However, D'Amato (1996) strongly opposes Ogbu's position, arguing that "resistance to school is not a phenomenon restricted to minority children but occurs among all school children for whom we have close ethnographic accounts" (p. 186). He points out that resistance occurs even among some Japanese schoolchildren and even among "decidedly upper-middle-class Jewish American school children under certain conditions" (p. 186). D'Amato concludes with other examples to show that "the castelike minority position is unable to explain why the children of castelike minorities do not always reject their teachers" (p. 186). D'Amato also rejects the cultural differences or communication process explanation, pointing out that certain immigrant children excel in school despite incongruities between the school and home cultures.

Noting that both Ogbu's position and the communications process explanation have received empirical support as well as "theoretical force," Erickson (1996) finds a synthesis of the two positions held by educational anthropologists as the most acceptable. He concludes, "As an educator I cannot accept the premise that there is nothing we can do to improve the educational situation of domestic minority students in the United States. The task is not only to analyze the structural conditions by which inequity is reproduced in society but to search out every possible site in which the struggle for progressive transformation can take place" (p. 45).

In fact, Erickson argues for "culturally responsive pedagogy" as part of the total solution. This pedagogy will "reduce miscommunication by teachers and students, foster trust, and prevent the genesis of conflict that moves quickly beyond intercultural misunderstanding to bitter struggles of negative identity exchange between some students and their teachers" (p. 48).

Approaches to Curriculum Reform

Geneva Gay (1995) has commented that multicultural education "teaches content about culturally pluralistic contributions to humankind and U.S. society; engages students actively and interactively with their own cultural identity and the cultural identity of others; and develops the kind of social consciousness, civic responsibility, and political activism needed to reconstruct society for greater pluralistic equality, truth, inclusion and justice" (p. 27).

In fact, the importance of integrating the content described by Gay into the curriculum has been stressed by Banks (1997). Banks (1995) has identified four approaches used to integrate ethnic content into the elementary and secondary curriculum: teaching about the contributions of diverse groups, adding content about diverse groups to the curriculum, transforming the curriculum, and social action. Heroes, heroines, holidays, foods, and discrete cultural elements are the focus of the contributions approach. In the additive approach, content, concepts, lessons, and units are added to the curriculum, leaving its basic structure unchanged. At the next level, the transformation approach, the structure of the curriculum is actually changed, enabling students to "view concepts, issues, events, and themes from diverse ethnic/cultural perspectives" (Banks, 1995, p. 13). The action approach provides opportunities for students to make decisions on personal, social, and civic problems and take action to find solutions. Some would insist that only the action approach is acceptable, while others view the four approaches as a continuum through which teachers often move. Ladson-Billings (1994) expresses the essence of the action approach in her discussion of culturally relevant teaching.

> Culturally relevant teaching is about questioning (and preparing students to question) the structural inequality, the racism, and the injustice that exist in society. The teachers I studied work in opposition to the system that employs them. They are critical of the way that the school system treats employees, students, parents, and activists in the community. However, they cannot let their critique reside solely in words. They must turn it into action by challenging the system. What they do is both their lives and their livelihoods. In their classrooms, they practice a subversive pedagogy. Even in the face of the most mundane curricular decisions these teachers make a stand. (p. 128)

Sleeter & Grant (1994) have also identified approaches to multicultural education. These include (1) teaching the exceptional and culturally different, (2) the human relations approach, (3) single-group studies, (4) multicultural education, and (5) education that is multicultural and social reconstructionist. In view of the limitations inherent in each approach, Sleeter & Grant (1994) favor the multicultural and social reconstructionist approach, which incorporates the strengths of all the other approaches. In their view, it "goes the furthest toward providing better schooling as well as creating a better society" (p. 243). We have summarized the approaches in Table 2.5.

The aim of curriculum reform has been to teach students to understand different racial, ethnic, and religious groups, which will ultimately improve relationships among all participants in the U.S. society, and to help students to build an ethnoracial identity (Heath, 1995). In her discussion of curriculum theory and multicultural education, Gay has explained that multicultural education has encompassed

> descriptive analyses of educational systems and conditions that ignore or deny the importance of cultural diversity; critical explanations are used to determine why those systems should be changed to be more representative of and responsive to cultural pluralism; and prescriptive recommendations suggest what the changes should embody in order for education to be maximally beneficial to an ever-increasing variety of culturally, ethnically, and socially pluralistic individuals, institutions and communities. (p. 27)

TABLE 2.5   Approaches to Multicultural Education

1. **Teaching the exceptional and culturally different:** The aim of those who favor this approach is assimilation of young people into the mainstream. The mainstream society is viewed as basically good and just by proponents of this approach. Sleeter and Grant point out that two orientations to difference exist within this group: a deficiency orientation and a difference orientation toward the exceptional and culturally different. Sleeter and Grant criticize this approach for its assimilationist orientation and the fact that it ignores structural and institutional racism as factors in the lack of progress for many families of color and poor families.
2. **The human relations approach:** The emphasis in this approach is on promotion of positive feelings among students and reduction of stereotyping, thereby promoting unity and tolerance in the diverse U.S. population. This approach focuses mainly on affective skills for students, for example, feeling good about themselves and the group to which they belong, and accepting and getting along with those who are different from themselves.
3. **Single-group studies:** The focus in this approach is on a single group. Examples include African Americans, Native Americans, Asian Americans, women, and children with disabilities. The goal of this approach is to empower the single group and promote their social equality and recognition.
4. **Multicultural education:** Sleeter and Grant describe this approach as promoting " social structural equality and cultural pluralism. Within the school, the goals are" equal opportunity, cultural pluralism and alternative life-styles, respect for those who differ, and support for power equity among groups. This approach is broader than the first three. Everyone is included in its goals since the aim is to reform schooling for all children.
5. **Education that is multicultural and social reconstructionist:** This is the most extensive approach. The goals include the promotion of social structural equality and cultural pluralism within the society. Within the schools the goals are to prepare students to work actively toward social structural equality and to promote cultural pluralism, alternative life-styles, and equal opportunity. Sleeter and Grant favor this approach. They point out that the approach has much in common with the multicultural education approach, and it also borrows from the others. However, the approach adds the preparation of students to take social action—to "change the rules of the game." Thus, it offers greater hope for the future. As Sleeter and Grant have noted, "Our thinking is based largely on social conditions that persist and that limit and often damage or destroy the lives of many people" (p. 243).

This is a very brief outline of the approaches and we strongly advise readers to consult the text by Sleeter and Grant for in-depth discussion of their analyses.

Sleeter, C., & Grant, C. (1994).

Curriculum reform has been especially focused on social studies and history. Before the 1960s, American history was white America's history, and students learned nothing of the participation of other groups in the building of this country (Heath, 1995). However, the ethnic studies movement in the 1970s resulted in the publication of textbooks and instructional materials that recognized the contributions of other groups (Banks, 1995). Private religious and racial–ethnic schools have also contributed to the development of new curricula and instructional materials.

Content Integration

In other approaches, literature has been used to enrich social studies and address multicultural goals (Davis & Palmer, 1992; Savage & Savage, 1993). For example, children can vicariously experience others' lives and develop em-

TABLE 2.6   Children's and Young Adult Multicultural Literature Related to the Cases in Bridging Multiple Worlds

BOOK AND AUTHOR	COPYRIGHT DATE	PUBLISHER	TOPIC AND GRADE LEVEL
Over Here It's Different: Carolina's Story by Mildred Leinweber Dawson	1993	Macmillan	Recent immigrants Grades 4 and up
Remix: Conversations with Immigrant Teenagers by Marina Tamar Budhos	1999	Henry Holt	Recent immigrants Grades 9 and up
Esperanza Rising by Pam Muñoz Ryan	2000	Scholastic	Migrant farmworkers Grades 5–8
My Heroes, My People by Ruth Katcher	1999	Farrar, Straus, & Giroux	African Americans and Native Americans in the West Grades 2 and up
Arab American Encyclopedia by Anan Ameri and Dawn Ramey (Eds.)	2000	Gale Group	Arab Americans Grades 5 and up
Native American Testimony: A Chronicle of Indian–White Relations from Prophecy to the Present, 1492–1992 by Peter Nabokov (Ed.)	1991	Penguin	Native Americans Grades 8 and up
Here Is My Kingdom: Hispanic-American Literature and Art for Young People by Charles Sullivan (Ed.)	1994	Harry N. Abrams	Latinos Grades 8 and up
All the Colors We Are: The Story of How We Get Our Skin Color by Katie Kissinger	1994	Redleaf Press	Race–ethnicity K–5

pathy for people of diverse cultures through carefully selected literature (Savage & Savage, 1993). A list of suggested children's and adolescent literature connected to the cases in this text is provided in Table 2.6.

Teachers can also create multicultural units using children's literature, thus helping students to learn about their multicultural world. Davis and Palmer (1992) have developed a model for supplementing textbook material in social studies with children's literature. Their model provides a series of steps that teachers can follow with a central focus on the concepts,

BOOK AND AUTHOR	COPYRIGHT DATE	PUBLISHER	TOPIC AND GRADE LEVEL
What Are You? Voices of Mixed-Race Young People by Pearl Fuyo Gaskins	1999	Henry Holt	Multiracial Grades 5 and up
The Kingfisher Book of Religions by Trevor Barnes	1999	Larousse Kingfisher Chambers	Religion Grades 3 and up
Joey Pigza Loses Control by Jack Gantos	2000	Farrar, Straus & Giroux	Attention deficit hyperactivity disorder Grades 5–8
From the Notebooks of Melanin Sun by Jackqueline Woodson	1995	Blue Sky Press	Homosexuality Grades 6 and up
Joyride by Gretchen Olson	1998	Boyds Mills Press	Migrant Grades 6 and up
Teaching with Folk Stories of the Hmong by Dia Cha and Norma J. Livo	2000	Libraries Unlimited	Hmong All grades
Migrant Worker: A Boy from the Rio Grande Valley by Diane Hoyt-Goldsmith	1996	Holiday House	Migrant farmworkers Grades 3 and up
The Norton Anthology of African American Literature edited by Henry Louis Gates and Nellie Y. McKay	1993	W. W. Norton	African American Grades 8 and up

facts, generalizations, values, and skills to be taught in social studies (Davis & Palmer, 1992).

Insisting that the best books for or about African American children must be both well written and sensitive to cultural and social realities, Sims (1982) and Sims Bishop (1997) provide useful guidelines for the selection of books. Noting that selection can be complicated, she points out that the sociopolitical premises of multicultural education make it important for us to reject some books. Those in which verbal or visual stereotyping exist or authenticity and authority, perspective, and world view or underlying ideology are unacceptable should be challenged and rejected.

Sims's earlier (1982) categories of books written for and about African American children include realistic fiction with a social conscience, melting pot fiction, and culturally conscious fiction. Realistic fiction attempts to "create a social conscience, mainly in non-African American readers, to encourage them to develop empathy, sympathy and tolerance for African American children and their problems" (p. 17). Melting pot books communicate that all people are the same, ignoring all differences except physical characteristics (Sims, 1982, 1997). According to Sims, without illustrations, one would never know that one of these books was about an African American child. This type of book is positive, however, in that images are usually positive and the grim social problems facing many minority children are omitted. In contrast, culturally conscious fiction comes closest to "constituting a body of literature about African American children and their lives" (p. 49).

In her later work, Sims Bishop (1997) refers to three areas of concerns about the selection of multicultural books: literary, sociopolitical, and educational. The literary includes the need for excellent visual artistry and the quality of the writing. Another concern is what the political message or viewpoint of the work is expressing. Is the book authentically based on cultural mores? Does the author have the authority to write the book? Her educational concern centers on what the book can contribute to the child's education.

Sims Bishop's categories or types of books can provide teachers with a guide for selecting books for their students according to the intended audience and intent of the author. Since teachers need to provide literature for and about diverse children, the definitions can aid the teacher in the selection process.

Oral history can also be utilized to modify the social studies curriculum. Olmedo (1993) presents steps for using oral history with bilingual and English as a second language (ESL) students who may lack the knowledge base or cultural background necessary to engage in social studies instruction. This approach "helps students understand that history is filled with stories" (Olmedo, 1993, p. 7). Steps begin with the identification of concepts, followed by preparation of an interview guide. The guide is then translated by students into their own native languages. Next, students practice by interviewing each other, even role playing various adult members of families. A guest speaker from the community is then interviewed by the class, providing a practice opportunity for the class to tape the speaker and transcribe or summarize the taped interview. Students then identify persons to be interviewed and conduct interviews individually or in small groups. Review, transcriptions, or summaries are then individually completed, followed by students' comparing and contrasting their experiences.

Other models of curriculum reform or content integration include programs such as Robert Moses' Algebra Project. The underlying premise of the project developers is that "all children can learn algebra" and "virtually all middle school students can learn algebra given the proper context" (Silva & Moses, 1990, p. 375). However, the project is especially concerned with the needs of inner-city minority students. The Algebra Project tries to change the way mathematics teachers construct their learning environment by producing teachers who are able to facilitate a math learning environment grounded in real-life experiences and to support students in the social construction of mathematics. Additional goals of the project include the development of

> mathematically literate, self-competent, and motivated middle school learners who are able to master the college preparatory high school mathematics and science curriculum and the mathematics necessary for mathematics- and science-related careers; and to build a broader community of individuals including parents, community volunteers, and school administrators who understand the problem of mathematics education as a problem of mathematics literacy and who understand the question of students' capability as learners as a matter of effective effort. (Silva & Moses, 1990, p. 379)

Success for All (Slavin & Madden, 2000) also focuses on mathematics, in addition to reading, and is currently used in many large, metropolitan school districts around the country. Aspects of this program are designed to allow increased movement, call and response strategies, and positive reinforcement in order to appeal to diverse minority groups, particularly African Americans. Observations by one of the authors in a classroom where the program had been implemented confirmed that African American students were enthusiastically engaged in learning. However, the program has been highly criticized in recent publications (Pogrow, 2000).

Publishers are also producing increasing quantities of new materials to address the needs of students to learn about and appreciate diverse groups in the society (see Table 2.6). Increasingly, curriculum materials are available that address diversity in the school-aged population.

An important note of caution is provided by Delpit in her book *Other People's Children* (1995), in which she writes of the cultural differences that must be understood in selecting instructional approaches and materials for teaching diverse students. She comments that "Appropriate education for poor children and children of color can only be devised in consultation with adults who share their culture. Black parents, teachers of color, and members of poor communities must be allowed to participate fully in the discussion of what kind of instruction is in their children's best interest" (p. 45). Delpit continues,

> [s]tudents must also be taught the codes needed to participate fully in the mainstream of American life, not by being forced to attend to hollow, inane, de-contextualized subskills, but rather within the context of meaningful communicative endeavors; . . . even while students are assisted in learning the culture of power, they must also be helped to learn about the arbitrariness of those codes and about the power relationships they represent. (p. 45)

However, the impetus for curriculum reform has come not only from social scientists and educators who seek a more equitable education for all students and an accurate portrayal of U.S. history that represents all groups in the society, but also from national, state, and local initiatives to raise academic standards and achievement for all students. The requirement to align the curriculum with the new state standards creates additional pressure on teachers, and the tendency to "teach to the tests" may well be counterproductive in teachers' efforts to improve the curriculum for diverse students. Nevertheless, time to plan, discuss, observe, and share ideas with colleagues, money to support the change process, support from colleagues and administrators, and information about assessment strategies and whole-class instructional strategies have been indicated by teachers as important needs in the curriculum change process (Teberg, 1999).

While support from colleagues and administrators is certainly required, a positive relationship between parents and educators is also critical (Konzal, 1997). In fact, to make major changes in curriculum, it is best to enlist the support of all stakeholders, and this includes the community served by the school. For example, an Iowa school district introducing a new middle school mathematics curriculum addressed the anticipated misgivings of parents early and made parents allies in the process (Meyer et al., 1996). In another study of curriculum reform, Anderson (1996) found that the technical, political, and cultural dimensions of curricular reform efforts required even broader consideration: a sufficient provision of time for teachers; changed values and beliefs about the school's goals of instruction and the means of fostering them; collaborative teacher learning; parent learning; new student roles and work; and a systemic view of reform by the entire school staff.

PREPARATION OF TEACHERS
FOR DIVERSE LEARNERS

Researchers in multicultural education have identified critical elements in preparing effective teachers for the increasingly diverse school-aged population in the United States. For example, teachers must consider the personal attitudes and experiences that they bring to teaching. In a review of the implementation of African and African American curriculum content reform in Buffalo, New York, Shujaa (1995), noted that "[teachers'] attitudes about their own and other people's ethnicity proved important for culturally relevant teaching" (p. 196).

In fact, Howard (1999) speaks eloquently to white teachers in multiracial schools in his book *We Can't Teach What We Don't Know*. Howard introduces the inner work of multicultural teaching for whites in the following passage:

> [T]here is a compelling need (particularly for White educators) to look within ourselves and realign our deepest assumptions and perceptions regarding the racial marker that we carry, namely Whiteness. We need to understand the dynamics of past and present dominance, face how we have been shaped by myths of superiority, and begin to sort out our thoughts, emotions, and behaviors relative to race and other dimensions of human diversity. (p. 4)

Culturally Responsive Teaching

Culturally responsive teaching, also referred to as culturally relevant teaching, has been defined by researchers in multicultural education in a variety of ways. The definition of Ladson-Billings (1994), provided earlier, focuses on questioning, critical thinking, and challenging the system. In his discussion of "situated teaching," Shor's (1992) definition reflects the same elements as that of Ladson-Billings. He notes that the teacher begins with what students bring to class—their knowledge, themes, cultures, conditions, and idioms. According to Shor, situated teaching "avoids teacher-centered syllabi and locates itself in the students' cultures" (p. 44). Describing a problem-posing pedagogy as empowering for students, the subject matter and learning process are adapted for the students so that they can develop critical thinking. Since all education is political, in Shor's view, "critical thought is married to everyday life by examining daily themes, social issues, and academic lore" (p. 44). In Shor's view, this pedagogy will "increase the chance that students will feel ownership in their education and reduces the conditions that produce their alienation" (p. 51).

Shor contributes further to our understanding of critical thinking through his definitions. For example, he notes, "To think critically in this framework means to examine the deep meanings, personal implications, and social consequences of any knowledge, theme, technique, text, or material" (p. 169).

Geneva Gay (2000) describes culturally responsive teaching as "using the cultural knowledge, prior experiences, frames of reference, and performance styles of ethnically diverse students to make learning encounters more relevant to and effective for them" (p. 29). An expanded list of characteristics reflects the teacher's recognition of the students' multiple worlds and the need to bridge these worlds to make the transitions easier for students (see Table 2.7).

TABLE 2.7   Characteristics of Culturally Responsive Teaching

1. Curriculum content and teaching strategies are "filtered through students' cultural frames of reference to make the content more personally meaningful and easier to master" (p. 24).
2. Culturally responsive teaching "acknowledges the legitimacy of the cultural heritages of different ethnic groups as worthy content to be taught in the formal curriculum" (p. 29). Students' cultural heritages influence their attitudes, dispositions, and approaches to learning.
3. Culturally responsive teaching "builds bridges of meaningfulness between home and school experiences as well as between academic abstractions and lived sociocultural realities" (p. 29).
4. Culturally responsive teaching uses a wide variety of teaching strategies that address different learning styles.
5. Culturally responsive teaching helps students to know and affirm their cultures.
6. Multicultural information, resources, and materials are incorporated throughout the curriculum.

From Gay, G. (2000).

Paulo Freire (1998) has also contributed to our understanding of culturally relevant or responsive teaching. In his discussion of "respect for what students know," Freire asks,

> "Why not take advantage of the students' experience of life in those parts of the city neglected by authorities to discuss the problem of pollution in the rivers and the question of poverty and the risks to health from the rubbish heaps in such areas?. . . Why not discuss with the students the concrete reality of their lives and that aggressive reality in which violence is permanent and where people are much more familiar with death than life?" (Friere, 1998, p. 6) However, the essence of culturally relevant teaching is found in the following question: "Why not establish an intimate connection between knowledge considered basic to any school curriculum and knowledge that is the fruit of the lived experience of these students as individuals?" (Friere, 1998, p. 36).

Classroom Discourse Patterns

Culturally relevant teaching may require modification of the classroom discourse patterns and participation structure as discussed earlier. Classroom discourse patterns can help or hinder a student's ability to respond to questions and participate in discussions. The teacher's manner of speaking to students and asking questions also contributes to students' successful communication and participation (Mehan, Lintz, Okamoto, & Wells, 1995). Many teachers, perhaps a majority in the United States, use what has been referred to as a "recitation script" (Tharp & Gallimore, 1988). This script involves the initiation of a communication by the teacher, the student's response, and the teacher's evaluation, or an IRE sequence. Most often, the sequence is directed to an individual student whose response is publicly evaluated. However, studies have shown that this pattern may not be appropriate for some diverse students and may represent discontinuity between the language patterns of the home and those of the school (Mehan et al., 1995). While patterns in Anglo families may be compatible with the recitation script, those in minority group families may not. The discontinuity in patterns could lead to lower achievement and higher dropout rates among minority students (Mehan et al., 1995).

For example, in a study reported by Phillips (1983), Native American children gave more effective performances in classrooms that minimized the public performances of individual students. In this study, the Indian teacher, who focused on groups to maintain classroom control, gave praise in public and criticism in private, and allocated turns so that students did not have to participate as individuals, demonstrated an effective classroom (Erickson & Mohatt, 1982).

Earlier studies reported in the 1980s include that of Puerto Rican students who also demonstrated more positive responses to group-oriented, turn-allocation strategies in which students volunteered their answers (McCullum, 1989). McCullum suggested that the instructional, "conversation-like" approach was more congruent with the conversational patterns in daily Puerto Rican life. Heath (1983) reported that white, middle-income teachers talked to low-income black elementary school students in the typical IRE pattern in contrast to the patterns used in the homes of these students. Parents at home did not ask known-information types of questions; rather, their questions requested nonspecific comparisons or analogies as answers (Mehan et al., 1995). In fact, while the IRE pattern as used in the homes of white students appears to prepare them for the classroom discourse pattern, it is not congruent with patterns used in the homes of low-income black children (Heath, 1983).

Modification of classroom discourse patterns to make the patterns congruent with those of the home has been found to improve academic performance (Piestrup, 1973; Mehan et al., 1995). Marva Collins, who has been widely recognized for her accomplishments at Chicago's Westside Prep School, has also been described as using a more congruent interaction style with her students. This includes rhythmic language, call and response, repetition, and deliberate body motions (Foster, 1989).

Traditional teaching not only uses the IRE script, but also frequently represents what Freire (1985) refers to as "banking education." This is the view of teaching and learning in which students represent vessels or depositories to be filled by teachers. The teacher is the expert or authority who knows everything, and the student knows nothing. This practice is contrary to the process of knowledge construction, one of the important dimensions of multicultural education (Banks, 1997). In the words of Freire (1998), "to teach is not to transfer knowledge but to create the possibilities for the production or construction of knowledge" (p. 30).

Culturally Relevant Teaching

The work of Ladson-Billings (1994) and others in multicultural education has shown that what Ladson-Billings refers to as "culturally relevant teaching" can facilitate the engagement of diverse learners in classroom learning activities. In a school described by Ladson-Billings, one fourth grade class studied how cities develop, took trips into the community to learn about branches of city government, and worked on solutions to specific problems in their city. They also wrote letters to the editor of a city newspaper about conditions in their neighborhood. Students participated in a community service program and parents participated in 20 hours of volunteer service to the school. This school also demonstrated some of the elements of culturally relevant schools defined by Ladson-Billings: providing educational self-determination, honoring and respecting the students' culture, helping African American students understand the world as it is, and equipping them to change it for the better (Ladson-Billings, 1994, pp. 137–139).

Another approach to culturally relevant teaching is available in the use of Mathematics Trails, a collection of activities that demonstrates how the study of math can be extended beyond the classroom and can involve teachers and students in investigative, problem-based experiences in the real world (Lancaster & Delisi, 1997; Ampadu & Rosenthal, Ampadu, 1999; E. Hofstetter, personal communication, December 2000). In this approach the teacher begins with a decision on the sites to be used, which may be found in the students' community or broader environment. Problems can be identified within the students' communities. Thus, students are involved not only in relating math to their real world, but also in tackling meaningful problems in their communities. Another rich example of relating the students' community to classroom instruction has been described by Moll, Velez-Ibanez, and Greenberg (1989). The teacher incorporated information about construction in the community (the barrio) in his reading instruction (see Table 2.8).

TABLE 2.8   An Example of Culturally Relevant Teaching

A sixth grade teacher conducted the following reading activity, incorporating the construction project in progress in a local barrio.

1. Students read library books on constructing houses and other types of buildings.
2. The teacher invited members of the community to speak to the class about building (several were parents of students in the class). A mason talked about how to mix mortar, measure straight lines, and stack bricks neatly. A carpenter talked about sawing and nailing and compared the strength of brick versus wood.
3. Students then applied what they had learned to building a model in the classroom.
4. They wrote about the learning experience. In their writing they used new vocabulary they had learned, described the skills used in building, and expressed appreciation for their parents' knowledge.

Adapted from Moll et al. (1989).

In her study on Amy, "a white, middle class teacher who consistently demonstrated culturally sensitive strategies," Powell (1997) described aspects of culturally relevant teaching as "acquiring cultural sensitivity, reshaping the classroom curriculum, and inviting students to learn" (p. 471).

> [Amy] sought ways to acquire a sensitivity for students' lives outside of school and for how their lives influenced her classroom curriculum. Specifically, she continuously explored students' cultural backgrounds and families, linked students' backgrounds to school culture, and assumed various leadership roles at school that were related to racial minority students. Although Amy viewed her classroom as an extension of students' cultural and family backgrounds when she began teaching, this kind of sensitivity became a preoccupation for her, and ultimately became a prevailing theme in her decision making about her classroom curriculum and instruction. (p. 473)

Teacher Preparation

However, the secretary of education under President Clinton has reported that only 20 percent of America's teachers feel very well prepared to teach children from diverse cultures (Riley, 1999). Included in four areas of special concern were addressing the needs of children with disabilities (21 percent) and of students with limited English proficiency (20 percent) and integrating educational technology into their teaching methods (20 percent) (Riley, 1999). The secretary also pointed out that students with limited English proficiency are "the fastest growing population served by the Elementary and Secondary Education Act with an increase of 67% between the 1990–91 and 1996–97 academic years." Educational researchers have supported the secretary's findings in other studies. For example, Taylor (1999) found that "few preservice and beginning teachers are prepared for the diversity of today's classrooms" (p. 1). Yet, by 2010, 40 percent of students will come from diverse groups (Taylor, 1999). In another study assessing the knowledge of preservice teachers and teacher educators regarding issues related to multicultural education, Taylor, (1999) found a significant difference between the multicultural knowledge levels of preservice teachers and teacher educators. Preservice teachers' knowledge levels were significantly below average, while those of teacher educators were almost average. Taylor concluded that both groups need to increase their multicultural knowledge. Yeo (1999) has also found a need for increased multicultural knowledge among teachers in rural schools, where the rural environment creates particular needs.

In an assessment of preservice teachers' attitudes and beliefs concerning cultural diversity, Schultz et al. (1996) found that a variety of experiences involving school and community were needed to bring preservice teachers into contact with cultural groups different from their own. In addition, a change in the roles of teachers from instructors and evaluators to cultural negotiators has been suggested (Stairs, 1996).

Other researchers have also pointed out weaknesses in current teacher education programs. For example, Tatto (1996) found that teacher education as currently structured in the United States is too weak as an intervention to alter views regarding the teaching and classroom management of diverse learners. He concluded that lay culture norms were strongly ingrained among education students.

In support of more effective teacher education, Cochran-Smith (1995) has identified five perspectives on race, culture, and language diversity that are essential to preparing teachers "who see themselves as both educators and activists," who work with others to do what (she) calls "teaching against the grain of institutions of schooling that are dysfunctional and inequitable. . . (1) reconsidering personal knowledge and experience; (2) locating teaching within the culture of the school and the community; (3) analyzing children's learning opportunities; (4) understanding children's understanding; and (5) constructing reconstructionist pedagogy" (p. 500). It is the reconsideration of personal knowledge and experience that can be so easily neglected in efforts to prepare teachers for diverse students. Opportunities to examine one's assumptions, stereotypes, and expectations of children from different languages, cultures, races, classes, and gender can help preservice and in-service teachers to begin to question their beliefs concerning the abilities, motivation, and behaviors of children from diverse backgrounds. Cochran-Smith suggests the use of personal narrative essays for that purpose.

Cochran-Smith also argues against the traditional lesson plan as the basis for instructional planning and proposes the inquiry method as a way for teachers to construct meaningful effective pedagogy for their students. She notes that the typical lesson plan "implies that both planning and teaching are linear activities that proceed from a preplanned opening move to a known and predetermined endpoint, suggesting that knowledge, curriculum and instruction are static and unchanging" (p. 496). On the other hand, an inquiry approach creates opportunities for prospective teachers to develop perspectives on teaching, learning, and schooling that are central to what she labels as "an activist's stance" (p. 495). Furthermore, according to Cochran-Smith, experienced teachers plan in ways that are "more recursive, cyclical, more learner-centered, and structured around larger chunks of content than those of a single lesson" (p. 495). Ultimately, she argues for generative ways for student teachers and teacher educators to "reconsider their assumptions, understand the values and practices of families and cultures different from their own, and construct pedagogy that not only takes these into account in locally appropriate ways but also makes issues of diversity an explicit part of the curriculum" (p. 493).

Another answer to the problems in teacher education is advanced by Darling-Hammond (1995), who stresses the need for the "professionalization of teaching" (p. 478). She points out that "the professionalization of an occupation raises the floor below which no entrants will be admitted to practice; and it eliminates the practices of substandard or irregular licensure that allows untrained entrants to practice disproportionately on underserved and poorly protected clients." She adds, it "increases the overall knowledge base for the occupation, thus improving the quality of services for all clients, especially those most in need of high-quality teaching" (p. 478).

Ladson-Billings (1995) has identified key elements from multicultural teacher education research in both mainstream and nonmainstream settings. The "wisdom of practice, the use of autobiography, restructured field experiences, and situated pedagogies" are included in these elements. Her notion of "culturally specific pedagogy" is described as "teachers' attempts to make the school and home cultures of diverse students more congruent" (p. 754).

In a recent practical discussion of the principles for teaching and learning in a multicultural society, Banks et al. (2001) reflect the goals of multicultural education and the work of researchers in this field. The 12 principles that they present include, among others, professional development programs to "help teachers understand the complex characteristics of ethnic groups within U.S. society and the ways in which race, ethnicity, language and social class interact to influence student behavior" (p. 198) and "the use of multiple, culturally sensitive techniques to assess complex cognitive and social skills" (p. 202). Several principles highlight equitable opportunities for students to learn and achieve high standards and curriculum that "helps students to understand that knowledge is socially constructed and reflects researchers' personal experiences as well as the social, political, and economic contexts in which they live and work" (p. 198). Other principles are concerned with the important areas of intergroup relations, students' knowledge of stereotyping and related biases, students' knowledge of values shared by all cultural groups, school governance, and equitable funding for all schools.

Challenges

Researchers in multicultural education continue to offer promising approaches for the challenges involved in educating an increasingly diverse school-aged population. However, critics have challenged the field in several areas. For example, Garcia (1995) argues that the educational research has been directed primarily at the problems encountered by diverse students—discrimination, desegregation, underachievement, low self-esteem, and limited English proficiency—and has lacked "substantive theoretical underpinnings" (p. 381). Furthermore, in his view, the widely used case study approach has resulted in the identification of generalized cultural characteristics that ignore the within-group diversity that exists in all cultural groups (Garcia, 1995). Therefore, from his point of view, much of the research that has identified some groups as field dependent versus field independent or cooperative versus competitive, for example, is problematic at best and bordering on creating stereotypes at worst. He raises two critical questions: What set of knowledge about diverse cultural groups is educationally important? And what overarching conceptualization of culture is useful in understanding the educational framework of culturally diverse groups? (p. 381).

Ogbu (1995), too, has challenged the field, insisting that multicultural education will not significantly affect the school-learning problems of minority students who traditionally underachieve due to the fact that the field is not based on a "good understanding of the nature of the cultural diversity or cultural differences of minority groups" (p. 582). Ogbu describes the emergence of multicultural education as, initially, a response to cultural deprivation theory and points out that many proponents of multicultural education have not studied minority cultures in minority communities. Furthermore, in his view, school success depends not only on what teachers do, but also on what students do. Some students are able to cross cultural and language boundaries and others are not. As discussed earlier in the chapter, it is those who are unable to cross boundaries with whom he is most concerned, those in groups he has classified as involuntary minorities. Ogbu suggests that teachers and interventionists should learn about the students' cultural backgrounds and use that knowledge to organize classrooms and programs. We can learn about students' cultures through observation of classroom and playground behavior, interviews of students about cultural practices and preferences, doing research on various ethnic groups with children in school, and the study of published works on children's ethnic groups (Ogbu, 1995, p. 589).

Critics on both the left (McCarthy, 1990; Ogbu, 1995; Olneck, 1995) and right (Ravitch, 1990a, b; Schlesinger, 1992; Sowell, 1993) have challenged multiculuralism as a philosophy and approach to education. Yet the responsibility of the education system in the United States to serve an increasingly diverse population of school-aged children, the unacceptable educational progress at this time, and the continuing need to create a more just and equitable American society underscore the power of the philosophy, goals, objectives, and pedagogy developed by researchers in multicultural education. Ladson-Billings (1995) insists that scholars in the field must engage in debate to challenge those who have misinterpreted, misperceived, or distorted the definition, goals, and research in multicultural education. Furthermore, she notes that "multicultural teacher education may well be the determiner of the fate of multicultural education" (p. 756).

REFERENCES

Ampadu, C., & Rosenthal, M. (1999). Making mathematics real: The Boston math trail. *Mathematics Teaching in the Middle School, 5*(3), 140–147.

Anderson, R. (1996). *Study of curriculum reform. Volume I: Findings and conclusions.* Boulder: Colorado University.

Au, K., & Mason, J. (1981). Social organizational factors in learning to read: The balance of rights hypothesis. *Reading Research Quarterly, 17*(1), 115–152.

Banks, J. A. (1995). Multicultural education: Historical development, dimensions, and practice. In J. Banks & C. A. McGee Banks (Eds.), *Handbook of research on multicultural education* (pp. 1–7). New York: Macmillan.

Banks, J. (1997). *Multicultural education: Issues and Perspectives* (3rd ed.). Boston: Allyn and Bacon.

Banks, J., Cookson, P., Gay, G., Hawley, W., Irvine, J., Nieto, S., Schofield, J. W., & Stephan, W. (2001). Diversity within unity: Essential principles for teaching and learning in a multicultural society. *Phi Delta Kappan, 83*(3), 196–201.

Barnhardt, C. (1982). "Tuning in" Athabaskan teachers and Athabaskan students. *Cross-cultural issues in Alaskan education, Vol. 2.* Fairbanks: University of Alaska, Center for Cross-cultural studies.

Carmichael, J. W., Jr., & Sevenair, J. (1991). Preparing minorities for science careers. *Issues in Science and Technology, 7*(3), 55–60.

Challenging the status quo: The education record 1993–2000. Washington, DC. U.S. Department of Education: Government Printing Office.

Cochran-Smith, M. (1995). Color blindness and basket making are not the answers: Confronting the dilemmas of race, culture and language diversity in teacher education. *American Educational Research Journal, 32*(3), 493–522.

D'Amato, J. (1996). Resistance and compliance in minority classrooms. In E. Jacob & C. Jordan (Eds.), *Minority education: Anthropological perspectives* (pp. 181–208). Norwood, NJ: Ablex Publishing.

Darling-Hammond, L. (1995). Inequality and access to knowledge. In J. Banks & C. A. McGee Banks (Eds.), *Handbook of research on multicultural education* (pp. 465–483). New York: Macmillan.

Davis, J., & Palmer, J. (1992). A strategy for using children's literature to extend the social studies curriculum. *The Social Studies, 83*(3), 125–128.

Delpit, L. (1995). *Other people's children: Cultural conflict in the classroom.* New York: The New Press.

Education Record, May 2000. *Challenging the status quo: The Education Record 1993–2000.* Washington, DC: U.S. Department of Education.

Erickson, F. (1996). Transformation and school success: The politics and culture of educational achievement. In E. Jacob & C. Jordan (Eds.), *Minority education: Anthropological perspectives* (pp. 27–52). Norwood, NJ: Ablex Publishing.

Erickson, F., & Mohatt, G. (1982). Cultural organization of participation structures in two classrooms of Indian students. In G. D. Spindler (Ed.), *Doing the ethnography of schooling: Educational anthropology in action* (pp. 132–175). New York: Holt, Rinehart & Winston.

Foster, M. (1989). "It's cookin now": A performance analysis of the speech events in an urban community college. *Language in Society, 18,* 1–29.

Fouad, N., & Spreda, S. (1995). Use of interest inventories with special populations: Women and minority groups. *Journal of Career Assessment, 3*(4), 53–68.

Freire, P. (1985). *The politics of education: Culture, power, and liberation.* South Hadley, MA: Bergin & Garvey.

Freire, P. (1998). *Pedagogy of freedom: Ethics, democracy and civic courage.* Lanham, MD: Rowman & Littlefield.

Garcia, E. (1995). Educating Mexican American students: Past treatment and recent developments in theory, research, policy, and practice. In J. Banks & C. A. McGee Banks (Eds.), *Handbook of research on multicultural education* (pp. 372–387). New York: Macmillan.

Gardner, H. (1993). *Multiple intelligences: The theory in practice.* New York: Basic Books.

Gay, G. (1995). Curriculum theory and multicultural education. In J. A. Banks & C. A. McGee Banks (Eds.), *Handbook of research on multicultural education* (pp. 25–43). New York: Macmillan.

Gay, G. (2000). *Culturally responsive teaching: Theory, research and practice.* New York: Teachers College Press.

Heath, S. B. (1983). *Ways with words: Language, life and work in communities and classrooms.* New York: Cambridge University Press.

Heath, S. B. (1995). Ethnography in communities: Learning the everyday life of America's subordinated youth. In J. Banks & C. A. McGee Banks (Eds.), *Handbook of research on multicultural education* (pp. 97–113). New York: Macmillan.

Howard, G. (1999). *We can't teach what we don't know: White teachers, multiracial schools.* New York: Teachers College Press.

Irvine, J. J., & York, D. E. (1995). Learning styles and culturally diverse students: A literature review. In J. A. Banks & C. A. McGee Banks (Eds.), *Handbook of research on multicultural education.* New York: Macmillan.

Konzal, J. (1997). *Teachers and parents working together for curriculum reform: Possibility or pipe dream?* Paper presented at the annual meeting of the American Education Research Association, Chicago, March 24–28.

Kozol, J. (1991). *Savage inequalities.* New York: Crown.

Ladson-Billings, G. (1994). *The dreamkeepers.* San Francisco: Jossey-Bass.

Ladson-Billings, G. (1995). Multicultural teacher education: Research, practice and policy. In J. A. Banks & C. A. McGee Banks (Eds.), *Handbook of research on multicultural education* (pp. 747–762). New York: Macmillan.

Lancaster, R., & Delisi, V. (1997). A mathematics trail at Exeter Academy. *Mathematics Teacher, 90*(3), 234–237.

Lau v Nichols 414 U.S. 563 (1974).

McCarthy, C. (1990). Race and education in the United States: The multicultural solution. *Interchange, 21*(3), 45–55.

McCullum, P. (1989). Turn-allocation in lessons with North American and Puerto Rican students. *Anthropology and Education Quarterly, 20,* 133–156.

McDermott, P., & Glutting, J. (1997). Informing stylistic learning behavior, disposition and achievement through ability subtests—or more illusions of meaning? *School Psychology Review, 26*(2), 163–175.

Mehan, H., Lintz, A., Okamoto, D., & Wills, J. (1995). Ethnographic studies of multicultural education in classrooms and schools. In J. A. Banks & C. A. McGee Banks (Eds.), *Handbook of research on multicultural education* (pp. 129–144). New York: Macmillan.

Meyer, M., Delagardelle, M. L., & Middleton, J. A. (1996). Addressing parents' concerns over curriculum reform. *Educational Leadership, 53*(7), 54–57.

Michaels, S., & Collins, J. (1984). Oral discourse styles: Classroom interaction and the acquisition of literacy. In D. Tannen (Ed.), *Coherence in spoken and written discourse.* Norwood, NJ: Ablex.

Miller-Lachman, L., & Taylor, L. S. (1995). *Schools for all: Educating children in a diverse society.* Albany, NY: Delmar.

Moll, L. C., Velez-Ihanez, C., & Greenberg, J. (1989). *Fieldwork summary: Community knowledge and classroom practice: Combining resources for literacy instruction.* Tucson: University of Arizona.

Mosteller, F., Light, J., & Sachs, J. A. (1996). Sustained inquiry in education: Lessons from skill grouping and class size. *Harvard Educational Review, 66*(4), 797–842.

Narvarro, M. (2001). For parents, one size doesn't fit all in bilingual education. *New York Times* METRO Section. p. B1, February 24, 2001.

National Center for Education Statistics (1996). National Assessment of Educational Progress. Retrieved November 1, 2001, from http://www.nces.ed.gov/nationsreportcard

Nieto, S. (1996). *Affirming diversity: The sociopolitical context of multicultural education* (2nd ed.). New York: Longman.

Nieto, S. (2000). *Affirming diversity: The sociopolitical context of multicultural education* (3rd ed.). New York: Longman.

Oakes, J. (1990). *Multiplying inequalities: The effects of race, social class and tracking on opportunities to learn mathematics and science.* Santa Monica, CA: The Rand Corporation.

Ogbu, J. (1995). Understanding cultural diversity and learning. In J. A. Banks & C. A. McGee Banks (Eds.), *Handbook of research on multicultural education* (pp. 582–596). New York: Macmillan.

Olmedo, I. (1993). Junior historians: Doing oral history with ESL and bilingual students. *TESOL Journal, Summer,* 7–10.

Olneck, M. (1995). Immigrants and education. In J. A. Banks & C. A. McGee Banks (Eds.), *Handbook of research on multicultural education* (pp. 310–330). New York: Macmillan.

Ovando, C. (1990). Politics and pedagogy: The case of bilingual education. *Harvard Educational Review, 60*(3), 341–356.

Phelan, P., Davidson, A. L., & Cao Yu, H. (1996). *Students' multiple worlds: Navigating the borders of family, peer, and school cultures: Renegotiating cultural diversity in American schools.* New York: Teachers College Press.

Phillips, S. (1983). *The invisible culture: Communication in classroom and community on the Warm Springs Indian Reservation.* New York: Longman.

Piestrup, A. (1973). *Black dialect interference and accommodation of reading instruction in first grade.* Berkeley, CA: Language Behavior Research Laboratory.

Pogrow, S. (2000). Success for all does not produce success for students. *Phi Delta Kappan, 82*(1), 67–80.

Powell, R. (1997). Then the beauty emerges: A longitudinal case study of culturally relevant teaching. *Teaching and Teacher Education, 13*(5), 467–484.

Ravitch, D. (1990a). Diversity and democracy: Multicultural education in America. *American Educator, 14*(1), 16–20, 46–48.

Ravitch, D. (1990b). Multiculturalism: E pluribus plures. *American Scholar, 59*(3), 337–354.

Riley, R. W. (1999). Statement of Secretary of Education before the U.S. Senate Committee on Health, Education, Labor and Pensions on the Reauthorization of the Elementary and Secondary Education Act of 1965. Washington, D.C. Feb. 9, 1999. http://www.ed.gov/speeches/02-1999/990209.html.

Savage, M., & Savage, T. (1993). Children's literature in middle school social studies. *The Social Studies, 84*(1), 32–36.

Schlessinger, A. M., Jr. (1992). *The disuniting of America.* New York: Norton.

Schultz, E., et al. (1996). Swimming against the tide: A study of prospective teachers' attitudes regarding cultural diversity and urban teaching. *Western Journal of Black Studies, 20*(1), 1–7.

Shor, I. (1992). *Empowering education: Critical teaching for social change.* Chicago: University of Chicago Press.

Shujaa, M. (1995). Cultural self meets cultural other in the African American experience: Teachers' responses to a curriculum content reform. *Theory into Practice, 34*(3), 194–201.

Silva, C., & Moses, R. (1990). The Algebra Project: Making middle school mathematics count. *Journal of Negro Education, 59*(3), 375–391.

Sims, R. (1982). *Shadow and substance: Afro-American experience in contemporary children's fiction.* Urbana, IL: National Council of Teachers of English.

Sims Bishop, R. (1997). Selecting literature for a multicultural curriculum. In V. J. Harris & C. A. Grant (Eds.), *Using multicultural literature in the K–8 classroom* (pp. 1–19). Norwood, MA: Christopher-Gordon.

Slavin, R. E., & Madden, N. A. (2000). Research on achievement outcomes of Success for All: A summary and response to critics. *Phi Delta Kappan, 82*(1), 38–40, 59–66.

Sleeter, C., & Grant, C. (1994). *Making choices for multicultural education: Five approaches to race, class, and gender.* Upper Saddle River, NJ: Merrill/Prentice Hall.

Sowell, T. (1993). *Inside American education.* New York: The Free Press.

Spener, D. (1988). Transitional bilingual education and the socialization of immigrants. *Harvard Educational Review, 58*(2), 133–153.

Stairs, A. (1996). Human development as cultural negotiation: Indigenous lessons on becoming a teacher. *Journal of Educational Thought/Revue de la Pensee Educative, 30*(3), 219–237.

Steinberg, J. (2000). In American education, bilingual means 'Learn English.' *New York Times,* The Nation Section, p. 3.

Tatto, M. T. (1996). Examining values and beliefs about teaching diverse students: Understanding the challenges for teacher education. *Educational Evaluation and Policy Analysis, 18*(2), 155–180.

Taylor, P. (1999). *Multicultural education issues: Perceived levels of knowledge of preservice teachers and teacher educators.* Paper presented at the Annual Meeting of the Mid-South Educational Research Association, Point Clear, Alabama, November 17–19.

Teberg, A. S. (1999). *Identified professional development needs of teachers in curriculum reform.* Paper presented at the Annual meeting of the American Educational Research Association, Montreal, Quebec, April 19–23.

Tharp, R. G., & Gallimore, R. (1988). *Rousing minds to life: Teaching, learning and schooling in social context.* New York: Cambridge University Press.

U.S. Department of Education. (1996). *The condition of education report.* Washington, DC: Government Printing Office.

U.S. Department of Education. (1999). *The condition of education report.* Washington, DC: Government Printing Office.

U.S. Department of Education. (2000). *Challenging the status quo: The education record 1993–2000.* Washington, DC: Government Printing Office.

Welner, K., & Oakes, J. (1996). Ability grouping: The new susceptibility of school tracking systems to legal challenges. *Harvard Educational Review, 66*(3), 451–470.

Yeo, F. (1999). The barriers of diversity: Multicultural education and rural schools. *Multicultural Education, 7*(1), 2–7.

TABLE OF CONTENTS

"Now more than ever, those who are committed to teacher education practice, research, and policy that includes language diversity need to understand and be strategic about the complex circumstances that threaten these agendas. This volume is a big step in the right direction."

—Marilyn Cochran-Smith, Boston College

PART I: KNOWLEDGE

PART II: PRACTICE

PART III: POLICY

To purchase a copy or receive more information on this title, please visit **www.routledge.com/9780805856989** or call **1-800-634-7064.**

ROUTLEDGE

Routledge
Taylor & Francis Group
an informa business

270 Madison Avenue
New York, NY 10016

****AUTO**MIXED AADC 07099 T12 P1 4430
Dale Linton
Field Placement Director And Assistant Professor O
Spring Arbor University
106 E Main St
School Of Education St 13
Spring Arbor, MI 49283-9799

PRSRT STD
U.S. Postage
Paid
Clifton, N.J.
Permit No. 1104

Language, Culture, and Community in Teacher Education

Edited by María Estela Brisk, Boston College

Language, Culture, and Community in Teacher Education addresses the pressing reality in teacher education that all teachers need to be prepared to work effectively with linguistically and culturally diverse student populations.

Emphasizing that culturally and linguistically diverse students, including immigrants, refugees, language minority populations, African Americans, and deaf students, have both common educational needs and needs that are specific, this volume is directed to the preparation of all teachers who work with culturally and linguistically diverse students. The focus is not only on how teachers need to change but how faculty and curriculum need to be transformed, and how to better train teacher education candidates to understand and work efficaciously with the communities in which culturally and linguistically diverse students tend to be predominant.

The American Association of Colleges for Teacher Education (AACTE) is a national, voluntary association of higher education institutions and related organizations. For more information on AACTE visit www.aacte.org.

Lawrence Erlbaum Associates/Taylor & Francis Group
October 2007: 368pp
Pb: 978-0-8058-5698-9: $29.95
Hb: 978-0-8058-5697-2: $80.00

Routledge
Taylor & Francis Group

LEA
Taylor & Francis Group

Serving Learners

CHAPTER 3

BUILDING PARTNERSHIPS
WITH DIVERSE FAMILIES
AND COMMUNITIES

The way schools care about children is reflected in the way schools care about the children's families. If educators view children simply as students, they are likely to see the family as separate from the school. That is, the family is expected to do its job and leave the education of children to the schools. If educators view students as children, they are likely to see both the family and the community as partners with the school in children's education and development. Partners recognize their shared interests in and responsibilities for children, and they work together to create better programs and opportunities for students. (Epstein, 1995, p. 701)

Proponents of multicultural education agree that family and community participation in the schools is of critical importance (Ladson-Billings, 1994; Heath, 1995). Epstein (1995) believes that "with frequent interactions between schools, families, and communities more students are more likely to receive common messages from various people about the importance of school, of working hard, of thinking creatively, of helping one another, and of staying in school" (p. 702).

School–family–community partnerships can improve school programs and climate, create a familylike school, provide support and family services, increase parent and family skills and leadership, serve as school–community liaisons, and help teachers (Epstein, 1995). Within the families and community, educators can also find support for school reform, curriculum reform, assistance in learning about the cultures of students, relevant content for instruction, volunteers as mentors for students, and support for immigrant families and students. Six types of parent involvement have been described by Epstein as parenting, communicating, volunteering, learning at home, decision making, and collaborating with the community (Epstein, 1995). The list was developed as a guide for schools, since each type of practice has certain limitations or problems to be resolved.

FAMILY INVOLVEMENT IN THE SCHOOLS

The Goals 2000 Educate America Act, passed by Congress in 1994, also encourages building partnerships with families and communities in an effort toward providing quality education for every child (U.S. Department of Education, 1994). Family involvement can benefit not only the child, but also the school, family, and community. As stated by Jeffie Frazier, "Community support also does wonders for the learning environment. Our school has extremely beneficial relationships with several community groups. There's a church right on the corner. The church adopted us many years ago. When we want to have a bake sale, they donate all of the ingredients, and all we have to do is bake and sell them. They also send people over to buy, and they advertise for us" (Comer, Ben-Avie, Haynes, & Joyner, 1999, p. 59).

Furthermore, the positive impact of parental involvement on student achievement and attitudes toward school has been well established (Donovan & Hodson, 1995; Griffiths, 1996; Keith et al., 1996; Leveque, 1994; Riley, 1999). However, parent involvement has been problematic in many schools across the country, particularly in the case of low-income and culturally diverse families (Comer, Haynes, Joyner, & Ben-Avie, 1996; Delgado-Gaitan, 1995).

Nevertheless, most low-income parents see education as a means to a better life for their children (Banks, 1999). Although teachers of children from low-income and culturally diverse families may often conclude that the parents are uninterested in participation in their children's education (Delgado-Gaitan, 1995), researchers have found that diverse families can be deterred by the school's climate and personnel.

Finders and Lewis (1994) found that some parents, for example, did not feel comfortable in the school's domain. They noted that parents' social, economic, linguistic, and cultural practices are often viewed as problems by the school, rather than as assets. In a two-way bilingual school, where both English-speaking and Spanish-speaking parents were interviewed, Zelazo (1995) concluded that (1) parents' comfort with the staff was critical in their becoming involved, (2) language played a major role in the nature of involvement, and (3) parents' views of their role in relationship to the school, their own level of schooling, and their present economic situation were critical factors in their involvement.

In fact, Delgado-Gaitan (1999) has noted that "strategies for parent involvement have been historically based upon deficit conceptions of [diverse] cultures and families and have thus been aimed at remedying perceived family deficiencies" (p. 139). The deficit perspective applies particularly to parents of children who are poor, to low-achieving children, and to children with special needs whose parents are often viewed as being unprepared to rear them.

Alternative approaches to promoting the involvement of families focus on their empowerment so that they can become decision makers. Recognition of the family as a system and of its strengths, cultural beliefs, expecta-

TABLE 3.1   Alternative Approaches for Parent–Family Involvement

1. Consider meetings in community facilities rather than the school.
2. Have parents and families collaborate with the school in setting the agenda for a meeting.
3. Invite members of the extended family who have an important role in the lives of the children.
4. Arrange meetings at times convenient for both the family and school personnel.
5. Consider assisting with transportation, child care, or other special challenges faced by the family.
6. Consider language differences and the possible need for a community liaison.
7. Facilitate the building of supportive networks for parents.
8. Become aware of families' strengths and the need for structures or opportunities for them to share their strengths with other families and school personnel.
9. Consider creative, nontraditional ways to bring parents into the life of the school.
10. Respect families' preferences for time and place of meetings.
11. Make opportunities for meaningful participation in the education of their children.
12. Know the community and its resources. Consider meetings at churches, neighborhood centers, and recreational facilities.
13. Consider occasional meetings conducted by parents–families.
14. Work to make families feel welcome, respected, and valued for their knowledge and experience.
15. Aim for collaboration with equal partners.

tions, and economic constraints can help the school facilitate the family's involvement (Table 3.1).

Families and communities of diverse groups, who may frequently encounter prejudice and hostility in the society, especially need to be met by school personnel who value their strengths and knowledge of their children. In a study of groups of Puerto Rican, African American, Chinese American, and Irish American families, all had experienced prejudice and discrimination in the United States because of their race, culture, or language (Hildago, Bright, Siu, Swap, & Epstein, 1995).

The Comer School Development Program (Comer et al., 1999) is one example of a widely used model for family involvement and school–community partnerships. A principal describes Comer's Program as "encouraging the collaboration of the home, the school, places of worship and the community to support the life of the school" (Comer et al., 1999, p. 53). The Comer School Development Program (SDP) involves parents and the community through a Parent Team and Comprehensive School Plan (see Figure 3.1). The parent team provides meaningful input and support for the School Planning and Management Team, which develops the Comprehensive School Plan, among other responsibilities. The SDP approach is described as having "parents and families at the center of change," a link that is often missing in efforts toward

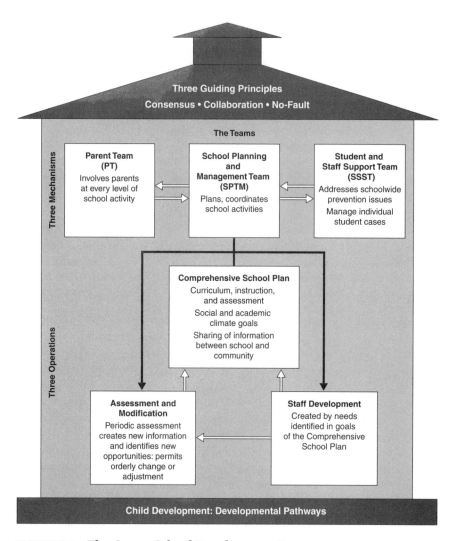

FIGURE 3.1   The Comer School Development Program

Reprinted by permission of the publisher from Comer, J., Haynes, N., Joyner, E., Ben-Avie, M., *Rallying the Whole Village: The Comer Process for Reforming Education,* (New York: Teachers College Press, © 1996 by Teachers College, Columbia University. All rights reserved.), p. 48.

school reform (p. 9). Most important are the guiding principles of the SDP, which are consensus, collaboration, and no-fault. These principles help to sustain the learning and caring community, a positive environment in which "all adults feel respected and all children feel valued and motivated to learn and achieve" (Comer et al., 1996, p. 9).

However, in many situations school personnel and community members will need to learn how to collaborate. As noted by Weast, Jones, and Howley (1999),

Everyone says that collaboration is a good idea, so why does SDP (School Development Program) invest so much time and effort training people in this guiding principle? The reason is that in our fragmented educational system, people don't actually know how to work together as a team because they haven't had opportunities to learn through trial and error. Elementary, middle and high school principals rarely even talk with one another, let alone plan together for the long term. At each school district's central office, staff members are usually too busy to take the time to build a team and change their work routines. (p. 256)

Yet it is critical to build collaborative teams in order to bring about change in a school. School reform requires the collaboration of all stakeholders—families, school, and community. However, families need a variety of meaningful opportunities for participation in the life of the school and the educational activities of their children. The Comer model, for example, provides possibilities for participation at different levels of intensity and responsibility. Even so, many families will be unable to enter into the type of ideal partnership so desired by school personnel. There are simply too many constraints due to changing family structures and economic pressures. In addition, researchers have found that family participation in the school takes different forms at different age levels and genders of the children involved (Muller, 1998). Researchers have also noted that parental involvement patterns vary according to parental racial/ethnic, social and economic characteristics (Casambis & Gartland, 1997). Nevertheless, educators should make every effort to develop collaborative relationships with students' families.

CHARACTERISTICS OF FAMILIES

Although changing family structures in the society make it difficult to assume a dominant family profile, all families are best understood as systems in which each individual affects all other members (Turnbull & Turnbull, 1997). According to Whitechurch and Constantine, modern systems theories about families have been derived from General System Theory, which is both a "transdisciplinary field of study and a theoretical framework with which theorists attempt to explain the behavior of complex, organized systems such as families" (Whitechurch & Constantine, 1993, p. 328). As we enter the 21st century, although a family might consist of mother, father, and children; single parents and children; or stepparents, first-married, same-sex parents, or grandparents as primary caretakers, the family is best understood as a system.

THE FAMILY SYSTEM

Three major components of the family system are its group and individual characteristics, its functions, and its life cycle.

Family Characteristics

Size and form, cultural background, socioeconomic status, and geographic location are examples of family characteristics. Individual characteristics of each member of the family may include educational level, employment, language proficiency, abilities, talents, and disabilities. In addition, families may be faced by special challenges, such as poverty, substance abuse, and HIV-AIDS.

The family system is further composed of parental, marital, sibling, and extended family subsystems. The extended family subsystem is a critical component in many culturally diverse families where economic, physical, and social support are provided by the extended family members. In some cases, extended family members may perform roles usually held by parents. Subsystems are separated by boundaries created by interactions within the family itself and with outsiders. When boundaries are very open, roles may be flexible and collaboration between the school and home will be easily accepted. On the other hand, boundaries may be closed to those outside and collaboration will be difficult to impossible (Turnbull & Turnbull, 1997). Boundaries also serve to define bonding relationships within the family. *Bonding* is referred to as cohesion, and it is a characteristic that exists on a continuum. When families have a very high degree of cohesion, they are extremely close and may risk the loss of individual autonomy. On the other hand, a family with low cohesion may be unable to provide adequate support and nurturance for its members. Assistance may be required in order to help them to more adequately meet these needs.

Adaptability, a term that refers to the family's ability to change in response to situational and developmental stress, also exists on a continuum. High control and structure are at one end, and low control and structure are at the other. Families in which control and structure are very low may live in chaotic conditions where no one is dependable, rules are nonexistent, leadership is absent, and roles and responsibilities are uncertain and constantly changing (Turnbull & Turnbull, 1997). School social workers or nurse educators may be called on to assist in efforts to obtain counseling for these families. Obviously, extreme degrees of family control and structure may inhibit individual initiative and independence and can result in immature children unable to function socially. Teachers can consult with other professionals with respect to making referrals, or families can be directed to the school social worker or counselor. In more complex situations, referrals to mental health professionals may be necessary. An action plan developed according to the Decision-Making Scaffold, which we will introduce in Chapter 4, would include such referrals.

Family Functions

The ease with which children can be engaged in school learning depends on the family's ability to carry out its functions and meet the needs of all its members. A family struggling to carry out its basic functions may be unable to meet the expectations of the school for participation in children's education. In some of the cases to follow, families are engaged in extreme efforts to meet economic, physical, and health needs and, consequently, the children involved are having difficulty progressing in school. A partnership in which the school and community provide services within the school can assist such families and children.

Functions of the family include (1) sharing verbal and physical affection and unconditional love, (2) developing self-esteem in its members, (3) meeting the family's economic needs, (4) meeting physical and health needs, (5) addressing the need for recreation and socialization, and (6) meeting members' educational needs (Turnbull & Turnbull, 1997). Although educators will be most concerned about the educational needs of children, other unmet needs will affect the family's ability to meet educational needs. Without intervention, for example, children without warm winter clothing or adequate medical care will lack the health, freedom, energy, and motivation to engage in school learning. The care of children and their education cannot be separated (Kagan, 1989). In developing a realistic plan of action to assist children, educators need to recognize the family as a system and recommend intervention accordingly.

Diverse families who are learning English may need assistance in identifying and accessing services in the community when carrying out their functions. Other families who face problems of living in poverty will also need to access services critical to the educational progress and success of their children. Citing the ecological relationship among schools, families, and communities, Crowson and Boyd (1993) point to the lack of concerted efforts to link human services into an "ecosystem for youth" (Timpane & Reich, 1997). Difficulties such as issues associated with "turf, client confidentiality, team-building, financial and budgetary agreements '' will challenge professionals who attempt to develop a model of coordinated, collaborative services for children (Lugg, 1994). Nevertheless, an "ecosystem—a total environment supporting the healthy growth and development of America's youth and contributing to their resilience" is needed for every student at this time of great stress in the society for all families, especially for those with the least resources (Timpane & Reich, 1997, p. 465) (see Figure 3.2).

The Family Life Cycle

Family functions are directly affected by the family life cycle, the third component of the family system. The life cycle refers to the changes in a family over time as it goes through certain predictable and stable stages with accompanying transition periods (Turnbull & Turnbull, 1997). Families generally experience birth, early childhood, childhood, adolescence, and adulthood, with the related tasks and responsibilities. Thus, a family with young children at the preschool age faces different responsibilities and challenges than the

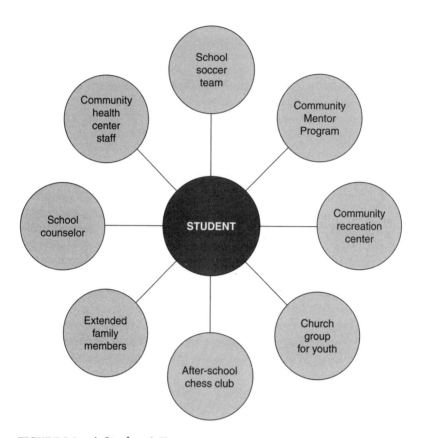

FIGURE 3.2   A Student's Ecosystem

family whose children have reached adolescence. Although theorists vary on the number of stages identified, most agree on at least three stages (Turnbull & Turnbull, 1997). Family life, in general, and family functions and priorities change according to the life cycle stage of its children and adult members. Birth and early childhood bring intense absorption of the family in adapting to and meeting the needs of growing children. During the elementary years, the horizons broaden for both children and families as they become more involved in the world outside. However, adolescence brings new tasks and challenges for children and families as rapid physical and psychological changes challenge the family's cohesiveness, balance of authority, and mid-life concerns of parents. Finally, adulthood usually brings autonomy, involvement in the community, and the challenge of change (Turnbull & Turnbull, 1997).

Special Challenges.   Some families may face special challenges that can affect the family system and subsystems. Homelessness, poverty, and disabilities of one or more family members can place undue stress on the family system. These challenges have been discussed in other chapters. However, refugee families also face special challenges. Refugees face numerous, complex challenges as they try to maintain the family system within a new cultural context. They must negotiate the employment and educational systems, understand immigration and naturalization laws, and try to access whatever social services might be available to them and their children (Huang, 1989). At the same time, they are challenged by the need to master a new language and social behaviors. Many refugee families are without the extended family members who could comprise a social and economic source of support. An additional challenge is the need to integrate their experience—the loss of home, land, family, and friends (Huang, 1989).

Researchers have found that those children who have fled with their families appear to adapt better than those who were unaccompanied (Huang, 1989). The latter group are at much higher risk for psychological problems such as depression, somatic complaints, sleep disturbances, violent antisocial behavior, tantrums, and withdrawals (Huang, 1989). Culturally diverse families may face all these challenges.

CULTURALLY DIVERSE FAMILIES

Diverse cultural groups in the United States differ as much within groups as they do between groups. Thus, generalizations are very risky. Although a great deal of research exists regarding diverse groups, we prefer to alert teachers to possible differences among parents and families in many areas of their lives and to encourage teachers to become familiar with the particular cultural groups in his or her school and classroom. Even then, it will be important to rely on community persons and families who can act as cultural informants to help the teacher to understand and appreciate the cultural differences among members of a community and to recognize that it is essential to know each family as individuals.

In fact, cultural differences among families may influence their responses to the changes and challenges involved at each stage of the life cycle. Families will differ in characteristics such as structure, child-rearing and discipline practices, behavioral and developmental expectations for their children, verbal and nonverbal communication patterns, English proficiency, and knowledge of the schools and "how they work" (Salend & Taylor, 1993). It is also important to point out that diversity within cultures is as prevalent as diversity among cultures. Therefore, even within a cultural group, each family must be known for its individual characteristics and preferences. Teachers will need to recognize these differences in order to build trust and establish positive relationships.

Discipline Practices

For example, cultural background may explain differences in a family's discipline practices or the extent to which they are concerned about developmental milestones (LaFramboise & Graff-Low, 1989; Ramirez, 1989). Differences in behavioral expectations may cause conflict between the home and school in some instances. When teachers are willing to collaborate with families to develop culturally appropriate and relevant programs that include mutually selected bicultural behaviors and cross-cultural criteria for measuring progress, the partnership is enhanced. Many families want their children to have bicultural competence so that children will show respect and behave appropriately in both the mainstream and their particular cultural group.

Teachers may be especially concerned about discipline. The level of noise and movement permitted in the child's home and community may differ from that in the school. Students who continue this practice at school may be viewed as behavior problems by uninformed teachers. A nonjudgmental approach will work best as teachers interview students and family members to learn about cultural practices. Students will need to learn that expectations for behavior may change across settings. The home–school differences in behavioral expectations should be considered to explain behavior that the teacher finds unacceptable before negative judgments are made or a referral for special education is decided on.

Home School Communication

Although differences in discipline methods between home and school can be problematic, effective home–school relationships will strongly depend on communication. Teachers will need to interpret parental verbal and non-verbal communication within diverse cultural contexts (Salend, 1990). Personal space, eye contact wait time, voice quality, vocabulary, facial expressions, and touching are forms of nonverbal communication that are likely to vary among cultures (Anderson & Fenichel, 1989). In addition, families from some cultural backgrounds may refrain from talking about their problems or concerns because this may be considered self-centered or "losing face" (Nagata, 1989). Similarly, other families may avoid discussion of the future of their children because they believe that negative or limiting comments about an individual's future may be self-fulfilling (Locust, 1988).

Culturally competent interpreters, community members who understand the family's culture, can help to minimize potential barriers to communication between culturally diverse families and educators. In fact, Brandenburg-Ayres (1990) suggests that schools employ such cultural informants to serve as liaisons among schools, families, and communities; to inform school personnel about relevant cultural variables; to help orient new families to the school; and to prepare culturally sensitive and relevant written documents.

Moreover, families whose cultures emphasize interpersonal relationships over personal expertise will respond best to meetings in which school personnel are warm, friendly, and nonjudgmental. With these families, effective communication will also require sufficient time for family members to express themselves. Demonstration of self-disclosure, respect, and humor by the teacher will be helpful (Anderson & Fenichel, 1989; LaFramboise & Graff-Low, 1989). Some families may prefer to be greeted with a handshake and to sit in close proximity to each other (Ramirez, 1989). Other families may emphasize professional expertise in their relations with professionals and view school personnel more impersonally. These families will prefer an environment that is structured and goal oriented, which helps participants to accomplish their goals (Nagata, 1989).

School Involvement

In her discussion of parent and community diversity, Banks (1997) points out that grandparents are assuming the role of parents in many families. Other families are headed by a single parent, and some parents have special needs. These groups may have difficulty with school involvement. However, flexible times for conferences, baby sitting services, procedures for acknowledgment and communicating with noncustodial parents, and using the correct surname for parents (which may differ from that of the student) will be helpful in increasing their involvement (Banks, 1997).

Low-income families are generally interested in the education of their children, but may face serious obstacles in their efforts to become involved. Migrant families, for example, face poor economic conditions at home and the need to travel to remain employed (Bressler, 1996). Migrant women work in the fields with the men, "doing nearly every kind of farm labor, including harvesting crops and sorting and packing produce" (Bressler, 1996). They also handle all the domestic responsibilities (Bressler, 1996). In the words of one Latina woman, "You work all day in the fields, and then in the afternoon, at night, you have to take care of the children, take them to the clinic, to the hospital when they get sick . . . (Bressler, 1996, p. 314). It is easy to appreciate the difficulties these families have with involvement in their children's education and the support they need in order to become involved. Furthermore, working in the fields brings income and creates an ambivalent situation regarding allowing the children to remain in school.

Acknowledgment of the low-income families' interest and concern for their children's education is the first step in building a positive school–home relationship. The adoption of the Comer School Development Program or a similar model, which provides many ways in which families can be involved, can also encourage, facilitate, and support families' involvement in the school. In addition, meetings in the neighborhood or community facility or provisions for transportation can be helpful. Even the time for meetings must be flexible since there is no such thing as personal days with pay for migrant workers.

Parents from non-English backgrounds may be reluctant to communicate with the school because they believe that they lack the proficiency in English that is expected or required. Furthermore, many schools lack bilingual

TABLE 3.2   Translators and Interpreters

1. Translators are needed for school–home communications, parent training activities, and family participation in school governance and decision making.
2. Examples of successful programs for parents–families of diverse groups include:
   - School–community councils, organized groups where bilingual teachers or volunteers attend the meetings
   - Parent handbooks published in the languages of the students
   - Home visits by parent volunteers or aides who can translate messages from teachers to parents
   - All school–home communications are published in the students' home languages.
   - All parent meetings and workshops are conducted in English and the other majority languages.
   - Technology (translation equipment) is available for parent meetings.
   - Local radio stations are used to announce coming events or meetings, broadcast educational programs for adults and children, make health-related public service announcements, and conduct interviews of school and community members about current issues or events. Announcements are mainly in the language of the majority of listeners.
   - Home–school liaisons who are fluent in the languages of most families conduct home visits monthly to address discipline, academic, and attendance problems and to help families with paperwork.

Source: National Parent Information Network (1997, October). *Family involvement in children's education: Successful local approaches* [Electronic version].

professionals who could communicate with parents in their own language. Interpreters or translators, preferably from the community, are needed to facilitate oral and written communication between the home and school. Interpreters can assist with oral language, while translators are essential for written communications. Where many languages are represented in the school district, the use of parent and community volunteers can be explored. In some school districts a regional survey for potential translators has led to a pool of translators and interpreters of various languages (Whittington-Couse, personal communication, 1998). However, the selection of interpreters and translators should be done with care and concern (see Table 3.2).

THE SCHOOL–FAMILY–COMMUNITY PARTNERSHIP

The dictionary defines *cooperate* as "to work or act together or jointly for a common purpose or benefit; to work or act with another or other persons willingly and agreeably," whereas the definition of *collaborate* stresses to work, one with another, as on a literary work (*Webster's New Universal Unabridged Dictionary,* 1994). The definitions imply working together as equals, where families are seen as having contributions to "bring to the table." Kampwirth's (1999) definition captures this essential meaning in the phrase, "mutual problem-solving by equal partners" (p. 72). Thus, in working with families and community members, educators should reflect their belief in Kampwirth's definition. The strong partnership that can be formed on this basis can help every child to progress.

The idea of community as a "web of relationships connecting individuals and institutions whose focus is ensuring that every child has a substantial opportunity to grow up successfully" is appealing (Timpane & Reich, 1997, p. 466). It makes a strong statement for the position of the school as a member of a network, working with other institutions to contribute to successful growth for the children and, often, revitalization of the neighborhood (Prager, 1993). As noted by Dryfoos (1994), "Schools in which quality education and comprehensive social services are offered under one roof have the potential to become neighborhood hubs, where children and their families want to be" (p. 18). Thus, the most appealing answer to the problems faced by many families and their children is the provision of coordinated services for children, through which the school works in collaboration with other community agencies and institutions to have services available in the school (Crowson & Boyd, 1993).

Models for the coordination of children's services include a school-based approach in which the school is the dominant institution, a school-linked model in which the school is a partner, and a community-based model with the school as a less dominant member (Behrman, 1992; Dryfoos, 1994). Lugg (1994) has differentiated among the models according to the degree of interdependence involved. Collaboration involves a high level of interagency participation, interdependence, and effort, whereas coordination implies moderate levels, and cooperation represents the lowest level of interdependence and interorganizational participation and high degrees of agency and school independence. In the community-based model, the school provides coordination with and referral to community agencies (Dryfoos, 1994). The school-linked approach involves a tighter relationship of the school with various social service agencies, but services remain outside the school. In the school-based model, a variety of social service agencies work together to provide integrated services within the school. Although Behrman (1992) notes that the school-linked model appears to be the most effective, there is no consensus at this time on the best model. From a practical point of view, the school-based model appears most practical because "that's where the children are."

It is important to note that families should be allowed to request assistance, rather than having it forced on them. Some may find community agencies and institutions intimidating and may need advocates to accompany them. Others will be inhibited due to previous negative experiences with mainstream personnel. Teachers can develop referral files to have quick, easy access to the information needed and also be prepared with names, phone numbers, and descriptions of the services offered. In many communities, directories may be available that provide this information. In any case, an investment in knowing the community and its resources can only serve to enhance the teacher–student–family relationship. While communities vary in the quantity and quality of services available, most will provide at

TABLE 3.3   Community Resources for Family Referrals

NEED	TYPE OF SERVICE	EXAMPLES: PUBLIC AND PRIVATE AGENCIES
Food	Soup kitchens Food baskets Food stamps Food banks	Churches, Salvation Army, Social services departments Community programs
Clothing	Clothing banks Thrift shops Consignment shops	Churches, Salvation Army Community centers Social service agencies
Shelter	Homeless shelter Battered women shelter Low-cost housing	Neighborhood agencies Churches Social services departments Habitat for Humanity
Furniture, household items	Flea markets Used furniture stores Yard, Garage sales Donations	Churches Private agencies Publications

Health care	Vision, hearing, medical,
	    dental problems
	Counseling, family therapy,
	    crisis intervention
		Lions Club
		Neighborhood clinics
		University and hospital clinics
		Local mental health agencies

Employment	Temporary employment Vocational assessment and training Work permits	Private agencies State department of labor Local businesses and industry Publications

Extended family substitutes	Role models, tutors,
	    advisors, counselors,
	    companions, child care
		Big Brothers
		Church groups
		Community organizations
		Support groups

Recreation	Afterschool programs and
	    activities, summer camps
	    and programs, family
	    recreation activities
		Public parks
		Schools
		YMCA, YWCA
		Local library
		Churches
		Some bookstores
		Neighborhood organizations

least some examples of the following categories of agencies, organizations, and institutions: educational, employment, child care, legal, health care, recreational, government, emergency food, clothing and shelter, and a variety of support groups. Table 3.3 presents a listing of frequently available community services.

NEED	TYPE OF SERVICE	EXAMPLES: PUBLIC AND PRIVATE AGENCIES
Support groups	Advocacy, support	Local chapters of national organizations for various disabilities Parent organizations
Legal assistance advocacy	Services for children with disabilities Housing disputes Miscellaneous infractions Minor problems involving individuals with limited proficiency in English	Parent organizations Tenants rights groups Rural poor and migrant advocacy agencies Neighborhood agencies
Education	Basic literacy English language instruction GED Technical and vocational training Parenting skills Early intervention Preschool programs Postsecondary programs Adult basic education Citizenship training	Public libraries Community colleges Vocational and technical schools High schools Literacy Volunteers of America Head Start Private preschools
Child care	Day care Special summer programs for children Respite care	Licensed private households Job-related programs

In some schools, social workers, nurses, and psychologists are expected to provide counseling and emergency assistance. Other schools may collaborate with the mental health system or a private agency to provide services in the school. The social services system may collaborate with the school to provide staff and other support that can allow the school social worker to work with a larger number of families and meet emergency needs for food, shelter, or clothing. In some instances, schools have developed their own clothing banks and food pantries. Families can be included in such activities as managers of clothing banks and food pantries. In a Chicago school, Principal Carol Edwards described this type of collaboration.

> We have a parent room on the first floor in the middle of the corridor. In the parent room are tables, chairs, bulletin boards, and some clothes in the back. If we have clothing to give away, we do it in that room. Parent meetings and parent training are held in that room. Specific parent activities, such as distributing books to children as part of the Reading is Fundamental initiative, are done in that room. Parents eat with the teachers in the lunchroom (Comer et al. 1999, p. 31).

In summary, students benefit when schools, families, and communities develop partnerships. Communities can provide support and resources to help schools to perform their missions, and communities can benefit from the availability of school facilities and programs. In addition, the real-life problems in the community may be resolved as students work with these problems in a context of learning. Families and communities also benefit from the educational progress of their members, who can contribute stability and richness to the community. Students must function in the world of the home, school, and community. A strong partnership can enhance the congruence among these worlds for students and facilitate their transitions among them.

REFERENCES

Anderson, P., & Fenichel, E. S. (1989). *Serving culturally diverse families of infants and toddlers with disabilities.* Retrieved June 1991, from http://www.eric.ed.gov

Banks, J. A., McGee, C. A., (1999). Parents and teachers: Partners in school reform. In J. A. Banks & C. A. McGee Banks (Eds.), *Multicultural education: Issues and perspectives* (3rd ed.). Boston: Allyn and Bacon.

Behrman, R. E. (Ed.). (1992). School-linked services. [Electronic version]. *Future of Children, 2*(1).

Brandenburg-Ayres, S. (1990). *Working with parents. Bilingual/TESOL Special Education Collaboration and Reform Project.* Gainsville: University of Florida.

Bressler, S. (1996). Voices of Latina mothers in rural Pennsylvania. In Judith LeBlanc Flores (Ed.), *Children of La Frontera.* (pp. 311–324). Charleston, West VA: Clearninghouse on rural education and small schools. Appalachia Education Laboratories.

Casambis, S., & Gartland, J. (1997). *Parental involvement in students' education during middle school and high school.* Report No. 181. Baltimore, MD: Johns Hopkins University; Washington, DC: Howard University, Center for Research on the Education of Students Placed At risk.

Comer, J. P., Ben-Avie, M., Haynes, N., & Joyner, E. T. (Eds.). (1999). *Child by child: The Comer process for change.* New York: Teachers College Press.

Comer, J. P., Haynes, N., Joyner, E., & Ben-Avie, M. (Eds.). (1996). *Rallying the whole village: The Comer process for reforming education.* New York: Teachers College Press.

Cooksey, E., & Fondell, M. (1996). Spending time with his kids: Effects of family structure on fathers' and children's lives. *Journal of Marriage and the Family, 58*(3), 693–707.

Crowson, R., & Boyd, W. L. (1993). Coordinated services for children: Designing arks for storms and seas unknown. *American Journal of Education, 101*(2), 140–179.

Delgado-Gaitan, C. (1999). In J. A. Banks & C. A. McGee Banks (Eds.), *Multicultural education: Issues and perspectives* (3rd ed.). Boston: Allyn and Bacon.

Donovan, R., & Hodson, J. (1995). Espanol aumentativo: *A transitional bilingual education program for secondary Hispanic preliterates. Evaluation report year four.* Houston, TX: Houston University; Spring Branch Independent School District.

Dryfoos, J. G. (1994). *Full-service schools: A revolution in health and social services for children, youth, and families.* San Francisco: Jossey-Bass.

Epstein, J. (1995). School/family/community partnerships: Caring for the children we share. *Phi Delta Kappan, 76*(9), 701–711.

Finders, M., & Lewis, C. (1994). Why some parents don't come to school. *Educational Leadership, 51*(8), 50–54.

Griffiths, J. (1996). Relation of parental involvement, empowerment, and school traits to student academic performance. *Journal of Educational Research, 90*(1), 33–41.

Heath, S. B. (1995). Ethnography in communities: Learning the everyday life of America's subordinated youth. In J. A. Banks & C. A. McGee Banks (Eds.), *Handbook of research on multicultural education* (pp. 114–128). New York: Macmillan.

Hildago, N., Bright, J., Siu, S. F., Swap, S., & Epstein, J. (1995). Research on families, schools, and communities: A multicultural perspective. In J. A. Banks & C. A. McGee Banks (Eds.), *Handbook of research on multicultural education* (pp. 498–524). New York: Macmillan.

Huang, L. N. (1989). *Children of color: Psychological interventions with minority youth.* San Francisco: Jossey-Bass.

Kagan, S. (1989). Early care and education: Beyond the school house doors. *Phi Delta Kappan, 71*(2), 107–112.

Kampwirth, T. (1999). *Collaborative consultation in the schools: Effective practices for students with learning and behavior problems.* Upper Saddle River, NJ: Merrill/Prentice Hall.

Keith, T. Z., et al. (1996). Effects of parental involvement on achievement for students who attend school in rural America. *Journal of Research in Rural Education, 12*(2), 55–67.

Ladson-Billings, G. (1994). *The dreamkeepers.* San Francisco: Jossey-Bass.

LaFramboise, T. D., & Graff-Low, K. (1989). American Indian children and adolescents (pp. 114–147). In J. Taylor-Gibbs & L. Nahme-Huang (Eds.), *Children of color: Psychological interventions with minority youth.* San Francisco: Jossey-Bass.

Leveque, D. (1994). *Cultural and parental influences on achievement among Native American students in Barstow Unified School District.* Paper presented at the National Meeting of the Comparative and International Educational Society, San Diego, CA, March

Locust, C. (1988). Wounding the spirit: Discrimination and traditional American Indian belief systems. *Harvard Educational Review, 58*(3), 315–330.

Lugg, C. A. (1994). *Schools and achieving integrated services: Facilitating utilization of the knowledge base.* Paper presented at the Annual Meeting of the University Council for Educational Administration, Philadelphia, October 28–30.

Muller, C. (1998). Gender differences in parental involvement and adolescents' mathematics achievement. *Sociology of Education, 71*(4), 336–356.

Nagata, D. K. (1989). Japanese American children and adolescents. In J. Taylor-Gibbs & L. Nahme-Huang (Eds.), *Children of color: Psychological interventions with minority youth* (pp. 67–113). San Francisco: Jossey-Bass.

Prager, K. (1993). Social capital: The foundation for education. *Issues in Restructuring Schools, 5,* 1–19.

Ramirez, O. (1989). Mexican American children and adolescents. In J. Taylor-Gibbs & L. Nahme Huang (Eds.), *Children of color: Psychological interventions with minority youth* (pp. 224–250). San Francisco: Jossey-Bass.

Riley, R. (1999). *Condition of Education Report.* Washington, DC: U.S. Department of Education.

Salend, S. J. (1990). Migrant education guide for special educators. *Teaching Exceptional Children, 22*(2), 18–21.

Salend, S. J., & Taylor, L. S. (1993). Working with families across cultural perspectives. *Remedial and Special Education, 14*(5), 25–31, 39.

Timpane, M., & Reich, R. (1997). Revitalizing the ecosystem for youth: A new perspective for school reform. *Phi Delta Kappan, 78,* 464–470.

Turnbull, A. P., & Turnbull, H. R. (1997). *Families, professionals, and exceptionality: A special partnership.* Upper Saddle River, NJ: Prentice Hall.

U.S. Department of Education (1994). Goals 2000 Educate America Act. Washington, DC: Author.

Weast, J. D., Jones, L. M., & Howley, J. P. (1999). A culture of collaboration. In J. P. Comer, M. Ben-Avie, N. Haynes, & E. T. Joyner (Eds.), *Child by child: The Comer process for change in education* (pp. 255–275). New York: Teachers College Press.

Webster's New Universal Unabridged Dictionary (1994). New York: Barnes & Noble.

Whitechurch, G., & Constantine, L. (1993). Systems theory. In P. Boss, W. Doherty, R. LaRossa, W. Schumm, & S. Steinmetz (Eds.), *Sourcebook of family theories and methods: A contextual approach* (pp. 325–349). New York: Plenum Press.

Zelazo, J. (1995). *Parent involvement in a two-way bilingual school.* Paper presented at the Annual Meeting of AERA, San Francisco, April 18–22. (ERIC Document Reproduction Number ED 383219).

CHAPTER 4

THE DEVELOPMENT AND USE OF CASES IN TEACHER EDUCATION

The use of cases as teaching and learning tools is frequently associated with the fields of medicine and law. The visual media have facilitated this phenomenon. Many people can remember nervousness in the voice of a third-year medical student who must present her first patient's case to the attending physician and peers on the clinical rotation in any number of television medical dramas. Movies such as the *Paper Chase* and television series such as *Family Law* create cases in which the fate of an individual depends on the knowledge, logic, and dramatic skills of the dueling attorneys. In both situations, cases are depicted as a vehicle for examining precedent and learning through deductive logic.

In medicine and law, the use of teaching cases as an effective pedagogy has its roots in the late 1800s (Doyle, 1990). More recently, the pedagogical approach that has provided the broadest platform is the one developed by the Harvard Business School MBA Program (Christensen, 1987). Faculty and graduate students have developed an extensive series of complex business cases that report the workings of actual companies and serve as the core of the MBA curriculum. The business faculty also has worked with other programs and universities to study and encourage the case study method in a variety of fields (Christensen, Garvin, & Sweet, 1991).

The field of education has recently reawakened to the tremendous benefits that cases can offer to preservice and in-service teachers. Although there is evidence that instructors used cases in teacher education as far back as 1864 (Doyle, 1990), most casebooks and discussions of how to teach using cases have been published in the last decade. There are several reasons for this renewed interest. First, many of the reports that have called for the reform of teacher education have advocated the use of cases to build skills in decision making and collaboration (Goodlad, 1990; Holmes Group, 1995; National Commission on Teaching & America's Future, 1996). Second, researchers are interested in discovering how experienced teachers develop their practical knowledge about teaching and learning by studying and analyzing their actions in the classroom. This type of case study research is based on a belief that we can learn about teaching by observing in classrooms, interviewing teachers about their beliefs, and reviewing relevant documents, rather than by trying to control and manipulate the classroom environment (Clandinin & Connelly, 1995; Lincoln & Guba, 1985). Finally, cases are essentially stories of teachers, students, parents, and other relevant individuals. Some would say that narrative is the best, if not only way, to really know how teachers think and learn (Doyle, 1997).

WHAT IS A TEACHING CASE?

The idea of what constitutes a case varies depending on the field of study and the medium employed. Cases can encompass a wide variety of problematic choice situations. A case can be the story of a family that is confronted with selling its commercial fishing operation (Wassermann, 1994) or a report about a community that is disputing the property rights of a resident who is unconcerned about the health of a 500-year-old oak (Simmons & Dunrud, 1994). A case also can be a video of a master teacher implementing an innovative teaching strategy in his classroom (Leinhardt, 1990) or a hypermedia program that teaches math problem solving (Lampert & Ball, 1990). Another example of a case is the report of a researcher who has observed, and sometimes participated in, a situation (e.g., school, business, or hospital) for the purpose of understanding how a professional thinks about problems (Schon, 1987, 1991).

The cases in this text are *teaching cases*. That is, we have written them to be read by and discussed primarily with preservice and in-service teachers and other participants in schools in order to facilitate connections between theory and practice. Furthermore, the content of these cases focuses on the challenges that school staff face in educating students who come from increasingly diverse cultural, linguistic, geographic, economic, religious, and educational backgrounds, an area that has been lacking in many teacher education programs (Allain & Pettus, 1998). We define a *teaching case* as a narrative that describes a specific, complex predicament that is written as an educational tool for exploring critical issues and developing a response. In the pages that follow we will use the terms *teaching case* and *case* interchangeably.

The cases in this book share a similarity in four features: authenticity, concrete detail, narrative form, and open-endedness (Hutchings, 1993). First, all the cases in this book are based on real events in real schools and classrooms. Admittedly, names and roles have been changed, but the narratives are true for those that have lived them. Keep in mind that a case is not intended to be representative of an entire group of people. Rather, a case is *one* example of a reality faced by teachers in one school setting that may not be generalizable across the country. However, certain aspects of the case may provide valuable learning for those who face similar situations.

Because these cases are authentic, the perceptions of one individual may conflict with those of another in the case. Although the cases include the voices of students, teachers, administrators, and community members, there are always other characters whose stories or actions related to the case may not be represented at all. Each character has certain beliefs, assumptions, and biases, and it is up to you to recognize these presuppositions.

Our purpose is to transport you outside the university classroom into the school and community. Therefore, we have attempted to include many concrete details that portray the situation physically, emotionally, and mentally. It is important that you hear the dialogue that unfolds between individuals and that you visualize the characters and the settings in which they live on a daily basis. We want you to experience the emotional impact of these situations as well as understand the "facts," since the joys and stress of teaching are as much a part of the decisions that individuals make as are the results of test scores and other more normative information. Therefore, these cases are more than short vignettes about teachers and students. They include individuals both in the school and the community who have a part in shaping a school's program and culture and whose opinions must be considered when making any decision.

Cases are written as narratives and therefore constitute a different way of learning than is common in university classrooms. Much of what you read and hear in teacher preparation has been described by Bruner (1986) as a *paradigmatic* mode of knowing. That is, it is information that leads to theory, analysis, proofs, arguments, principles, and empirical discovery. This type of learning is generalized knowledge; it is useful as a guide, but not as a specific prescription. Bruner also encourages teachers to investigate a *narrative* mode of knowing, because narratives are sensitive to the unique contexts in which teachers work and are most helpful in connecting understanding with action.

Narratives have a form or syntax, such as beginning–middle–end or situation–transformation, that is related by time. They are written specifically to communicate to someone else what the narrator believes happened (Herrenstein-Smith, 1981). It is this social aspect of narratives that is particularly important to teaching cases. Their value is the analysis and response that cases evoke when discussed in a social setting. This uniqueness of each participant's experiences, understandings, values, and beliefs adds to the richness of the discussion and leads to differences in opinion regarding the issues at stake and the course of action that should be followed. Simply put, cases don't have one answer, and there is no presumption on the part of the authors that there is a "best" answer. The response that a group will make depends on the individuals making the decision and the particular context described in the narrative. However, there *is* such a thing as a bad answer. Knowledge of theory and research should guide the class's deliberations.

These cases are open-ended; the class must tell the rest of the story. Teaching cases are a slice of a problem, question, or concern that individuals in a school are encountering. There may be hints about the options that a character is considering and suggestions of the uncertainties that they feel, but the cases do not come to a resolution. The participants must decide if a narrator's view is adequate or if a character has been fully developed. It is often necessary to step back from the immediate picture and try to get a more comprehensive view. These activities, as well as the enhanced perspective provided by the class dynamic, will contribute significantly to the learning experience. Ultimately, the class will decide on a plan of action.

Cases, then, tell at least part of the story of several individuals' actions, words, and reflections concerning the challenge of a particular student or school situation. It is up to you to create a resolution. As we discuss next, we believe that the creativity and engagement that case discussion demands will help you be better teachers, not just better storytellers.

WHY ARE CASE DISCUSSIONS VALUABLE?

How many times have you heard the maxim "experience is the best teacher"? Is "getting out there and trying it" the best way to learn to teach? Or is there a certain body of knowledge related to subject matter, curriculum, instruction, educational contexts, learners, and the purposes and ends of education that must be mastered before starting to teach (Shulman, 1987)?

This dichotomy, the supposed chasm between theory and practice, is the separation that has challenged teacher education throughout history. As teacher educators, we strongly endorse the need for teachers to be grounded in a professional knowledge base. The critical question becomes how this grounding takes place. We believe that school observations, home visits, field experiences, practica, and other school-related assignments can be an invaluable part of teacher education when carefully integrated with coursework. Cases provide another way to experience the real world of teaching, with the additional benefit of inviting the whole class to observe, discuss, and learn from the events that transpire. They are a middle ground in which the sometimes dizzying pace of a classroom can be viewed as a video: slowed down, replayed, and analyzed frame by frame.

Another rationale for case discussions can be drawn from what we know about expert teachers. Researchers have found that expert teachers have practical knowledge, a "complex practically oriented set of understandings which teachers actively use to shape and direct the work of teaching" (Connelly & Clandinin, 1988, p. 19). Teachers cannot always describe this knowledge in terms of theories or beliefs, yet they seem to know intuitively how to proceed in the midst of very complicated and ambiguous situations. When asked to describe the rationale for their actions, they are more likely to tell a story to explain what they know and believe about their teaching.

Practical knowledge is that intuitive, artistic, experiential knowledge that often seems most essential yet elusive to beginning teachers. However, much evidence suggests that expert teachers are not simply those who have taught for many years. Rather, expert teachers are those who are "reflective practitioners" (Schon, 1987). By this, Schon means that expert teachers think about their teaching in one of two ways. When a teacher is surprised by an unexpected result in the classroom, he may look back at a later time to understand what factors in that complex situation, or "swampy lowland," led to this result. Schon terms this "reflection-on-action." Or a teacher may think through the surprise without interruption so that he can reshape the situation while in the midst of it. Schon calls this more immediate response "reflection-in-action." This reshaping of a situation is also referred to as *framing* the problem or bringing all of one's educational and experiential background, values, and understandings to configure the issues in a certain pattern.

Case discussions allow the readers to reflect on the action of other professionals who are mucking through the swampy lowlands of an ambiguous and multifaceted situation. These cases are unique and therefore will not replicate readers' exact experience. However, we have chosen them because they point toward and illustrate larger theoretical, conceptual, or descriptive categories. Lee Shulman (1996) reminds us that one question we should continually ask ourselves when reading and discussing a case is this: "What is this a case of?" Furthermore, he concedes that cases are so complex and rich that we can create an entire network of associations between theory and practice. While we know that you will not encounter the specific circumstances described in these cases, we are confident that the principles that you extract from them will be applicable in today's diverse classrooms.

Case discussions allow participants to practice the communication skills and cultural competence needed by effective teachers. Progressive school districts are implementing programs that involve team teaching, collaborative planning, peer coaching, and cross-grade or subject teaming. A case is "nonego invested" because participants are discussing the uncertainty and frustration of someone else's teaching (Hutchings, 1993). Once trust and a culture that supports reflection have been established, it is easier to reveal concerns about one's own teaching or the challenging situations that shape students' lives.

Cases are also an excellent vehicle for discussing issues of professionalism and social justice. Teaching is a moral endeavor. Teachers are constantly modeling what they believe to be important and good for their students and the many individuals with whom they interact each day. What they teach, and how they teach, and how they relate to students and others are testimony to these values and beliefs. It is one thing to write a philosophy of education on paper and quite another to enact that personal ethic in the classroom and community. Cases will not provide a standard of ethical conduct, but they will allow participants to test out the horizons of their beliefs and the cost that they may entail.

Cases force individuals and groups to think somewhat differently than they have before. Theories, concepts, and techniques are examined in the light of the real challenges that teachers meet in schools. By reflecting on these situations with peers and choosing viable alternatives, teachers broaden their own practical knowledge and test their beliefs.

HOW DO PARTICIPANTS ANALYZE A CASE?

We have established that one of the marks of an expert teacher is the ability to reflect on practice (Schon, 1987, 1991). Furthermore, we believe that reflection-on-action can occur in a vicarious way through the reading and discussion of teaching cases. But what do we mean by reflection? Is it simply a moment to stop and think in the midst of the ongoing stream of events and dialogue? If teaching is indeed an art, does that mean we must simply wait for inspiration? Is there a scaffold that can support our decision-making process that will promote a well-considered response? We would suggest several aspects that constitute a framework or scaffold for reflecting on a case. This scaffold that we have developed is not meant to be a step-by-step process that you must systematically follow in order to "crack the case." We recognize that thinking rarely occurs in such a linear fashion and, frequently, our thinking processes consider several ideas simultaneously and revisit others recursively. Similarly, there are considerations in the scaffold that participants will omit altogether in some cases and spend a great deal of deliberation on in others, depending on experience and familiarity with similar problems.

The Case Decision-Making Scaffold has five components (see Table 4.1). The following is a description of each aspect of this reflective process.

Recognize the Problem

As simplistic as it may sound, a reflective practitioner must first recognize that there is a problem, or a discrepancy between what he expects and what is actually occurring. We have found that it is helpful to identify the major characters or groups within the case and determine, for each, if they perceive a discrepancy between their expectations and real occurrences. At this stage of

TABLE 4.1   A Case Decision-Making Scaffold

RECOGNIZE THE PROBLEM
Is there a trigger event that causes an individual to recognize a problem?

What facts do we know about the individuals, the school, the family, and the community?

What discrepancies exist between the individuals' expectations and actual events?

FRAME THE PROBLEM
What perspective of the problem or issues is held by various individuals?

What underlying assumptions, values, or beliefs do individuals involved hold individually and in common?

How can we reframe the problem to address the important issues?

SEARCH FOR ALTERNATIVES
What can we learn about the issues from those who have experience and expertise?

What alternative goals might address the important issues involved in the cases?

What short- and long-term consequences will each alternative goal have for the student, school, family, and community?

Which goals best address the important issues?

DEVELOP AND IMPLEMENT A PLAN OF ACTION
How can we prioritize the goals to facilitate implementation?

What activities, referrals, resources, and strategies must be included in the plan of action to address the goals?

Who is responsible for performing the various components of the plan of action?

What criteria will we use to evaluate progress?

EVALUATE PROGRESS
What progress has been made based on established criteria?

Are all individuals and groups satisfied with the progress?

What new problems have developed?

What revisions to the plan of action need to be made?

decision making, it is important to stick to facts that the case presents without making interpretations regarding beliefs, motivation, and actions. Sometimes there is a trigger event that points to the problems involved. Participants should make statements regarding the problems involved based on evidence within the case. For example, if Mr. Levitt states that he expects Emanuel to complete all homework to get a passing grade and Emanuel's parents tell him he must work 20 hours a week to support the family, there is a real discrepancy in expectations. Once problems are identified, it is possible to better understand these issues by examining the framework that each individual utilizes to view the problem.

Frame the Problem

As discussed in previous chapters, people frame problems based on their own values, culture, experiences, and assumptions. While there may be agreement that there is a problem, there may not be agreement on the issues involved or how to resolve them in an ethical and equitable manner. When a teacher modifies an assignment for Nicholas, who has a severe learning disability, Greg may feel that the teacher is "letting him off" too easily or showing favoritism. The teacher may see the issue as Greg's inability to understand the need for individualized instruction. Similarly, we may make assumptions about the aims of education that simply aren't workable or valued in a particular setting or context. Mr. Bellows may believe that all students in middle school science classes should complete a project for the science fair at home, but this may not be realistic for some families in which staying warm, clothed, and fed is a daily struggle.

This framing stage of decision making is often ignored. Values and beliefs strongly influence the actions of individuals and groups. They are often accompanied by strong emotion. While knowledge and logic must inform decision making, we must also carefully consider the individual's past experience and the emotions involved in this experience. Decision making that ignores these aspects may, at best, receive tacit agreement from those involved, but may ultimately enact little change.

Schon (1987) suggests that part of reflection-on-action is reframing the problem. To institute meaningful change, one must see a problem from multiple perspectives. An important part of the reframing process is considering the values and beliefs that govern action. When we inquire into important issues, they "have at their core fundamental beliefs, values, and human interests at stake (Sirotnik, 1991, p. 244). This need for examining varying perspectives does not imply that we can or should attempt to alter basic values. Rather, it suggests that by understanding the core beliefs that teachers, students, and families can mutually adhere to we are better able to reconstruct the problem and seek viable and acceptable alternatives.

Search for Alternatives

The experience and expertise of others from different backgrounds (students, parents, or school staff) are particularly valuable when you are searching for an alternative plan of action. As educators, it is incumbent on us to be knowledgeable about the research in the field of education that addresses the situations that we face. Therefore, part of our task in searching for alternatives is reading the professional literature, attending educational conferences, consulting experts in the field, and conducting action research in the classroom. Although each situation is unique, the issues involved in these situations are accessible in the professional literature. We enhance our understanding and multiply our options when we use these rich resources to our advantage. In the first three chapters we described some of the important issues and research that will help to guide your problem solving. Furthermore, each succeeding chapter starts with pertinent background information that will supply you with specific information and research regarding the teaching cases.

The expertise of parents, other school staff, and community members is also valuable when we are searching for alternatives. Each person's ability to see the situation through a different lens strengthens the outcome. There must be an agreement on the general goals that are to be accomplished and an understanding that all ideas are welcome and respected. While some in the group may have expertise in a particular area, all members have practical knowledge of their own roles and must be treated with parity. This type of collaborative approach provides a broad repertoire of alternatives.

When a problem is newly encountered or very complex, a thorough search for alternatives may be necessary (Engel, Blackwell, & Miniard, 1995). However, once individuals have gone through an extended problem-solving process, they tend to make related decisions automatically. This may be part of what is occurring when teachers are said to reflect-in-action. They see a discrepancy between what they expected and what is happening, but can quickly reframe the problem and seemingly choose a viable alternative in seconds. This may be because they have encountered many similar situations in the past and have a rich repertoire of workable alternatives from which to choose. However, most of these cases involve many participants and will require more than a single teacher making a decision.

Once an individual or a group has generated a list of alternatives, choices must be made. This requires examining the short- and long-term consequences of each decision for all the stakeholders. Often, complex ethical issues are involved. For example, Ms. Simmons may believe that it is unconscionable to allow Jesus to be promoted to second grade when he is still reading in English on a preprimer level. However, knowing that Spanish is the primary language in Jesus's home and that holding students back rarely improves their academic skills in the long run (Smith, 2001), the consequences of retaining Jesus in the same grade the next year must be carefully considered.

When several alternatives seem acceptable within a shared ethical and cultural vision, some criteria for prioritization must be established based on the needs of the child and other stakeholders, the philosophy and legal mandates that govern the school, the constraints of the setting, and the abilities and style of the teacher. Criteria such as excellence, equity, feasibility, cost effectiveness, and legality all must be considered as possible criteria in the decision-making process.

Develop and Implement a Plan of Action

Once the major goals for implementing a change process have been chosen and prioritized, the steps for achieving these goals must be delineated. A plan of action may involve specific classroom, school, or community activities, referrals to school personnel or outside agencies; additional resources; or alternative instructional strategies. Each goal will be accomplished through one or more of these activities. Furthermore, tasks must be clearly assigned to one or more individuals who are capable of following through. A plan of action will fail without such built-in accountability. Furthermore, criteria should be established to determine whether the plan has been successfully executed. How will you know if your goals have been accomplished? What changes do you expect to see in individuals? What changes in attitude and actions are reasonable?

Activities and criteria for achievement must be carefully determined and, in many cases, recorded in some fashion. This may take the form of an entry in a teacher's journal, a revised lesson plan, a contract with a student, an addition to the student handbook, or a mission statement for a district-level task force. Even if the plan of action involves only a teacher and student, writing down the plan still allows both parties to understand the terms to which they are consenting. When multiple people have roles in implementing the plan, it is helpful to have a clear statement of what these responsibilities entail. Admittedly, many alternatives are chosen and successfully implemented without a written document. Likewise, some cases that participants discuss in class will not be carried through to the plan of action. However, we would encourage you to think seriously about possible follow-up activities. We believe that action is an integral part of reflection. If teachers do not take steps to change those situations that cause the problem, they will constantly submit themselves to a substandard professional experience and, eventually, may burn out or leave the profession.

Evaluate Progress

One reward that accrues to a reflective practitioner is the satisfaction that comes from seeing positive change. Once criteria are established for choosing an alternative, these criteria can be used to assess progress. This may be as simple as seeing a student react with excitement when a lesson includes some literature about her cultural heritage or as complex as having the final draft of a district policy on inclusive education after a year's worth of meetings with teachers, administrators, and community members.

Of course the outcome of this process of reflection is actually a continuation of the process. Even successful plans must be modified when the context inevitably changes and new variables are introduced into the equation. It is a mistake to institute a plan that does not allow for ongoing evaluation and modification.

In conclusion, this Case Decision-Making Scaffold is a tool to use while reading, discussing, and responding to the cases in this text. We have no desire to squelch intuition or reduce an art to a skill. Others have contributed valuable ideas for discussing cases, conducting critical inquiry, and developing teacher leadership, and we commend them to you (Shulman, 1996; Silverman and Welty, 1996; Sirotnik, 1991). The scaffold may be most helpful initially when case discussion is unfamiliar and there is a tendency to devise solutions before thoroughly considering aspects of the issues involved. Later, it may be less necessary to refer to the scaffold as the process of reflection becomes more internalized. We offer it as a scaffold for thinking that should be removed once you have determined your own decision-making process.

HOW DO PARTICIPANTS DISCUSS A CASE?

Often your instructors will ask you to read a case before meeting together and be ready to discuss the study questions at the end of the case or other questions that he or she has provided. In using these cases with in-service and preservice teachers, we have observed that it is important to read the cases carefully, highlighting important facts or taking notes as you proceed. Facts should be separated from opinions. If characters seem to hold certain assumptions, determine if these beliefs are based on reality. You should analyze your own interpretations and see if you can support them from data in the case. The Case Decision-Making Scaffold may be a good reference to help you to organize thoughts and feelings while thinking through this process.

Some of our students have formed informal study groups that would meet before class to discuss study questions and get a general sense of each individual's reaction to the case. In doing so, they have a better sense of the various perspectives that the case can evoke. By spending time on the initial analysis (that is, recognizing and framing the problem) outside class, they increase the possibility that class discussion will include all aspects of the decision-making process. In class, your instructor may first ask you to examine the case in small groups. This is another opportunity to learn how others have framed the case and is an excellent chance to practice those communication skills that are so critical to collaborative teaming in schools.

A benefit to discussing cases is that the process can encourage the development of a community of learners. People will frame the issues of the case differently based on their own background and beliefs. This diversity of ideas will provide for an interesting exploration of assumptions and feelings that you may not have considered. Undoubtedly, differences of opinion will surface. You must address all these perspectives before the group can progress and formulate a plan of action.

It can be exhilarating to observe the breadth of ideas that a group of reflective individuals can generate, but there is hard work involved in fleshing out these sometimes disparate notions into a workable plan. People will respond with their intellect and their emotions; both the cognitive and affective aspects of decision making must be considered. However, we agree with Kleinfeld (1998) that it is preferable to discuss the potentially emotionally unsettling situations that relate to diverse student populations through case studies before encountering similar events through direct experience. Confrontations in the school can harden teacher's prejudices, rather than create empathy. Within a community of learners, the passion that often accompanies debate can be channeled into mutual understanding and reasoned response.

During both small- and large-group discussions, it is important to establish an atmosphere of cooperation and mutual trust. As previously discussed, many issues will arise on which participants will have very different views, and emotions will inevitably surface. However, the point of case discussion is not to generate a debate and see who can win. The purpose of these cases is to come to some mutual understanding of the complex issues involved and to an informed and promising plan for addressing them. For example, once a school planning team has analyzed a problem that they are confronting through divergent thinking, the focus must switch to those alternatives around which stakeholders can reach some degree of consensus. Without agreement on an action plan, nothing is likely to change.

Perhaps the most important skill needed in group discussions is listening. Everyone has had the experience of having the person who follows in a discussion repeat almost exactly the same ideas. This is probably because the person who followed was too focused on his or her own ideas to listen to the speaker. It is difficult to truly understand what someone is saying (and what he or she may mean but is not saying) while simultaneously constructing a response. More deliberate displays of poor listening are apparent when individuals keep their hand up the entire time that someone is speaking or simply interrupt the speaker. When people feel strongly about something, they are tempted to block out what others are saying and concentrate on getting their own point across. All members must develop the skills of encouragement, clarification, and summarization, which can facilitate an acceptable solution.

It is true that a listener's thoughts are constantly racing in front of the speaker. People simply can't speak as quickly as they can think. However, this allows the astute discussion group member to accomplish several things. She can check the notes from her reading for facts or interpretations, listen carefully and take notes on significant points of agreement or disagreement, and write down ideas that she would like to contribute. When recognized by the discussion leader, she is able to first check with the previous speaker about the accuracy of her own perceptions by reflecting or paraphrasing that person's contribution or asking a clarifying question. Then she can go on to expand on the topic or offer an alternative idea. This is a complicated skill, yet one worth cultivating, since it will also determine the success of your class discussions as a teacher and a member of a collaborative team. There are many extended treatments of the skills needed to develop the art of discussion (Christensen, Garvin, & Sweet, 1991; Friend & Cook, 1992; Miller & Kantrov, 1998) and we would highly recommend them.

One caveat we would offer is that there are many reasons why individuals modulate the amount and intensity of their contributions to the group. One factor can be a person's own racial or cultural identity. Our experience is that individuals who are not part of the racial or culturally dominant group in the class are not always comfortable with sharing their opinions and experiences. This may be because they are still forming their own racial identity or because they do not feel it is appropriate to speak for others. For example, an individual from an upper-class family in Puerto Rico may have very different experiences and opinions from the child of an undocumented Mexican farm worker. While all class members must be made to feel that their contributions are welcome, those who prefer to remain quiet should be allowed to pass. On the other hand, some individuals have repeatedly experienced racial injustice and may want to make others aware that there is not always equal treatment under the law. However, voicing such inequities in a public forum is always a risk for the speaker. Within the first few classes, all participants should agree on discussion ground rules. For example, we would suggest that all discussion be kept within the group unless permission is granted otherwise. Furthermore, revealing difficult personal experiences can evoke strong emotions of anger or sorrow. All participants must be willing to support each other when emotions overflow and understand that the listeners are not the objects of that emotion.

The cases in this text portray the questions and quandaries that perplex both novice and experienced teachers. The characters represent diverse cultural, linguistic, economic, educational, and religious backgrounds, and the events of these narratives extend beyond the classroom and include the community. You are now familiar with the Case Decision-Making Scaffold and can use it to think through these complex cases. Furthermore, you can utilize the guidelines for discussing the cases to improve the quality of your class interactions. Chapter 5 presents a case and discusses how using the Case Decision-Making Scaffold enables the class to conduct a comprehensive analysis of the case and determine an action plan.

REFERENCES

Allain, V. A., & Pettus, A. M. (1998). *Teaching diverse students: Preparing with cases* (Fastback 429). Bloomington, IN: Phi Delta Kappa Educational Foundation.

Bruner, J. (1986). *Actual minds, possible worlds.* Cambridge, MA: Harvard University Press.

Christensen, C. R. (1987). *Teaching and the case method: Text, cases, and readings.* Cambridge, MA: Harvard Business School Press.

Christensen, C. R., Garvin, D. A., & Sweet, A. (1991). *Education for judgment: The artistry of discussion leadership.* Cambridge, MA: Harvard Business School Press.

Clandinin, D. J., & Connelly, F. M. (Eds.). (1995). *Teachers' professional knowledge landscapes.* New York: Teachers College Press.

Connelly, F. M., & Clandinin, D. J. (1988). *Teachers as curriculum planners.* New York: Teachers College Press.

Doyle, W. (1990, Winter). Case methods in teacher education. *Teacher Education Quarterly,* 7–15.

Doyle, W. (1997). Heard any really good stories lately? A critique of the critics of narrative in educational research. *Teaching and Teacher Education, 13*(1), 93–99.

Engel, J. F., Blackwell, R. D., & Miniard, P. W. (1995). *Consumer behavior* (8th ed.). New York: Harcourt Brace.

Friend, M., & Cook, L. (1992). *Interactions: Collaboration skills for school professionals.* White Plains, NY: Longman.

Goodlad, J. I. (1990). *Teachers for our nation's schools.* San Francisco: Jossey-Bass.

Herrenstein-Smith, B. (1981). Narrative version, narrative theories. In W. Mitchell (Ed.), *On narrative* (pp. 209–232). Chicago: University of Chicago Press.

Holmes Group (1995). *Tomorrow's schools of education.* East Lansing: Michigan State University School of Education.

Hutchings, P. (1993). *Using cases to improve college teaching.* Washington, DC: American Association for Higher Education.

Kleinfeld, J. S. (1998). The use of case studies in preparing teachers for cultural diversity. *Theory into Practice, 37*(2), 140–147.

Lampert, M., & Ball, D. L. (1990). *Using hypermedia technology to support a new pedagogy of teacher education (Issue Paper 90–5).* East Lansing: National Center for Research on Teacher Education, Michigan State University.

Leinhardt, G. (1990). Situated knowledge and expertise in teaching. In J. Calderhead (Ed.), *Teachers' professional knowledge* (pp. 146–168). London: Falmer.

Lincoln, Y. S., & Guba, E. G. (1985). *Naturalistic inquiry.* Newbury Park, CA: Sage.

Miller, B., & Kantrov, I. (1998). *A guide to facilitating cases in education.* Portsmouth, NH: Heinemann.

National Commission on Teaching & America's Future. (1996). *What matters most: Teaching for America's future.* New York: Author.

Schon, D. (1987). *Educating the reflective practitioner.* San Francisco: Jossey-Bass.

Schon, D. (1991). *The reflective turn: Case studies in and on educational practice.* New York: Teachers College Press.

Shulman, J. H. (1996). Tender feelings, hidden thoughts: Confronting bias, innocence, and racism through case discussion. In A. Colbert, P. Desberg, & K. Trimble (Eds.), *The case for education: Contemporary approaches for using case methods* (pp. 137–158). Boston: Allyn and Bacon.

Shulman, L. S. (1987). Knowledge and teaching: Foundations of the new reform. *Harvard Educational Review, 57,* 114–135.

Shulman, L. S. (1996). Just in case: Reflections on learning from experience. In J. A. Colbert, P. Desberg, & K. Trimble (Eds.), *The case for education: Contemporary approaches for using case methods* (pp. 197–217). Boston: Allyn and Bacon.

Silverman, R., & Welty, W. M. (1996). Teaching without a net: Using cases in teacher education. In J. A. Colbert, P. Desberg, & K. Trimble (Eds.), *The case for education: Contemporary approaches for using case methods* (pp. 159–172). Boston: Allyn and Bacon.

Simmons, S. R., & Dunrud, R. (1994). *The worth of an oak tree.* Unpublished manuscript, University of Minnesota.

Sirotnik, K. A. (1991). Critical inquiry: A paradigm for praxis. In E. C. Short (Ed.), *Forms of
curriculum inquiry* (pp. 243–258). Albany, NY: State University of New York Press.

Smith, D. D. (2001). *Introduction to special education: Teaching in an age of opportunity* (4th ed.).
Boston: Allyn and Bacon.

Wasserman, S. (1994). *Introduction to case method teaching: A guide to the galaxy.* New York: Teachers College Press.

CHAPTER 5

PUTTING IT ALL TOGETHER: ANALYZING AND DISCUSSING A CASE

The case studies in subsequent chapters are organized under six issues of diversity: race and ethnicity, poverty and socioeconomic status, language and culture, exceptionalities, gender and sexual orientation, and religion. Each chapter begins with an overview of the issue, with background information and research that we believe to be important to a thorough discussion of the case. The primary issues involved in the cases are clearly related to the chapter title. Other issues will inevitably be relevant. Life, teaching, and these cases are complex.

This chapter is illustrative. It presents the case of Jesus Gonzalez and demonstrates how the authors would employ the Case Decision-Making Scaffold (see Table 4.1 on page 73). We provide relevant background information about migrant farmworkers before the case. We also encourage you to read the overview material in Chapter 8, since the primary focus of this case is language and culture.

ISSUES REGARDING MIGRANT FARMWORKERS AND THEIR FAMILIES

Migrant workers are individuals who travel to work in agricultural, dairy, or fishing industries. Although they often live in camps near their work and are relatively invisible to the surrounding community, their labor is essential to the quality and low cost of fruits, vegetables, and other food products in the United States (Whittaker, Salend, & Gutierrez, 1997).

Migrant workers usually fall into one of two groups based on their movement patterns (Martin, 1996). The largest group consists of workers who usually work in one location in the United States and then return to their homes in Mexico, Central America, or the Caribbean. Another group travels from state to state within the same *stream* from year to year. The three major streams in the United States are the eastern, mid-continent, and western streams (Shotland, 1989). Many migrants bring their families with them, and often both parents and children work in the fields. Family members are often close-knit and take their responsibilities to one another very seriously (Garcias, 2001). Of the 650,000 migrant students who live in the United States, approximately 90 percent live in households where a language other than English is spoken (Salend, 1990, 1998). This means that many of the children are English language learners in school, but may not receive appropriate instruction in English. Migrant students come from many cultural backgrounds: Hispanics, 79%; white, 11%; black, 4%; Asian–Pacific Islander, 3%; and Native American or Native Alaskan, 2%.

Sometimes workers are asked by their employers to stay year round. Understandably, if a job exists, migrant farmworkers who are offered a place to live and a minimum wage for physically demanding work often decide to stay in a community all year. Often these circumstances, while unacceptable to most Americans, are better than those that they encounter in their country of origin. These families are often known as *resettled* migrants by the government agencies that provide services for them.

Migrant families face difficult socioeconomic conditions (Salend, 2001). They can work six or seven days per week for ten or more hours a day. Wages are low. When adjusted for inflation, these farmworkers often have less purchasing power than they "enjoyed" in the 1960s. Often they face poor sanitation in the fields and work camps, overcrowded or substandard housing, exposure to pesticides, and limited health care. Children are often expected to take over household chores and child care and may even be faced with the difficult decision of remaining in school or working in the fields to help to support the family. They usually live on the farms or in a nearby town or city with several families in one apartment. Usually they depend on others for transportation.

It is not surprising that children of migrant workers often face educational difficulties. Because of their mobility, they may attend schools that have very different educational requirements, programs, and organizational patterns (Salend, 1990, 2001). Furthermore, they have to adjust to new peers each time that they move. Unfortunately, migrant students report that they are sometimes teased and ostracized because of cultural, linguistic, or economic differences. Approximately 25 percent of migrant students enroll in school more than 30 days after school begins. Each year that they continue in school, migrant students have a tendency to fall behind academically. In some parts of the country their dropout rate is as high as 49 percent.

The federal government provides limited funding to assist migrant farmworkers. States in which migrants work have a network of agencies that provide health, legal, and educational services to the families. For example, health clinics are available to provide children and adults with basic dental and health care since families do not have health insurance. Furthermore, Migrant Head Start provides preschool programs and transportation for 3- to 5-year-olds in some areas. In the past, educational centers provided tutoring for migrant children during the school year and a full-day summer program. However, due to federal funding cutbacks, many centers have changed to a family advocacy model. This service model assists families by assigning a caseworker who can help the family to access community resources such as literacy training or accompany them when interfacing with school or government agencies. However, individual tutoring for children is less available and summer programs are shorter. In general, families who have resettled in an area lose services after 3 years.

It is incumbent on teachers to be aware of the challenges that the children of migrant and resettled workers face and to help them to feel welcome in their classrooms. Too often these children are ignored because they are expected to leave soon or are viewed as problems due to their linguistic differences. At other times, teachers are unaware of the assistance available to farmworkers through local and state agencies (Collaborative, 2001). Unless teachers and school staff advocate for these children, many will not receive the educational support that they deserve.

THE CASE OF JESUS GONZALEZ

My first graders had just returned from gym. I knew from hearing their loud voices coming down the hall and seeing their sweaty foreheads as they careened into the classroom that I needed to read them a story before we began the social studies lesson on community helpers that afternoon. All the children were gathered around me on the rug as I read them *The Hungry Little Caterpillar.*

We had just finished the part where the caterpillar had gorged himself and wasn't feeling so well. I looked up from the story, sensing that someone was at the door. A short, sturdy man in dusty jeans and a John Deere feed cap with a "visitor" button on his sweatshirt was waiting there. Not recognizing his face, I rose and approached him.

"May I help you?" I asked.

"Si. I come to get Jesus," he responded, looking beyond me.

Then I remembered that the office had told me that Jesus had to leave early on family business that day.

"Of course," I replied, being sure to smile. "Jesus, get your backpack and jacket."

The rest of the class stayed in their circle, but strained to see the visitor.

"Hey, Jesus. Is that your dad?" queried the ever-curious Michael.

Jesus ignored him and quickly went to his desk to collect his things. I turned to Mr. Gonzalez, hoping to make him feel welcome.

"It's nice to meet you. I enjoy having your son in class."

Mr. Gonzalez took a step backward and smiled. Jesus was still reaching into the black hole he had created in his desk.

"Vamanos! Es la hora, Jesus!" his father commanded.

Jesus's surprised face appeared from behind his desktop. Clearly embarrassed, Jesus screamed out, "Stop talking Spanish in here!"

Mr. Gonzalez was speechless. He stepped outside the door and Jesus quickly followed.

Jesus's father was halfway down the hall with Jesus running after him before I realized that I had not even said goodbye. My feeble attempt to do so went unheeded. I was so thrown by this brief interchange that I simply could not respond.

What should I have said? "Adios, senor?" This was about the extent of my Spanish. Should I have told Jesus that all languages were welcome in this classroom? Would I be usurping Mr. Gonzalez's parental role by interfering, not to mention embarrassing him further? What should I say to the other children? This kind of situation had never come up in my four years of teaching first grade.

But then, I told myself, why would it? Jesus was the first culturally and linguistically diverse student I had had in my first grade class. In fact, there were only a handful of these students in the entire school. In our small midwestern town of 7,500 about 98 percent of the population was white and came from European heritage. We live in an area with many truck farms, so Mexican families come here to pick tomatoes and other vegetables. However, most of them leave before school starts. Those who stay on for a few weeks in September often wait until they return home to enroll the children in school. These families usually live on the farms and, although I might see them at the supermarket on Friday evenings cashing their checks and buying groceries, I had little contact with them.

I knew from several conversations with Jesus's kindergarten teacher from last year, Susan Bigelow, that Jesus had been identified as speech impaired and that was why he went for speech therapy for half an hour three times per week. He had not progressed academically or socially as the teacher had hoped, and there was discussion about having him repeat kindergarten. However, a compromise was reached, and during this school year Jesus is with me in the morning and with Carolyn Davis, a different kindergarten teacher, in the afternoon. It was hoped that he would be able to make the transition to first grade more smoothly if he could experience it more gradually. Of course, we also knew that he might need to stay in first grade for another year after this. After 4 months of working with Jesus, I have little reason to hope that he will be able to manage second grade in the fall.

Besides being pulled out for speech, Jesus goes to ESL instruction with Ms. Vanderpool for half an hour three times a week during our language arts time. Ms. Vanderpool is not a certified bilingual teacher nor does she speak Spanish. However, I think she has been helping him with vocabulary. Susan Bigelow is the one teacher in the school who can speak basic Spanish, and she could talk with the family if I needed to communicate with Jesus's parents. Truthfully, however, up until Mr. Gonzalez's appearance at my door, we had had no contact.

I felt somewhat guilty about this because Jesus was having some problems in my classroom. It seemed that Jesus's oral language was improving, but he was still behind in reading, simple addition, and handwriting skills. He lacked organizational skills and was having difficulty working independently. I also was concerned that he often did not have homework completed. Part of me felt that he should have remained in kindergarten where he could develop socially one more year and learn how to "do school."

I could tell that Jesus desperately wanted to be accepted by his peers. This outburst was just one example of his desire to be just like everyone else. He seemed to get along with Michael and Scott and stayed close to them on the playground. However, he was very quiet and shy around most of the other children. He wasn't disliked by anyone; however, he remained on the fringes of the social scene.

After this encounter with Jesus and his father, I decided that I had better talk with Jim McIntyre, our district social worker. He, in turn, put me in touch with Luis Torres, an outreach worker from the Migrant Center, a state-funded agency that helps migrant farmworkers to connect with social and educational agencies when they work in our area. Luis had visited Jesus's family in their home and knew something of their family history. He was extremely helpful in providing information about Jesus's family, which helped me to better understand the ways in which they valued school and the expectations that they had for their son.

Luis explained that Jesus lives with his father, mother, and 4-year-old brother in a small trailer located behind a large packing house on a farm. His father, who is in his early thirties, is a foreman who does odd jobs on the farm, and Mrs. Gonzalez works in the packing plant. Although they are paid only minimum wage, the family is pleased with the arrangement because they live in the trailer rent free with all utilities paid all year around. Therefore, they are able to save some money and hope to buy their own home someday. Mrs. Gonzalez likes working near home so that she can meet the school bus each day.

Mr. and Mrs. Gonzalez came from Mexico 7 years ago in search of a better life. Jesus lived in Mexico with his grandmother for 9 months when he was 2, but he has been in the United States the rest of his life. The Gonzalezes wanted their children to be born and raised in the United States so that they could get a good education and not have to rely on farmwork to sustain themselves.

Although the family views the educational opportunities in the United States as a benefit, they are worried about the influence that U.S. culture may have on their children. They have extended family in a town about an hour away, but see them only once every other month. Their social contacts, though few, are primarily with other Mexican and Jamaican farmworkers. Jesus is very close to his younger brother and spends most of his time after school playing Nintendo or watching television with him. Just recently, Jesus has been allowed to invite his best friend over to visit once a week if he behaves and does his schoolwork. When he does not complete his work, his parents remind him that if he fails school they will have to return to Mexico where Jesus will have to tend cows for a living and work in the fields all day long.

It was enlightening to know more about Jesus's family life, but I couldn't help but feel that the child I saw in school was not necessarily the same child his parents saw at home. Behind those dark brown eyes that peered out from under a thick fringe of straight, brown-black hair, was a developing mind that I did not fully understand. Yesterday in class was no exception. I asked Jesus for his completed homework and he simply responded, "I forgot." I rummaged through his desk to find his folder and pulled out all the assignments he had not completed. Hoping that he would make up his work in class, I numbered them in the order in which they should be completed and asked him to get to work. Within 5 minutes, Jesus was wandering around the room. He picked up a fallen art project and walked over to my desk.

"Here, Mrs. Kniffen, someone dropped this."

"Thank you, Jesus. Now please go back to your seat and get to work," I responded without looking up.

"But I didn't do it. I just found it on the floor," he interjected.

"Give it to me and I'll put it away. Thank you," I responded, trying to be patient.

Jesus never made it back to his seat. He sat next to Michael and played with his ruler for awhile. Then he grabbed a pencil from his desk, sharpened it for 2 minutes, and strolled around the room looking at everyone else's work.

"Jesus, you are already behind. Now get back to your desk and finish your work," I said firmly.

I wish that I could say that he finally responded to me, but, in fact, he was up again, ostensibly looking for math manipulatives, in another 2 minutes. However, he passed them by and continued to wander. Not until Mrs. Adams, my teaching assistant, gave him the box of manipulatives did he sit down and start to work.

I finally decided that I must have a parent conference and asked the Gonzalezes to come to school. Mr. Torres agreed to come and translate when they had difficulty understanding my English. Mrs. Gonzalez arrived with Mr. Torres at the scheduled time, but said that her husband had to work. I started by telling her how much I liked her son and how well he seemed to get along with his small circle of friends.

"He is a very friendly boy who loves people," she said, smiling slightly.

"I am afraid, however, that he is not very organized in school and often does not bring in his homework," I added.

Mrs. Gonzalez agreed, but said that they always insist that he do his homework each evening. However, she admitted that more recently he has been leaving the kitchen table before he is done to watch television. She is bothered by this disobedience and insists that he return to his work. Then she reported that one evening last week, when she told him to return to his work, he screamed, "No!" He proceeded to slam the refrigerator door and pouted for 2 hours. Although she has tried letting him go to bed and complete his work in the morning, this plan is rarely successful. She promised that she would force him to complete his work at the table and tell him his best friend would not be able to come over if he did not.

I wanted to impress on Mrs. Gonzalez that Jesus is becoming more fluent in English, but that he is easily distracted and lacks many skills in reading and mathematics. Once again I stressed that, because of his immaturity, he was better off being in first grade half the day. She seemed unsure of this, but yielded to my expertise.

Mrs. Gonzalez wanted me to understand that she was doing the best that she could with her son, but that her own limited English proficiency made it difficult for her to do more. What she did see as her area of control was Jesus's social life. She said that they have kept Jesus and his brother away from the prejudiced people outside the farm and associate with Jamaicans and African American farmworkers that they work with who share their circumstances. They maintain their culture by speaking only Spanish at home and buying Mexican foods in the city nearby. She said that she did not want her children to be exposed to the bad influences that she observed in some local children, although she didn't elaborate.

Although Mrs. Gonzalez and I had ended our meeting with a considerable amount of good will, I found myself staring out the window as she and Mr. Torres left the parking lot. I could not help but feel that there were many things that she was probably expressing to Luis that she would never say to me.

I could empathize with Jesus's mother, yet I wondered if we had made any real progress. We agreed that I would stay in contact with her regarding Jesus's progress and homework completion. However, I doubted that this would have any effect on his performance in school, particularly when she simply could not help him that much. I was haunted by the few defiant outbursts that came from this usually good-spirited boy. Nor could I understand the quiet defiance he displayed by being a nomad in my classroom.

USING THE CASE DECISION-MAKING SCAFFOLD

Recognize the Problem

The trigger event that alerts us to a problem is Jesus's demand that his father speak English in school. Although Mrs. Kniffen, Jesus's teacher, has been very aware of the academic and behavioral difficulties, this event prompts her into action. For us to determine the source of the problems involved, it is important to identify the relevant information that the case provides regarding each individual or constituency.

The facts that we can garner from the case regarding Jesus are that he is below first grade level in reading, math, and handwriting, although his oral language skills in English seem to be improving. He lacks organizational skills, is easily distracted, doesn't work well independently, and often does not complete homework. Furthermore, Mrs. Kniffen believes that he is socially immature and notes that he has only two friends in the class.

The school responded to Jesus's difficulties in kindergarten by placing him part time in first grade and kindergarten during this school year. He also has speech and language services three times a week for half-hour sessions and an equivalent amount of time with the English as a Second Language teacher, who does not speak Spanish. The school has a social worker and has placed a teaching assistant in Mrs. Kniffen's classroom, although we know little of their involvement with Jesus.

The community is a small, midwestern farming town the population of which is 98 percent white. Most farmworkers come for the summer growing season and harvest and leave in the fall. It appears that they live on the farms and have very little contact with community members.

Mrs. Kniffen is a first grade teacher who has never before had a student who is culturally and linguistically diverse. She doesn't speak Spanish and is unsure of how to interact with the Gonzalez family, although she does feel guilty about it. She notes that she has had minimal contact with the Mexicans that do come in the summer. She tells Mrs. Gonzalez that it is good for Jesus to be part time in kindergarten and first grade, but also lists the multiple academic and social problems that he is having.

The Gonzalez family is living in the United States because the wages that they earn are better than what is available in Mexico. Both parents work on a local farm, where the grower provides them with a trailer for housing. They speak Spanish and need a translator to communicate with school staff. Jesus has a younger brother who is his primary companion at home, although occasionally another friend is allowed to visit. Their social life is confined to other farmworkers and occasional contact with relatives in another town. Lately they have been experiencing difficulty getting Jesus to complete his homework.

There are many discrepancies between various individuals' expectations and actual events. Mrs. Kniffen clearly expects that Jesus should pay attention in school, complete his homework, and make academic progress, given the program that the school has provided and the curriculum that she has established. At this point, we can only make conjectures about Jesus's lack of academic engagement. However, he obviously wants to please his teacher and make friends. He does not want to be different from the other children and reacts strongly when his father speaks to him in Spanish in front of his peers.

Like Mrs. Kniffen, Jesus's parents want him to complete his homework and do well in school, especially since this is one of the major reasons they came to the United States. They also want him to be a respectful child and obey their requests. However, they would prefer that his social contacts be limited to families of other farmworkers and relatives.

The school expects that children like Jesus will progress within the standard school curriculum and educational program. Obviously, they view the services performed by the ESL and speech language teacher as appropriate for his needs. The school has decided that it is reasonable and, in fact, beneficial for Jesus to be in kindergarten and first grade half-days.

Frame the Problem

To frame the problem, we must look beyond the facts to the values and beliefs of the individuals involved, since understanding these perspectives is critical to finding effective solutions. When individuals come from different cultures and must speak through a translator, the chances that their assumptions will differ or not be fully communicated increase. A culturally responsive teacher will be aware that her perspectives are culturally bound and make every attempt to understand those of students and parents who come from other cultures.

Jesus's parents place a high value on education. They see it as the only way to avoid the very poor conditions of their own childhood and the difficult, physically demanding labor that they both perform. At the same time, they are proud of their Mexican roots, language, and culture. Yet they live in a community in which few speak Spanish, and the Mexican culture is not celebrated or even apparent. As is true of most Latino families, one of their highest values is family unity. The Gonzalezes believe that their life-style is not acceptable to the community at large, and they have deepened this marginalization by choosing to keep to themselves.

In traditional Latino families, the father is the provider and protector of the family and is to be respected. Therefore, we can assume that Jesus's outburst in response to his father's request in Spanish was very disturbing to Mr. Gonzalez, both because of his place in the family and his high regard for his first language. Perhaps Mr. Gonzalez viewed this as just one more indication that, while school is a place to gain an education, an American school will also expose his son to many bad influences. Mrs. Gonzalez certainly said that she didn't want Jesus to be exposed to the negative behavior that she observed in local children.

The fact that Jesus would dare reprimand his father in public demonstrates the extent to which he is struggling to negotiate the worlds of home and school. For half the day he lives in a white, English-only environment that espouses the values of academic success and individual achievement. He undoubtedly knows that his dual placement is an indication of his academic failure. He, like most children, wants to be accepted by his peers, but is unable to communicate enough to make significant social contacts. He is trying to acculturate, but knows that his parents would rather that he avoid the children who surround him all day. The rest of the day he lives in a Mexican, Spanish-only environment that is quite isolated. His frustration in trying to negotiate these two worlds may explain his refusal to complete homework when asked by both his parents and teachers. Neither parents nor teachers really seem able to help him academically.

Mrs. Kniffen and the other school staff assume that the school is providing for Jesus's needs in a way that exceeds what is provided to the typical student. They view the ESL and speech language pullout services as adequate and therefore don't understand why Jesus is not making greater progress. They see the split-day schedule as a positive approach compared to retention, the first option that they had considered. Mrs. Kniffen views Jesus's nomad behavior as a kind of quiet defiance from an otherwise kind boy. Even after the conference with Mrs. Gonzalez, she doubts that Jesus's performance will improve. While she promises to stay in contact with Mrs. Gonzalez, she does not discuss any concrete methods for communicating with her in the future, despite their language differences. There is no indication that Mrs. Kniffen has included information in the curriculum that explains Mexican culture or history in order to help Jesus feel comfortable with his culture and language and gain recognition from the other children. Furthermore, the school sees no reason to provide more extensive ESL or bilingual services. There is no discussion of what is reasonable to expect in terms of language acquisition when a child's only language prior to entering school was Spanish. The assumption is that the problem lies with Jesus and not with the school.

Although no open hostility is apparent in this case, there is a great deal of misunderstanding and mistrust beneath the surface. It is critical that all the individuals involved have the opportunity to understand and communicate these differences in beliefs and find those things that they can agree on. The promising aspect of the case is that both the parents and the school seem to agree that it is important for Jesus to progress in school and receive an education. Given that common ground, they must attempt to discuss alternatives that will accomplish this goal without compromising their basic beliefs.

Search for Alternatives

The issue of how to work with students who come from culturally and linguistically diverse backgrounds is new to Mrs. Kniffen, but it is an issue with which many schools across the country have dealt, some with great success. Although many of these districts lie in urban areas where there is a more diverse population than described here, many areas of the United States will face similar challenges in the next 10 years. Therefore, it is critical to be informed about programs, practices, and instructional approaches that improve the educational process for children like Jesus.

In addition, we must understand that there may be immediate, short-term actions that can make a difference for Jesus. However, for students like Jesus to be successful, the district must consider a model to implement comprehensive school reform that will sustain positive educational programs over time (McChesney & Hertling, 2000). Ultimately, changes that assist Jesus must be supported by an entire school program that will promote high standards for all students, including those who are culturally and linguistically diverse. Thus, we must understand those factors that currently impede his progress and design a program that will eliminate these barriers.

Research tells us that Jesus faces multiple barriers to learning. First, while he is acquiring basic interpersonal communication skills (BICS) in English, he has only been exposed to the English language consistently for a little over a year and to ESL instruction for several months. We know that most children need cognitive academic learning proficiency (CALP) to achieve in school and that this type of language proficiency may take up to 7 years to acquire (Cummins, 1984). We also know that second language learners often present academic difficulties that appear to be learning disabilities, but actually result from the normal process of language acquisition, while others actually are delayed in both languages (Ortiz, 1997). Furthermore, immigrants go through stages of adjustment and sometimes exhibit a "silent period" during which they listen to a new language, but say little (Igoa, 1995). Proper assessment and comprehensive planning that support Jesus's understanding of Spanish while he acquires English are clearly needed (Baca & Cervantes, 1998; Salend, 2001). Several studies have found that when students are taught in their first language it is easier for them to learn a second language as well as keep up with peers in the content of the general education curriculum (Ramirez, 1992; Thomas & Collier, 1998). The controversy over whether children learn best in bilingual education programs continues to rage; however, the practical reality is that there are not enough students in Jesus's school and age range to financially support such a program. Therefore, it is critical that all teachers, not just the ESL teacher, differentiate instruction by using effective ESL approaches (Salend, 2001).

"Student academic motivation, commitment to democratic values, and resistance to problem behaviors all depend on their experience of the school as a community" (Schaps & Lewis, 1999, p. 215). It is difficult for students who do not hear their first language in school, do not see their culture and history in their textbooks or classroom walls, and do not see teachers of their racial group to experience a caring community. Yet this Euro-centric experience of school is still the norm in schools today (Bohn & Sleeter, 2000). One way that teachers can create community is by including the languages, traditions, and histories of their students in the curriculum.

We also know that a key component to student success is the support of families and the community. Although Jesus's parents want desperately to see Jesus succeed in school, they face many barriers in their attempt to achieve this. Parents who do not speak English and know little about the culture of American schools are not likely to be involved in their child's education (Salend & Taylor, 1993). They are limited in the extent to which they can offer their child academic assistance at home or advocate for their child at school. If they feel uncomfortable in the school or experience prejudice from the community, there is little likelihood that they will be willing to use the regular communication channels (parent–teacher conference, phone calls, notes, parent–teacher organization meetings, volunteering and the like).

Long-term solutions for this situation involve examining the academic subject areas across grade levels, implementing research-based changes, sharing common goals, providing professional development, aligning resources across grade and content areas, and facilitating parent and community involvement (Education Commission of the States, 1998). In particular, the district must determine how it can best design programs for students who do not reach state or local standards and students who are second language learners. Furthermore, it must involve community members, including parents whose first language is not English, as it sets goals and determines priorities. Teachers must be provided with in-service education that will assist them in incorporating the principles of multicultural education into their

teaching philosophy and introducing research-based instructional strategies
for second language learners.

Develop and Implement Plan of Action

The task of choosing and prioritizing goals that will address the issues in this
case must be accomplished collaboratively by the family, school district, and
community. This joint effort should be based on the belief held by all stakeholders that it is important for Jesus to gain an education. Therefore, for goals
to be chosen, the school must first establish a workable method for communication between the school and home.

It is essential that a plan of action be developed that clearly defines each
goal, establishes methods to implement the goal, assigns responsibility to specific individuals, and determines criteria and time lines for evaluation. The
goal of establishing communication might be accomplished by identifying a
translator for all parent–teacher meetings, determining a method for other
communications, establishing regular planning meetings, and finding a bilingual advocate for the Gonzalez family from the community (see Table 5.1). If
the parents are desirous, the school can inform them of community agencies
that provide English language instruction. While accomplishing each of these
action steps will undoubtedly require the services of various individuals in
the school and community, it is important to assign responsibility for each
step to one or two individuals. Similarly, workable criteria and a time line are
critical for evaluating progress.

Once an effective communication system is established, it will be possible to determine an action plan that includes both short- and long-term goals
for improving the educational program for Jesus and other students like him.
As stated previously, cases do not have one answer. Each time we discuss
these cases with participants, outcomes vary based on the beliefs of the discussants, access and exposure to research and expertise, individual experience, and time available. However, the goals that discussants establish are
frequently similar. In this case, additional goals often include redesigning an
educational program for Jesus, professional development for teachers in
strategies for teaching students who are culturally and linguistically diverse,
infusing multicultural education throughout the curriculum, and establishing a district task force to examine resources and programs for all students.
An example of one plan of action for accomplishing these goals is listed in
Table 5.2.

Evaluate Progress

The evaluation of progress is essential to the success of any action plan. The
evaluation process is tied to the discussion of teacher reflection in Chapter 4.

TABLE 5.1   Goals of Home and School Communication

ACTIVITY, REFERRAL, RESOURCE, STRATEGY	PERSON(S) RESPONSIBLE	CRITERIA FOR EVALUATION	TIME LINE
1. Identify translator for parent and teacher meetings	School social worker	Translator attends each meeting and parent indicates understanding of conversation	Two weeks
2. Establish regular parent–school meetings to develop and implement a program for Jesus	Mrs. Kniffen School social worker	An educational program that results in academic and social improvement for Jesus	Monthly
3. Identify bilingual advocate for Jesus's family who can attend school meetings and assist	Luis Torres Migrant Center staff School social worker	Advocate attends all meetings at request of parent	As needed
4. Determine method for communication between parents and school beyond regular meetings (e.g., oral or written translation of school notices)	Luis Torres School social worker	Parents receive communication from school in Spanish	As needed

While we have chosen to display evaluation as the last part of the Case Decision-Making Scaffold, evaluation or reflection is an ongoing process that all individuals concerned must undertake individually and collectively. Regular meetings of stakeholders formalize the reflection process and establish a means for revising the plan of action when needed.

In the cases presented in the following chapters, we have presented one slice of a real teaching situation. We have chosen not to present follow-up information for these cases so that the discussants can analyze the case from their own perspectives. However, occasionally we have been able to follow up on a case. Because we believe that evaluation is a critical component of change, we have chosen to present further information about Jesus so that readers will be able to evaluate the progress of the plan of action that was actually undertaken.

TABLE 5.2   Goals and Plan of Action for Case of Jesus Gonzalez

ACTIVITY, REFERRAL, RESOURCE, STRATEGY	PERSON(S) RESPONSIBLE	CRITERIA FOR EVALUATION	TIME LINE
GOAL: REDESIGN AN EDUCATIONAL PROGRAM FOR JESUS			
1. Assess Jesus's academic abilities in English and Spanish	Mrs. Kniffen, Ms. Vanderpool (ESL teacher)	Written report of standardized and informal assessments	Within 2 weeks
2. Meet with Child Study Team, Jesus's teachers, and parents to discuss assessment and determine appropriate educational program	Child study team coordinator	Plan of Action designed at Child Study Team meeting	Within 2 weeks
3. Establish collaborative program that utilizes present school staff and community resources to educate Jesus	Mrs. Kniffen School social worker	Meeting of school staff and community agencies to coordinate instructional program for Jesus	Every month
4. Determine Jesus's educational needs that are not met by present school program and program development needs for students who are culturally and linguistically diverse for the principal and board of education	Child study team coordinator	Written report of program development need for students who are culturally and linguistically diverse for principal and board of education	Within 3 months
GOAL: PROVIDE PROFESSIONAL DEVELOPMENT FOR TEACHERS IN STRATEGIES FOR TEACHING STUDENTS WHO ARE CULTURALLY AND LINGUISTICALLY DIVERSE			
1. Assess school staff needs for professional development	Building leadership team coordinator	Survey of professional development needs	Within 1 month
2. Identify in-service approach and qualified professionals to facilitate professional development	Building leadership team coordinator	Evaluation of professional development	Within 6 months
3. Establish professional development plans for school staff that include implementation of professional development	Principal and staff	Professional development plans for teachers	Within school year

ACTIVITY, REFERRAL, RESOURCE, STRATEGY	PERSON(S) RESPONSIBLE	CRITERIA FOR EVALUATION	TIME LINE
GOAL: INFUSE MULTICULTURAL EDUCATION THROUGHOUT THE CURRICULUM			
1. Assess multicultural content of school curriculum	Curriculum committee coordinator	Comparison of district curriculum with national, state, and professional standards for multicultural education using curriculum mapping	Within 6 months
2. Present results of curriculum mapping to school staff for comment and revision	Curriculum committee coordinator	Revision of curriculum mapping by staff	Within school year
3. Develop report on curriculum mapping and curriculum resource funding need for board of education	Curriculum committee coordinator and principals	Written report to board of education	Within 1 year
4. Present report on multicultural education to board of education for funding	Curriculum committee coordinator and principals	Minutes of board of education meeting	Within 1 year
5. Establish implementation procedures for multicultural education curriculum funding	Superintendent, principals, and district task force	Written implementation plan	Within 2 years
GOAL: ESTABLISH A DISTRICT TASK FORCE TO EXAMINE RESOURCES AND PROGRAMS FOR ALL STUDENTS			
1. Develop and approve mission statement and membership for district multicultural education task force	Board of education, superintendent, principals, and curriculum committee	Mission statement and membership roles	Within 15 months
2. Meet regularly to discuss issues related to multicultural education within the district and community	Multicultural education task force chair	Minutes of meetings	Within 16 months and then every 2 months
3. Implement curriculum funding for multicultural education and ongoing professional development	Superintendent and multicultural education task force chair	Minutes of meetings and survey of professional development needs	Ongoing

FOLLOW-UP ON JESUS GONZALEZ

As I thought more about my meeting with Mrs. Gonzalez and Mr. Torres, I decided that I would make an attempt to include more of the Spanish language and Mexican American culture in my classroom. However, I did not have the background in second language acquisition or curriculum resources in my classroom to give Jesus the support and recognition that he needed. Certainly, I could consider getting additional training in working with students like Jesus, but that was a long-term solution. I needed help now. Mrs. Vanderpool was doing what she could three times a week for Jesus, but I wanted to know what I should do the other 28½ hours each week when Jesus was with me.

I called Mr. Torres the next day and asked if he had any ideas or suggestions, since I thought he might have spoken to Mrs. Gonzalez further after our meeting. He suggested that I try to encourage Jesus to talk about his family, culture, and language with the rest of the class so that they would understand more about Jesus. I agreed that it would be important for Jesus' self-concept to be able to share these things with the others, but that he resisted any attempts I had made to get him to speak to me privately about his language and culture; I doubted that he would talk to the whole class. Then he had a wonderful suggestion. He said that he knew that there was a graduate program in education at Clearwater State that was designed to encourage students to get their master's in multicultural education. He knew of someone in the program who used to work with him and thought perhaps I could find out more through her.

It wasn't easy making the contacts, but within 2 weeks Estrella Cortez was on her way to my classroom to observe Jesus. She was enrolled in the graduate program that Mr. Torres had mentioned and was interested in observing and possibly designing a curriculum unit for my class to fulfill a class assignment. The first time Estrella came she just sat in the back of the class, observed, and took copious notes. Jesus was off task at least half of the time she was there. The next week she sat with Jesus as he was trying to complete his reading worksheet and noted the words that he could not read or write. She also spent time just talking with him about his family and told him about her memories of first grade in Puerto Rico. Although she did not try to speak to Jesus in Spanish, I'm sure he realized from her accent that her first language was Spanish, too.

We spent time after school discussing Jesus's areas of strength and weakness. I told Estrella about the incident in class with Mr. Gonzalez, as well as of my conversation with Mr. Torres and Mrs. Gonzalez. She suggested that she come to my class weekly for a month and read children's literature that related to his culture and language to the whole class. Then she would plan activities that related to the books. She wouldn't single him out unless he volunteered. I readily agreed, since I knew the number of books in the school library about Mexican Americans was limited; at least it wouldn't hurt.

The first week Estrella read *Radio Man,* the story of a Mexican American family that travels from Texas to the Pacific Northwest to pick crops. The son always listens to the local radio stations and sends messages in to these stations about his arrival to an area. He hopes that his best friend will hear the message and contact him. It is a bilingual text, so Estrella read both languages to the children and they were spellbound. They wanted to know how to say different words in Spanish, and Estrella was happy to respond and obviously proud of her first language. Afterward she asked if anyone knew a migrant worker or spoke Spanish. Jesus did not say a word and she did not press him.

Estrella decided she would use the story in *Radio Man* to conduct a class sociogram. She asked the students to write down which two people they would send a message on the radio to if they were traveling and wanted to see their friends. Jesus put down Scott and Michael and they were the only ones to put down his name.

Fortunately, Estrella wasn't easily discouraged by Jesus's lack of response. She said that she understood what a big risk it is to talk about being different in any way when you want so much to be accepted. The next week she brought in the book *Con Mi Hermano,* a delightful bilingual text about two brothers who love to be together. She began to read the English and then the Spanish. Then she asked if there was anyone who would like to help her read. I'm still not sure whether it was because the book was on an easy reading level or because it was about two brothers or because Jesus had seen the children enjoy Estrella reading in Spanish last week. But Jesus volunteered to read—in both English and Spanish! The children applauded when he was through and he was beaming. During snack time, the children crowded around Jesus; they wanted him to talk in Spanish and teach them new words.

Estrella said that she wanted to visit Jesus's family in their home, and I said it was fine with me, if his parents consented. Mrs. Gonzalez agreed to have Estrella visit after school the next week. Estrella talked about the progress she thought Jesus was making both in staying on task and in his willingness to speak Spanish. Of course, Mrs. Gonzalez was very pleased. Estrella took her several books that were in English and Spanish that she could read with her son. Mrs. Gonzalez said that it was hard for her to visit the school— that there were too many Anglos there. However, she was grateful for the help that Jesus was getting and recognized that, to some extent, he was going to be Americanized.

I knew things were changing for Jesus when Estrella read *Amazing Grace* to the class. Grace is a willowy African American girl who wants to be Peter Pan in the school play, but is told that she can't since Peter Pan is white. Ultimately, she gets to star in the show and says, "No one can tell me I can't." Estrella set up a role play in class in which the main character needed to speak Spanish. Jesus immediately volunteered. When asked by the classmate in the role play, "What if someone told you that you couldn't speak Spanish?" Jesus boldly replied, "No one can tell me I can't."

FIGURE 5.1   Jesus's Poster

The last week Estrella came to class she asked the students to draw a poster with a picture of themselves on it. They were supposed to write down things that they could do and that they liked about themselves. Jesus had several things written on his poster, but the one that I will always remember is "Yo hablo Espanol" (see Figure 5.1).

Evaluation of Follow-up to the Case of Jesus Gonzalez

The follow-up to the case portrays a much more hopeful view of Mrs. Kniffen's approach to Jesus's education and his attitude toward school. Mrs. Kniffen recognizes that she is lacking in the professional knowledge and curriculum materials needed to assist Jesus. She acknowledges that she needs additional professional development in instructional approaches for English language learners. However, she also wants immediate assistance and uses contacts through the Migrant Center and the local university to identify a graduate student, Estrella, who is able to serve as a role model for Jesus, implement effective instructional approaches, and provide appropriate children's literature that celebrates Jesus's language and culture. Estrella's demonstration of ESL approaches also serves as an excellent model for Mrs. Kniffen to use in planning her future lessons.

When we read Jesus's confident assertion that no one can tell him not to speak Spanish, we must admit that Jesus's attitude toward his first language has undergone significant change. This is a major breakthrough that can fuel motivation toward further academic and social progress. However, if we examine the goals identified in the plan of action, we must also recognize that the short-term solutions enacted so far are only a start. Although Estrella has contacted Mrs. Gonzalez, the communication process between school staff and the family is unchanged. Similarly, while Mrs. Kniffen now sees the academic and social benefits of using multicultural literature with her class, she still needs professional development in strategies for working with culturally and linguistically diverse students. Furthermore, apart from the changes that have occurred due to Estrella's presence in the classroom, Jesus's educational program remains the same. In fact, the goals that are most likely to institute long-term change in the district have not even begun. The entire school staff needs professional development in multicultural education through regional workshops or from national professional organizations, the curriculum must be redesigned to include a diverse curriculum, and a district task force on multicultural education has yet to be established. Clearly, the case of Jesus is one that requires systemic change.

The cases in the following chapters are equally as complex as that of Jesus and require a comprehensive response. As demonstrated, the Case Decision-Making Scaffold provides participants with a guide for thoroughly discussing and reflecting on each case. Furthermore, we trust that it will provide a helpful support for your deliberations as you face other equally challenging cases in your teaching career.

REFERENCES

Baca, L. M., & Cervantes, H. T. (1998). *The bilingual special education interface* (3rd ed.). Upper Saddle River, NJ: Merrill/ Prentice Hall.

Bohn, A. P., & Sleeter, C. E. (2000). Multicultural education and the standards movement: A report from the field. *Phi Delta Kappan, 82,* 156–159.

Collaborative for the Study of Migrant Children and Their Families (2001). Resources Addressing the Education of Migrant Students. Retrieved July 12, 2002, from SUNY New Paltz website: http://www.newpaltz.edu/collaborative/

Cummins, J. (1984). *Bilingualism and special education: Issues in assessment and pedagogy.* San Diego, CA: College-Hill.

Education Commission of the States. (1998). *Comprehensive school reform: Identifying effective models.* Denver, CO: Author.

Garcias: Farmworkers That Travel (2001, October 12). Retrieved July 12, 2002, from SUNY New Paltz website: http://www.newpaltz.edu/collaborative/

Igoa, C. (1995). *The inner world of the immigrant child.* New York: St. Martin's Press.

Martin, P. L. (1996). Migrant farmworkers and their children: What recent labor department data show. In J. L. Flores (Ed.), *Children of LaFrontera: Binational efforts to serve Mexican migrant immigrant students* (pp. 19–24). Charleston, WV: Clearinghouse on Rural Education and Small Schools.

McChesney, J., & Hertling, E. (2000). The path to comprehensive school reform. *Educational Leadership, 57*(7), 10–15.

Ortiz, A. A. (1997). Learning disabilities occurring concomitantly with linguistic differences. *Journal of Learning Disabilities, 30*(3), 321–332.

Ramirez, J. D. (1992). Executive summary. *Bilingual Research Journal, 16*(1&2), 1–63.

Salend, S. J. (1990). A migrant education guide for special educators. *Teaching Exceptional Children, 22*(2), 18–21.

Salend, S. J. (1998). *Effective mainstreaming: Creating inclusive classrooms* (3rd ed.). Upper Saddle River, NJ: Merrill/Prentice Hall.

Salend, S. J. (2001). *Creating inclusive classrooms: Effective and reflective practices.* (4th ed.). Upper Saddle River, NJ: Merrill/Prentice Hall.

Salend, S. J., & Taylor, L. (1993). Working with families: A cross-cultural perspective. *Remedial and Special Education, 14*(5), 25–32.

Schaps, E., & Lewis, C. (1999). Perils on an essential journey: Building school community. *Phi Delta Kappan, 81,* 215–218.

Shotland, J. (1989). *Full fields, empty cupboard: The nutritional status of migrant farmworkers in America.* Washington, DC: Public Voice for Food and Health Policy.

Thomas, W. P., & Collier, V. P. (1998). Two languages are better than one. *Educational Leadership, 55*(4), 23–26.

U.S. Department of Education. (1998). *Profiles of successful schoolwide programs.* Washington, DC: Author.

Whittaker, C. R., Salend, S. J., & Gutierrez, M. B. (1997). "Voices from the fields": Including migrant farmworkers in the curriculum. *Reading Teacher, 50*(6), 482–493.

CHAPTER 6

RACE AND ETHNICITY

Race should not be understood as a bundle of genetically determined traits that generate of themselves social differences—a view that has been repudiated by the vast majority of social scientists—but as a kind of social classification used by members of a society. (Borgatta & Borgatta, 1992, p. 575)

CURRENT CONCEPTS OF RACE

Although earlier social scientists addressed the contradictions and inherent weaknesses of race as a category for classifying human beings, the recognition of and respect for contributions by social scientists of color who emerged after the 1960s resulted in a more diverse and balanced literature on race in America (Borgatta & Borgatta, 1992). Thus, the concept of race has changed over time, although social scientists continue to differ on its meaning. Noting that the term *race* was used at the beginning of the 20th century to refer to any "geographical, religious, class-based or color-based grouping," Barkan (1992) believes that a shift in the concept of race from "a part of the natural order based upon real or assumed racial distinctions to that of racism as an oppressive and dogmatic ideology" was due to the scientific discourse on race among a small group of British and American anthropologists and biologists, probably considered "outsiders." The change in the concept of race represented an awareness on the part of some members of the British and American societies that racial terminology was not value free and that social organization based on a racial hierarchy was repugnant (Barkan, 1992). As Michael Omi (2001) has pointed out, "over time, the idea of race as a biological construct was increasingly discredited in academic and scientific circles" (p. 12).

Nevertheless, as we enter the 21st century, some dictionaries continue to define race as other than a socially constructed concept, and some social scientists continue to propose previously discounted biological theories in attempts to explain racial differences. An example from a current dictionary defines race as "a group of persons related by common descent, blood or heredity; a subdivision of a stock, characterized by a more or less distinctive combination of physical traits that are transmitted in descent: the Caucasian race; the Mongoloid race" (*Webster's New Universal Unabridged Dictionary,* 1994). Similarly, social scientists who cling to outdated and refuted views of race usually ignore the increasing diversity and intermarriage among Americans. In particular, the intellectual, emotional, and behavioral stereotypes associated with outdated racial categories cannot be supported in the current diverse, multiracial American society. Furthermore, the stereotypes conflict with portraits of multiracial individuals across the country (Gaskins, 1999; Loury, 1995; also see Box 6.1).

In an interesting example of the difficulties inherent in racial categorization, Loury (1995) notes that "racial identity in America is inherently a social and cultural construct, not simply a biological one—it necessarily involves an irreducible element of choice" (Loury, 1995, p. 2). He describes a friend whose pale skin color made him unacceptable as "black" to many African Americans, yet he was also uncomfortable when categorized as "white." Unable to cope with the ambiguity, Loury's friend suffered isolation and alienation.

Interestingly, the U.S. Census continues to use racial categories although Omi (2001) has pointed out that the categories are "rife with inconsistencies" (p. 12). One of the terms is specifically racial, one is cultural, and one "relies on a notion of affiliation or community recognition" (Omi, p. 12). Furthermore, Omi (2001) notes that the official categories have changed nine times in the past 10 U.S. census counts and the Census Bureau also faced demands for changes in the Census 2000. Nevertheless, the U.S. Census in 2000 did describe race as a "sociopolitical construct" although the following racial "categories" were listed: White/Black/, American Indian, Eskimo, Aleut/ Asian, Pacific Islander/Hispanic origin/and Not of Hispanic origin—White, Black, American Indian, Eskimo, Aleut, and Asian, Pacific Islander. In recognition of the fluid, sometimes arbitrary, nature of race and racial identification, census takers were instructed to accept whatever racial classifications were chosen by an individual. For the first time, one could name all the races that describe her, supporting the view that "race" is a personal choice, a social construct (Loury, 1995; Marable, 1995; Webster, 1992). Although it is difficult to determine the actual percentage of Americans who identify themselves as multiracial, the results of the 2000 U.S. Census support the fact that 1.9 percent (excluding Hispanic or Latino) identified themselves as "two or more races"; and of the Hispanic or Latino group, 1.3 percent chose "two or more races."

Marable (1995) has captured the essence of race as a paradoxical fixture in American society which has changed over time. In his words, "The racial prism creates an illusion that race is permanent and finite, but, in reality, "race" is a complex expression of unequal relations which are dynamic and ever-changing" (p. 9).

Other social scientists have observed that the significance of race in America has declined (Wilson, 1987, 1997). Wilson has pointed out that socioeconomic differences among groups in the society are superceding race in importance. Furthermore, Webster (1992) charges that the continuation of racial classifications of social groups in America in itself creates a racist society obsessed with race and racial conflicts.

Ethnicity

The concept of ethnicity, like race, appears to be fluid and subject to different perceptions and definitions. Race and ethnicity are frequently interchanged, yet some define race as a special case of ethnicity (van den Berghe, 1981). In this view, ethnic groups share a common ancestry and culture. Language, religion, styles of clothing, and foods would identify persons of a certain ethnic group. According to Borgatta and Borgatta (1992), members of ethnic groups frequently marry within their group, share a sense of solidarity, identify themselves as members of the group, and are so identified by others. On the other hand, Weber (1922, cited in Borgatta & Borgatta, 1992) has provided a classic definition of ethnicity in which he maintains that

> an ethnic group is one whose members entertain a subjective belief in their common descent because of similarities of physical type or customs or both, or because of memories of colonization and migration. It does not matter whether or not an objective blood relationship exists. Those who view race as a form of ethnicity describe an ethnic group as one whose members are believed by others, if not also by themselves, to be physiologically distinctive. (Borgatta & Borgatta, 1992, p. 576)

Ethnicity, as with race, has been viewed from different perspectives. D'Alba (1990) favors the view of symbolic ethnicity. This refers to the fact that ethnic identities of many whites are actually a symbol of the emergence on the American scene of a new ethnic group. D'Alba points to the belief among scholars and lay persons that ethnic differences "form a possible permanent substructure in the society" (1990, p. 2). The belief was especially prominent during the 1960s and 1970s when an "ethnic revival" and cultural pluralism emerged, according to D'Alba. In contrast to earlier views that assimilation would decrease group differences, the ethnic revival at that time heightened ethnic assertiveness in the United States (D'Alba, 1990). He noted that an ethnic hierarchy based on staggered arrivals, economic success, and varied backgrounds has occurred. Thus, ethnicity, too, like race, has been a source of unequal progress for some groups. Ethnicity and race also interact, resulting in differential treatment for many. Since race and ethnicity are frequently used synonymously in the literature, we have chosen not to differentiate the terms as we continue to discuss the cases in the text.

RACIAL AND ETHNIC IDENTITY

The integration of race into personal identity varies among individuals. For some, it becomes a dominant component of their identity, while for others it is subservient to membership in other groups (Cross, 1995). Tatum (1997) notes that children become aware of physical differences very early in their development. In the early preschool years they notice differences in color and other physical characteristics and may try to account for them with assumptions such as "Eddie says my skin is brown because I drink too much chocolate milk" (Tatum, 1997, p. 70). She recommends that an adult could give the child a simple explanation about melanin in order to correct the misunderstanding. Or a child may attribute a darker skin to dirtiness and, again, according to Tatum, an adult should correct this misperception based on the cognitive ability and developmental stage of the child. A direct response, rather than quieting the child or expressing embarrassment, is preferred in order to prevent the child's development of a negative self-image.

The issue of racial identity becomes more critical in adolescence when important questions such as "Who am I?" and "Who can I be?" occur. Some adolescents must also answer "What does it mean to be black, or Asian, or Latino?" In pointing out that black students may sit together in the school cafeteria in answer to their developmental need to explore the meaning of their identity with others engaged in the same process, Tatum (1997) provides a rationale for that phenomenon. As an alternative, she suggests a daily group meeting for students in the company of a supportive adult where they can discuss identity issues together. The opportunity to get together with others facing the same challenges is needed. As Tatum has suggested, educators need to provide students with "identity affirming experiences and information about their own cultural groups" (Tatum, 1997, p. 71).

Cross (1995) has also contributed to an understanding of racial identity development in African Americans. He has identified five stages in the development process: (1) pre-encounter, (2) encounter, (3) immersion–emersion (4) internalization, and (5) internalization–commitment. Cross points out that one must have an encounter that stimulates or triggers an individual's conscious awareness of race and that race will vary in its importance to an individual within any racial group.

White children will also need to integrate a positive racial identity so that their identity will not be developed at the expense of children of color. A close relationship exists between white racial identity and racism (Helms, 1990). Thus, according to Helms, an important aspect of the development of a positive racial identity for white children is the elimination of racism. White racial identity models have been developed by other social scientists; however, Helms' model may serve as an example. She has developed a stage or phase model that begins with the elimination of racism in the individual, followed by the development of a positive white racial identity. Stages include contact, disintegration, and reintegration, which comprise phase 1; and pseudo-independence, immersion–emersion and autonomy, which comprise phase 2.

Children of Mixed Race or Ethnicity

Racial or ethnic identity can be most challenging for children of mixed heritage, who now make up a significant proportion of the multiracial population. In at least 10 states, multiracial school-aged residents comprise at least 25 percent of the population (AP News Service, 2001). Interestingly, the percentage of all school-aged Americans, regardless of racial background, is only 19 percent. "More than 100,000 biracial babies have been born every year after 1989. This increase is true across racial and ethnic groups: black/white, Japanese/white, racially mixed Native American, Hispanic mixes and other Asian American mixes" (Wardle, 2000, p. 1). Wardle attributes the increase in biracial births to the 1967 Supreme Court decision outlawing state laws against interracial marriage, increased interaction among the races at school and in the workplace, and an increased acceptance of interracial marriage by Americans. As immigration patterns continue to increase the number of people of color and social contact and interaction among diverse groups continue, multiracial families and children are likely to continue to increase. Although we do not have an accurate count of multiracial, multiethnic children in our schools, educators will need to understand the issues that these families and children must confront and provide the necessary sensitivity and support. As Gladwell (1998), the son of an English father and Jamaican mother, has written, "I go back and forth between my two sides. I never feel my whiteness more than when I'm around West Indians and never feel my West Indianess more than when I'm with whites. And when I'm by myself, I can't answer the question at all, so I just push it out of my mind" (p. 123).

Fukuyama (1999) has written, "Being biracial, it is impossible for me to fit into one category" (p. 3). Biracial children share the culture and language of both parents and sometimes face difficulty in developing a sense of their own identity. This dilemma is illustrated later in the case studies where the question "What am I?" arises early from the children as well as their peers at school. We seem to have the need to categorize or classify each other, as illustrated again in the words of Johanna, a girl who is white and Puerto Rican. When a new black friend asked what race she was, she commented, "People are always asking, 'What are you?' and I don't really like it. I told him I'm half white and half Puerto Rican, and he said, 'But you act black.' I told him, 'You can't act like a race.' He said I would have a point if he'd said African American, because that's a race, but black is a way of acting" (Lewin, 2001, p. 153).

The task of integrating two ethnic identities and, often, two different cultural backgrounds may be particularly challenging in some families and becomes critical for adolescents (Gibbs, 1989; Kerwin & Ponterotto, 1995). In fact, interracial families face several major issues. Primary, perhaps, is the task of transmitting a cultural heritage and racial or ethnic identity to their children (Gibbs, 1989). Obviously, parents must agree on how and what will be transmitted. In Lisa's case, which is presented later in this chapter, the family solved the problem by agreeing to recognize one of the cultures as dominant in their family and ignoring the other. In other cases, the family has tried to recognize and teach both cultures to their children (see Box 6.1). In some

■ ■ ■ ■ ■ ▬▬▬▬▬▬▬▬▬▬▬▬▬▬▬▬▬▬▬▬▬▬▬▬▬▬

BOX 6.1

OTHER VOICES

When kids ask "What are you?" we answer, "Native American, African American, European, and French Canadian. That's the answer that mother gave us when we asked her "What are we?" Mother is French Canadian and Dad is African American and Native American. We have been learning some things about the Native American culture, although we don't know which tribe we're from. . . . We only know that it is a southeastern U.S. Native American tribe, probably Seminole." (Andre, age 11, August 2000)

One day a classmate saw me with my Dad, and she had already met my mom. . . . She asked me if that was my Dad and said, "Oh, now I understand why you're the color that you are." (Angie, age 12, August 2000)

Angie's and Andre's Mom described their current school experience. "Angie and Andre have attended a magnet school (in the Midwest) that focuses on community cultures and environmental science. The school is multiage and multiracial and every student takes a community cultures class. Since they entered when the school was only a year in operation, its reputation was yet unknown and requests to enter were not excessive. There was no problem in admission. Now there's a long waiting list. The school serves a very diverse population of students where there is no majority. We have all been pleased with it."

"The school has good, empowering leadership by the principal, and standards and testing are not important at the school. However, I'm worried about next year because, although Andre will continue at the magnet school, Angie will attend a traditional middle school for seventh grade where 97 percent of the students are white. The school, grades 7 and 8, is located in a white suburb. We expect that there will be some difficulties including questions like 'What are you?' Hopefully, she can handle them since she has learned good responses in a special program she attended. Kids in that program were taught how to take social action, how to stand up for what they think is right. Angie has had experience with protests and she participated in the Children's March on Washington, so I hope that she will be able to manage." (Emily Green, mother of Angie and Andre, August 2001) cases, historical differences among groups, for example, whites and African Americans in the United States, may make it difficult for parents to understand, share, and teach each other's perspectives.

Furthermore, interracial families continue to encounter problems in community acceptance and approval, social isolation, and job discrimination. Although published reports of extreme hostility appear to have diminished, families continue to report the experience of "stares" and refusal by some neighbors to recognize their presence (see Lisa Golden's case). Biracial or multiracial youth may also suffer differential treatment or rejection by some family members, peers, and communities (Fukuyama, 1999; Gibbs, 1989; McBride, 1996; Wardle, 2000). Again Fukuyama has shared that, "Race did not have personal meaning for me until, as a young child (age 4 or 5) I was mocked by another child for the shape of my eyes" (1999, p. 1). Wardle (2000) has noted that children of mixed heritage "experience harassment from mainstream society and from members of minority groups" (p. 4). Direct assaults on their identity from students and insensitive, hostile interactions from educators occur (Wardle, 2000).

In fact, even educators who take multicultural education courses do not often learn about multiracial or multiethnic children (Wardle, 2000). Filling out school forms that ask for racial or ethnic identification, for example, is difficult for many of these children. "Students or parents who refuse to designate a single identity, or who select an alternative response may be harassed, accused of being uptight about their racial identity, or denied entrance into a program (Wardle, 2000). This author makes an important point in noting that, historically, schools have viewed these children as having the racial or ethnic identity of the parent of color. However, as seen in "Other Voices" (Box 6.1) parents may choose to have the children identified according to all the groups to which they belong. In any case, schools can make these students feel invisible and uncomfortable.

Like all other students, multiracial or multiethnic students need familiar images in textbooks and instructional materials, interracial hands-on activities, posters and literature, and extracurricular activities such as special clubs that are inclusive.

Referrals may be necessary for adequate counseling to facilitate the development of a positive self-concept and resolution of conflicts. School personnel can assist the children to lead productive and fulfilling lives. The parents and children's views to be read later in this chapter illustrate their needs.

RACISM

The widely quoted, prophetic words of W. E. B. DuBois (1953) which communicated that "The problem of the twentieth century is the problem of color-line," continue to be applicable as we enter the twenty-first century

(p. vii). One can only hope that one day we will no longer find his words so relevant. Yet, Derrick Bell (1992), among others, has described racism as a "permanent component of American life" (p. 13).

Racism at the individual, institutional, and societal levels continues to plague our society. In a traditional dictionary definition, racism is based on "A belief that race is the primary determinant of human traits and capacities and that racial differences produce an inherent superiority of a particular race" (*Webster's Ninth New Collegiate Dictionary*, 1990). Harris (1999) supports this definition in his more recent publication, where he notes that "racists believe that the human family is divided into stable racial categories of superior and inferior kinds from birth" (p. 17). However, Wilson's (1999) perception differs somewhat in that he adds the role of rationalizations based upon one's belief. One's belief in a group's biological or cultural inferiority is used to rationalize or prescribe that "inferior" group's treatment in the society and to "explain its social position and accomplishments" (p. 14).

In many definitions of racism, white dominance is a key ingredient. Joe Feagin and Melvin Sikes, in *Living Racism, The Black Middle Class Experience*, state that "we generally use the term in a broad sense to refer not only to the prejudices and discriminatory actions of particular white bigots, but also to institutionalized discrimination and to the recurring ways in which white people dominate black people in almost every major area of this society" (p. 3). Sivanandan agrees that "racism is about power not prejudice" (Sivanandan, cited in Garcia, 1999, p. 398).

Garcia (1999) provides a more extensive description of racism in the following passage:

> a vicious kind of racially based disregard for the welfare of certain people. . . . In its central and most vicious form, it is a hatred, ill-will directed against a person or persons on account of their assigned race. In a derivative form, one is a racist when one either does not care at all or does not care enough (i.e., as morality requires) or does not care in the right ways about people assigned to a certain racial group, where this regard is based on racial classification. (p. 399)

Yet, discrimination is inherent in all definitions. Barkan (1992, p. 3) has defined it as "prejudicial action based on racial discrimination" while Marable (1995) offers an even more expansive definition in the following passage:

> Racism is not just social discrimination, political disenfranchisement and acts of extralegal violence and terror which proliferated under Jim Crow segregation. At its essential core, racism is most keenly felt in its smallest manifestations: the white merchant who drops change on the sales counter, rather than touch the hand of a Black person, the white salesperson who follows you into the dressing room when you carry several items of clothing to try on, because he or she suspects that you are going to steal; . . . the white taxicab driver who speeds by you to pick up a white passenger. (1995, p. 7)

Examples of Racism

Cornell West, the distinguished Harvard professor, speaks of the "New York taxicab experience" in the introduction to his book *Race Matters* (1993). In his words, "I waited and waited and waited. After the ninth taxi refused me, my blood began to boil. The tenth taxi refused me and stopped for a kind, well dressed, smiling female fellow citizen of European descent. As she stepped in the cab, she said, "This is really ridiculous, is it not?" (p. x).

Berger (1999) also offers vivid examples of white racism and its black victims. For example, in a 1996 incident in Philadelphia, an African American woman found racial epithets and ketchup spread on her front steps. The extreme harassment and picketing forced her to give up and move out. This scene is frequently repeated around the country, as in St. Paul, Minnesota, where a cross was burned on the front lawn of an African American home. The beating of Rodney King, police brutality, and racial profiling of people of color by the police in New Jersey are recent, highly publicized examples of racism.

Berger (1999) also describes racism in the media, where black male models are restricted to photo shots in which they appear "gangsterlike"; and the film industry's discrimination in the films and roles that black actors are allowed to play. Other examples of individual racism are seen in the experience of a photographer on Long Island who wore dreadlocks. She was mistakenly identified as Whoopi Goldberg because "We all look alike." The condescension of a white professor who listened politely to an African American colleague while exchanging knowing glances with a white colleague also in the room is another example (Berger, 1999). These incidents comprise a short list of the small, daily expressions of racism experienced by African Americans in the society.

Racism exists also in the schools where it is reflected in tracking students of color into lower-level classes while white students dominate the higher levels (Gordon, 1998; Oakes, 1985). The overrepresentation of African American and some Hispanic students in special education, especially classes for students with emotional or behavioral problems, and the underrepresentation of these students in programs for gifted children provides another illustration. In addition, the disproportionate rate of minority students in many school districts, particularly African Americans, who are suspended and expelled from school also provides examples (Gordon, 1998). Furthermore, the dismal conditions in many urban, inner-city, largely minority schools as compared with suburban, predominantly white schools can also be attributed to institutional racism.

Racism in the society is perpetuated, at least in part, by myths and media hype. In Berger's (1999) words, "The subject of race, perhaps more than any other subject in contemporary life, feeds on myth. Myth[ic] is the sinister adjective of the white supremacist, delineating a whiteness that is superior, moral, wholesome, stable, intelligent, and talented and a blackness that is inferior, stupid, shiftless, lazy, dishonest, untrustworthy, licentious, and violent" (1999, p. 97).

Although some myths may appear positive, such as Asians as a "model minority," in reality even this positive myth is dangerous in that it deprives each individual of unique characteristics and may obscure very real needs and issues. In essence, myths, along with stereotypes such as "Arabs are terrorists," deprive many Americans of recognition of the individual uniqueness that they deserve. The result is a reduced quality of life for too many American citizens.

Resisting Racism

We can combat racism through more open dialogue on race. The message of Cornell West (1993) is relevant where he speaks of "our truncated public discussions of race, [that] suppress the best of who and what we are as a people because they fail to confront the complexity of the issue in a candid and critical manner" (p. 2). However, West also points out that "To engage in a serious discussion of race in America, we must begin not with the problems of black people, but with the flaws of American society—flaws rooted in historic inequalities and longstanding cultural stereotypes" (p. 3). "To establish a new framework, we need to begin with a frank acknowledgment of the basic humanness and Americanness of each of us" (p. 4).

Gary Howard (1996) has also offered several thoughts on what a new framework for race relations will require. In his words: "A peaceful transition to a new kind of America in which no ethnic or cultural group is in a dominant position will require considerable change in education and deep psychological shifts for many White Americans" (p. 324).

From a somewhat different perspective, Peggy McIntosh (1988) has written of the privilege associated with white skin. In order to eliminate racism, one thing that must take place is the recognition of this privilege. In her words, "It seems to me that obliviousness about white advantage, like obliviousness about male advantage, is kept strongly inculturated in the United States so as to maintain the myth of meritocracy, the myth that democratic choice is equally available to all" (p. 4). In fact, an important aspect of the "inner work" that teachers must do, as counseled by Gary Howard (1999), is to raise their consciousness of white privilege and its effect.

All children and adolescents will need knowledge and understanding of racism in order to resist the myth of meritocracy and other myths and stereotypes associated with racial classifications in the United States. Children will need information about how racial myths and stereotypes operate in order to combat them. They will also need affirming racial identity opportunities as recommended by Tatum (1997). Through multicultural education, an appreciation for diverse races and cultures can be promoted and enhanced by teachers. An abundance of curricular materials and pedagogy is available for schools that aim to help their students to learn to live in a democratic nation in which equality for all is assured. As Marable (1995) has noted, "We must rethink old categories and old ways of perceiving each other. We must define the issue of diversity as a dynamic, changing concept, leading us to explore problems of human relations and social equality in a manner which will expand the principles of fairness and opportunity to all members of society" (Marable, 1995, p. 118).

Educators who understand the evolution of racism, current concepts of race and ethnicity, the development of racial and ethnic identity, and the issues faced by an increasing population of multiracial or multiethnic students will be able to effectively address the issues faced by their students and create a truly inclusive classroom where all students can learn.

THE CASE OF JIM PETERSON

Jim had begun student teaching only a week ago and his enthusiasm was already beginning to wane. Mrs. Fitzgerald, the cooperating teacher, was strict and inflexible with the students, in Jim's opinion, and he felt that she treated him that way, too. Nevertheless, she was the wife of the principal, and Jim wanted to make a very positive impression on her so that she could, hopefully, make positive comments about him to the principal. Jim had waited so long to get a regular teaching job and, as an older student at 35, he was desperate for any hopeful situation.

Jim thought of himself as "laid back," easy to get along with, and usually liked by the adolescents with whom he had previously worked. He believed that when the curriculum addressed students' interests and needs behavior problems would be minimal. The key to good classroom management, in Jim's opinion, was a relevant curriculum. Furthermore, the profanity used by some students and talking out without permission by many did not really bother Jim as long as the behaviors were not too disruptive. Yet these were the very behaviors that Mrs. Fitzgerald would not tolerate.

Mrs. Fitzgerald explained her inflexibility to Jim as necessary because "These students have serious behavior problems and you cannot let up or they'll take over." She repeated to Jim many times that "Behavior management is more important than anything else you do." The principal agreed with her in his comments to the teacher and students and in his expectations. Mr. Fitzgerald insisted that all classroom doors remain open at all times. He would patrol the corridors frequently to shout at students out of class without permission or to intervene in a noisy classroom. At close to 7 feet tall, his height and deep voice easily intimidated both students and teachers.

The 8-week summer program served students with disabilities who were eligible for 12-month educational services. Thirteen classes were located in the bright, cheerful building of U-shaped corridors painted in vibrant colors.

However, there was no air conditioning and life in the building became difficult for students and staff on many sultry afternoons. There was a school-wide discipline system in which students began each day with 100 points and lost them for various infractions throughout the day, a response cost system. At the end of the week, points were exchanged for rewards. Mr. Fitzgerald expected every classroom to operate accordingly.

Mrs. Fitzgerald's class consisted of seven students, ages 11 to 13, who were classified seriously emotionally disturbed. Six students were African American and one was white. However, the composition of the class did not represent the population throughout the region. In each county of this semi-rural and small urban region, minority students were only 3 to 5 percent of the school population and in some areas they were less than 1 percent. The largest numbers of students of color came from the older urban areas of the region. Mrs. Fitzgerald's class did represent, however, the disproportionate placement of African American students in classes for students who are emotionally or behaviorally disturbed, which exists throughout the country. Also, because it was a summer program, students came from many schools in several counties, and Mrs. Fitzgerald's students did not know each other, a fact that Mrs. Fitzgerald did not consider important. Nor did she consider important the fact that she was white, as were the majority of teachers in the school.

She preferred to begin academic lessons the first day of school and she used traditional materials and methods. Thus, when Jim began to plan instruction, she told him, "I use basal readers and various easy paperback books. There are teacher editions available for the science, social studies, and mathematics texts that I use, and they will be helpful to you in planning lessons. Jim silently disagreed with her traditional approach and he looked forward to being more creative.

Jim believed that he had a good understanding of the students' interests and needs. In fact, Mrs. Fitzgerald's students reminded Jim of others who he had recently tutored at the college he attended. Actually, Jim thought of himself as an experienced teacher, since he had also worked the past summer at a school for adolescents with serious emotional disabilities. He had been a child care and residential counselor and later a teacher's aide at the school. Many of the students with whom he had worked were African American and Latino, and Jim felt that he had been very successful with them. Although Jim was white, he had worked in many situations in which he was in the minority. He had worked as a sergeant in the military and had no problems with discipline. Jim's other jobs included work in a restaurant and convenience store. He felt quite proud of the experience he had accumulated and his preparation for teaching.

Actually, as the time for student teaching approached, Jim had smiled when his classmates expressed anxiety about beginning student teaching. "I don't feel any nervousness at all," he told one classmate. "I have worked with lots of students like those I will have in my student teaching." In fact, he also expressed his confidence and experience to Mrs. Fitzgerald on the first day. However, he was somewhat disappointed when she responded, "Don't forget that you are a student teacher, after all, with lots to learn, and the students here are very challenging."

Jim searched for some way to remain optimistic and he found it in the makeup of the class. The majority of the students were African American, and Jim became excited about implementing many of the ideas that he had learned about in his courses on multicultural education. He had learned about materials that he could use immediately.

His first responsibility in Mrs. Fitzgerald's classroom was to take over the reading instruction. Jim believed that stories about African American sports heroes would motivate the students and hold their interest. As required, he met with Mrs. Fitzgerald to discuss his plans. It was obvious to Jim that she was not too pleased when she said, "You can try the material, but you must remain firm and consistent and maintain control. I do not want chaos in my classroom."

On the following Monday morning Jim began reading instruction with the story on Jackie Robinson. All the students were present and curious about the new material. Motivation was not a problem. They were all seated at a rectangular table and, after Jim introduced the story, students took turns reading aloud as he provided cues and prompts. After each chapter of the story, there was a brief discussion, which Jim led using stimulating questions. This procedure was followed each day until Thursday, when the classroom fell into chaos.

The single white student in the group jumped out of his seat, threw his material on the floor, and shouted, "I ain't reading this no more. I'm sick of niggers!"

Two of the African American students immediately responded with, "We'll whip your ass."

The white student ran out of the room with Jim running close behind. Mrs. Fitzgerald remained in the classroom.

As he returned to the room holding the student by the shoulder, Jim could see that Mrs. Fitzgerald was angry. She shouted at him, "Mr. Peterson, put away that material immediately and do not plan to use it again!" Jim found her words really piercing when she added, "You have created chaos in my classroom!"

He was devastated. All he could think of was how well prepared he had been and that he never anticipated this kind of problem. What went wrong? His good intentions, his knowledge of multicultural education, his prior teaching experience, all the training in working with students who have emotional disabilities—all seemed useless. He hated to think about tomorrow and his shaken confidence. Sure, he would ask for a conference with his university supervisor, but Mrs. Fitzgerald was obviously unhappy with him. He did not believe that he could change that.

Besides, he had some questions that he couldn't answer about diversity and multicultural education. What happened in this situation? Was it too risky to use such materials in a group where only one student was different? What should he have done with that student? The practicum was only 8 weeks and already 2 weeks were completed. Would he make it through? He needed a job so badly . . . should he ask to start over in another placement?

DISCUSSION QUESTIONS

1. Describe the students' classroom situation and the particular aspects that might prove challenging for any teacher.
2. What discrepancies exist between Jim's expectations for his student teaching and what actually occurred? What discrepancies exist between what Mrs. Fitzgerald expected and what actually occurred?
3. What perceptions did Jim have of himself when he began student teaching? What were the beliefs he held about multicultural education, instructional approaches, and classroom management?
4. How did Jim's beliefs about teaching conflict with Mrs. Fitzgerald's? With the students' views of what and how they were to learn?
5. What do we know about multicultural education and culturally responsive classroom management from experts in the field that would help to guide the decisions that need to be made in this situation?
6. How could the university supervisor reframe the issues in this conflict to help Jim and Mrs. Fitzgerald move forward in the student teaching experience?
7. What goals should Jim and Mrs. Fitzgerald set for themselves and for the class from this point on?

THE CASE OF LISA GOLDEN

James McBride (1996) has written a moving story about his interracial family, with emphasis on his mother as a single parent. The following quote from his book *The Color of Water: A Black Man's Tribute to His White Mother*, reveals an occasion on which he wants to know "What am I?"

> One afternoon I came home from school and cornered Mommy while she was cooking dinner.
> "Ma, what's a tragic mulatto?" I asked.
> "Where'd you hear that?" she asked.
> "I read it in a book."

"For God's sake, you're no tragic mul . . . What book is this?"
"Just a book I read." "Don't read that book anymore." She sucked her teeth.
"Tragic mulatto. What a stupid thing to call somebody."
"Don't you ever use that term."
"Am I Black or White?"
"You're a human being," she snapped. "Educate yourself or you'll be a nobody."
"Will I be a Black nobody or just a nobody?"
"If you're a nobody," she said dryly, "it doesn't matter what color you are."

(James McBride, 1996, p. 92)

Lisa's mother, Mrs. Golden, echoed the dilemma when she expressed her frustration: When your children are mixed, how do you find the middle? What is the middle? For Lisa's sake, her father and I need to determine the answer. Children at school are constantly asking her, "What are you?" and we need the best possible answer. Although both Lisa and Tommy asked questions about their skin color and hair very early, our former answer to them doesn't seem sufficient now. Since Lisa is "browner" and Tommy is "whiter," we explained then that they were a mixture of daddy and mommy. The kids at school who keep pestering Lisa obviously want a different answer.

Lisa is now 12 years old and will begin seventh grade this September at Kennedy Junior High School. In fifth and sixth grade at the elementary school, she appeared to be trying to identify first with a group of white kids and then with a group of African American kids. I believe that she has been trying to find out "where she belongs," as well as to find friends with whom she feels comfortable. Earlier this year during sixth grade she became friendly with an African American girl who needed tutoring, and soon they had a small group of four African American girls and Lisa who hung out together. However, Lisa eventually tired of helping the girl, describing her as "needing too much tutoring." The other girls became angry with Lisa when she stopped the tutoring. They thought that she should continue and sometimes help them, too. That ended the friendship. It was difficult, but, after all, Lisa is an outstanding student who is so academically driven that her father and I decided to enroll her in a swimming class to provide more balance in her life. Now she's just as driven about excelling in swimming!

Her teacher, Mrs. Johanssen, has been quite concerned about Lisa's difficulty in developing a racial identity and a sense of belonging. However, Lisa has a nice group of friends now who happen to be all white.

We really like the diversity in the school district and in the individual schools. Although the district's desegregation plan was initially court mandated, the plan has resulted in diversity throughout the district schools. Furthermore, the magnet school choices appeal to most parents, and the lottery system used to place students according to their choices seems to work fairly. At the beginning of each school year you fill out a form stating your six choices of programs at the various magnet schools (Box 6.2). For example,

■ ■ ■ ■ ■

BOX 6.2

MAGNET SCHOOLS

The U.S. Supreme Court mandate in 1954 for school desegregation in *Brown* v. *Board of Education* resulted in a search by many school districts across the country to develop strategies to accomplish integration of schools since "separate but equal" was declared unacceptable. Although avoidance strategies such as the development of private "academies" for white children, refusals to obey the law, and home schooling were some tactics utilized by those who opposed the ruling during the 1970s and 1980s, the focus of desegregation was on the physical integration of African American and white students.

Magnet schools, one of those options, appear to encourage more cooperation than other measures such as busing. It appears that, if a school district can develop programs that are sufficiently appealing to its constituents, white parents will choose to send their children to schools attended by black students as well as other minority groups. Lisa's school district has chosen consolidation of the city and suburban schools into an enlarged school district, as well as magnet schools, to achieve integration of the students and positive responses of all district parents and families.

A magnet school has been defined as "a public school with any grades K–12, that offers 'whole-school' or 'program-within-a-school' programs characterized by the following: special curricular theme or method of instruction designed to attract students district-wide; enrollment on a district-wide basis; and some type of racial/ethnic enrollment goals or controls" (Blank & Archibald, 1992, p. 82). The schools are usually classified according to the curriculum content or instructional approaches. Schools generally try to use methods to determine admission to the schools or programs that will seem most fair to parents and students. The magnet schools are usually created and regulated by the state and public school district.

It is important to add that there is a disturbing trend described by Weiler (1998), who has pointed out that, although many of the above efforts are continuing in school districts across the nation, courts are declaring more and more large urban districts "unitary," thus moving toward resegregation. The term unitary refers to the release of school districts from court supervision of their desegregation efforts (Weiler, 1998). This has been more extensively discussed in Chapter 2.

Lisa wanted the magnet school offering programs in the fine and performing arts as her first choice for seventh grade. We just learned that she will not get the first choice, but her second choice was granted.

We are very pleased with this system since we are accustomed to diversity in our community and schools. We moved here from a large, metropolitan area where there were all kinds of people. Both children were born there and Tommy attended kindergarten in that community. When we moved here, Lisa was just ready to begin kindergarten and Tommy was ready for first grade.

This is a small city, with many characteristics and problems of older, urban areas. I just read in the paper that the unemployment rate in our city is approximately 8 percent and the population of approximately 26,000 includes about 51 percent whites. Blacks and Hispanics constitute the largest percentages of the remaining 49 percent. The city population has decreased over the past 10 years while the suburbs have grown. We actually live in a nice fringe area of the city in which most of our neighbors are white. Only one family appears to respond to us negatively, never coming too close when we meet them outside. However, I must say that many times when I attend meetings or community events people look surprised when they learn that I am Mrs. Golden. Many people do not expect a brown-skinned person with that name!

The school population includes a total of approximately 12,000 students of which about 10 percent are considered English language learners and 43 percent are eligible for free lunch. To be able to achieve racial–ethnic and socioeconomic diversity in the schools, the district decided to enlarge to incorporate the surrounding, newer suburban areas. This provided more white students and more students of middle-income levels for integration of the schools. Yet most of the teachers remain white. Our children have had only two African American teachers and no Hispanic teachers so far. One possible explanation is that, until recently, there were no bilingual programs in their school. It seems that bilingual education programs can provide some culturally diverse teachers who are bilingual.

Interestingly, Tommy is getting along fine as he begins high school. Tommy is now 14 years old and has a circle of friends who have accepted him. Although the circle of friends happens to be white, Tommy gets along with all types of kids. He moves easily among all the different racial–ethnic groups. His cultural background is not a major concern for him.

However, the question of our family's racial and ethnic heritage became an issue for us when we first enrolled the children in school here. We had to decide how to identify the children just in case there was an advantage in being Hispanic. Although the lottery was in use, we thought that our racial–ethnic designation just might mean whether or not we got the kids into the magnet school of our choice. It was painfully difficult to decide on "Hispanic–Puerto Rican" as opposed to "Caucasian," because we thought that the first choice just might give us an advantage. The school officials assured us that only the lottery was used, but it was hard for us to believe that they didn't take some other things into account. Although my husband doesn't feel as strongly about his German–Jewish heritage as I do about my Puerto Rican background, I think it's still important to recognize both sides of the family. Fortunately, we did get our first choice, the magnet school for gifted and talented children.

Although Lisa's teacher now is concerned about helping her in response to her classmates' questions, I believe that the development of racial or ethnic identity in children is personal and private and mainly the responsibility of the family. My husband agrees that schools and teachers should not try to be guides for the development of racial or ethnic identity in children. It is too easy for teachers to "step on parents' toes," since parents will differ in their views and choices. In addition, teachers will vary in their preparation and may be completely unprepared to deal with such issues as racial or ethnic identity.

Another consideration is the increasing emphasis on testing and standards across the country. Many teachers are overloaded already, "teaching to the tests," and dealing with curricula for social skills and violence prevention. They have little time for one more area of responsibility. The district does not have a multicultural education curriculum or program. They do, however, have a "culture day" when all students get a chance to share aspects of their culture. We think that this is very helpful, but don't see how teachers could find time for a multicultural education curriculum.

Teachers can be most helpful when they teach children about all the different cultures in the community so that children who do not learn about their culture at home, for example, can gain knowledge of it at school. In addition, all children can learn to appreciate and respect the diversity of cultures represented. Teachers need awareness and knowledge of the diverse cultures in order to teach about them responsibly and accurately (see Box 6.3).

Since major questions such as "What will be the family traditions?" and "Which culture will we practice?" can only be decided by the family, and each family will have its own unique responses, it is obvious that teachers can make no assumptions about children of mixed heritage. In our family, my husband and I agreed early that the Puerto Rican culture would be dominant. Since my husband's German mother taught him very little of that culture, it has been essentially lost. However, since we both practiced the Lutheran religion when we married, we did not have to make a choice of religion for the family.

My husband and I firmly believe that a family of mixed races and cultures, in which parents' cultures and values are shared and taught to the children, the children learn about tolerance and how to respond to and deal with intolerance, and, above all, the parents really love each other, can cope successfully with all of society's challenges and demands.

Lisa's teacher, Mrs. Johanssen, called me again this morning to discuss her concern about dealing with the students' questions about Lisa's heritage. She mentioned that positive racial or ethnic identity development in children is very important, and she feels that she cannot ignore such important questions from the students. In her opinion, students need opportunities to dis-

■ ■ ■ ■ ■

BOX 6.3

WHAT TEACHERS CAN DO:
Suggestions Made by Angie, 12, and Andre, 11, Multiracial Siblings Who Attend a Midwestern Public School

- Teachers can study the cultural backgrounds of the kids in the school and teach about each culture over the school year.
- Teachers should be trained to understand that "Just because your ancestors were 'like that'—alcoholics, for example—doesn't mean that you will be like that."
- Teachers should expand their knowledge of cultures.
- Teachers can ask their students how they feel about current events.
- Teachers can visit museums, attend cultural events, conduct interviews, and read books to learn about other cultures.
- Teachers should get copies of the book, *How Rude,* and have it available for their students to read. It is published by Free Spirit Publications.
- It's important to have a variety of literature available for students.

cuss race and ethnicity and their concerns about it. We strongly believe that she should ignore their questions, referring them to their families for assistance. We know best how we want Lisa to answer such questions for others and for herself. I only hope that Mrs. Johanssen and I can find a way to resolve this disagreement. I hope that our relationship won't be damaged by this difference in our viewpoints.

DISCUSSION QUESTIONS

1. What discrepancies exist between parent and teacher expectations for how racial identity should be addressed in school? What underlying assumptions follow their expectations?
2. Based on expert opinions, should teachers respond to students' questions about racial and ethnic identity?
3. To what extent does Mrs. Johanssen have the responsibility to help her students in their search for racial or ethnic identity?
4. To maintain a positive relationship with this family, how should the teacher respond to Lisa's parents' request to ignore the students' questions about Lisa's heritage?
5. In view of the rapidly increasing diversity in the United States and the rate of intermarriage, how should schools respond to help children to understand and appreciate the nature of this diversity?

REFERENCES

Associated Press. (2001, June 20). Census: Multiracial population is young. Kingston Freeman, p. D5.

Barkan, E. (1992). *The retreat of scientific racism.* New York: Cambridge University Press.

Bell, D. (1992). *Faces at the bottom of the well.* New York: Basic Books.

Berger, M. (1999). *White lies: Race and the myth of whiteness.* New York: Farrar, Straus & Giroux.

Blank, R. K., & Archibald, D. (1992). Magnet schools and issues of education quality. *Clearing House, 66*(2), 81–86.

Borgatta, E. F., & Borgatta, M. L. (Eds.). (1992). *Encyclopedia of sociology,* Vols. 2, 3. New York: Macmillan.

Cross, W. (1995). The psychology of Nigrescence: Revising the Cross model. In J. Ponterotto, J. M. Casas, L. A. Suzuki, & C. M. Alexander (Eds.), *Handbook of multicultural counseling* (pp. 93–122). Thousand Oaks, CA: Sage.

D'Alba, R. (1990). *Ethnic identity: The transformation of white America.* New Haven: Yale University Press.

DuBois, W. E. B. (1953). *The souls of Black folk.* New York: The Blue Heron Press.

Fukuyama, M. (1999). Personal narrative: Growing up biracial. *Journal of Counseling and Development, 77*(1), 12–14.

Garcia, J. L. A. (1999). The heart of racism. In Leonard Harris (Ed.), *Racism: Key concepts in critical theory* (pp. 398–434). Amherst, NY: Humanity Books.

Gibbs, J. Taylor. (1989). Black American adolescents. In J. Taylor Gibbs & L. Nahme Huang (Eds.), *Children of color: Psychological interventions with minority youth* (pp. 179–223). San Francisco: Jossey-Bass.

Gordon, R. (1998). *Education and race.* Oakland, CA: Applied Research Center.

Harris, L. (1999). *Racism: Key concepts in critical theory.* Amherst, NY: Humanity Books.

Helms, J. (Ed.).(1990). *Black and white racial identity: Theory, research and practice.* Westport, CN: Praeger.

Howard, G. (1996). Whites in multicultural education: Rethinking our role. In James A. Banks (Ed.), *Multicultural education: Transformative knowledge and action: Historical and contemporary perspectives* (pp. 323–334). New York: Teachers College Press.

Howard, G. (1999) *We can't teach what we don't know: White teachers, multiracial schools.* New York: Teachers College Press.

Kerwin, C., & Ponterotto, J. G. (1995). Biracial children. In J. G. Ponteritto, J. M. Casas, L. A. Suzuki, & C. M. Alexander (Eds.), *Handbook of multicultural counseling* (pp. 199–217). Thousand Oaks, CA: Sage.

Lewin, T. (2001). Growing up, growing apart. In Correspondents of the *New York Times, How race is lived in America: Pulling together, pulling apart.* New York: Times Books, Henry Holt & Co.

Loury, G. (1995). *One by one from the inside out.* New York: The Free Press.

Marable, M. (1995). *Beyond black and white: Transforming African American politics.* London: Verso.

McBride, J. (1996). *The color of water: A black man's tribute to his white mother.* New York: Riverhead Books.

McIntosh, P. (1988). *White privilege.* Wellesley Center for Research on Women: Working papers. Wellesley, MA: Wellesley College.

Oakes, J. (1985). *Keeping track: How schools structure inequality.* New Haven, CT: Yale University Press.

Omi, M. (2001). Counting in the dark. *Color lines,* Spring, 2001, pp. 12–14

Tatum, B. (1997). *Why are all the black kids sitting together in the cafeteria? And other conversations about race.* New York: Basic Books.

U.S. Bureau of the Census. (2000). Washington, DC: Government Printing Office.

Van den Berghe, P. (1981). *The ethnic phenomenon.* New York: Elsevier.

Wardle, F. (2000). Children of mixed race—no longer invisible. *Educational Leadership,* 57(4), 68–72.

Webster, Y. (1992). *The racialization of America.* New York: St. Martin's Press.

Webster's New Universal Unabridged Dictionary. (1994). New York: Barnes and Noble.

Webster's Ninth New Collegiate Dictionary (1990). Springfield, MA: Merriam-Webster.

West, C. (1993). *Race matters.* Boston: Beacon Press.

Weiler, J. (1998). Recent changes in school desegregation. ERIC/CUE Digest Number 133. (ERIC Document Reproduction Number ED419029).

Wilson, W. J. (1987). *The declining significance of race: Blacks and changing American institutions.* Chicago: University of Chicago Press.

CHAPTER 7

ISSUES OF CULTURE
AND LANGUAGE

The influence of culture and language on the lives and actions of individuals in many of the cases in this text is prominent. However, we have chosen to include two cases in this section as exemplars of the issues that arise when bridges between the multiple worlds of culturally and linguistically diverse students have not been adequately built. The first is a report of the events that occurred in the Onteora School District in Boiceville, New York, when community members requested that the board of education re-evaluate the choice of an Indian as a school mascot. The second is an account of the obstacles that a refugee girl who is Hmong faced trying to learn in a U.S. school. While these two cases are prototypes of the barriers that cultural and linguistic differences can present in the schools, you will find similar threads running through many of the cases in this book.

Important issues regarding culture and language are addressed in previous chapters that are relevant to these cases. First, we discuss the processes of acculturation and assimilation. Especially relevant to the second case is the insight that refugees, in particular, frequently experience marginalization when they are transplanted from their own language and culture without the educational experience, background, or cultural awareness necessary to manage in the United States. Then we discuss the inequities that many English language learners and those from nondominant cultures face and argue for the need for multicultural education. Finally, we describe the cultural divide that can exist between the home and school and suggest bridges across a child's multiple worlds. Our purpose in this chapter is to define culture and language, review perceptions of children who are cultural and linguistically different, and briefly discuss effective educational strategies and programs for these students. In addition, we will provide background information on Native American mascots and the Hmong culture to better inform your discussion of the cases that follow.

DEFINITION OF CULTURE

> Culture consists of the values, traditions, social and political relationships, and worldview created, shared, and transformed by a group of people bound together by a common history, geographic location, language, social class, and/or religion. (Nieto, 2000, p. 139)

For the purposes of this text we would like to adopt Nieto's definition of culture because it emphasizes the values and abstract aspects of culture. In doing so, we recognize that, while there is disagreement among social scientists as to what constitutes a culture, it may be somewhat easier to determine the characteristics of culture in general. Gollnick & Chinn (1998) characterize culture as that which is learned throughout life by participation in the family and society, is shared by an identifiable group, is developed to accommodate to environmental conditions and resources, and is dynamic. Because cultures change over time based on complex circumstances, it is difficult if not harmful to determine a fixed view of a culture. At best, such descriptions lead to stereotypes (McDermott, 1997).

Historically, the dominant culture in the United States has been Western European. Our political system and language derive from Great Britain. In general, the dominant culture values individualism, competition, freedom, and industriousness. As with all individuals in a particular culture, those in the dominant society often view their culture as the "only" or "correct" viewpoint. This "inability to view other cultures as equally viable alternatives for organizing reality" is known as ethnocentrism (Gollnick & Chinn, 1998, p. 8). Without an ability to look through other cultural lenses, individuals and cultures will frequently misunderstand each other. Such misunderstandings are often the roots of mental anguish, verbal conflict, and physical harm.

The subgroups within cultures vary in significant ways from one another. The national or shared culture of the nation-state or society of the big culture can be referred to as the macroculture, whereas subcultures or microcultures may have distinctive cultural patterns while sharing some traits and values of the macroculture (Banks, 1999; Gollnick & Chinn, 1998). Microcultures defined by gender, ethnicity, race, class, language, religion, ability, and geography exist within the greater macroculture. An individual's cultural identity is formed by the interaction of microcultures in the person's experience and the degree of importance of each microculture at a particular time.

DEFINITION OF LANGUAGE

Language is a vehicle for communication, a means of shaping cultural and personal identity, and a way to socialize an individual into a cultural group (Gollnick & Chinn, 1998). Communication can be verbal or nonverbal. Nonverbal communication may involve the degree of social space between speakers; the body language conveyed by facial expressions, posture, and gestures; vocalizations such as pitch or intensity; or vocal qualities such as rhythm or articulation. Linguists have determined that American Sign Language is a language although it is not oral (Box 7.1).

Language development in one's first language (L1) depends on many complex variables (Merino, Trueba, & Samaniego, 1993). In any kindergarten class there will be a significant range among students of the sounds that they articulate correctly and the number of words in their vocabulary (Bos & Vaughn, 2002; Smith, 2001). In addition, English, as well as other languages, has dialectical differences that vary from the standard language. While no dialect should be considered inferior to another, a child who enters a classroom speaking a different dialect from the rest of the children can experience social isolation. Although Standard English is supposedly the acceptable language in schools, no one dialect can be identified as standard.

Language development becomes even more complicated when the child is introduced to a second language (L2). The continuing immigration from non-English-speaking countries ensures that all school districts will have students whose first language is not English. In fact, in many major cities in the United States over 100 languages are spoken. For many immigrants in these larger cities, it is possible to survive by understanding a minimal amount of English because their jobs are primarily menial and their first language is commonly spoken in their neighborhood. The degree to

■ ■ ■ ■ ■

BOX 7.1

AMERICAN SIGN LANGUAGE

Deafness is viewed in different ways by different individuals and groups. Many hearing people consider deafness a disability, a pathological condition. To many Deaf people, deafness is one aspect binding a minority group together, a minority group rich in culture, history, language and the arts. The language of the Deaf community is American Sign Language (ASL), a language that uses signs, has all of the elements (grammar, syntax, idioms) of other languages, and is not parallel to English in either structure or word order. ASL is not a mere translation of oral speech or the English language (as is Signed English): it is a fully developed language. In fact, many states allow ASL as an option to meet the high school foreign language requirement, and the same is true at many colleges and universities. As the language of the Deaf community, ASL is used in all aspects of their culture. For example, plays are written in ASL and performed by deaf theater groups around the world, and a base of folk literature has also developed over the years (Smith, 2001, p. 432).

which an immigrant family speaks English at home is another influence on a child's language development. Historically, some families have encouraged their children to speak their first language while learning English. Others, primarily for economic and social reasons, have encouraged their children to speak only English. Because second language acquisition is positively correlated with the degree of first language acquisition (Cummins, 1981; Snow, 1993), a child whose family comes to the United States when the child is quite young and discourages use of the primary language may unknowingly retard English acquisition because a threshold of language proficiency in the first language is needed to learn the second language. In addition, if older children come from a strife-ridden country where there is little or no schooling, their chances of competing successfully with middle-class American students may be significantly decreased (Suárez-Orozco & Suárez-Orozco, 2001).

Language and culture are inseparable (Trueba, 1993). To learn a language, one must learn the culture, and vice versa. Both are needed to participate successfully in a society. Furthermore, the process of acquiring a new language and culture will inevitably change the nature of the first. For example, the Spanish spoken by Mexican immigrants varies from that in Mexico, and their life-styles are typical of neither the white mainstream nor the individuals in their homeland. The extent to which the first language and culture can be preserved is related to the degree of national tolerance for pluralism in the receiving country. For children, this includes the degree to which their language and culture are accepted and respected in schools.

CULTURAL AND LINGUISTIC DIFFERENCE

Educators and social scientists have proposed three major orientations or theories toward understanding individuals who are outside the dominant culture and/or whose first language is not English. These frameworks have been termed a deficiency orientation, a difference orientation, and a political orientation or stand.

Deficiency Orientation

A deficiency orientation toward those who come from culturally and linguistically diverse backgrounds focuses on what attributes the individual lacks (McDermott, 1997; Sleeter & Grant, 1999). This negative view holds the values of the dominant culture (e.g., time orientation, high English literacy skills, independence) as important for success and classifies those who lack these skills as at risk, disadvantaged, or culturally deprived. Children from poor or ethnic backgrounds have been variously described as deficient in achievement, IQ, social skills, sensory stimulation, rich or elaborated language, and moral stability. The assumption is that something is lacking either within the individual or in the individual's environment.

This was certainly the orientation that Jesus's teacher, Mrs. Kniffen, held in regard to Jesus in Chapter 5. His teacher did not view his bilingualism or biculturalism as strengths, and this ethnocentric bias was communicated to the entire class. Jesus understood this all too well and, enculturated with the middle-class values of school, he responded to his father and his native language with shame and anger.

Difference Orientation

A cultural difference orientation views cultural and linguistic diversity as strengths and builds on the knowledge and skills that students bring with them (Sleeter & Grant, 1999). Multiculturalism and multilingualism are viewed as desirable traits that should be encouraged. Differences in communication and cognitive styles are recognized and accommodated. If children have problems learning, the assumption is that the main limitation is inappropriate teaching. This orientation suggests a celebration of differences, rather than a denigration of them.

Estrella, the graduate student who visited Jesus's classroom at Mrs. Kniffen's invitation, adopted this orientation. As a person from a Latin culture who spoke Spanish, Estrella broke whatever stereotypes Mrs. Kniffen or her students had about the competence of culturally different individuals. Furthermore, Estrella brought a culturally responsive curriculum and pedagogy to the classroom that encouraged Jesus to not only participate, but to excel in the classroom.

Political Orientation

The political theory grows out of an attempt to understand the reasons behind school failure (McDermott, 1997). School failure is often attributed to those who are defined as poor, culturally or linguistically different, or intellectually subnormal. This theory suggests that we must change the unit of analysis from the individual to the culture. In other words, school failure is a cultural fabrication that must be understood in terms of the battle for access and resources by all groups. Furthermore, the dominant society must question the markers that measure school success: grades, standardized tests, high school completion, college graduation. Rather than look only at the schools for change, one must confront the systemic problems of the society as a whole. This view parallels Banks's (1999) characterization of the social action approach to multicultural education and education that is multicultural and reconstructionist as described by Sleeter & Grant (1999).

IMPLICATIONS FOR EDUCATION

In Chapter 2 we discussed many of the components of teacher education programs and school programs that must be in place to effectively educate students from culturally and linguistically diverse backgrounds. The following are examples of several approaches to pedagogy and curriculum that seem relevant to the cases in this chapter.

A starting point for effecting change in schools for students who are culturally and linguistically diverse is to view bilingualism, bidialectalism, and biculturalism as strengths. Using the child's native language does not impede the acquisition of English; rather, it offers many advantages (August & Hakuta, 1997). Businesses today view an individual who speaks two languages and is cross-culturally competent as an asset and will frequently offer a higher salary for these skills (Suárez-Orozco & Suárez-Orozco, 2001). Research suggests that children who are bilingual have advantages over monolinguals of the same socioeconomic background in their linguistic, cognitive, and social development. However, acquiring the proficiency needed in the second language for academic success takes from 5 to 7 years and a threshold proficiency in the first language (Collier, 1987; Cummins, 1981). Teachers must recognize that there are phonological, morphological, and syntactical differences among all dialects and languages that will take time to learn (Table 7.1).

TABLE 7.1   Comparison of Spanish and English Languages

PHONOLOGICAL	MORPHOLOGICAL	SYNTACTICAL
Spanish has fewer vowel sounds: No short *a* (hat), short *i* (fish), sort *u* (up), short double *o* (took), or schwa (sofa)	In Spanish, *de* (of) is used to show possession: Joe's pen becomes the pen of Joe	In Spanish, *no* is used for *not:* He no do his homework. In Spanish, there are no auxiliary verbs: She no play soccer.
Spanish has fewer consonant sounds: No /j/ (jump), /v/ (vase), /z/ (zipper), /sh/ (shoe), /ng/ (sing), /hw/ (when), /zh/ beige	In Spanish, *más* (more) is used to show comparison: *faster* becomes *more fast*	In Spanish, adjectives come after nouns: the car blue In Spanish, adjectives must agree: the elephants bigs

Source: Adapted from C. S. Bos & S. Vaughn (2002). *Strategies for teaching students with learning and behavior problems* (5th ed.). Boston: Allyn and Bacon.

Bilingual Education

Given the educational research, it seems clear that the decision being made in some states to dismantle bilingual education is often based on economic, cultural, and political agendas, instead of on what is best for the learners. This is not to say that this is an unequivocal issue. The variety of programs that exists even within the framework of transition, maintenance, total immersion and English as a Second Language programs makes comparative research difficult. However, educational research continues to show that bilingual education that supports the maintenance of the second language has a positive effect in promoting achievement among bilingual students (Ramirez, 1992; Merino, Trueba, & Samaniego, 1993; Thomas & Collier, 1997).

Yet the practical aspects of actual implementation of bilingual education are far from ideal. Even in states where bilingual education is still offered, certified bilingual teachers are in short supply and most are Spanish speakers (Merino, Trueba, & Samaniego, 1993; Suárez-Orozco & Suárez-Orozco, 2001). Furthermore, some programs are characterized by poor administrative support, inadequate resources, segregation from English language models, and basic secondary content courses that place students on a separate track from those who are college bound (Suárez-Orozco & Suárez-Orozco, 2001).

Bilingualism can be viewed as additive or subtractive (Trueba, 1993). Additive bilingualism sees both language and cultures as complementary and positive aspects of a child's development. Subtractive bilingualism views acquisition of the second language as more important and minimizes the value of the first. Although some programs in the United States have truly adopted an additive approach (e.g., Cuban Americans in Florida), many programs, even those categorized as maintenance programs, are essentially subtractive. Furthermore, while approximately 75 percent of all English language learners are Spanish speakers, the diversity of languages spoken in some school districts makes bilingual education impossible, given the lack of bilingual teachers for all those languages. Consequently, English as a Second Language instruction is the only viable alternative. Nevertheless, approaches such as cooperative learning, role playing, readers theater, visual representation, total physical response, and peer tutoring can be used to offer the contextual support needed (Cummins, 1996; Douville & Wood, 2001). In fact, all general education teachers should employ these approaches rather than "dumbing down" the curriculum.

Communication Style

Nieto (2000) suggests that communication style in a classroom in which culturally subordinated students are taught by culturally dominant teachers can be a barrier to achievement. Communication breaks down simply by virtue of each group behaving in ways that their subcultures see as "normal" (Heath,

1983). However, when teachers employ some of the discourse patterns of the students, communication improves. For example, Foster (1992) found that African American students were highly responsive and more likely to re-member the information when the teachers used "performances," stylized ways of speaking that resemble African American preaching styles, to inter-pret abstract concepts.

Sometimes students find the classroom culture very different from sim-ilar settings that involve interactions with adults in their own culture. Often the classrooms in their countries of origin are more teacher centered and structured, and they find the student-centered approach common in many U.S. classrooms to be disconcerting (Suárez-Orozco & Suárez-Orozco, 2001). Nieto (2000) gives an example of a teacher who asks her students if they un-derstand the lesson and observes that her students from Puerto Rico wrinkle their nose. Not understanding that this is a cultural sign for "I don't under-stand," the teacher continues without explanation. Siddle Walker (1992) dis-cusses possible cultural barriers implicit in the process approach to writing. This approach assumes that students are comfortable sharing personal nar-rative with the teacher and peers when, in fact, children may be hesitant to write in a personal mode when they sense a lack of cultural synchronization between themselves and their teacher or peers. In addition to differences in discourse patterns and cultural norms, differences in nonverbal communica-tion patterns can cause misunderstanding. These communication mis-matches, while certainly not the only cause for school failure, can further explain the confusion, and sometimes antagonism, that students display in the classroom.

Communication mismatches and a deficiency view of culture can result in very real conflict in the school and community. One area in which conflicts are ongoing across the United States is that of using Native American sym-bols as team mascots.

NATIVE AMERICAN MASCOTS

The issue of using Native American names and symbols for school and team mascots is an ongoing national controversy. Many universities and school dis-tricts have changed their names over the years. For example, Stanford went from the Indians to the Cardinals, Dartmouth changed from Indians to the Big Green, and Miami University of Ohio retired the Redskins for the Red Hawks. However, other national sport teams (e.g., Washington Redskins, Kansas City Chiefs) and universities (e.g., University of Illinois's Chief Illini-wek, University of North Dakota's Fighting Sioux) persist in having such mas-cots (see Table 7.2). As many as 2500 schools in the United States still have mascots that employ Native American images (Staurowsky, 1999).

TABLE 7.2   University of Illinois Mascot Chief Illiniwek

For 75 years, Chief Illiniwek has danced onto the field during half-time at football games. Typically, he is a white male in buckskin and a turkey feather headdress who ends his performance by saluting the Illini fans. In response, some in the stands yell repeatedly "chieeef," while others boo. The following is a brief chronology of the events that have surrounded the controversy.

1989	Charlene Teters, an art student and member of the Spokane Nation, calls for the elimination of Chief Illiniwek mascot and receives support from the minority affairs committee of the student government. The student government adopts an amended resolution supporting her.
	The University of Illinois asks the pep club, cheerleaders, and marching band to refrain from wearing "war paint" at athletic events.
1990	University of Illinois trustees vote seven to one to retain Chief Illiniwek as the university's mascot.
1991	The student government adopts a resolution calling for the removal of Chief Illiniwek and offers a declaration of apology to Native Americans.
	The Alumni Association announces that alumni will be polled concerning the mascot issue.
1994	Representative Rick Winkel of the Illinois House of Representatives introduces a bill to protect Chief Illiniwek as an "honored symbol" of the University of Illinois.
	Staff members and students at the university file race discrimination complaints with the U.S. Department of Education, Office of Civil Rights.
1995	The Illinois House of Representatives votes 80 to 26 in favor of the Winkel bill to protect Chief Illiniwek.
	The U.S. Department of Education rules that the mascot does not create a hostile environment for American Indians at the university.
1998	The University of Illinois Senate, composed of 200 faculty members and 50 students, votes March 9 to eliminate the Chief Illiniwek mascot. The vote is advisory. The board of trustees has the final say on the issue.
1999	North Central Association of Colleges and Schools concludes that the mascot issues need to be resolved as part of its reaccreditation report.
	The board of trustees begin a "dialogue," soliciting 18,000 opinions via e-mails, letters, and a public session.
2000	The results of the board of trustees survey showed overwhelming support for the chief. A committee was formed to study the problem further.
	The U.S. Commission on Civil Rights, in a 5 to 2 vote, said Indian names and mascots could be viewed as "disrespectful and offensive" and could create "a racially hostile educational environment for Indian students."

Adapted from Indian Mascot (2001), Molin (1999), and Spilky (2001).

Proponents for maintaining Indian mascots and names usually advance a number of arguments for their position (Molin, 1999). First, the polls of alumni and fans often report that a majority is in favor of keeping the mascot. They view the mascot, along with the logos, nicknames, or rituals that accompany it, with nostalgia and resist the idea of losing a part of their past. Second, supporters say that they are honoring indigenous peoples and have respect for their mascot or they would not continue using it. Sometimes individuals who claim Native American descent put this argument forth. Finally, some maintain that the movement to change mascot names is just another exercise in political correctness by overly sensitive groups.

Those who want to eliminate the use of Native American names and mascots for sports teams and schools argue that those who view a mascot with nostalgia are, at best, exhibiting dysconscious racism (Pewewardy, 1999). Dysconscious racism is an uncritical habit of mind (i.e., perceptions, attitudes, assumptions, and beliefs) that justifies inequity and exploitation by accepting the existing order of things as given (King, 1991). It is an ethnocentric view that assumes that the values and myths of the dominant society are correct and justifiable. If an individual has grown up with Hollywood images of cowboys and Indians, corporate images of Cherokee Jeeps and Land of Lakes butter, and stereotypical school celebrations of the first Thanksgiving, they assume that such symbolism is acceptable and correct.

There is real irony in objecting to the loss of a school mascot as an elimination of some part of one's personal history, when so much of the history and culture of indigenous peoples has been ignored or distorted. Deculturalization, the educational process of eliminating cultures, is a common strategy used by one country or group to dominate another (Spring, 1994). Deculturalization is implemented by segregating a people, forcing a change of language, imposing the dominant culture through the curriculum, denying expression of the dominated group's culture, and using teachers from the dominant group.

For example, the federal government's policy toward Indian education from the Revolutionary War until the publication of the Meriam Report in 1928 was one of deculturalization (Spring, 1994). Native Americans were removed to reservations as a result of the Indian Removal Act of 1830 and, thereby, segregated from whites. At first, schools were established primarily on reservations, and the purpose of the curriculum, taught by white teachers, was to promote the "dignity of labor" and the values of "civilization." However, reservation schools were not always viewed as successful in accomplishing these goals, so many nonreservation boarding schools were founded. The philosophy was that children should be removed from their families and tribal customs and learn vocational skills, English, American history, and U.S. government. In the 1920s, investigators were often horrified by the conditions that they found in Indian schools, and finally the publication of the Meriam Report began the process of reversing many of these repressive policies.

The argument that fans show respect by having Indian mascots is viewed by opponents as disingenuous. "Invented behavior like the tomahawk chop and dancing around in stereotypical Hollywood Indian style makes a mockery of Indigenous cultural identity and causes many young Indigenous people to feel shame about who they are as human beings, because racial stereotypes play an important role in shaping a young person's consciousness" (Pewewardy, 1999, p. 178). Furthermore, harm is done to all children when stereotypes go unchallenged and the sacred or cultural symbols of any group are trivialized. Such ignorance is symptomatic of a public school curriculum that marginalizes or distorts the history, culture, and spirituality of Native Americans and other nondominant groups (Loewen, 1995).

Therefore, opponents assert, the movement to eliminate Native American mascots cannot be trivialized as simply an attempt at political correctness. Rather, understanding and respecting Native American history and culture are an important part of promoting cultural literacy in our schools. It is hypocritical to include a character education curriculum that emphasizes values of truth, democracy, and justice and simultaneously to omit information about the inequitable treatment our society has meted out to Native Americans. President Clinton's Race Initiative Advisory Board reported that Native Americans experience more pronounced levels of racism in the form of economic and physical abuse than any other identified group (Staurowsky, 1999). One step toward ameliorating this unacceptable treatment is to own all of U.S. history and include it in our textbooks.

Many governmental, professional, and Native American organizations have criticized the use of Indian names and mascots. The Commission on Civil Rights issued a position on the use of Indian team names at non-Indian schools, saying they could be viewed as disrespectful and offensive and could create a racially hostile environment (Indian Mascot, 2001). The National Education Association, the NAACP, and the NCAA have issued statements supporting the elimination of Indian names and mascots (Pewewardy, 1999). Similarly, the National Congress of American Indians, the National Indian Education Association, and the National Coalition for Racism in Sport and Media have opposed what they see as a dehumanizing practice (Staurowsky, 1999). In spite of these strong statements from so many political and educational groups, the conversation about the use of Indian mascots is far from over in the wider society, as the case study of the Onteora Indian will show.

ASIAN AMERICANS AND THE HMONG CULTURE

Although many Americans perceive all Asians as the same, the population is actually quite diverse. Four subgroups have been identified based on their geographical origins: East Asians, Southeast Asians, South Asians, and Pacific

TABLE 7.3   Representative Asian–Pacific Subgroups in the United States

EAST ASIANS	SOUTH ASIANS	SOUTHEAST ASIANS	PACIFIC ISLANDERS
Chinese	Indian	Burmese	Hawaiian
Japanese	Pakistani	Cambodian	Guamanian
Korean		Laotian	Samoan
Taiwanese		Thai	Tahitian
		Vietnamese	
		Malaysian	
		Filipino	

Islanders (Wan, 1996) (see Table 7.3). The population of Asian–Pacific Islanders in the United States increased by 95.2 percent between 1980 and 1990 (U.S. Census Bureau, 1990).

The Asian American subgroups differ in their reasons for immigration, level of schooling in the home country, place of residence in the United States, socioeconomic status, experiences in the home country, and level of assimilation or acculturation (Pang, 1990; Pang & Evans, 1995). East Asians appear to be the most established of the four groups, their ancestors having settled in the United States since the mid-1800s. However, most Southeast Asians have come as refugees fleeing war or oppression, without literacy in their own languages and unprepared for the immigration experience (Gougeon, 1993). At the end of 1990, approximately 1,302,000 Southeast Asian refugees were included in the U.S. population (U.S. Census Bureau, 1990). Although the U.S. government had planned to disperse the refugees throughout the country, Southeast Asians are actually concentrated in the West with 39.2 percent in California, 7.6 percent in Texas, and 4.7 percent in Washington. Others are scattered throughout the states. Locations have been determined by such factors as employment opportunities, the attraction of established communities, desirability of welfare benefits in some states, and reunification with relatives (Huang, 1989). Due to such problems as examination and certification requirements in some professions, language difficulties, lack of transportation, and discrimination, the jobs found by refugees in the United States have been generally inferior to those held in their home country.

Model Minority Myth

Although Asian Americans are diverse in many ways, they are likely to share the risk of treatment according to the "model minority" stereotype that is held by many Americans. According to the stereotype, Asian American students are high achievers and have identical appearances and cultures (Wan, 1996). Yet studies refute these myths. In the Seattle School District, for example, high school dropout rates for Vietnamese and other Southeast Asian students was "twice or more those of Japanese and Chinese students" (Wan, 1996, p. 3). Sixty-nine percent of the Asian students fell below the 50th percentile in reading and 35 percent were below the 50th percentile in math. This is only one example of the importance of recognizing individual differences among these students, particularly those who may need special help. In fact, ignoring individual differences and special needs among Asian American students is the greatest danger fostered by the stereotype. Parents of some Asian American students have noted that it is particularly in the area of social–emotional needs and skills that their children are most likely to be shortchanged (S. Tung, personal communication, 1997). Students need encouragement and guidance to participate fully in extracurricular activities and social events so that they can acquire social skills and develop socially as well as academically. Other data concerning poverty, high school graduation rates, and the need for educational and psychological services among Asian American youth also serve to discredit the model minority myth (Wan, 1996).

It is also important for teachers to understand the insult to an Asian student when her identity is not correctly recognized. A Korean American student who is described as Chinese is likely to be offended by the mistake (Wan, 1996). Historical animosity and conditions of war among Asian groups may impede cooperation and friendships. The long-term conflict between Vietnam and Cambodia, for example, has resulted in mistrust between the two groups (Wan, 1996).

Despite the obvious diversity among Asian Americans, certain cultural patterns are shared by all, primarily controlling one's expression and dealing with confrontational situations (Wan, 1996). Teachers will have to be more patient in giving the students opportunities to express themselves and in dealing with them in a conflict situation. The control of emotions is a cultural characteristic that should not be attributed to lack of interest, boredom, or poor motivation. Cross-cultural competence will help teachers to acquire appropriate communication skills, use empowering curricula in the classroom, and build strong connections to students' homes and communities (Wan, 1996).

The Hmong

One group of Southeast Asian refugees whose culture and language are strikingly different from that of mainstream American is the Hmong. They have lived in remote, mountainous regions of Laos, where they cooperated with the American forces against the communists during the Vietnam War. After 1975, when the communists took over, many Hmong fled to Thailand on rafts and inner tubes. From Thailand's refugee camps, many came to the United States, where resettlement programs attempted to scatter them throughout the states. However, of the over 94,000 Hmong in the United States, many have moved to warm-weather states such as California, where more than 50 percent have settled, especially in agricultural areas such as the San Joaquin Valley (Kitano & Daniels, 1995; Rumbaut, 1995). However, there are also Hmong in Seattle, Providence, Minneapolis–St. Paul, and Milwaukee in smaller numbers.

The Hmong have been described as seminomadic people who are thought to have origins in Mongolia and who settled in northern China 4,000 years ago. They eventually migrated north, south, and west into the highlands, where their distinct cultural and linguistic characteristics were intensified (Trueba, Jacobs, & Kirton, 1990). Patrilineal clans, large families, residence with the husband's family, a model of male domination, interdependence of clan members for subsistence, ancestor worship, animism, and the important role of elders are cultural characteristics that have endured (Kitano & Daniels, 1995; Trueba et al., 1990). In China, the Hmong are recognized for their special talents, free and powerful spirit, and enjoyment of their unique music and dancing. They use the gong, drums, pipe organs, and leaf blowing.

The Hmong who have come to the United States, for example, have had to adapt to big cities, modern appliances and conveniences, commerce, supermarkets, and other aspects of modern American society that have made their adjustment confusing and difficult. Without a written language and with difficulty understanding written symbols, the acculturation process has been painful, especially for the older refugees. In addition, the Hmong have encountered racism, prejudice, and discrimination. In the Fresno, California, area, Hmong refugees have experienced considerable discrimination from residents and from other immigrant groups who feel threatened by the newcomers (Kitano & Daniels, 1995). In some cities they have settled primarily in African American areas, where there tends to be less resistance to their densely populated housing and other cultural practices. Many Hmong have tried farming in California and Minnesota, but their methods have been very different, and money and marketing methods have also been serious problems. Thus, employment has been problematic and many have resorted to selling handicrafts. In fact, the unemployment rate among the Hmong has been established at 90 percent with most receiving welfare (Kitano & Daniels, 1995). Their median family income has been reported as $14,327 per year (Rumbaut, 1995). Furthermore, while only 1.7 percent of Hmong individuals over age 15 are divorced, 76 percent of female-headed Hmong households live below the poverty level (Fong, 1998).

Like many refugees, the Hmong experience many physical and mental health problems (Fong, 1998). Depression is widespread among the group as they struggle to begin their lives again in a new culture and language and find new ways to make a living. Recently, a "sudden death syndrome" has been described among healthy Hmong men, which may be related to some of the difficulties in their lives (Fong, 1998; Kitano & Daniels, 1995). Interestingly, the fertility rate of Hmong women ages 35 to 44 may be the highest in the United States, at 6.1 per woman compared to a U.S. fertility rate of 2.0 (Rumbaut, 1995). This means that the Hmong median age is 12.7.

Hmong children may be unable to talk about school activities at home or cultural and home activities at school. Many children are rapidly losing their native language, which may weaken communication with their families even more. In the rapid adjustment to American society, the children may "find themselves lost in school, feeling ambivalent about their self-worth and identity, yet their desire for upward mobility is seen in the aggressive competitiveness to excel in school" (Trueba, Jacobs, & Kirton, 1990, p. xix). Furthermore, Hmong children may be ambivalent about wanting to belong to their own people and at the same time wanting to become mainstream Americans (Trueba et al., 1990). They may feel culturally isolated, perhaps marginalized, and stereotyped in school and in the community. In addition, they may face conflict in their classroom where their behaviors are culturally different. In an interesting study of Hmong adult classroom behavior, Kang, Kuehn, & Herrell (1994) observed cultural characteristics identified by Hmong cultural informants who participated in the study. Table 7.4 presents

TABLE 7.4   Classroom Behaviors Observed in Adult Hmong Students

1. Students display cooperative learning behavior. Students learn from each other, often providing unsolicited assistance at the first sign of a problem. They pair up or form groups without teacher direction.
2. Explicit directions are needed from the teacher. Students learn through demonstrations and examples.
3. Students' answers to questions or completion of tasks are prefaced by expressions of lack of ability or knowledge.
4. Laughter is a common behavior in the classroom, indicating several different things: when a student makes a mistake, is having problems, or is not sure of what he or she is doing or of the answers given. Others laughed with the student in order to show support, "soften the mistake," or help a student to save face.
5. Students are reluctant to perform in front of others due mainly to fear of making mistakes or looking bad or foolish.
6. Students depend on the teacher for direction. Out of respect, they rarely ask the teacher for help or tell the teacher what to teach.
7. Students constantly read aloud as they read and speak aloud as they write, regardless of their ability level. They read aloud when reading alone or in pairs or when copying from the board.
8. The use of imagery as a memory aid is a consistent learning strategy.

Adapted from Kong, Kuehn and Herrell (1994).

the list of significant behaviors identified as culturally determined by cultural informants. While the students involved were adults, it is possible that younger students may also share these behavioral characteristics.

In their oral cultural tradition, important Hmong values, such as sharing and loyalty, family stability, long-term commitment, and love, are reflected in some of their folktales (Trueba, Jacobs, & Kirton, 1990). Obedience to parents, tolerance, and patience are virtues of women that are also extolled in folktales. A cooperative approach to resolution of family conflicts and economic problems is maintained, and family privacy is protected along with the protection of young people from outside influences (Trueba, et al., 1990). These cultural traditions will be severely challenged as the Hmong population encounters the acculturation process in America.

In the following cases we focus on issues of culture and language for Native Americans and American Hmong. Of course, there are hundreds of Native American nations in the United States, but they share similar values about the sacredness of their symbols. On the other hand, the Hmong represent a relatively small percentage of Asian Americans, yet they are experiencing some of the greatest educational, economic, and social hardships within that demographic category of people. We hope that as you explore the concepts of culture and language related to these cases you will gain greater insight into the challenging but critical task of becoming a culturally responsive educator.

THE CASE OF THE ONTEORA INDIAN

In 1952 the Onteora Central School District was incorporated. The largest district in New York State, Onteora encompasses rural areas in the Catskill Mountains and the town of Woodstock, made famous by the 1960s festival and now a popular home for those in the arts community.

Onteora is a high-performing district. Historically, the percentage of students passing state-mandated exams has exceeded both county and state averages. The high school offers advance placement courses in a considerable number of areas, and 60 to 80 percent of the students attend college after graduation.

During the 2000–2001 school year, the district served 2,277 students. Of that number, 307 received free lunch and 130 received reduced-priced lunch. The racial distribution of the district is American Indian or Alaskan Native (1), Asian or Pacific Islander (53), Black (81), Hispanic (72), White (2070).

The major highway running through the district is Route 28, also known as the Onteora Highway, and it is from this supposed Indian word that the district chose its name and mascot, the Onteora Indians. However, the historical record does not support the existence of Indian settlements in the area. The Esopus and the Mohicans were the nearest Native Americans who settled along the Hudson River and may have sent hunters to the area in the fall to find deer and turkey.

Dennis Yerry, a parent in the district, questioned the use of an Indian as a school symbol in 1998, but he received no subsequent support from the school board at that time. By the 1999–2000 school year, there was enough public support to raise the issue once again (see Box 7.2 and Figure 7.1).

■ ■ ■ ■ ■

BOX 7.2

INDIAN MASCOTS DRAW CRITICISM
Some See Images as 'Derogatory'

In the Onteora school district, the Board of Education is expected to vote Monday on whether to abolish the longtime symbol of its teams.

By Jonathan Ment
Freeman Staff

The Onteora school board is expected to vote Monday on whether to eliminate the American Indian as a school symbol.

The district's athletic teams are nicknamed the Indians, an annual dance and the high school yearbook sport the name "Tomahawk," and a muscular American Indian breaking through a cinder block wall is painted on the wall of the high school gymnasium.

Dennis Yerry, who says he's "part Seneca, part Dutch and part Irish," stepped forward two years ago to protest the use of American Indian images.

"I don't feel it's a sports issue or a popularity issue," said Yerry, a 1977 Onteora graduate who now has an 8-year-old in the school district. "I feel it's an education issue. The term 'Indians,' as the mascot for the sports team and the logos on the wall, have become curriculum for students at the high school."

Yerry said seventh-graders have two weeks of planned study on American Indian life and culture; third-graders have about a month.

"According to the school, there's not much in the curriculum from ninth to 12th grade," Yerry said. "The only thing they get is the mascot and the totem pole in the cafeteria. . . . The bottom line is I don't think any group of people should be used as the mascot for a sports team."

Although Yerry let go of the issue locally when he "felt no support from the (school) board," others have come forward to champion the cause, and in greater numbers. Yerry is now active in the issue nationally.

The issue has received enough attention across New York state to prompt the Education Department to begin evaluating the use of American Indian images in schools.

"There were some concerns communicated to the department from around the state," said Bill Hirschen an Education Department spokesman. "There are no conclusions, but there's a survey (circulating) to determine the extent of this in the state . . . and to gather the opinions of school officials."

On January 10, 2000, the Onteora school board revisited the issue of the school name and accompanying images after receiving a letter of discontent from parents and a citizen's group known as Community: One Love One Race (COLOR). The board decided to hold a public hearing on the issue at the January 24 regular meeting of the school board and then vote on whether to retire the name.

FIGURE 7.1   Mural of Onteora Indian

Hirschen said there's no time limit for the study and no related state Education Department Policy.

Onteora school board President Marty Millman said the logos in the building and on the playing field "have disturbed a great deal of the local people."

Daily Freeman, Kingston, N.Y.

The meeting began at 7:00 at the junior–senior high school with a thorough report on the district technology programs and accompanying budgetary needs of the district, but few questions regarding the report were asked. The board then moved to public comment and gave each speaker who had called the district office ahead of time 2 minutes to speak. Over 200 people attended the January 24 meeting and 50 of them were on the list to speak. Throughout the crowd there were people wearing armbands with a red circle and slash crossing out the words "racist stereotypes," which had been distributed by COLOR. The board did not provide a microphone for the speakers, so it was difficult for the audience to hear their statements.

Speakers from outside the district came, as well as community members. Ray Tin-Koshyula, a Lakota Indian from the Pine Ridge reservation in South Dakota, began by presenting the board with several red and blue feathers as a symbol of friendship and showed them an empty liquor bottle with the brand name Crazy Horse to emphasize how names could be demeaning to American Indians. Later, Kay Olan, a teacher in a local district and member of the Mohawk Nation, said that, although she believed that no harm was meant in establishing the symbol originally, human decisions must be reconsidered when people become more enlightened. She emphasized the need for all involved to talk and listen with open minds and include these discussions in the school curriculum.

A coach from the district stated that he felt that the name was not discriminatory and had been chosen out of respect. A community member supported his view saying that the determined, muscular Indian figure painted on the gymnasium wall in 1997 was an inspiration to all school teams and that they had done well under the eye of that figure. Another man from the community stated that it was ridiculous to change the images just because a politically correct group in the community said they were racist or insensitive. He called the wall painting a work of art and said that removing it would be censorship. He called those objecting to the image thin skinned and dysfunctional.

A black man with dreadlocks who wore an armband said that there was no question that the symbols used by the school were racist and were an insult to the First Nation. He received a great deal of applause. Then a woman who was a graduate of Onteora suggested that it would be a shame to wipe out the tradition of the Indian and that it would be possible to change the images without changing the name. Later, a man who identified himself as 25 percent Indian, stated that his wife had graduated from Onteora and that no one in his family found the mascot objectionable. He felt the Indian promoted spirit and school tradition and wished that people were as concerned about the drug problem as they were about this issue. He said that racism was not a problem in the district and encouraged the board to put the issue up for a public referendum.

A woman who stated that her husband is part Native American and part Latino said that her children had been subjected to demeaning comments about their ethnicity. Another speaker who identified himself as a Jewish American reminded the audience that symbols could be used to dehumanize people and justify genocide. He stated that a person should not be used as a mascot and also called for better information within the school curriculum regarding the history of native peoples in the United States.

Josh Telson, the vice-president of the Student Affairs Council, said that most students at Onteora didn't care whether the mascot was kept or not. He did point out that the cost of changing school uniforms would be considerable and urged the board to fund the change if they made it.

After over 2 hours of public comment, the board voted to retire the Indian. It was a 4 to 3 vote, with school board president Martin Millman in the minority. The board received a standing ovation from some in the audience. Superintendent Hal Rowe commended the audience for its eloquence and said that if any image disturbs the people that it represents it should be eliminated.

The school board's decision was the beginning, not the end, of a long and often heated debate over the Onteora Indian. Because of the outcry against the decision that surfaced over the ensuing week, the board agreed to hold another hearing at their meeting on February 7 to determine whether voters should decide the question of retiring the symbol by holding a referendum in May. That morning about 200 middle and high school students conducted a 45-minute sit-in in the cafeteria to protest the board's decision. The day after the vote, students had begun to circulate a petition to support a return to the Indian mascot and were continuing to get signatures during the sit-in. A controversy arose when 11 students were given a 5-day suspension for refusing to return to class (see Box 7.3).

At least 300 people attended the February 7 meeting, and the overwhelming majority of the 40 who spoke were in favor of keeping the Indian symbol. Trustees were given petitions containing more than 2,000 signatures opposing their decision to retire the Indian. Sadie Finkle, president of the Student Advisory Council, stated that the majority of students wanted to keep the Indian name and perhaps change the images. Josh Telson took a different view: "When people realize the issue here is respect, they'll change their minds and realize it's no big deal. It's time to move on. If students develop a new name themselves, they'll have school spirit over that" (Twine, 2000). Eighth-grader Rachel McCallum wore face paint and a decorated headband, with a sign that read "Proud of My Indian Heritage (descendant of the Moon family) and My School Emblem." At the end of the meeting the Onteora Board of Education voted 4 to 3 against trustee Joseph Doan's resolution for a public referendum along the same lines as the previous vote.

■ ■ ■ ■ ■

BOX 7.3

STUDENTS WHO CUT CLASSES FOR
PETITION DRIVE ARE SUSPENDED

*Onteora officials discipline 11 youngsters who were collecting signatures in
support of keeping the school's Indian symbol.*

by Cynthia Werthamer
Freeman Staff

BOICEVILLE, FEBRUARY 9, 2000 — Eleven Onteora High School students received
five-day out-of-school suspensions Tuesday for cutting classes while they circu-
lated petitions asking the school district to keep the school's Indian mascot.

Tommy Clare of Boiceville, one of those suspended, called the punishments
disrespectful of the students' rights. His mother said the students were promised
school time to circulate the petitions but didn't get it.

School authorities said the students were told three of them could continue
circulating the petitions but that any others refusing to return to class would be
suspended.

The students began asking for petition signatures Tuesday, the morning after
the Onteora school board, by a 4–3 vote, stood by its earlier decision to stop using
the Indian as the district's symbol. About 200 students protested the retirement of
the symbol Monday morning by staging a 45-minutes sit-in in the school cafeteria.

Three of the 11 suspended students had spoken at the board meeting's public comment session, supporting retention of the mascot, Clare said.

The students were promised a longer homeroom period than usual so they
could seek signatures, but the period wasn't extended, said Barbara Clare, mother
of the 15-year-old freshman.

"A democracy is not always the will of the majority of people who have
the right to vote," stated Marino D'Orazio, a trustee. "In our system, bodies
of elected officials vote based on the best information they have and ultimately, their conscience. That's because in a democracy people are not usually willing to make changes. Tough decisions are always unpopular because
they go to the heart of what we live by" (Twine, 2000).

After this and other board of education meetings, it was discovered that
cars had been damaged. Tires were punctured, among other things. No one
was ever caught in connection with these incidents.

In subsequent months the issues raised by these two meetings resur-
faced in countless conversations throughout the area in homes, schools, and
other community settings. Local editorial pages frequently contained strong
words on both sides of the debate, although supporters of the Indian mascot

The group moved to the cafeteria, then into the hallway, effectively spending most of their school day soliciting names, Tommy Clare said.

"The principal (Thomas Jackson) saw us in the morning and said, 'Just make sure you spell everything right' on our posters. He was pretty sarcastic," he said. "Then he tried to split us up, suggesting three representatives stay out. But it was important that we stick together. It was like a sit-down strike.

"I think we were treated very unfairly," Clare said. "I know I cut (class), but we were standing up for our rights. We have the right to speak our minds, and we weren't getting respect from the principal and the higher authorities."

He added that the group did not encourage others to cut class, warning those who choses to join that they risked being suspended.

Assistant Principal Vincent Bruck said the students were not singled out because of their speeches the night before. "In fact, this morning on the PA (public address system), we complimented the students who attended the board meeting," he said. "We also said we expect students to be in classes today or face the consequences. We gave them ample opportunity to go back to class, which they didn't do."

He said the administration agreed to requests by students on Monday that they be allowed to meet with members of the school board about the mascot decision and that they be allowed to vote on the mascot in a school referendum, with the results to be given to the board.

Clare said students were upset both by the removal of the Indian, which he said has been the school's symbol for 49 years, and the fact that students weren't consulted before the board's decision.

"We are supporting their process," Bruck said. "But this type of process, in my opinion, isn't helping their cause one bit."

Daily Freeman, Kingston, N.Y.

---

seemed most vocal. Editorials accused the board of catering to special interest groups, ignoring majority opinion, abandoning their educational mission, and modeling poor parliamentary procedures.

Although most teachers agreed with the board's decision to change the mascot, some were upset by the process. They, like the students, felt that a democratic process was not followed and that teachers should have been polled or consulted more thoroughly regarding the issue, since they were the ones who had to live with implementing any changes and dealing with the repercussions. However, few teachers attended school board meetings or voiced their opinions at those meetings. Teachers on both sides of the issue were reluctant to speak up.

State and federal governmental groups became involved. For example, in March a representative from the U.S. Community Relations Service, a branch of the U.S. Justice Department, met with Superintendent Hal Rowe and other district leaders to discuss possible solutions. One idea was to bring in trained mediators who would meet with middle and high school students to resolve some of the differences in opinion regarding the board decisions. In April, consultants in conflict resolution affiliated with Rutgers University met with seven middle and high school students to determine the students' perceptions of the issues regarding the Indian mascot. However, this was the only time that mediators met with the students.

That same month, Andrian Cooke, acting coordinator of the Native American Education Unit for the New York State Education Department, wrote to the Onteora board commending their courageous stand against racism. He wrote, "Our children must be taught not to demean certain groups of people with who(m) they must coexist in today's society. The images presented by [Onteora yearbook] pictures create negative feelings toward Native American people within the community" (Kemble, 2000a). New York State Department spokesman Tom Dunn indicated that an official position on Indians as school mascots was expected to be released by Commissioner Richard Mills, which would provide school districts with guidance in dealing with these issues.

At the April 3 board meeting, Josh Telson reported on the process for choosing a new mascot. Students would soon be surveyed in homeroom for their top three choices, with the understanding that the symbol cannot be racially derogatory. Then a list would be generated based on frequency, originality, color scheme, and school atmosphere. The top three choices would be voted on. Once chosen, students would be involved in developing the logo and mascot costume. This process never occurred. However, in April a policy was passed to prohibit the use of racial "images and artifacts" in the district.

On May 8 the board held a hearing for the 2000–2001 Onteora Central School District budget scheduled May 16 for a vote. The proposed budget was approximately $35,500,000, a 6.94 percent increase over the previous year. In addition, voters were given the opportunity to vote on three propositions: school buses, maintenance vehicles, and computer equipment. About 30 people attended the meeting, but few comments were made about the actual expenditures. However, community members raised concerns that voters would vote down the budget because of their displeasure with the mascot issue. May 16 was also the evening when district residents would vote for school board trustees. Two of the three individuals running against incumbents were in favor of restoring the Indian mascot.

The predictions about the results of the May 16 election in Onteora were accurate. The budget was voted down, albeit by a vote of 2,099 to 2,057. The only proposition to pass involved technology support. Of the nine school districts in the county, only four school budgets were approved. However, the budgets that were rejected had higher spending increases than Onteora's, and the district that had a comparable budget received approval. Furthermore, the two candidates that had run on a pro-Indian platform were elected to the board. The night of the election there was a physical altercation between one of the successful candidates and the boyfriend of a woman who ran unsuccessfully. Stories were conflicting regarding fault, and both members were required to appear in town court, although the judge eventually determined no penalties or jail time.

On June 5 one of the first actions of the new school board was to rescind the January resolution to eliminate the use of the Indian name and symbols after the 1999–2000 school year with a vote of 5 to 1. In addition, trustees passed the first reading of a policy that would delete language referencing the use of ethnic images and artifacts as district symbols. There was disagreement over whether the board could approve the first reading without discussion of the language. Attorneys with the American Indian Movement, a Minnesota-based organization, later stated that they would file a lawsuit against the district if racially based images were used as district mascots and symbols.

In addition, the new school board decided to put the budget up for another vote. According to New York State law, if a budget is defeated a second time, the district is forced to adopt an austerity spending plan that puts a 2.64 percent limit on increases in nonmandated spending. Mandatory spending includes salaries and expenditures for academic programs. Given the narrow margin of defeat and the belief by many that the mascot controversy influenced voters, the new board decided to put a slightly reduced budget of $35.46 million up for vote on June 20.

At the June 19 school board meeting, attended by about 175 people, members of the community criticized Superintendent Hal Rowe and other district officials on a variety of issues. These included failure to take seriously a female student's charges of sexual assault, overcrowding in school buildings, and creating dissension by openly taking sides in controversial issues and hiding others. Other parents supported the administration, saying Dr. Rowe was caring and cooperative and that the criticisms were unfair. On June 20 the budget was defeated by a 1,438 to 1,348 vote, requiring the board to cut approximately $800,000 from the 2000–2001 budget.

Over the summer a vote on rescinding the policy on racial images and artifacts was delayed based on advice from the New York State attorney general's office and the school board attorney. Likewise, a suggestion to form a three-person committee to study the infusion of Indian history and culture into the curriculum was not enacted. Also during the summer, the board received a lengthy letter from the state attorney general's office outlining the district controversy and similar case decisions across the country (Kemble 2000b). The letter advised the board to review the U.S. Civil Rights Act of 1964 before rescinding the policy enacted by the previous board to prohibit a race of people or its symbols or artifacts from being used as district symbols. The letter outlined relevant legal issues (see Box 7.4).

■ ■ ■ ■ ■

BOX 7.4

STATE WARNS OF CONSEQUENCES
OF KEEPING INDIAN MASCOT

Onteora school officials are advised to carefully consider the legal implications of rescinding the policy banning the use of racial images or artifacts as district symbols.

By William J. Kemble
Correspondent

BOICEVILLE — A five-page letter from the state Attorney General's Office to the Onteora school board outlines the history of the district's mascot controversy and advises trustees to review similar cases where court action has been threatened over the use of Indian symbols

The letter, written by state Civil Rights Bureau Chief Andrew Celli, was released by state officials Wednesday after school district representatives denied the *Freeman's* request for a copy.

To emphasize how other school districts have adapted to changing sensitivity over the issue, Celli cited a U.S. Department of Justice investigation of a North Carolina school district and the decisions of school systems in Dallas and Los Angeles to cease the use of Indian mascots.

"The degree to which the maintenance of 'Indian' team nicknames, the use of 'Indian' imagery, the use of native religious symbols, gestures or chants in a secular (and potentially demeaning) context and/or the maintenance of an 'Indian' mascot implicate the anti-discrimination laws under these and other relevant statutes can only be determined on a case-by-case basis, with careful attention to the facts," Celli wrote.

Onteora trustees were advised to review the U.S. Civil Rights Act of 1964 carefully before voting to rescind a policy enacted by the previous board to prohibit "a race of people or its symbol or artifact" from being used as district symbols.

"It is the view of the (Attorney General's Office) that these considerations, as well as others, should be borne in mind when a decision about the Onteora Indian and related imagery is made," Celli wrote.

Investigators for the state attorney general have attended the past two Onteora school board meetings, and Celli said the situation will continue to be mon-

In the fall of 2000 the school board voted 5 to 2 to rescind the policy banning the use of racial images in the district. This was done despite considerable progress on a compromise policy being negotiated by representatives of the state attorney general's office. The American Indian Movement stated that it would proceed with a lawsuit against the district challenging all federal funding that the district receives.

itored. He also offered recommendations for reviewing policy involving the Indian mascot, saying the "relevant legal issues" to consider include:

- The nature of the team nickname and whether it is "patently offensive" in how it uses or refers to American Indians as hostile or warlike.
- Use by athletic teams of Indians items of historical or religious significance, such as a feather headdress, face paint, totem poles or tomahawks, in a non-religious event or in a manner that may have the effect of demeaning American Indian traditions.
- Depictions of American Indians in a comical fashion, as cartoon characters or with aggressive or hostile features or expressions.
- Allowing the language or gestures of American Indian culture to be distorted, including the use of a person dressed as an Indian to lead cheers.
- The extent of efforts by the district to educate students about American Indian history and traditions, with an emphasis on discerning fact from the stereotypical images that have been depicted by schools with Indian mascots.

Paul Larrabee, a spokesman for the Attorney General's Office, said the letter was intended to provide Onteora board members with factual information without threatening court action.

School board members, however, weren't given copies of the letter by the schools' attorney at their meeting Tuesday. A state official said Wednesday that the findings should not be so secret that even school board members have to make an appointment to see them.

"Who's making the rules here?" said Robert Freeman, executive director of the state Committee on Open Government. "The school board is the governing body, the attorney is not. If the school board chooses not to disclose it . . . that's its choice."

Trustees discussed the letter during an executive session, with board President Martin Millman saying the material involved litigation and could involve board legal strategy. Freeman agreed the meeting could be closed on that basis, but he said the document itself should largely be available to the public.

Millman said school district attorney John Donoghue had given one copy of the letter to trustees during the closed session but took it back to avoid having "copies floating around."

Daily Freeman, Kingston, N.Y.

At the writing of this case, the Commissioner of the New York State Department of Education, Richard Mills, has issued a letter to all public schools that states: "I have concluded that the use of Native American symbols or depictions as mascots can become a barrier to building a safe and nurturing school community and improving academic achievement for all students. I ask the superintendents and presidents of school boards to lead their communities to a new understanding on this matter" (Kemble, 2001a). Furthermore, in April 2001 the U.S. Commission on Civil Rights urged schools to stop using Indian team names and mascots, saying that the practice may violate antidiscrimination laws (Kemble, 2001b). On May 15, 2001, the school board authorized a nonbinding referendum asking residents if the Onteora Indian should remain the title of all sports teams and all other student athletic activities (Kemble, 2001c). Despite statements from the New York State Education Department that ballots for issues such as these were not appropriate, the referendum was held. The results showed that 1,950 individuals were for keeping the Indian mascot and 1,883 were against it.

DISCUSSION QUESTIONS

1. Regarding the use of the Onteora Indian as a name and symbol, what are the views of each of the following groups: students, teachers, community members, board of education trustees, and administrators? Does there appear to be any consensus within or between groups?
2. What underlying beliefs motivate those who want to eliminate the Indian name and what underlying beliefs motivate those that want to maintain it?
3. To what extent are the views of the student body sought or represented in this case?
4. How has the controversy over the Indian mascot affected other aspects of the school program?
5. If you were teaching in this district, what would be your personal response to the situation?
6. What could teachers and administrators do individually or corporately to work toward resolution of this issue?

THE CASE OF MALEE VANG

Terrified, I always sit in the back of the bus while the bus driver jokes with the boys and makes fun of me. This day is no different from all the others as we drive through many nice neighborhoods of this big city. The big, fat bus driver and all of the boys often talk about me as if I'm not even present. But, whenever one of the boys comes back to talk to me, I turn away and stare out the window, scared to death.

Although the driver picks up five Hmong students every morning, I am the only girl on the bus and I feel very alone and frightened.

As we approach my school, the neat, ordinary houses that line the streets become a blur as I begin to worry about how the day will go in my classes. When I finally arrive at the old brick school building and enter my classroom I don't feel much better than I did on the bus.

Now that I'm no longer in ESL classes, I don't have Hmong students in most of my classes and the white kids seem indifferent to me. I just feel invisible except when Miss Halvorsen holds me up to the other students. "Why can't everyone finish homework like Malee?" she'll ask the other students. "Why can't the rest of you complete your work as quickly and as neatly as Malee?"

Every time she brings attention to me as the "best student," I can feel my classmates' anger and it gets worse every time she makes a "Malee statement." It's as if she doesn't know that no one in the class likes me. She just doesn't seem to realize that I hate those public displays. When I finally worked my way to the mainstream and no longer had to suffer the stigma of going to ESL classes and having a Hmong teacher, I thought life in school would be great. After all, if you're not in the mainstream you're considered stupid. But eighth grade is the worst! Some days when Miss Halvorsen is especially emotional she will yell at the students because no one has chosen me for a group. "Malee is obedient; she listens; she's a good student," Miss Halvorsen will shout. "Include her in your projects or you won't get recess."

Sometimes, Miss Halvorsen will direct me to get into a certain group whether the students want me or not. When she gets very emotional, it's embarrassing for me. I usually remain alone. I guess that you could call me a loner. Maybe it would be better if I were not the only Hmong student in my class. I think sometimes, too, that the fact that I'm at least a year older than everyone else may make a difference. I was placed in second grade when I arrived in this country even though I was 10 years old. I've always been older than most kids in my class have and now I'm 16 in eighth grade. The kids here at school seem mainly concerned about their peers. Everyone wants to be liked and popular. My classmates simply ignore me unless Miss Halvorsen calls their attention to me. But, that only happens in her English/homeroom.

It's really difficult for me to understand and accept the rules for socializing and being popular. I'm not even sure that I want to be a part of it. I don't like pretending to like kids that I really don't like just to be popular, and I don't know if I want to be part of the American culture.

Other things about eighth grade bother me, too. My advanced math and science classes, for example, move so fast that I wish I could slow the pace. In my enriched Earth Science class the students are very smart, and I feel that my communication skills are lacking and I'm trailing behind. The teacher, Mr. Jensen, a white middle-aged man, is nice but he is only interested in the subject matter. He usually does a demonstration and then we do it, sometimes in pairs. The class is very competitive and we have no group activities. There are two other Hmong girls in my science class who speak excellent English and seem very Americanized. I sometimes resent their Americanization. I just feel that everything is spinning out of control for me.

My mom can't help either. She plays no role whatever in my school-work and decisions. Since my mother divorced my father several years ago, something unheard of in the Hmong culture, she must take care of six children alone. Although there is a large Hmong community in the city, we are really isolated and shunned. So, we live a very secluded life. Although all of us are in school—my youngest brother is in kindergarten—my mom has a lot of work to do for six kids ages 19, 17, 16, 13, 10, and 8, and we all help after school. There is always cooking, dishes to wash, and helping with the younger children for me after school. My mom has no outside contacts and seldom goes out. She has very little money since our family is on welfare. Sometimes, my sister and I bike around the neighborhood or to the Target store, but our time is usually spent in the house.

According to the newspaper, more than 70,000 Hmong live in this city, with 18 clans and leaders, all men, who act as mediators and judges. The newspaper said recently that approximately 7,500 Hmong children are in the public schools, but we don't live near the large Hmong community either, so it is difficult to even try to find people who understand. I feel sorry about my mother's plight as a non-English speaking woman trying to raise and understand her children and their struggles in this American society. Life is lonely for her. I really want to grow up and help ease her burden of raising the children alone.

Even though I do hate eighth grade, school has been fun at times and we've done a lot of things that I've enjoyed. We've had lots of field trips to museums, picnics, and roller blading. There are a lot of Hmong students here and some Hmong teachers, too. But now that I'm no longer in ESL I don't have many Hmong students in my classes and I have no Hmong teachers. If it were not for two Hmong ESL teachers to whom I can talk sometimes, I would be even lonelier. Until last year I had a best friend named Ping, but she got married in 7th grade to a Hmong teacher, with her family's approval, and disappeared without even saying good-by. My only friend now is an African American girl who no one likes, so we are both outcasts. Often, we walk down the halls together and one day a male Hmong teacher saw us and said, "No wonder we don't see you much anymore, Malee. You're friends with an African American now and you think you're cool." I felt terrible. I only wanted a friend.

Of all the things that have happened to me this year, the worst experience of my whole life has been the band. Everyone at school must play an instrument and they gave me a flute to play. First, it was such a culture shock because, although I had heard music, I had never been around people playing music before. Second, I am the worst flute player ever and everyone in the band hates me. I always play the wrong notes and spoil whatever they are playing. This is terrible when we are playing in the auditorium for everyone. And, for the first time, it bothers me that the other students in the band don't like me.

At home, I cry sometimes and try to get my mother to understand how I feel. But mom has six kids to worry about and doesn't know the language. She also believes that whatever decisions my teachers make are good for me. As I struggle to make sense of my new home and identity in America, I feel great confusion. School and home are so different. I'm expected to be docile and obedient at home while I have to be assertive to be recognized at school. Too often, I feel like I don't belong to either the Hmong or the American culture. Will I ever belong somewhere?

DISCUSSION QUESTIONS
1. What are the major issues in the case?
2. How would you describe the impact of the acculturation process on Malee and her family?
3. To what extent is the teacher, Miss Halvorsen, responsive to Malee's cultural differences?
4. How would you describe Malee's terror on the bus?
5. Identify several important goals based on the issues in the case.
6. How do the perspectives of Malee, her teachers, and family differ with respect to Malee's problems?

REFERENCES

August, D., & Hakuta, K. (1997). *Improving schooling for language minority children: A research agenda.* Washington, DC: National Academy Press.

Banks, J. A. (1999). *An introduction to multicultural education.* Boston: Allyn and Bacon.

Bos, C. S., & Vaughn, S. (2002). *Strategies for teaching students with learning and behavior problems.* Boston: Allyn and Bacon.

Collier, V. P. (1987). Age and rate of acquisition of second language acquisition for academic purposes. *TESOL Quarterly, 21,* 617–641.

Cummins, J. (1981). The role of primary language development in promoting education success for language minority students. In California State Department of Education (Ed.), *Schooling and language minority students: A theoretical framework* (pp. 3–50). Los Angeles: Evaluation, Dissemination and Assessment Center, California State University.

Cummins, J. (1996). *Negotiating identities: Education for empowerment in a diverse society.* Ontario, CA: California Association for Bilingual Education.

Douville, P., & Wood, K. D. (2001). Collaborative learning strategies in diverse classrooms. In V. J. Risko & K. Bromley, *Collaborative strategies for diverse learners: Viewpoints and practices.* Newark, DE: International Reading Association.

Fong, T. P. (1998). *The contemporary Asian American experience: Beyond the model minority.* Upper Saddle River, NJ: Prentice Hall.

Foster, M. (1992). Sociolinguistics and the African-American community: Implications for literacy. *Theory into Practice, 31*(4), 303–311.

Gollnick, D. M., & Chinn, P. C. (1998). *Multicultural education in a pluralistic society* (5th ed.). Upper Saddle River, NJ: Prentice Hall.

Gougeon, T. D. (1993). Urban schools and immigrant families: Teacher perspectives. *Urban Review, 25*(4), 251–287.

Heath, S. B. (1983). *Ways with words: Language, life and work in communities and classrooms.* New York: Cambridge University Press.

Huang, L. N. (1989). Southeast Asian refugee children and adolescents. In G. T. Gibbs & L. J. Huang (Eds.), *Children of color: Psychological interventions with minority youth* (pp. 278–321). San Francisco: Jossey-Bass.

Indian mascot opponents pleased. (2001, April 15). *New York Times,* Sports Section, p. 6.

Kang, H. W., Kuehn, P., & Herrell, A. (1994). The Hmong literacy project: A study of Hmong classroom behavior. *Bilingual Research Journal, 18* (3 & 4), 63–68.

Kemble, W. J. (2000a, April 26). State education official praises Onteora's Indian mascot vote. *Daily Freeman,* p. A3.

Kemble, W. J. (2000b, August 3). State warns of consequence of keeping Indian mascot. *Daily Freeman,* pp. A1, A4.

Kemble, W. J. (2001a, April 6). "Indian" days are numbered. *Daily Freeman,* pp. A1, A4.

Kemble, W. J. (2001b, April 14). No more Indian names, civil rights panel urges. *Daily Freeman,* pp. A1, A8.

Kemble, W. J. (2001c, April 25). Onteora duo wants "Indian" off May ballot. *Daily Freeman,* pp. A1, A6.

King, J. E. (1991). Dysconscious racism: Ideology, identity, and miseducation of teachers. *Journal of Negro Education, 60*(2), 133–146.

Kitano, H. H. L., & Daniels, R. (1995). *Asian Americans: Emerging minorities* (2nd ed.). Upper Saddle River, NJ: Prentice Hall.

Loewen, J. W. (1995). *Lies my teacher told me: Everything your American history textbook got wrong.* New York: Simon & Schuster.

Ment, J. (2000, January 23). Indian mascots draw criticism. *Daily Freeman,* pp. A1, A8.

McDermott, R. (1997). Achieving school failure: 1972–1997 (3rd ed.). In G. D. Spindler (Ed.), *Education and cultural process: Anthropological approaches* (pp. 110–135). Prospect Heights, IL: Waveland Press.

Merino, B. J., Trueba, J. T., & Samaniego, F. A. (1993). Toward a framework for the study of the maintenance of the home language in language minority students. In B. J. Merino, H. T. Trueba, & F. A. Samaniego (Eds.), *Language and culture in learning: Teaching Spanish to native speakers of Spanish* (pp. 5–25). Washington, DC: Falmer Press.

Molin, P. F. (1999). American Indian mascots in sports. In A. Hirschfelder, P. F. Molin, & Y. Wakim (Eds.), *American Indian stereotypes in the world of children: A reader and bibliography* (2nd ed.) (pp. 175–184). Lantham, MD: Scarecrow Press.

Nieto, S. (2000). *Affirming diversity: The sociopolitical context of multicultural education* (3rd ed.). New York: Longman.

Pang, V. O. (1990). Asian American children: A diverse population. *Educational Forum, 55*(1), 49–65.

Pang, V. O., & Evans, R. W. (1995). Caring for Asian Pacific American students in the social studies classroom. *Social Studies and the Young Learner, 7*(4), 11–14.

Pewewardy, C. (1999). From enemy to mascot: The deculturation of Indian mascots in sports culture. *Canadian Journal of Native Education, 23,* 176–189.

Ramirez, J. D. (1992). Executive summary. *Bilingual Research Journal, 16* (1 & 2), 1–63.

Rumbaut, R. G. (1995). Vietnamese, Laotian, and Cambodian Americans. In P. G. Min (Ed.), *Asian Americans: Contemporary trends and issues* (pp. 232–270). Thousand Oaks, CA: Sage.

Siddle Walker, E. V. (1992). Falling asleep and failure among African-American students: Rethinking assumptions about process teaching. *Theory into Practice, 31,* 321–327.

Sleeter, C. E., & Grant, C. A. (1999). *Making choices for multicultural education: Five approaches to race, class, and gender* (3rd ed.). Upper Saddle River, NJ: Prentice Hall.

Smith, D. D. (2001). *Introduction to special education: Teaching in an age of opportunity* (4th ed.). Boston: Allyn and Bacon.

Snow, C. (1993). Bilingualism and second language acquisition. In J. B. Gleason and N. Ratner (Eds.), *Psycholinguistics* (pp. 392–416). Fort Worth, TX: Harcourt Brace.

Spilky, S. (2001, April 8). Dancing with critics. *New York Times,* Education Life Supplement, p. 12.

Spring, J. (1994). *Deculturalization and the struggle for equality: A brief history of the education of dominated cultures in the United States.* New York: McGraw-Hill.

Staurowsky, E. J. (1999). American Indian imagery and the miseducation of America. *Quest, 51,* 382–392.

Suárez-Orozco, C., & Suárez-Orozco, M. M. (2001). *Children of immigration.* Cambridge, MA: Harvard University Press.

Thomas, W. P., & Collier, V. P. (1997). *School effectiveness for language minority students.* Washington, DC: National Clearinghouse for Bilingual Education.

Trueba, H. T. (1993). Culture and language: The ethnographic approach to the study of learning environments. In B. J. Merino, H. T. Trueba, & F. A. Samaniego (Eds.), *Language and culture in learning: Teaching Spanish to native speakers of Spanish* (pp. 26–44). Washington, DC: Falmer Press.

Trueba, H. T., Jacobs, L, & Kirton, E. (1990). *Cultural conflict and adaptation: The case of Hmong children in American society.* New York: Falmer Press.

Twine, R. (2000, February 8). "Indian" fans lose bid for referendum. *Daily Freeman,* pp. A1, A6.

U.S. Census Bureau. (1990). *Census of the population of the United States.* Washington, DC: Bureau of the Census.

Wan, Y. (1996). *Bearing the image of model minority: An inside look behind the classroom door.* Paper presented at the National Association for Multicultural Education, Sixth Annual Conference, San Diego, CA. (ERIC Document Reproduction Service No. ED 404 432.)

Werthamer, C. (2000, February 9). Students who cut classes for petition drive are suspended. *Daily Freeman,* pp. A1–A2.

CHAPTER 8

EXCEPTIONALITY

The term *exceptionality* has been used in the education field to refer to students who are recognized as disabled or gifted and are eligible for services under the Individuals with Disabilities Education Act (IDEA), 1990, or the 1988 Gifted and Talented Students Education Act (P.L. 100-297) Gifted and Talented Act. IDEA defines a student with a disability as one who meets the criteria specified by at least one of the following classification areas: specific learning disabilities, speech or language impairments, mental retardation, serious emotional disturbance, autism, hearing impairments, multiple disabilities, orthopedic impairments, other health impairments, visual impairments, deaf-blindness, or traumatic brain injury (Salend, 2001). P.L. 100-297, on the other hand, applies to students who are described as gifted and talented. These are students who possess demonstrated or potential high-performance capability in intellectual, creative, specific academic, and leadership areas or in the performing and visual arts and require services or activities not ordinarily provided by the school to develop such capabilities (Friend & Bursuck, 1999).

IDEA, because of its specificity, is a more powerful piece of legislation than P.L. 100-297. It mandates that all students that meet the definitions are entitled to a free, appropriate public education regardless of the nature and severity of the disability. Each student has an individual education program (IEP) based on a multifactored assessment of his or her strengths and weaknesses. In contrast, P.L. 100-297 does not mandate specific services for gifted and talented students; therefore, programs depend more on the legislation and allocations made by individual states and the types of programs developed by school districts.

ISSUES OF DEFINITION, IDENTIFICATION, AND APPROPRIATE PROGRAMS

Many have questioned the system that these laws have created (Dunn, 1968; Sailor & Skritic, 1995; Wang & Reynolds, 1997). IDEA requires that students be assessed using multiple standardized or criterion-referenced assessments

156

and that a team of individuals determine whether the child is eligible for services. Of course, there is a fair amount of controversy about the criteria and scope of the definitions stated in the laws for a number of reasons. These include the stigma that a label can engender, the varying interpretations of the definitions, the reliability and validity of the assessments used to determine eligibility, and the lengthy process involved in referral, assessment, and program determinations. Yet the law provides services that are available only to those students who go through this process. Prior to the enactment of IDEA, many students were not receiving an appropriate education and some were not being educated at all. This law has changed that situation dramatically, but some or all of the previously mentioned problems can affect its participants.

Another serious issue regarding identification is the disproportionate representation of minority students in special education. For example, data from the U.S. Department of Education (1998) show that while approximately 17 percent of the school population is African American, African Americans make up the following percentages of students in the following special education categories: mental retardation (31%), emotionally disturbed (25%), and learning disabled (17%). This means that nationally, black students are two and a half times more likely to be identified as having mild mental retardation and about one and a half times more likely to have behavioral disorder when compared to their peers (Oswald, Coutinho, Best, & Singh, 1999). Considerable debate surrounds this issue given the multiple factors involved (Reschly, 1997; Patton, 1998). As discussed in Chapter 2, the achievement of African American students and Hispanic students falls behind that of their peers. This must be placed in the context of the relatively low income of many of these students and the higher incidence of disabilities associated with poverty, often due to poor health care and environmental factors.

Some groups are underrepresented in special education (Burnette, 1998). For example, Asian–Pacific Islanders are underrepresented in the categories of learning disabilities, mental retardation, and emotional disturbance, and Hispanics are underrepresented in the categories of mental retardation and emotional disturbance, (see Table 8.1) (Smith, 2001). Given the data on overrepresentation and underrepresentation, the U.S. Office of Special Education Programs and the U.S. Office for Civil Rights are concerned that students may be unserved, receive inappropriate services, or be misclassified and that their placement in special education may be a form of discrimination. To address these problems, it is critical that schools offer early intervention programs, promote family involvement, make the general education classroom conducive to success for all children, increase the accuracy of referral and evaluation, provide and monitor appropriate services, and include the community in policy-making bodies (Burnette, 1998).

As with students with disabilities, students who are gifted also face problematic situations. Presently, about two-thirds of the states are mandating

TABLE 8.1   Percentage and Number of Students in Special Education by Race–Ethnicity and Disability: 1994

	WHITE, NON-HISPANIC	BLACK, NON-HISPANIC	HISPANIC	AMERICAN INDIAN	ASIAN–PACIFIC ISLANDER	TOTAL
Learning disabilities	5.7% 1,287,918	5.7% 407,848	5.7% 308,136	7.3% 32,413	2.0% 31,968	5.5% 2,368,283
Mental retardation	1.2% 350,699	2.6% 109,885	0.9% 50,091	1.6% 7,152	0.5% 8,197	1.4% 607,024
Emotional disturbance	0.8% 214,442	1.1% 80,253	0.5% 25,514	0.9% 4,227	0.2% 2,786	0.8% 327,222
Total student population by race–ethnicity	28,039,068	7,193,038	5,425,976	445,105	1,588,124	42,691,311

Source: U.S. Department of Education, Office for Civil Rights, 1994 Elementary and Secondary School Compliance Reports; as reported in *Twentieth Annual Report to Congress on the Implementation of the Individuals with Disabilities Education Act,* U.S. Department of Education, 1998.

either identification of or services for students who are gifted (Turnbull, Turnbull, Shank, & Leal, 1999). Individual districts determine an identification system for students who are gifted, and such assessments may include IQ tests; standardized achievement test scores; teacher-, parent-, peer-, and self-nomination; and evaluation of students' work or performance (Hallahan & Kauffman, 1997). Researchers are concerned that assessments do not always take into account the effects of language, culture, and socioeconomic status, so the reliability and validity of the assessment instruments are questioned. Presently, African Americans, Hispanics, Hawaiians, and Native American students are underrepresented in gifted education (Ford, 1998).

Another issue associated with defining exceptionality is the question of whether such a concept exists at all. Some view exceptionality as a social construct based on a determination by the dominant members of society of what is normal or acceptable behavior. By determining that some individuals are exceptional, it is possible to place differing values on them as people and consequently limit or enhance their access to educational programs. Rather than view the individual as abnormal, it is argued that society can change its physical, financial, governmental, and educational structures to accommodate the needs of all within the society. Such an approach would be based on a system that would provide services based on educational need, rather than on the numbers of individuals that fit into a definition category.

THE INCLUSION CONTROVERSY

A recent manifestation of this controversy regarding definitions and appropriate educational services is the inclusion movement. Lipsky and Gartner (1996) have defined inclusion as the "provision of services to students with disabilities, including those with severe impairments, in general education classes, with the necessary support services and supplementary aids (for the child and teacher) both to assure the child's success—academic, behavioral and social—and to prepare the child to participate as a full and contributing member of the society" (p. 763). Furthermore, inclusive schools are to espouse a philosophy that everyone belongs and is accepted by peers and other members of the school community (Stainback, Stainback, & Stefanich, 1996). While this definition emphasizes the need for supportive services from special education personnel, some charge that inclusion is merely the dumping of special education students into the general education classroom without the assistance of a special education teacher (Fuchs & Fuchs, 1994; Smelter, Rasch, & Yudevitz, 1994) and without differentiation of curriculum or instructional practices (MacMillan, Gresham, & Forness, 1996).

In analyzing this debate, we can appeal to the law and legal precedents, to research on the outcomes of inclusion, and to philosophical and ethical considerations. IDEA mandates that students be placed in the least restrictive environment with proper supplementary aids and services (Etscheidt & Bartlett, 1999). States must assure that, to the maximum extent appropriate, students with disabilities are educated with children who do not have disabilities, and that removal from the general education classroom occur only when the disability is so severe that the curriculum and instruction of the general education classroom cannot be adapted to achieve satisfactory results (McLeskey, Henry, & Axelrod, 1999). Furthermore, the rulings in the overwhelming number of cases in which parents have sued school districts to keep children with more severe disabilities in the general education classroom have been settled in favor of the family (Etscheidt & Bartlett, 1999; Yell & Shriner, 1996).

Those who have examined the rapidly accumulating body of research related to inclusive schooling have generally concluded that the effect of inclusion on the academic and social performance of students with disabilities is mixed (Salend, 2001; Salend & Duhaney, 1999). When inclusion is properly implemented, rather than seen as a way to cut costs by eliminating special education personnel, the majority of studies yield positive results in a variety of areas (Moore, Gilbreath, & Maiuri, 1998; Scruggs & Mastropieri, 1996). Placing students with disabilities in general education and providing structures that promote positive peer interactions result in improved social competence and communication skills (McGregor & Vogelsberg, 1998). Friendship is facilitated by long-term membership in the class and school activities. However, the degree of social acceptance experienced by students with disabilities often varies depending on the degree of severity of the disability, the age of the student, and the teacher's ability to promote positive social interaction and differentiate instruction (Roberts & Zubrick, 1992; Sale & Carey, 1995; Salend, 2001).

Similarly, studies on the academic performance of students with disabilities show varied results. Research indicates that students with mild disabilities can show positive achievement gains in the general education classroom (Baker, Wang, & Walberg, 1995; Jenkins et al., 1992; Lipsky & Gartner, 1996; Moore, Gilbreath, & Maiuri, 1998). These gains are apparent on standardized test scores, reading performance, mastery of IEP goals, and grades (Salend, 2001). However, there continues to be strong reservations by teachers, researchers, and professional organizations about the suitability of providing services in the regular classroom, including for students with learning disabilities (Vaughn & Schumm, 1995), students with severe disabilities (Scruggs & Mastropieri, 1996), and students who are gifted and talented (Gurcsik, 1998; Kearney, 1996). Much of this concern is related to the degree to which general education teachers have the knowledge, time for planning and collaboration, and willingness to differentiate instruction for students of all abilities. Students with mild disabilities who are not given "specially designed instruction" in inclusion programs may perform better academically in pull-out resource programs (Baker & Zigmond, 1995; Marston, 1996; Manset & Semmel, 1997). Reports involving students with moderate to severe disabilities indicate higher levels of academic engagement and participation in academic content areas than in segregated classrooms (Hunt, Farron-Davis, Beckstead, Curtis, & Goetz, 1994; Ryndak, Jacqueline, & Morison, 1995). Finally, the effects on typical peers in inclusive classrooms have been positive in that their academic performance has not been compromised, they improve in social cognition, and they benefit from the instructional strategies and organizational approaches that teachers initiate in inclusive classrooms (Manset & Semmel, 1997; McGregor & Vogelsberg, 1998).

Perhaps the most intractable aspect of the inclusion controversy is the philosophical issues involved. In fact, Paul and Ward (1996) would argue that the conflicts are essentially paradigmatic rather than scientific. They categorize those who question inclusion as part of a comparison paradigm that uses quantitative data to compare different settings to determine the most appropriate placement based on academic and social criteria. Those on the other side of the debate are characterized as being part of an ethics paradigm, who see inclusion as a moral right for all students and who use primarily qualitative data to answer the question of how we can reduce barriers to inclusion. Given the very different nature of the research questions asked and methods employed, as well as the disparate views of what is morally imperative, there appears to be little promise that these sides will find much room for compromise.

CREATING INCLUSIVE SCHOOLS FOR STUDENTS WITH DISABILITIES

Despite the ongoing controversies, school districts are faced with the realities of implementing school programs in ways that are satisfactory to the stakeholders involved: student, parents, and teachers. We have already discussed the responses of students with and without disabilities. In general, parents have been supportive of the inclusion movement, especially because of the greater acceptance by peers and elevated self-esteem that their children experience (McGregor & Vogelsberg, 1998). Parents who oppose inclusion question the level of individual attention available in an inclusive classroom. Those who are initially hesitant to see their child moved to a less segregated environment have usually been pleased with the positive results for their child by the end of a school year if the teachers are able to differentiate instruction.

When inclusion was first introduced, many general teachers were skeptical, if not negative, about having students with disabilities in the classroom. They felt they were unprepared to respond to the range of student needs, because they were used to planning for the whole class, relied primarily on large-group instruction, and saw adaptations as more desirable than feasible. However, most research indicates that having students with disabilities in the classroom increased the teachers' ownership and involvement with the students and willingness to try it again (Giangreco, Dennis, Cloninger, Edelman, & Schattman, 1993). In fact, teachers who believe that they have received adequate training, resources, time for collaboration, and administrative support are genuinely positive about inclusion (Moore, Gilbreath, & Maiuri, 1998; Villa, Thousand, Meyers, & Nevin, 1996). Regrettably, this level of support has not been made available in all districts.

For teachers, the question becomes one of differentiating the curriculum and instruction in a manner that is both effective and feasible, given the time and resources available. Although researchers have suggested many different strategies for designing more inclusive classrooms, there are some broad areas of agreement as to what these approaches should encompass (McGregor & Vogelsberg, 1998; Moore, Gilbreath, & Maiuri, 1998; Wang & Reynolds, 1997). First, diversity must become the new norm, given the changing racial, economic, and linguistic characteristics of our population. Therefore, classrooms will become less homogeneous. Second, teachers will need to work more collaboratively with teams of professionals to plan and implement appropriate programs. In addition, students will be better served when they are working collaboratively in small groups or pairs (Logan, Bakeman,

& Keefe, 1997) and when instruction is active, meaningful, and integrated and promotes problem solving (Monda-Amaya & Pearson, 1996; Zemelman, Daniels, & Hyde, 1993). Third, flexible school structures must be implemented, such as alternative scheduling, multiage classrooms, or schools within schools. Finally, assessment must be authentic and performance based. This is certainly possible on the classroom level, but becomes increasingly difficult given state mandates that require that all students pass the same tests. Fortunately, these suggestions for inclusive schools are in alignment with the goals of many school restructuring plans and can be implemented as part of the overall school program, thereby benefiting all students.

Certainly, student differences in learning style and cognition necessitate differentiation of approach. For example, the literature on metacognition indicates that some students, including those with learning disabilities, must be taught specific strategies for learning (Deshler & Schumaker, 1986). These strategies assist students in everyday academic tasks, such as comprehending text, writing narrative and expository text, taking notes, solving a mathematical word problem, or taking a test. Once students learn and utilize strategies, they often show academic progress. Furthermore, teachers must be able to modify instruction in terms of interest level, amount of content, complexity, performance criteria, material used, and level of assistance (Kame'enui & Simmons, 1999; Lenz & Schumaker, 1999; Schumm, 1999). While such considerations may appear to involve a high degree of individualization, it is less so if special education and general education teachers work together on initial planning so that lessons incorporate some of these approaches up front and require less adjustments after the fact (Heron & Jorgenson, 1994; Udvari-Solner, 1995).

Another group of students that must be considered are the gifted and talented, who often are stuck in the inflexible age–grade classrooms of most public schools. Kearney (1996) points out that schools must provide intellectual access for gifted students to the full range of the curriculum. However, multiple issues related to identification, assessment, and programming must be recognized by those planning inclusive school programs.

ISSUES IN THE EDUCATION OF STUDENTS WHO ARE GIFTED AND TALENTED

School programs for students who are gifted and talented have increasingly come under attack for failing to identify, include, and appropriately serve an expanding list of students. In fact, because many gifted programs have been havens for upper-middle-class white students, some would suggest that this may be a subtle form of racial and ethnic discrimination (Gallagher, 1995). There are adequate data to confirm that many students of color are underrepresented in programs for gifted learners (U.S. Department of Education, 1993). About half of the proportion of black and Hispanic students in the general population are represented in programs for gifted students on the elementary and middle school levels, whereas Asian students are overrepresented (Gallagher, 1995; Patton, 1997). Likewise, students who are bilingual or limited English proficient often are not included in such programs (Barkan & Bernal, 1991). Not all inequities relate to race or language. For example, girls still have not been equally represented in advanced mathematics classes (Gallagher, 1995; Reis & Callahan, 1989). Not surprisingly, low socioeconomic status also is a factor in the exclusion of children from programs for the gifted (Frasier, 1991).

Causes of Underrepresentation

There are multiple reasons for these discrepancies: limiting definitions of giftedness, assessment measure and techniques that are not culturally sensitive, inadequate preparation of teachers in issues and practices appropriate for the multicultural school population, and negative stereotypes and inaccurate perceptions of the abilities of children of color (Maker, 1996; Patton, 1997; Tomlinson, Callahan, & Lelli, 1997). The issue of identification and assessment is particularly thorny. Although there has been a paradigm shift in gifted education, which views intelligence as having multiple forms and as being developmental and process-oriented, rather than stable and unchangeable, there remains a need to develop and implement inexpensive, valid, and reliable measure of the abilities found in a variety of cultural and linguistic groups (Frasier, 1991; Maker, 1996; Rueda, 1997). The still common reliance on IQ scores and teacher nomination has effectively precluded the classification of many students, and even the use of checklists designed for diverse and disadvantaged populations, quota systems, and a matrix to weigh data from multiple sources has not changed disproportionate representation (Frasier, 1991; Johnson, 1994).

The identification process must be guided by a knowledge of culture, language, values, and the world view of culturally and linguistically diverse learners and their parents (Patton, 1997). Evaluators need sensitivity to intragroup differences within each group as well. It is becoming increasingly evident that intelligence must be studied by observing how individuals recognize and solve problems in their own environment from a young age, and several researchers are pursuing the development of such tools (Frasier, 1991; Maker, 1996; Tomlinson, Callahan, & Lelli, 1997).

Teacher Attitudes and Family Involvement

Even with improved identification procedures, children from culturally and linguistically diverse groups have not always been successful in programs because their behavior did not fit with the teacher's beliefs about giftedness or the behavior of the child (Barkan & Bernal, 1991; Ishii-Jordan, 1997; Maker, 1996). For example, it is assumed that a child must have attained a certain level of English proficiency before he or she can be considered for gifted education. The same framework that guides new assessments must guide program development or students who are not high achievers in the traditional curriculum will receive inappropriate instruction, become frustrated, and fail or drop out.

Family involvement is a definite factor in the achievement of gifted students of color. Clark (1983) found that black students from low socioeconomic groups who were achieving had parents who were assertive in parent involvement efforts, kept track of their child's progress, and perceived themselves as having effective coping mechanisms. These parents set high and realistic expectations for their children, held achievement-oriented norms and role boundaries, engaged in experiences that promoted achievement, and had positive parent–child relations. However, parent educational level does not appear to be a predictor of gifted student's academic performance (Ford & Thomas, 1997).

Programming for Gifted and Talented Students

Gifted education is still struggling to determine the extent to which gifted learners can thrive in the regular education classroom (Tomlinson, Coleman, Allan, Udall, & Landrum, 1996). Differences have emerged over instructional and programmatic models such as acceleration, heterogeneous groups, cooperative learning, block scheduling, and the middle school concept. Furthermore, there is great concern that few programs exist for young gifted learners.

Academic acceleration is one alternative for precocious youth that has been supported in the research literature as positive (Kulik & Kulik, 1984; Van Tassel-Baska, 1991). However, many educational practitioners appear to be unaware of this research and, relying on common sense and little personal experience, report being opposed to acceleration (Southern, Jones, & Fiscus, 1989). Their concerns seem to center around potentially hurrying the child through school and risks to social and emotional development. Admittedly, the effect of acceleration on affect has not been well researched for various types of acceleration and the particular age of the child (Cornell, Callahan, Bassin, & Ramsay, 1991; Van Tassel-Baska, 1991). However, it appears that careful screening for social and emotional maturity, as well as academic aptitude, can assist in making a decision for or against acceleration in the primary grades (Cornell et al., 1991; Feldhusen, Proctor, & Black, 1986).

Cooperative learning has been questioned by some in gifted education as inappropriate for, if not exploitive of, students who are gifted (Gurcsik, 1998). It is charged that cooperative learning provides training in cooperation at the expense of learning higher-order thinking skills and challenging content. Others would counter that students who are gifted can benefit academically and socially from being involved in cooperative learning activities (Sapon-Shevin, 1995). Many cooperative learning structures do promote higher-order thinking skills. Furthermore, using cooperative learning in the classroom does not preclude the use of other instructional strategies, such as curriculum compacting, independent projects, mentoring, thematic instruction, and enrichment clusters (Buckner, 1997). In fact, these strategies should be incorporated into all classrooms.

A final area of concern is a dearth of programming for young students who are gifted and little research on programs that do exist. When programs are nonexistent, concerned parents can only request that teachers provide changes in curriculum and approach for their child. Unfortunately, teachers are not always receptive to parental requests that their gifted child receive curriculum modifications, especially when the child may present challenging social behaviors (Mooij, 1999). When a more engaging curriculum for the gifted learner is absent, young children can react with negative emotions toward teachers and school as well as become underachievers. However, children who show precocity even in kindergarten can be encouraged by allowing them to pursue their academic interests, work with one or more other students or projects or alone, and accomplish tasks that promote independence and responsibility. If students are reading, writing, or pursuing other learning experiences that typically are introduced in later grades, Mooij would argue that access to materials and resources should be provided, as well as stimulation of developmental activities and free play.

One program that shows promise for gifted students in general education is the Enrichment Triad Model (Beecher, 1995; Buckner, 1997; Renzulli & Reis, 1997), a model that establishes three types of activities in the classroom. Type I activities, such as guest speakers, performances, and field trips, are designed to make connections to the regular curriculum. In addition, all students are involved in creative thinking and problem-solving activities (Type II). Then Type III enrichment activities allow students to apply their interests and knowledge by pursuing a self-selected area for independent or group study.

In addition, several instructional approaches and model programs have been developed for students of color and those from low economic backgrounds who are gifted (Ford & Thomas, 1997). Some approaches suggest that students experience success when curricula and instruction are designed to be culturally and linguistically compatible (Cummins, 1986; Tharp & Gallimore, 1988; Tharp, 1989). Instruction and projects that can be accomplished using multiple intelligences and concept-based instruction also hold promise for these students (Armstrong, 1994). Results from one model have demonstrated that gifted children of color, particularly those who come from low-income backgrounds, flourish when they are involved in a mentorship

program and when their family attends family outreach programs (Tomlinson, Callahan, & Lelli, 1997). During this program, children met weekly with an adult mentor who exposed the child to new ideas and experiences and encouraged thinking skills, perseverance, and self-esteem. In addition, parents attended and appreciated a variety of programs that allowed them to take part in activities with their children and gave them ideas for becoming more effective parents. Another promising practice is the development of early programs designed to stimulate cognitive, mathematical, and perceptual abilities for minority and low-income children while they are still in preschool (Gallagher, 1995).

While there continues to be a need for research on how best to identify and serve children who are identified as disabled or gifted and talented, this much that is already known is not being applied in districts across the country. Whether the reasons are a lack of knowledge, resources, legislative mandates, or political support, many students will not reach the educational levels that they are capable of unless schools rethink their identification procedures and program models.

ISSUES IN THE EDUCATION OF STUDENTS WITH ATTENTION DEFICIT HYPERACTIVITY DISORDER

Another area of the field of special education that has engendered great controversy in the last 10 years is the assessment and treatment of attention-deficit/hyperactivity disorder (AD/HD). AD/HD is the most commonly diagnosed childhood psychiatric disorder in the United States (Turnbull, Turnbull, Shank, & Leal, 1999). AD/HD is defined as "a persistent pattern of inattention and/or hyperactivity–impulsivity that is more frequent and severe than is typically observed in individuals at a comparable level of development" (American Psychiatric Association, 1994, p. 78). The symptoms must have been present before the age of 7, be present in at least two settings, and show clear interference with developmentally appropriate functioning.

There are three subtypes of AD/HD. The predominantly inattentive type describes children who have difficulty paying attention, appear apathetic, seem internally occupied, are socially neglected, may be anxious or depressed, and are often underachievers (Barkley, 1990; Lahey & Carlson, 1991). The predominantly hyperactive–impulsive type includes children who often talk excessively, have difficulty sitting still, often challenge boundaries, interrupt and blurt out answers, and can be accident prone (Turnbull, Turnbull, Shank, & Leal, 1999). This type is most frequently observed in young children who often challenge parents' child-rearing skills (Aust, 1994). Children who are described as having the combined type may be inattentive as well as hyperactive and impulsive.

The identification and treatment of children with AD/HD has been particularly controversial. In 1995 the Drug Enforcement Administration reported that the U.S. production and use of Ritalin, the stimulant most frequently used to treat AD/HD, had increased sixfold since 1990 (Hadnot, 1997). Furthermore, the United States consumes 80 percent of the world's supply of Ritalin. Children and Adults with Attention Deficit Disorders (Ch.A.D.D), an organization that provides advocacy and education about AD/HD, estimates that 3 to 5 percent of the school-aged population has AD/HD, but in some areas of the country, particularly urban areas, the percentages are much higher (Turnbull, Turnbull, Shank, & Leal, 1999). While some argue that this increase is due to an awareness of the condition, others believe the drug is overprescribed and are concerned about possible side effects, such as insomnia, headaches, irritability, moodiness, nausea, and weight loss. They also wonder if the fact that two to four times as many boys as girls are diagnosed is related to teacher perception of acceptable behavior.

Diagnosis of AD/HD is fairly complicated, because identification depends on the use of several assessments, including behavior rating scales, a medical history, functional assessment, continuous performance tests, and parent and teacher reports (Reid & Maag, 1998; Turnbull, Turnbull, Shank, & Leal, 1999). Cultural, ethnic, and economic factors can result in overdiagnosis or underdiagnosis (Reid, 1995; Williams, Lerner, Wigal, & Swanson, 1995). Overdiagnosis may occur because some students have activity levels that are different from same-aged peers in the majority culture. Furthermore, some of the characteristics of AD/HD are also found in students who are depressed or live in chaotic homes or potentially violent situations (Salend, 2001). Students who may be underdiagnosed include those who do not have access to health care and girls. In addition, gifted children who have AD/HD pose a different set of challenges regarding identification and treatment (Guenther, 1995; Lovecky, 1999).

Some students with AD/HD will be identified as needing special education services under IDEA, some may receive reasonable accommodations under Section 504 of the Rehabilitation Act, and others will not receive any support through federally mandated laws. Nevertheless, general education teachers will need to determine how to assist these students in learning. At present, researchers believe that children who take some combination of stimulants or other medications for AD/HD should show signs of improvement relatively quickly, or the regiment or diagnosis should be reevaluated (Schlozman & Schlozman, 2000). Stimulant medication can improve ability to control motor behavior, increase concentration, improve self-regulation, decrease aggression, and increase the amount and accuracy of work (Swanson et al., 1993; Prater & Pancheri, 1999). However, there may not be significant improvement of specific skills, such as reading or social skills. Likewise, stimulants may not result in long-term improvement of academic achievement.

Therefore, educators should strongly consider interventions such as behavior management, organizational training, counseling, peer tutoring, and task modifications (DuPaul & Eckert, 1998; Prater & Pancheri, 1999; Turnbull, Turnbull, Shank, & Leal, 1999; Schlozman & Schlozman, 2000; Salend, 2001). Finally, it is essential that parents, physicians, teachers, school nurse, and counselors collaborate to evaluate the effectiveness of all interventions.

Special education and gifted education have undergone dramatic changes in the past 25 years. Understanding the research and issues that influence educators, parents, and communities today as they attempt to provide services for students who are exceptional will be critical for designing successful outcomes for individuals such as those in the case studies that follow.

THE CASE OF SELINA JAMES

It was 8:34 A.M. and Carol, the social worker; Yvonne, the art teacher; Lillian, the reading specialist; and Sharon, the computer lab teacher, were gathered around a table with me. We were making small talk: Lillian's new home, Yvonne's daughter's dance lessons, weekend plans, the school board elections. I looked toward the door, wishing that I would see Norma, a first grade teacher and the only teacher of color on the faculty, coming through it. I felt her presence was important to the outcome of the meeting.

Carol began, "I think we should start even though Norma isn't here yet. Ann Elliott has asked me to call this Student Review Team meeting to discuss Selina James. As all of you know, Selina is a very bright kindergartner whose reading skills far surpass most of the students in Ann's class. I thought we should start by having Ann explain her concerns about Selina."

"Selina doesn't present the typical scenario for calling a meeting, but I think it's important that we address her needs as well as those who struggle academically. Selina is a gifted student; there's no doubt about that. She can read books that are on a second or third grade level independently. With help, she has been reading even more complex texts. Once she learns to read and spell a word she doesn't forget it. And her comprehension is exceptional. She can retell a story with all the important events in sequence. It's even more impressive when you realize she was born in August and, although she doesn't look it, is one of the youngest five-year-olds in the class."

Norma walked through the door and took a seat. She looked striking in her dress and heels, but I knew that the night before she had been directing the youth choir at the neighborhood African Methodist Episcopal Church and inside she was dragging.

"I am concerned that I am not challenging Selina enough. She thrives on adult attention, but I just don't have the time to devote to her exclusively very often and none of the other children are close to her reading level. I have given her permission to read whatever books she chooses from the library and she reads voraciously. I've also asked her to tutor some of the children who need assistance, but I don't want to take advantage of her in that way. I try to listen to her read when I have a few spare minutes and she loves the attention. In fact, she loves being able to read to any adult who will listen.

"But I'm not sure that these things are enough, and it's starting to show up in her relationships with other children. For example, last week Bridgett was showing me a wonderful picture of a lion in the cage that she had drawn, and I complimented her saying, 'You're a good artist, Bridgett!' Immediately, Selina chimed in and said, 'But I'm a GREAT artist!' I'm glad she's proud of her own accomplishments—she has every reason to be—but I don't want her to build her own self-esteem at the expense of other children."

This is how I presented Selina's case to the team last Friday. I'm still unsure about which of their recommendations I can live with. We have a policy at Stevenson Elementary that the team can make any suggestions that they may think of, but the teacher directly involved ultimately decides whether the ideas are workable. Possible suggestions that included involving Selina in circle time in Norma's first grade classroom two days a week, including her in the afterschool book group sponsored by the librarian, having an older child or adult carry on an e-mail conversation with her weekly, contacting community youth theater or music programs to see if Selina could receive a scholarship, and promoting her to second grade next year.

The latter suggestion was the most extreme option, and I'm just not sure I could live with the ramifications of such a move. The long-term social implications of promotions are serious: Selina would be a senior at 16. However, I did like the idea of her becoming involved in the first grade circle activity if Norma and I can coordinate it. The afterschool book discussion is a great idea if Selina's parents will allow her to stay. The e-mail idea is a good one, but our school has e-mail within, not among, classes right now. It is difficult to get a child to consistently come to the room and write Selina a message. The theater group may not have scholarships; they are struggling to stay afloat.

These are the alternatives that have been swimming through my head over the last few days. We're having a follow-up meeting next Monday and I have to decide which of these options we should pursue. As I look at the diverse needs of the class I have this year, sometimes I feel like I should have a Student Review Team meeting each week on a different child. There are 10 white, 8 African American, 1 Hispanic, and 4 biracial children in the class. Thirteen are boys and 10 are girls. But these statistics are only an obvious way of looking at the children's diversity.

This is my twenty-fourth year of teaching in Howard City Schools, with 14 of them spent in kindergarten. Although I have many years of instructional ideas to draw on and adequate materials and supplies, it seems that I never have enough human resources to call on. I am fortunate to have had Donna, my teaching assistant, with me full time for 4 years now and can count on her to reinforce the instruction that I deliver. Isabella Myers, the consultant teacher, comes in for 45 minutes every day during language arts time, so we can do some small-group work then. I'm thankful for her help, but that's a small part of the day.

A teacher and a teaching assistant just can't get around to 23 students adequately when their social and cognitive skills range from 3 to 8 or 9 years old. Two children were retained last year and now are in kindergarten again since we don't have a "transition" class. Right now there are 10 students who have IEPs in my classroom, with labels including learning disabled, emotionally disturbed, and mentally retarded. Four students had been in preschool special education programs before they entered kindergarten, but since two had received those services and then were removed from special education, I didn't see their files and didn't know until I asked the parents directly. Two children aren't in special education, but do receive speech services. I'm hoping that the IEP team will agree that at least three students no longer need services this spring at the annual review since they've made considerable progress.

I love my students, but some of them can really be a challenge. Take Shakeem, for example. His dark brown eyes are beguiling, yet he sometimes has tears running down his chocolate cheeks. He came to me at the beginning of the year with behaviors that were typical of a 3-year-old. He would crawl around the room, scream, and have tantrums. Initially, we had to remove him several times a day from the classroom. He had been in a special education preschool and still is receiving services in my classroom. In September he knew none of his letters and sounds and now, in March, he knows about half of them. During journal time, he still prefers to draw. He'll try writing the alphabet independently if he's in a good mood, but he needs one-on-one assistance to write a word, much less a sentence. The one thing that keeps him on task for long periods of time is the computer. He's learned concepts, like "same" and "different," and most of the letters and sounds of the alphabet that he knows from computer programs. However, he's come a long way in the area of social skills and tantrums are rare.

Then there is Larry. He also received special education services during his preschool years and still has an IEP. At the beginning of the year he seemed like just a small, pale face hiding behind his glasses; he wouldn't talk at all. Then there would be days when he would kick or pinch Donna. He's talking now, but he's made minimal improvement on reading skills. He only knows about five letter sounds consistently. He'll still bite or pinch when there's more change in the classroom (e.g., substitutes, schedule variations) than he can manage. I think that he will need to be retained this year.

Destiny is a large African American girl who has a very difficult time attending to task and following directions. She is immature in her socialization skills and can be "clingy" with adults. Although the IQ and achievement scores suggest that she should be labeled as mentally retarded, I feel that the category of learning disabled is more appropriate. She was in a preschool special education classroom when she was 3 or 4, but was then taken out of special education the year before coming to kindergarten. Her number and letter recognition skills are very weak. Her parents would like to see her mainstreamed in the regular classroom next year without special education services, but I'm afraid that's not what is best for her.

I could go on and on. Each child has special needs whether or not they are in special education. And they range from the ridiculous to the serious. Last week Lamont's dad asked if I would get the snot out of Lamont's nose since he can't manage it himself. I told him to talk to the nurse. Over the weekend Patrick's dad died of a heart attack at age 40, leaving four children to survive on their mother's minimum wage job. In one day my emotions can flip-flop between joy and depression with one phone call or one child's remark.

These are some of the concerns that cross my consciousness while I'm trying to teach this morning. My 23 kindergarten students sit cross-legged in a semicircle around the easel. I have put a morning message on newsprint in a cloze format for the children to read. Next to the message there are letters and numbers on individual pieces of Post-It notes. The children can choose one of these to fill in the blanks.

To_ay is Tues_ay, _arch, 19_ _. _ix baby ch_cks have

_atched from the e_gs. We _ave _rt class t_day.

Six chicks are cheerily chirping from their cage under the warming light. The children loved turning the eggs each day until they hatched and now are actively involved in feeding them. I have structured a fair amount of my curriculum around the chick's presence over the last two weeks.

As I wait for all the children to direct their eyes toward me, I am reminded of what an impossible expectation such undivided attention might have been back in September. Six months ago Larry might have been climbing under his table trying to avoid circle time completely. Shakeem might have still been in the cafeteria finishing his breakfast. Today I knew that if I simply praised those who were attending to me, the rest would quickly follow suit. I was pleased with the considerable progress that they had made in socialization skills.

Donna is sitting between Selina and Shakeem, the two extremes of my class's ability spectrum. Selina's alert, dark eyes are constantly scanning her surroundings. Shakeem is dressed in the finest in kindergarten wear and is playing with the ties on his high top Nikes. Donna's wonderful skills as a teaching assistant are evident once again. She knows that these two students need her attention and places herself accordingly.

I explain that they should raise their hands if they know what letter or number belongs in the blank. We start with the first word and immediately about two-thirds of the children raise their hands. I know that raised hands do not necessarily mean that they know the answer, but it does indicate their willingness to try.

I choose Larry because he often does not even attempt to raise his hand. As I suspected, he has no immediate response when I call on him, but once I tell him to look around the room to see if he can see the whole word, he finds it. He comes to the board with a slight smile when he sees the answer. He holds his shoulders a bit straighter as he returns to his place in the circle.

We go on to the next word. Selina is waving her hand high into the air and, I know, whispering the answer to Donna. I decide to call on her next, and she confidently places the correct letter in the blank. Her light brown cheeks seem to grow even more rounded with pleasure when I applaud her correct response. Other children do not have Selina's facility with letters, words, and syntax, but I make a conscious effort to call on all the students equally, regardless of their abilities.

I go on to call on other children and find that I have to give a fair number of prompts to help them to choose the right symbol for the blank. I believe that it is important for them to be successful, so I try to direct them to environmental print and other visuals posted around the room to give them clues. Of course, this takes time. I can tell that Donna has her hands full. Shakeem is beginning to bounce on his knees while making animal sounds. Simultaneously, Selina is waving her hand in the air and whispering answers in Donna's ear.

Several of the children seem to be reaching the outer limits of their attention span, so I try to finish up. I called on Destiny to fill in the last blank and notice that Selina pulls down her hand in disgust.

"Mrs. Elliott doesn't call on me because I'm smarter than the other kids," Selina complains to Donna, loud enough for me and several of the other children to hear. Donna leans over and speaks to her. I know she is reminding Selina that I can't call on her each time she has her hand up.

I ignore Selina's remark and quickly move on to the next activity I had planned, a class read-aloud of the big book *The Little Red Hen*. It is the first time we have read the book as a class. I know this is a favorite activity and will get everyone involved. While some of the students can read along only when we read the repetitive sections, others surprise me by recognizing words that we have not discussed in class before. I know that they were using their decoding skills. There is only one child that reads practically every word along with me—Selina.

During our planning time I express my frustration to Donna about Selina's snobbish comment. I certainly had not ignored her.

"The more attention you give her, the more she wants," agreed Donna. "That's not the first time I've heard her say things that are hurtful to the other children."

"Miss Humble. And it's not as if everything she does is perfect. Yesterday she rushed through that writing assignment so she could read a book. Her handwriting was sloppy and she only wrote one sentence," Donna replied.

"But look at Selina's reading skills!"

"I know. I know. But Selina's got to learn not to put down the other children by flaunting her own abilities. She has to follow the instructions, too. She seems to think that she's special and deserves extra attention. There are too many children who demand my attention now. I don't see how I can give her any more," Donna answered.

"Selina is gifted in some areas, but not all," I agreed. "She certainly needs more help with aspects of her interpersonal intelligence."

As I drive home, I try to imagine what changes can be made to improve Selina's social interactions and also keep her interested and challenged in school. It is hard to remain positive, however, when I think about all the demands that the children in the class place on me. It is clear that they need this full-day kindergarten program since so many are below developmental norms. At least the school district recognizes that.

This year at Stevenson Elementary we added a third kindergarten because of the large enrollment. In spite of this my class size is over the 22-student limit "directive" established by the school district. Contractually, I could have 30 in this class. Every classroom in the school is used and, while my classroom is adequate in size, I could always use more room, especially when Isabella comes in and we divide into small groups. However, there is no room to create additional classrooms or programs.

We are a neighborhood school situated in one of the poorest sections of the city. Eighteen of my children receive free lunch. We try very hard to promote the values of kindness, respect, and responsibility that seem important to most of our parents. To promote respect for our backgrounds, this year our faculty has worked hard each quarter to decorate our school display case with artifacts representing the various cultures from which our children or their families have immigrated, whether recently or in the distant past. Yet we are faced with the reality that some parents cannot give their children the educational and financial support that they need. Some of them became parents when they were 15 years old.

Recently, we had a citywide vote on two school district issues. The expenses for "noncontingent" items (extracurricular activities, sports, music and art programs, the gifted program) were part of that budget. Second, five places on the school board were up for a vote and there were five members of the local taxpayers group who ran against incumbents on a platform to cut future budget expenditures. The outcome was that the noncontingent budget passed by a narrow margin. However, four of the five candidates from the taxpayers group were elected.

This certainly does not give me much hope that I'll be getting any more resources, human or material, to help with the diversity in my classroom. If anything, I'll be lucky to hang on to what I have now. It's even conceivable that the funding for the gifted program and some of the afterschool enrichment programs at Stevenson Elementary will be reduced or eliminated in the future. Although our gifted program does not extend to the kindergarten level, such a cut would mean that Selina would not be able to be involved in such programs in the future. As it is now, the basic skills coordinator is in charge of the gifted program. However, she also is responsible for the mentor program for students who need academic and social development, the Title I program, individual and group reading instruction, and any other assignment that the principal asks her to accomplish.

I'm not sure that Selina's family has the financial resources to provide her with the music lessons, theater classes, or other special training that more affluent parents might insist on. She has three older siblings and her mother just had a baby girl one month ago. Her mother is from Puerto Rico and her father is African American. While they seem to be a solid family, with only Mr. James working as a maintenance person in the city recreation program, they certainly can't afford too many extras. They live in public housing that is clean and well cared for, but crowded for seven people. Selina's dad often picks her up after school and walks her and her older sister home. He says that she went to a pre-K program for 2 years and knew her alphabet and could count to 100 before kindergarten. She taught herself to read.

The only thing that I can think of to do at this point is to make sure that at least some of the suggestions of the Student Review Team are implemented. But which ones? And will incremental changes like these really make a difference? Our state has a miserable record for funding gifted education and we have few resources to rely on. However, I feel strongly that a child like Selina should be challenged to meet her own potential. At the same time, I also believe that many students with disabilities can make tremendous behavioral and academic gains when placed in a general education setting. But one of the many attacks on the idea of including students with disabilities in the regular classroom is that other children will not receive adequate attention. I do not want that to be the case in my classroom, yet I realize how difficult it is to keep a balance.

DISCUSSION QUESTIONS
1. Describe Selina's academic and interpersonal abilities.
2. What do we know about the abilities of other students in the classroom?
3. What options are presently available for Selina for this year and beyond?

4. What does the research indicate regarding the assessment and placement of students of color in programs for the gifted?
5. What does Ann believe might be the best program for Selina? For the children who achieve at a much lower level?
6. What assumptions and underlying values does the school district hold regarding the inclusion of students from a broad ability range in the regular classroom?
7. What issues must be addressed to provide an appropriate education for Selina? Who should be involved in determining and providing this program?
8. What type of professional development or support does Ann need to continue to find kindergarten teaching fulfilling and meaningful?
9. What district, state, and national policies affect Selina's education?

THE CASE OF MATTHEW SIMPSON

"If I can't leave by the door, I'll leave by the window," Matthew shouted as he ran toward the windows in the classroom. I dashed to the window and slammed it, wondering if Matthew had taken his Ritalin that morning. On his worst days he had usually left home without it. Today, like so many other days, I had kept Matthew in for recess because he had called out all morning. Only today, I had to lock the door when he tried to leave despite my directions to remain seated.

As an African American teacher, I worry about Matthew and many other African American students who should not be in special education. It's so obvious to me that students are often placed in my classroom because of behavior. Sometimes my 15 years of experience here at Stevens Elementary School and my MS degree in special education seem almost useless in dealing with some of the students. The challenges are greater every year. Yet I refuse to alter my philosophy because students of color are so disproportionately placed in special education, and I believe that it is my duty to prepare as many as possible to return to the mainstream. Thus, unlike too many special education teachers, I stress academics in my classroom and I use the regular curriculum. Each year, in June, I always feel elated at the end of the school year when I can recommend that several of my students return to mainstream classes in sixth grade when they graduate to middle school.

However, there are times when Matthew really tries my patience and tests my philosophy. He can disrupt the entire class when he insists on calling out, conversing with students seated nearby, asking multiple questions, or giving endless answers to one of my questions. On rare occasions when I lose it, I actually shout, "Shut up, Matthew! That's enough!"

My self-contained special education class consists of 15 children aged 9 to 11. There are 9 African American students (including Matthew), 5 Latinos, and one white child. Although the grade levels supposedly range from 3 to 5, students are functioning academically from grade 1.0 to 7.7 in reading and math. The highest scores belong to Matthew, who is 11 years old and should be in fifth grade. With so many levels in reading and math in my classroom, how can I possibly individualize work for Matthew? I have five reading groups and, of course, he is in the top group; however, that group is only on the fifth grade level. Often he has read the story earlier and already knows all the answers. This means that he raises his hand for every question asked, and sometimes he blurts out the answer without raising his hand. When he doesn't take his Ritalin, Matthew shouts out all the answers and the day is usually unbearable.

Matthew really stands out in my classroom, not only because he is the tallest, but also due to his academic ability and behavior. One day I sent him out into the hall to sit in a chair because I had to speak to him too many times that morning. When I looked out to check on him, he was pacing the floor. Then he came to the door, stuck his head in, and asked if he could sharpen his pencil. I shouted "No" before I thought. He needed the pencil in order to do some work! Matthew is often out of the room, in the principal's office or sent home for the same unacceptable behaviors—calling out, talking back, and not listening. Sometimes he even complains that he's bored and that's the reason he talks so much. I can't totally disagree with Matthew. In school, he's not being challenged. At home and in the community there is little for a bright, active child to do.

The surrounding neighborhood, in which all the children live, suffers the problems of many inner-city communities. There is a lack of decent housing, excessive crime and drug activity, and a scarcity of recreational activities. No playground or park is available in the area. An organized neighborhood group does try to make a difference, but appears to be powerless in dealing with the political structure of the city. For example, the group has tried to fight drug activity through the presence of a community police office. However, the office remained unstaffed for 6 months and was finally closed despite letters to the mayor and other politicians. Interestingly, there are several large, formerly all white churches in the neighborhood that are struggling with how to develop better relationships with the community, and progress has been very slow, thus far.

Matthew lives with his mother, Mrs. Simpson, who has a full-time job. She has no phone at home, but did call me once when I sent a note home with Matthew that I wanted to speak with her. After expressing some of my concerns about Matthew's behavior and above-average intelligence, she told me that she, too, had had problems in school.

"But I was a fighter," she said. "I fought with everyone and got put in a special school. It was one of the teachers there that was good to me and helped me graduate," she insisted.

She continued to tell me that most of the time Matthew is left in the care of his grandmother. He has a sister aged 23, a brother who is 19, and a 5-year-old sister.

Recently, when Matthew was absent for an entire week, I realized how peaceful my classroom could be. The class was working quietly in their reading groups the following Monday when the door opened suddenly and Matthew entered, followed by the guidance counselor, who held the door. Matthew's right leg was bandaged in bright blue from ankle to groin and around the blue bandage were wide white bands. He hobbled on two crutches. Surprised to see him after a week's absence, several students and I asked in unison, "Matthew, what happened to you?"

He responded proudly, "I pulled a ligament in my leg; in fact, I tore two ligaments."

Matthew always loves the class's attention and he appeared to relish their interest in his leg. However, one student muttered, "Uh-oh, the class comedian is back." I told Matthew to get his book for reading, a fourth grade basal reader, and he joined my reading group who were engaged then in reading *Charlotte's Web,* a story that Matthew seemed to know already. After 5 to 10 minutes, having answered every question that I asked, Matthew announced, "I'm so bored."

Nevertheless, he remained cooperative throughout the remainder of the period. This was admirable, given his frequent distractibility, impulsivity, and endless chatter. In fact, when you ask Matthew a question, it's necessary to plan for a 5-minute answer. He never stops with a simple answer, but is forever elaborating on and expanding his initial response.

Matthew is classified as emotionally disturbed, although his recent test scores indicated that he is very capable of mainstream work. Not only is he currently reading at a grade-level of 7.7, but his grade-level mathematics score is 7.3. However, on an older WISC intelligence test, which was administered 5 years ago, his full scale IQ was 82. Matthew seems much brighter than the old IQ score, and his academic abilities are certainly higher than would be expected for a student with those scores.

I had a talk with Matthew one afternoon immediately after our science lesson. During the lesson it had been evident that he already knew much of the material on the earth's composition and had volunteered, as usual, to answer each question that I asked, in his lengthy manner of providing three times the quantity of information expected. He also volunteered to help distribute materials to the class and was very cooperative throughout the lesson.

However, he appeared very subdued, almost drugged, and I wondered if the Ritalin was responsible.

The day before Matthew had become impossible in class. I had tried every behavior management technique my 15 years of teaching had provided and nothing seemed to be working, so I sent him down to the office. Apparently, Mrs. Arnold, the principal, was also at the end of her rope. She called his mother at work to say, "Come and get him. He can't come back until his behavior is manageable."

I wondered if an increase in the Ritalin was responsible for Matthew's sluggish behavior. I decided to talk with him to see what he thought about taking the medication.

"Matthew, do you think taking Ritalin helps you in school?" I asked.

"Now that I take Ritalin, I can concentrate better. Before, the other kids around me would bother me and it was hard to finish my work," insisted Matthew.

I thought it might be helpful to find out more about Matthew's background. Maybe it would help me to stay calm when he was driving me nuts to know some of his history.

"Matthew, have you always lived here in Sagamore City?'

"No, I was born in Vermont. I went to preschool and kindergarten there. I liked kindergarten, 'cause I could play games and make things. But I had to come here to live with my grandmother because my mother had too many fights with my father. I started first grade at Truman School and they put me in special ed.

"After first grade I began to hang out with my cousin, Noah. He taught me how to steal bikes and do other bad things. One time we found a pile of hay and got some matches. What a fire! We ran away 'cause it just kept getting bigger and we were scared. But someone saw me and I ended up in big trouble. I was kicked out of school and placed on probation. I negotiated the probation. The police said to me, 'Take your choice. You either go to jail or go on probation.' I told them, 'I'm only eight years old. Put me on probation.' "

Matthew was just getting warmed up, so I quickly interjected, "Did you eventually go back to Truman?"

"No, we moved to a different apartment and I went to Collingswood. But the kids beat me up all the time. Then the principal threw me out."

"So when did you come to Stevens Elementary?"

"I was in third grade. All the grown-ups liked me but the kids picked on me because I have a big nose and big head. I got in a lot of fights. My grandmother told me, 'Tell the kids to stop messing with you only twice. The third time, you take care of it.' "

I knew that many fights and trips to the office had followed. I wondered if Matthew had any outlets for his frustrations and boundless energy.

"Matthew, what do you do after school?"

Matthew described his activities after school with a bored facial expression. "I go out to play or go to the YMCA, but there really isn't much for kids to do. I don't stay in the house much, but sometimes when I do I read some of my mom's old books. The Y is the only place to go but they don't have much—a few games, Ping-Pong and basketball. There's nothing for kids to do after school. I wish we could start a boys' and girls' club."

I knew that Matthew liked to play basketball, but he had many interests, including art and inventing. He certainly did not mention any family travel or visits to museums or special events that would give him the opportunity to develop these aspects. I had a feeling his family was too poor to finance special lessons, trips, or summer camps.

"Matthew, what would you like to do as a career someday?" I asked hoping to find out ways to motivate him.

"Oh, I'd like to be a computer specialist, baby doctor, real doctor, karate teacher, store owner, jet pilot, technology specialist, or creator of suits for people to wear in space. I'd also like to buy a house someday."

Despite Matthew's long history of totally unacceptable behavior, you couldn't help but like Matthew when you talked with him on a one-to-one basis. But it seemed that Matthew needed that kind of adult attention all day long to keep him out of trouble. It bothered me that Matthew was on Ritalin at all, but even more so when I saw him so sluggish. I also recognized that Matthew's complaints about being bored didn't stem from a lack of motivation or low cognitive abilities. In fact, at 11 years old Matthew was well aware of the problems faced by his community and he is motivated to help to change things.

We are approaching the end of the school year and Matthew will go to sixth grade at the middle school. I have decided to recommend him for placement in a regular sixth grade program. I'm very concerned about his placement next year because I want him to succeed. This was my reason for disagreeing with the guidance counselor at our recent meeting when she favored recommending Matthew for the middle school gifted and talented program. I worry that the demands of the gifted and talented program, a new school, and the mainstream classes may be overwhelming for Matthew. After all, he has been in segregated special education classes since first grade. I prefer the Pace Program, an enriched reading pull-out program available for sixth grade readers. The annual meeting at which these recommendations will be formally made is only a week away and I must be ready to make and defend my position.

Meanwhile, my students have made a great deal of progress this year and my poetry unit was a great success. Their behavior has calmed down so much, and they can listen to me attentively during my lessons. However, our big, end of year field trip to the museum was disappointing because some of the students did not behave appropriately. Nevertheless, I'm looking forward to the graduation ceremony for the fifth graders, including Matthew.

DISCUSSION QUESTIONS

1. What are the major issues in the case?
2. How does this teacher perceive Matthew's problems?
3. What is Matthew's perception of his difficulties in class?
4. What responsibility does the school have for providing an educational program for Matthew?
5. In planning for Matthew's promotion to sixth grade, what are some critical needs?
6. In an action plan, what would several goals and objectives for Matthew include?

REFERENCES

American Psychiatric Association. (1994). *Diagnostic and statistical manual of mental disorders,* (4th ed.). Washington, DC: Author.
Armstrong, T. (1994). *Multiple intelligences in the classroom.* Alexandria, VA: Association for Supervision and Curriculum Development.
Aust, P. (1994). When the problem is not the problem: Understanding attention deficit disorder with and without hyperactivity. *Child Welfare, 73,* 215–227.
Baker, E. T., Wang, M. C., & Walberg, H. J. (1995). The effects of inclusion on learning. *Educational Leadership, 21*(4), 33–35.
Baker, J. M., & Zigmond, N. (1995). The meaning and practice of inclusion for students with learning disabilities: The issues and implications from five cases. *Journal of Special Education, 29*(2), 163–180.
Barkan, J. H., & Bernal, E. M. (1991). Gifted education of bilingual and limited English proficient students. *Gifted Child Quarterly, 35,* 144–147.
Barkley, R. A. (1990). *Attention deficit hyperactivity disorder.* New York: Guilford Press.
Beecher, M. (1995). *Developing the gifts and talents of all students in the regular classroom: An innovative curricular design based on the enrichment triad model.* Mansfield Center, CN: Creative Learning Press.
Buckner, C. (1997). *Meeting the needs of gifted students in the inclusion classroom.* St. George, UT: Bloomington Hills Elementary (ERIC Document Reproduction Service No. ED 409687).
Burnette, J. (1998). *Reducing the disproportionate representation of minority students in special education.* Reston, VA. ERIC Clearinghouse on Disabilities and Gifted Education.
Clark, R. (1983). *Family life and school achievement: Why poor black children succeed and fail.* Chicago: University of Chicago Press.
Cornell, D. G., Callahan, C. M., Bassin, L. E., & Ramsay, S. G. (1991). Affective development in accelerated students. In W. T. Southern & E. D. Jones (Eds.), *The academic acceleration of gifted children* (pp. 74–101). New York: Teachers College Press.
Deshler, D. D., & Schumaker, J. S. (1986). Learning strategies: An instructional alternative for low-achieving adolescents. *Exceptional Children, 52*(6), 360–364.
Dunn, L. M. (1968). Special education for the mildly retarded—is much of it justifiable? *Exceptional Children, 35,* 5–22.
DuPaul, G. J., & Eckert, T. L. (1998). Academic interventions for students with attention-deficit/hyperactivity disorder: A review of the literature. *Reading and Writing Quarterly: Overcoming Learning Difficulties, 14*(1), 59–82.

Empowering minority students: A framework for intervention. *Harvard Educational Review, 56*(1), 18–36.

Etscheidt, S. K., & Bartlett, L. (1999). The IDEA amendments: A four-step approach for determining supplementary aids and services. *Exceptional Children, 65*(2), 163–174.

Feldhusen, J. F., Proctor, R. B., & Black, L. N. (1986). Guidelines for grade advancement of precocious children. *Roeper Review, 9*(1), 25–27.

Ford, D. Y. (1998). The underrepresentation of minority students in gifted education: Problems and promises in recruitment and retention. *Journal of Special Education, 32*, 4–14.

Ford, D. Y., & Thomas, A. (1997). *Underachievement among gifted minority students: Problems and promises.* Reston, VA: ERIC Clearinghouse on Disabilities and Gifted Education (ERIC Document Reproduction Service No. ED 409660).

Frasier, M. M. (1991). Disadvantaged and culturally diverse gifted students. *Journal for the Education of the Gifted, 14*, 235–245.

Friend, M., & Bursuck, W. D. (1999). *Including students with special needs: A practical guide for classroom teachers.* Boston: Allyn and Bacon.

Fuchs, D., & Fuchs, L. (1994). Inclusive schools movement and the radicalization of special education reform. *Exceptional Children, 60*(4), 294–309.

Gallagher, J. J. (1995). Education of gifted students: A civil rights issue? *Phi Delta Kappan, 79*, 408–410.

Giangreco, M. F., Dennis, R., Cloninger, C., Edelman, S., & Schattman, R. (1993). "I've counted Jon": Transformational experiences of teachers educating students with disabilities. *Exceptional Children, 59*(4), 359–372

Guenther, A. (1995). What educators and parents need to know about—ADHD, Creativity, and gifted students (Practitioners' Guide A9814). Storrs, CN: National Research Center on the Gifted and Talented (Eric Document Reproduction No. ED 429 415).

Gurcsik, B. (1998). Inclusion: A wrong turn for the gifted in the 21st century. *Gifted Education Press Quarterly, 12*(1), 5–8.

Hadnot, I. J. (June 22, 1997). A prescription for controversy. *Dallas Morning News*, p. 1J [Online]. Available: http://elibrary.com/getdoc.cig.

Hallahan, D. P., & Kauffman, J. M. (1997). *Exceptional learners: Introduction to special education* (7th ed.). Boston: Allyn and Bacon.

Heron, E., & Jorgensen, C. M. (1994). Addressing learning differences right from the start. *Educational Leadership, 54*(4), 56–58.

Hunt, P., Farron-Davis, F., Beckstead, S., Curtis, D., & Goetz, L. (1994). Evaluating the effects of placement of students with severe disabilities in general education versus special classes. *Journal of the Association for Persons with Severe Handicaps, 19*(4), 290–301.

Ishii-Jordan, S. R. (1997). When behavior differences are not disorders. In A. J. Artiles & G. Samora-Duran (Eds.), *Reducing disproportionate representation of culturally diverse students in special and gifted education* (pp. 27–46). Reston, VA: Council for Exceptional Children.

Jenkins, J., Jewell, M., Leicester, N., O'Connor, R. E., Jenkins, L., & Troutner, N. M. (1992). Accommodating for individual differences without classroom ability groups: An experiment in school restructuring. *Exceptional Children, 60*(4), 344–359.

Johnson, N. E. (1994). *Use of the WISC-R with disadvantaged gifted children: Current practice, limitations, and ethical concerns.* San Diego, CA: San Diego State University (ERIC Document Reproduction Service No. ED 368097).

Kame'enui, E. J., & Simmons, D. C. (1999). *Toward successful inclusion of students with disabilities: The architecture of instruction.* Reston, VA: Council for Exceptional Children.

Kearney, K. (1996). *Highly gifted children in full inclusion classrooms.* Ames: Iowa State University (ERIC Reproduction No. 425575).

Kulik, J. A., & Kulik, C. C. (1984). Effects of accelerated instruction on students. *Review of Educational Research, 54*, 409–425.

Lahey, B. B., & Carlson, C. L. (1991). Validity of the diagnostic category of attention deficit disorder without hyperactivity: A review of the literature. *Journal of Learning Disabilities, 24*(2), 110–120.

Lenz, B. K., & Schumaker, J. B. (1999). *Adapting language arts, social studies, and science materials for the inclusive classroom.* Reston, VA: Council for Exceptional Children.

Lipsky, D. K., & Gartner, A. (1996). Inclusion, school restructuring, and the remaking of American society. *Harvard Educational Review, 66*(4), 762–796.

Logan, K. R., Bakeman, R., & Keefe, E. D. (1997). *Inclusion and school reform: Transforming America's classrooms.* Baltimore, MD: Paul H. Brookes.

Lovecky, D. V. (1999). *Gifted children with AD/HD.* Paper presented at the Annual CHADD International Conference, Washington, DC October 8, 1999 (ERIC Reproduction No. ED439 555).

MacMillan, D. L., Gresham, F. M., & Forness, S. R. (1996). Full inclusion: An empirical perspective. *Behavioral Disorders, 21*(2), 145–149.

Maker, C. J. (1996). Identification of gifted minority students: A national problem, needed changes and a promising solution. *Gifted Child Quarterly, 40*(1), 41–50.

Manset, G., & Semmel, M. (1997). Are inclusive programs for students with mild disabilities effective? *Journal of Special Education, 30,* 121–132.

Marston, D. (1996). A comparison of inclusion only, pull-out only, and combined service models for students with mild disabilities. *Journal of Special Education, 30*(2), 121–132.

McGregor, G., & Vogelsberg, R. T. (1998). Inclusive schooling practices: Pedagogical and research foundations: A synthesis of the literature that informs best practices about inclusive schooling. Pittsburgh, PA: Allegheny University of the Health Sciences (ERIC Document Reproduction No. ED418559).

McLeskey, J., Henry, D., & Axelrod, M. I. (1999). Inclusion of students with learning disabilities: An examination of data from reports to Congress. *Exceptional Children, 66*(1), 55–66.

Monda-Amaya, I. E., & Pearson, P. D. (1996). Toward a responsible pedagogy for teaching and learning literacy. In M. C. Pugach & C. L. Warger (Eds.), *Curriculum trends, special education and reform: Refocusing the conversation* (pp. 143–163). New York: Teachers College Press.

Mooij, T. (1999). Integrating gifted children into kindergarten by improving educational processes. *Gifted Child Quarterly, 48*(2), 63–74.

Moore, C., Gilbreath, D., & Maiuri, F. (1998). Educating students with disabilities in general education classrooms: A summary of the research. Eugene, OR: Western Regional Resource Center (Eric Document Reproduction No. ED 419 329).

Oswald, D. P., Coutinho, M. J., Best, A. M., & Singh, N. N. (1999). Ethnic representation in special education: The influence of school-related economic and demographic variables. *Journal of Special Education, 32,* 194–206.

Patton, J. M. (1997). Disproportionate representation in gifted programs: Best practices for meeting this challenge. In A. J. Artiles & G. Samora-Duran (Eds.), *Reducing disproportionate representation of culturally diverse students in special and gifted education* (pp. 59–86). Reston, VA: Council for Exceptional Children.

Patton, J. M. (1998). The disproportionate representation of African Americans in special education: Looking behind the curtain for understanding and solutions. *Journal of Special Education, 32,* 25–31.

Paul, P. V., & Ward, M. (1996). Inclusion paradigms in conflict. *Theory into Practice, 35*(1), 4–11.

Prater, M. A., & Pancheri, C. (1999). What teachers and parents should know about Ritalin. *Teaching Exceptional Children, 31*(4), 20–26.

Reid, R. (1995). Assessment of ADHD with culturally different groups: The use of behavioral rating scales. *School Psychology Review, 24*(4), 537–560.

Reid, R., & Maag, J. W. (1998). Functional assessment: A method for developing classroom-based accommodations and interventions for children with ADHD. *Reading and Writing Quarterly: Overcoming Learning Difficulties, 14*(1), 9–42.

Reis, S. D., & Callahan, C. (1989). Gifted females: They've come a long way—or have they? *Journal for the Education of the Gifted, 12,* 99–117.

Renzulli, J. S., Reis, S. M. (1997). The schoolwide enrichment model: New directions for developing high-end learning. In N. Colangelo and G. A. Davis (Eds.) *Handbook of gifted education* (2nd ed., pp. 136–154). Boston: Allyn and Bacon.

Reschly, D. J. (1997). Utility of individual ability measures and public policy choices for the 21st century. *School Psychology Review, 26,* 234–241.

Roberts, C., & Zubrick, S. (1992). Factors influencing the social status of children with mild academic disabilities in regular classrooms. *Exceptional Children, 59*(30) 192–202.

Rueda, R. (1997). Changing the context of assessment: The move to portfolios and authentic assessment. In A. J. Artiles & G. Samora-Duran (Eds.), *Reducing disproportionate representation of culturally diverse students in special and gifted education* (pp. 7–25). Reston, VA: Council for Exceptional Children.

Ryndak, D., Jacqueline, I., & Morison, A. (1995). Parents' perceptions after inclusion of their children with moderate or severe disabilities. *Journal of the Association of Persons with Severe Handicaps, 20*(2), 147–157.

Sailor, W., & Skritic, T. (1995). Modern and postmodern agendas in special education: Implications for teacher education, research, and policy development. In J. L. Paul, H. Rosselli, & D. Evan (Eds.), *Integrating school restructuring and special education reform* (pp. 418–432). Fort Worth, TX: Harcourt Brace.

Sale, P., & Carey, D. M. (1995). The sociometric status of students with disabilities in a full-inclusion school. *Exceptional Children 62*(1), 6–19.

Salend, S. J. (2001) *Creating inclusive classrooms: Effective and reflective practices* (4th ed.). Upper Saddle River, NJ: Merrill/Prentice Hall.

Salend, S. J., & Duhaney, L. G. (1999). The impact of inclusion on students with and without disabilities and their educators. *Remedial and Special Education 20*(2), 114–126.

Sapon-Shevin, M. (1995). Why gifted students belong in inclusive schools. *Educational Leadership, 52*(4), 64–70.

Schlozman, S. C., & Schlozman, V. R. (2000). Chaos in the classroom: Looking at ADHD. *Educational Leadership, 58*(3), 28–33.

Schumm, J. S. (1999). *Adapting reading and math materials for the inclusive classroom.* Reston, VA: Council for Exceptional Children.

Scruggs, T. E., & Mastropieri, M. A. (1996). Teacher perceptions of mainstreaming/inclusion, 1958–1995: A research synthesis. *Exceptional Children, 63*(1), 59–74.

Smelter, R. W., Rasch, B. W., & Yudevitz, G. L. (1994). Thinking of inclusion for all special needs children? Better think again. *Phi Delta Kappan, 76*(1), 35–38.

Smith, D. D. (2001). *Introduction to special education: Teaching in an age of opportunity (4th Ed.).* Boston: Allyn and Bacon.

Southern, W. T., Jones, E. D., & Fiscus, E. D. (1989). Practitioner objections to the academic acceleration of gifted children. *Gifted Child Quarterly, 33,* 29–35.

Stainback, W., Stainback, S., & Stefanich, G. (1996). Learning together in inclusive classrooms. *Teaching Exceptional Children, 28*(3), 14–19.

Swanson, J. M., McBurnett, K., Wigal, R., Pfiffner, L. J., Lerner, M. A., Williams, L., Christian, D. L., Tamor, L., Willcutt, E., Crowley, K., Clevenger, W., Khouzam, N., Woo, C., Crinella, F. M., & Fisher, T. (1993). Effect of stimulant medication on children with attention deficit disorder: A review of reviews. *Exceptional Children, 60*(2), 154–161.

Tharp, R. G. (1989). Psychocultural variables and constraints: Effects on teaching and learning in school. *American Psychologist, 44*(2), 349–359.

Tharp, R. G., & Gallimore, R. (1988). *Rousing minds to life: Teaching, learning, and schooling in social context.* New York: Cambridge University Press.

Tomlinson, C. A., Callahan, C. M., & Lelli, K. M. (1997). Challenging expectations: Case studies of high-potential, culturally diverse young children. Gifted *Child Quarterly, 41,* 5–17.

Tomlinson, C. A., Coleman, M. R., Allan, S., Udall, A., & Lundrum, M. (1996). Interface between gifted education and general education: Toward communication, cooperation, and collaboration. *Gifted Child Quarterly, 40,* 165–171.

Turnbull, A., Turnbull, R., Shank, M., & Leal, D. (1999). *Exceptional lives: Special education in today's schools* (2nd ed.). Upper Saddle River, NJ: Merrill/Prentice Hall.

Udvari-Solner, A. (1995). A process for adapting curriculum in inclusive classrooms. In R. A. Villa & J. Thousand (Eds.), *Creating an inclusive school* (pp. 110–124). Alexandria, VA: Association for Supervision and Curriculum Development.

U.S. Department of Education. (1993). *National excellence: A case for developing American's talent.* Washington, DC: Office of Educational Research and Improvement.

U.S. Department of Education. (1998). *Twentieth annual report to Congress on the implementation of the Individuals with Disabilities Education Act.* Washington, DC: U.S. Government Printing Office.

Van Tassel-Baska, J. (1991). Identification of candidates for acceleration: Issues and concerns. In W. T. Southern and E. D. Jones (Eds.), *The academic acceleration of gifted children.* (pp. 148–161). New York: Teachers College Press.

Vaughn, S., & Schumm, J. (1995). Responsible inclusion for students with learning disabilities. *Journal of Learning Disabilities, 28,* 264–270.

Villa, R. A., Thousand, J. S., Meyers, H., & Nevin, A. (1996). Teacher and administrator perceptions of heterogeneous education. *Exceptional Children, 63*(1), 29–45.

Wang, M. C., & Reynolds, M. C. (1997). *Progressive inclusion: Meeting new challenges in special education.* Philadelphia: Mid-Atlantic Lab for Student Success (ERIC Document Reproduction No. ED420134).

Williams, L., Lerner, M., Wigal, T., & Swanson, J. (1995). Minority assessment of ADD: Issues in the development of new assessment techniques. *Attention!, 2*(1), 9–15.

Yell, J. L., & Shriner, J. G. (1996). Inclusive education: Legal and policy implications. *Preventing School Failure, 40*(3), 101–116.

Zemelman, S., Daniels, H., & Hyde, A. (1993). *Best practice: New standards for teaching and learning in America's schools.* Portsmouth, NH: Heinemann.

CHAPTER 9

POVERTY AND SOCIOECONOMIC CLASS

Socioeconomic diversity among the school-aged population affects the overall quality of students' lives as well as their educational outcomes. In his gripping book, *Savage Inequalities*, Kozol (1991) provides striking pictures of the differences between schools for suburban, mostly white students and those of inner-city, lower-income minority families, primarily black and Hispanic students. Linda Darling-Hammond (1995) also refers to the continuing segregation of African American and Hispanic students in schools of the central cities where substandard funding, tracking systems, inadequately prepared teachers, fewer counselors, the lack of sufficient technology, and curriculum all contribute to unequal educational outcomes for these students.

In addition, teachers' attitudes may reflect negative, lower expectations for students of lower-income families. In effect, the students who are most in need of enriched school experiences and a highly trained and experienced teaching staff are least likely to receive them. Furthermore, these students may suffer most from their inability to meet the general expectations of the school, arriving unprepared with the home experiences, behaviors. and resources required.

EXPECTATIONS AND REALITIES

Teachers need to realize that the realities of the children's lives may easily conflict with the expectations of the schools. This is particularly true when we consider that the orientations of the majority of schools and teachers in the United States can be best described as either middle income–middle class or aspiring to belong to the middle class. Not only will teachers need to recognize that all children will not be able to meet the school's demands for appropriate clothing, school supplies, family involvement, good health care, extracurricular expenses, and outside experiences; they will also need the attitudes, knowledge, and skills required when they must address these difficulties with the children and their families. Furthermore, all members of the family system are affected by such conditions. The school's expectations for parents and families can be totally unrealistic when families in poverty are without telephones, transportation, access to health care and funds for medication, child care, and jobs that grant time off for personal business or sickness.

The difficulties faced by children in poverty are abundant. Newspapers, particularly during holidays and special drives for the "needy," often publish profiles of individuals and families in dire circumstances. News magazines also publish stories and reports on Americans in poverty. Although we are all familiar with these portraits, current facts on school-aged children among the poor can be informative for both preservice and in-service teachers as they prepare to assure progress for these children in our schools. Furthermore, it is likely that teachers will encounter children from groups in the society who are disproportionately represented among the poor. Therefore, recent data on the composition of the poor in the United States will be helpful.

In addition, the most current information on the impact of poverty on children's ability to learn, even to become engaged in school learning activities, and to meet both the academic and social–behavioral expectations of teachers is critical knowledge for teachers if they are to engage and guide these students with skill, sensitivity, and success. Furthermore, where the rights of children have been established, for example, the rights of children who are homeless, these rights must be observed and teachers will need to be appropriately informed.

Since the state and federal governments attempt to assuage the effects of poverty on children and families, a review of government programs provided for low-income families can also provide important information. Finally, a brief review of what schools are doing and what they can do to assure the success of children who come to school with very limited resources is important, not only to educators, but to all Americans. Therefore, this chapter is organized according to the following important dimensions of poverty's meaning for educators: (1) current facts on children in poverty in the United States; (2) the impact of poverty on school-aged children; (3) state and federal regulations for those in poverty, including the rights of children who are homeless; and (4) what schools are doing and can do.

CURRENT FACTS

> Over 13 million children live in poverty and the number of children living in poverty has increased by 3 million since 1979. The child poverty rate grew by 15 percent from 1979 to 1998. (National Center for Children in Poverty, January, 2001)

Definitions

Children in poverty live with families whose incomes fall below that required by families of various sizes. Thus, in 1997, the federal poverty threshold, which is adjusted for family size and annual cost-of-living increases, was $10,473 for a family of two, $12,802 for a family of three, and $16,400 for a family of four (National Center for Children in Poverty, 2001). The U.S. Census Bureau includes the following types of income in determining who is to be considered poor: wages and salary, nonfarm and farm self-employment, Temporary Assistance to Needy Families (TANF), and general assistance, Social Security, Supplemental Security Income, unemployment compensation, worker's compensation, veterans' payments, interest, dividends, rent, survivor's income, disability, retirement income, child support, education benefits, and financial assistance payments (Bennett, Li, Song, & Yang, 2001).

Other terms in use that are also based on income levels include working poor, near poverty, and extremely poor. The *working poor* refers to families whose income remains within the poverty range despite employment. According to the National Center for Children in Poverty, (2001), 39 percent of American children live in or near poverty. *Near poverty* is defined as income that falls below 185 percent of the poverty line, a designation referring to families served by a number of government assistance programs for low-income people. Examples of such programs include Medicaid, the School Lunch and School Breakfast Programs, and the Special Supplemental Nutrition Program for Women, Infants and Children (WIC) that use 185 percent of the poverty line as the upper limit to determine eligibility (National Center for Children in Poverty, 2001). Seven percent of children in the U.S. live in extreme poverty. *Extreme poverty* is determined as family income that falls 50 percent below the poverty line (National Center for Children in Poverty, 2001).

However, broader definitions of poverty consider the lack of resources other than income that can enable individuals to climb out of poverty. Emotional resources such as stamina and perseverance, mental resources required to deal with the challenges of daily life, and physical, spiritual, and supportive resources or systems can be equally important (Payne, 1998). Payne describes emotional resources as the stamina to withstand difficult and uncomfortable emotional situations and feelings. Mental resources are needed to access and use information from many different sources. A support system can provide individuals to whom one can turn for help in a crisis or emergency. All the resources identified by Payne and others can contribute to an individual's resilience. Resilient families and children are able to bounce back from crises and hardships. Payne (1998) also refers to hidden rules that exist in all socioeconomic classes in the United States. In her view, an individual's knowledge of these hidden rules can also be considered a resource. She describes these rules as the "salient, unspoken understandings that cue the members of the group that this individual does or does not fit" (Payne, 1998, p. 18). Suggesting that people in poverty comprise a socioeconomic class or group, she identifies hidden rules among those living in poverty, such as acceptance of high noise levels, the importance placed on nonverbal information, and the value placed on an individual's ability to entertain.

The danger in this author's viewpoint on hidden rules among classes is her implied acceptance of the outdated and highly debatable concept of a "culture of poverty." People living in poverty are as diverse as members of any other group in society. Nevertheless, the behaviors described by Payne may be confused with a behavior disorder or emotional disturbance when exhibited by children in school.

Furthermore, research has shown that the length of time spent in poverty varies among individuals and families. While some families and children may be in and out of poverty for brief periods, others may be trapped for long periods of time. A 1998 report by the U.S. Census Bureau pointed out that "Over a three year span, 30.3 percent of the population lived below the poverty level for at least two months. But just 5.3 percent of them stayed poor for two full years" ("Report: U.S. Poverty," 1998). The information described poverty as "a trap door for a few and a revolving door for many." On average, people were poor for 4.5 months. However, the most likely to be poor at that time were families headed by single mothers who lived in poverty for at least two months in a row, more than three times the rate for married couples. Among the chronically poor, single mothers were eight times as likely as married couples to live in poverty for at least 2 years. In fact, according to Cheal (1996), "No type of poverty is more characteristic of discussions of postmodern family life than that of the female-headed, sole-parent family" (p. 2).

Poverty rates also continue to differ dramatically by race (Chinyavong & Leonard, 1997). Blacks, Hispanics, and children are among the poorest groups in the nation. As Cheal (1996) has noted, "The entrenched nature of poverty today has become a major political issue and a major topic for social research, especially in the U.S. Inevitably, it has also become linked to, and confounded with, prominent issues in the U.S. policy discourse concerning race, crime and urban decay" (p. 2).

Cheal (1996), in fact, refers to a "new poverty," which seems to be economically and politically intractable. In his words, this "new poverty appears to be a curious conjunction of increased family instability and increased employment instability" (p. 180). This view is also supported by Bauman (1998), who notes that "the present day economy does not need a massive labor force, having learned how to increase not just profits, but the volume of products while cutting down on labor and its costs" (p. 90).

Bauman describes the poor as "such people as are not fed, shod and clad as the standards of their time and place define as right and proper; but they are above all people who do not live 'up to the norm,' that norm being the ability to meet such standards" (Bauman, 1998, p. 86). The words of Bauman reflect the influence of society's norms and standards, particularly in the United States, which relegate those who are unable to consume at adequate levels to the ranks of the poor. Norms and standards in the United States are based on high levels of consumption or consumerism, and those who are unable to display the signs of acceptable levels of consumption may be considered poor. Bauman expands his view in this comment: "Contemporary society engages its members primarily as consumers; only secondarily, and partly, as producers. To meet the social norm, to be a fully fledged member of society, one needs to respond promptly and efficiently to the temptations of the consumer market" (p. 90). In fact, Bauman's discussion is helpful in our understanding of the stigma, sense of alienation, and rage that can result from living in conditions of poverty. Again, in Bauman's words,

> The phenomenon of poverty is also a social and psychological condition; as the propriety of human existence is measured by such standards of decent life practiced by any given society, inability to abide by such standards is itself a cause of distress, agony and self-mortification. . . . Poverty means being excluded from whatever passes for a "normal life." It means being "not up to the mark." This results in a fall of self-esteem, feelings of shame or feelings of guilt. Poverty also means being cut off from the chances of whatever passes in a given society for a "happy life." . . . This results in resentment and aggravation, which spill out in the form of violent acts, self-deprecation, or both." (p. 37)

In one of the cases to follow, the parents of Maria and her sisters become targets for charges of child abuse and neglect because the children have come to school in the winter wearing clothes described as flimsy, the medication for Maria has not been purchased as prescribed, and the family is without an automobile for transportation. Although they lack things that are considered essential in the United States, the lack of these things may not be considered abusive or neglectful to children in many other parts of the world.

Who Are the Poor?

The highest, most extreme poverty rate in our society exists among children under 6. "It continues to exceed the rate for older children, ages 6 through 17, and is more than double the rate for adults, ages 18 through 64, and the elderly, ages 65 and above" (Bennett, Li, Song, & Yang, 2001, p. 2). An examination of the poverty rates by age for 1975 to 1997 vividly portrays a picture of the 42 percent of children under age 6 living in poverty or near poverty in 1997. According to the National Center for Children in Poverty, one in ten young children was extremely poor in 1997.

A breakdown of those living in poverty in 1997 shows that the largest racial or ethnic group was white, followed by Hispanic, non-Hispanic black, and other. However, black and Hispanic young children were disproportionately poor in 1997, with rates three times as much as those for white children. Urban areas suffered the highest rates of poverty, followed by suburban and rural rates. Children under age 6 in urban areas had the highest rate in 1997, followed by rural and suburban areas. However, the rate of poverty has risen most rapidly in suburban areas.

In addition to residence, factors such as single parenthood, low education level of parents, and part-time or no employment also contribute to the risk of poverty for young children. Children who lived with a single parent in 1997 were five times as likely to be poor as those living with two parents. While children under age 6 with two unemployed parents or a single parent who was unemployed faced extremely high rates of poverty, part-time employment of a single parent was not sufficient to change the poverty status of most young children (National Center for Children in Poverty, 2001). Furthermore, the facts that wages have not kept pace with inflation, the number of families headed by single parents has increased, and the level of government assistance for poor families with children has decreased provide additional explanations (Ohlson, 1998).

Despite the fact that 65 percent of poor young children had at least one employed parent, "a figure that is higher than at any time in more than 20 years," the high poverty rate continues (National Center for Children in Poverty, 2001). The substantial decrease in public assistance provided to families of young children in poverty can only intensify the harsh conditions of their lives (Ohlson, 1998). The changes in welfare provisions will be discussed later. Nevertheless, parental education does make a difference. As the parental level of education increases, the poverty rate for young children in the family decreases. The poverty rate in 1997 among children under 6 whose "better educated parent had earned a college degree was only three percent" (National Center for Children in Poverty, 2001). In contrast, the rate among children whose parent or parents lacked a college degree increased by 31 percent. "The powerful combination of single motherhood, relatively low educational attainment, and less than full-time employment results in extremely high poverty rates" (National Center for Children in Poverty, 2001, p. 13).

Migrant Families

One group that suffers a high level of poverty is migrant families. As they move from location to location, these families and children suffer "poor sanitation in the fields and work camp facilities, overcrowded, substandard housing and poor diets, exposure to pesticides and other hazards of agricultural work (particularly hazardous to pregnant women and young children), limited health care and low wages" (Salend, 1998, p. 39). In the case of Maria to follow, the family can be described as "resettled migrants" who no longer travel constantly to seek work. Nevertheless, their living conditions and income meet the definitions of poverty.

The educational progress of children who are migrants may be negatively affected. Migrant workers, their families, and children are frequently provided substandard housing where conditions do not allow for areas of privacy, independent activities, homework and studying, or recreation. Children sometimes help in the fields while they try to attend school. Fortunately, advocacy groups in various areas of the country where migrant labor is utilized often protest the conditions in which migrant families and children must live (Witt, 2001).

Jose Martinez tells his story in *With These Hands: The Hidden World of Migrant Farmworkers Today* by Daniel Rothenberg (1998):

> I was in second grade the first time I stepped into a field to work. . . . It was difficult to work and go to school at the same time. Since we'd come up to Michigan before the end of the regular school year, I had to complete two months of extra school work before we left Texas. Then, when school started again, we'd enroll here in Michigan, stay until early November, and then go back to Texas. Sometimes, the school in Texas wouldn't accept Michigan's work or vice versa. (p. 273)

Rothenberg (1998) notes that the Martinez family of 10 members has picked asparagus, strawberries, cherries, blueberries, grapes, and apples at a family income of about $15,000 a year.

Homeless Families and Children

Homeless families and children are also included among the poor. In fact, over 2 million men, women, and children were homeless in 2000. Within the diverse homeless population, 37 percent were families with children and 25 percent were children. Other groups included veterans (30%), drug- or alcohol-dependent persons (40%), persons with mental disabilities (25% to 30%) and workers (25% to 40%) (National Law Center on Homelessness and Poverty, 2001). Many homeless persons belong to more than one subgroup, which accounts for the fact that the numbers cannot be added to 100 percent.

High levels of absenteeism and tardiness are common among homeless children, who are constantly moving, often without dependable transportation and knowledgeable advocates for their needs. Nevertheless, homeless children do have rights that must be recognized by the schools (see Table 9.1).

In view of the numerous factors involved in a family's socioeconomic condition, it is essential for the school to consider a variety of important explanations for the fact that children are unable to meet the school's expectations for preparedness to learn. Full-service schools, as described in Chapter 3, where the educational and support needs of families and children can be met, are sorely needed.

TABLE 9.1   What Teachers Need to Know about the Rights of Homeless Children

- Children do not need a permanent address to be enrolled in school.
- Families have a choice of school placement. The child may remain at the same school she or he attended before becoming homeless or enroll at the school serving attendance area where the family is receiving temporary shelter.
- A homeless child cannot be denied school enrollment just because school records or other enrollment documentation are not immediately available.
- The child has the right to participate in all extracurricular activities and all federal, state, or local programs for which the child is eligible, including food programs; before- and after-school care programs; vocational education; Title I; and other programs for gifted, talented, and disadvantaged learners.
- The child may have a right to transportation services to and from school.
- A child cannot be isolated or separated from mainstream school environment solely due to homelessness.
- If parents do not agree with the educational placement of their child, they and their child have the right to receive prompt resolution of any dispute.
- The state has the responsibility to ensure that barriers to enrollment, attendance, and success in school of homeless children are removed.

Adapted from: "What you need to know about the rights of homeless children." National Law Center on Homelessness and Poverty. Retrieved November, 2001 from http://www.nclchp.org/rights.htm

IMPACT OF POVERTY ON SCHOOL-AGED CHILDREN

Children are expected to enter school being able to learn in groups; to cope with public evaluation of their academic and social behaviors, which may be culturally different from those expected by the school; to learn to compete with other students, which may also be culturally alien; to respond as expected to the authority of teachers and other school personnel; and to socialize with their peers. In addition, they are expected to be adequately and appropriately clothed, fed, and sheltered so that they can attend school regularly and be punctual, be able to engage in learning activities at school, have the necessary space and tools with which to complete school tasks at home, and have parents who are free to help their children at home and participate in necessary activities and conferences with teachers at the school. As we consider the limitations on families living at the poverty level, it is easy to anticipate the conflicts between the conditions of their lives and the expectations of the school.

Although some may view the federal definition of poverty as too narrowly based on income, money does buy essential things for children. Good food, safe and decent shelter, opportunities to learn, reduced family stress and conflict, a decent neighborhood, health care, health supplies and safety devices, healthy recreation, transportation, communication, and economic opportunity are essential resources that depend on income (Sherman, 1994). One might also add a sense of stability and predictability in one's life that contributes to the freedom to learn.

Poverty increases the risks that children must face and threatens their determination, self-discipline, and resilience. Children in poverty are more likely to suffer health problems and learning problems, attend inferior schools, live in substandard housing, move more often, and even face earlier deaths than those whose families have sufficient economic resources (Sherman, 1994). Health problems and the risk of disabilities are particularly critical. As cited by Ohlson (1998), many researchers have found that "children in low-income families are more likely to experience chronic illness and disability" (p. 192).

Impact on Brain Development

Since school-aged children are primarily engaged in learning experiences, it is important to consider the potential impact of poverty on brain development. Inadequate nutrition, substance abuse, maternal depression, exposure to environmental toxins, trauma and abuse, and quality of day care may negatively affect brain development in young children (National Center for Children in Poverty, 2001).

Thus, children in poverty may begin their school years with impaired development. As noted by Shore (1997), "Researchers have gathered new evidence on the importance of the first years of life for children's emotional and intellectual development" (p. 4). Despite the resilience found in many children, impaired brain development may be unavoidable. During the period when the brain is most sensitive to environmental stimulation, children in poverty may be exposed to risk factors affecting brain development (Shor, 1997).

Chinyavong and Leonard (1997) have pointed out that persistently low-income children have an average IQ score 9 test points lower than that of children in never-poor average families who are similar in ethnicity, family structure, and parental education. They are also 11 to 25 percentiles lower in academic achievement scores; 1.3 times more likely to have learning disabilities; 2 or 3 percentage points more likely to be placed in special education; and 2 times more likely to drop out than middle income youths (p. 4).

Inadequate nutrition, for example, can result in lower scores on tests of vocabulary, reading comprehension, arithmetic, and general knowledge (Brown & Pollitt, 1996). Malnutrition also causes social withdrawal, delayed motor skills development, and delayed physical growth, which may lead to lower expectations from parents and teachers (Bennett et al., 2001). Research has also linked poor brain development to substance abuse, which may exist in families living in conditions of poverty. Stunted neurons in the brain and a lack of brain cells in crucial developmental stages may result from the harmful effects of nicotine, alcohol, and drugs (Mayes, 1996). Maternal depression, exposure to environmental toxins, trauma and abuse, and the poor quality of daily care are additional risks associated with poverty that may result in impaired brain development in children (see Figure 9.1).

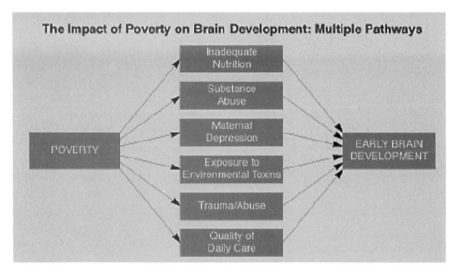

FIGURE 9.1   **The Impact of Poverty on Brain Development: Multiple Pathways**

Source: National Center for Children in Poverty. Retrieved January, 2002 from http://cpmcnet. columbia.edu/dept/nccp/brain.html

STATE AND FEDERAL PROVISIONS

As we enter the 21st century, families in poverty also suffer the impact of welfare reform. President Bill Clinton, who promised to "end welfare as we know it," signed the Personal Responsibility and Work Opportunity Reconciliation Action (PRWORA) in August 1996. According to Ohlson (1998), "The intent of the legislation is to remove incentives to remain on welfare that many believe were inherent in the Aid to Families with Dependent Children (AFDC) program, and to encourage the personal responsibility of welfare recipients by mandating work" (p. 191). Federal funds for AFDC, food stamps, and Supplemental Security Income have been reduced. Actually, AFDC has been replaced by the Temporary Assistance to Needy Families (TANF) program, through which the federal government provides states a block grant that is capped with a fixed level of funding (Ohlson, 1998). TANF includes a work requirement provision in which "states may require individuals who have received TANF for 2 months to participate in community service or risk loss of benefits." Unfortunately, "allowable work" does not include attending school, so parents who have limited education cannot improve their employment situation through additional education (Ohlson, 1998).

The law does allow a "hardship" provision, which permits states to waive work requirements for up to 20 percent of its TANF recipients. However, there is a lifetime limit of 5 years of assistance. Other provisions of the PRWORA that are especially harsh include the fact that, under the new Supplemental Security Income (SSI) changes, many children with disabilities will lose their SSI benefits. Ohlson (1998) points out that SSI has "historically assisted many impoverished parents to manage additional expenses related to their child's disability" (p. 194). Another provision for those in poverty, Medicaid, has not been changed under PRWORA. However, child care assistance for all families participating in welfare-to-work provisions is limited by the Child Care and Development Block Grant, which uses a fixed funding formula that limits the amount of funding available to the states.

Major cuts have been made in the food stamps program and the Federal Child Nutrition Program, which, in part, reduce the amount of funds for day care providers operating in low-income areas. Funds are also cut under the Social Services Block Grant, which supports several programs for families who are homeless, among others. In addition, the immigrant provisions of PROWRA denies many legal immigrants TANF and SSI and restricts the provision of "means tested federal benefits to legal immigrants who arrived in the U.S. after August 22, 1996" (Ohlson, 1998).

Becker (2001) has reported that private food charities are trying to fill the gaps created by reduced federal aid to the poor. In fact, more people are getting food from private charities over the course of the year than are participating in the federal food stamp program (Becker, 2001). There has been a decrease from 21.9 million people using federal food stamps in 1997 to 17.7 million in 2001. "Emergency feeding sites around the country serve more than 7 million people in a given week. Both the U.S. Senate and House are recommending increases in the food stamp program" (Becker 2001, p. A14). Religious groups, who run most of the private programs, are also supporting an increase in money for food stamps. Results of a survey by the Mathematica Policy Research group showed that nearly one-half the households receiving aid included children, working families made up 40 percent of those seeking aid, women accounted for nearly two-thirds of adults who sought emergency food aid, and nearly one-third of those seeking emergency food assistance also received food stamps (Becker 2001).

Ohlson (1998) points out that families already in poverty who are struggling to raise children will be under additional stress due to the changes in welfare. Increased levels of stress in the families will affect parents' ability to care for their children and to meet the demands of the schools. An expansion of the cost-effective prevention programs is needed.

WHAT CAN SCHOOLS DO?

The full-service schools described in Chapter 3 can answer the needs of many children whose families are caught in the harsh circumstances of poverty with only reduced state and federal assistance available. For example, in several New York City schools where dental services are now available, principals have found that dental health has led to improved academic performance

(Bahrampour, January, 2001). In Maria's case, which follows, the health services, eye test, and medication that she needed and the lack of eyeglasses that prevented her progress in school could have been obtained in a school where community agencies, in collaboration with the school, provide critical services to children. In view of the limited assistance available to families and children in poverty, it is urgent to remember Kagan's comment that "the education of children cannot be separated from their care" (1989, p. 189).

Maeroff (1998) has argued for the importance of connectedness, a support system or network that most students need "to succeed in education" (p. 426). He notes that "when students gain a sense of connectedness to the people and institutions whose guidance and assistance will help them to advance themselves, their social capital increases" (p. 426). In his view, the school is perceived as part of the ecosystem that includes all parts of a student's life. Thus, the school's linkages with the home and community is essential. In Chapter 3, we have discussed the critical importance of building a strong school–home–community relationship. Mayeroff (1998) reinforces this view in his comment that social capital "the whole system of networks, values, norms and trust may count for as much as book learning and have as much to do with finding a place in the mainstream" (p. 432). Ultimately we want every child to find a place in the mainstream.

THE CASE OF MARIA RAMIREZ

As she dressed for school on Monday morning, Mrs. Corea felt energetic for the first time in many weeks. Finally, the multidisciplinary team at Washington Elementary School was meeting to consider Maria Ramirez's eligibility for special education. It was now February, and Mrs. Corea had been frustrated with Maria since the school year began. It seemed as if nothing that she tried made a difference for Maria, and it had been impossible to communicate with the parents who did not speak English.

Mrs. Corea took her usual route to Washington Elementary School, a lovely drive along the river that avoided the poorest area of the city where the Ramirez family lived. Mrs. Corea thought about the contrast of Maria's neighborhood with that of the majority of students at Washington and wondered how the Ramirez children could find friends. The Ramirez's neighborhood had the appearance of a war-torn city where abandoned houses, small businesses, and factories were boarded up, windows broken, and structures gutted. The street on which Maria's family lived was typical of many. Broken sidewalks and potholed streets were littered with broken glass, rocks, and other debris. Signs of neglect were everywhere. At one end of the street there were eight small houses of two stories, several with occupants who sat on the front steps, their faces expressing sadness or boredom as they watched the passing cars or the children who sometimes played in the street.

The Ramirez building was sandwiched between two abandoned factories. Directly facing their house, on the other side of the street, another empty factory stood as a reminder of the jobs lost to the community. Neither grass nor trees enlivened the surroundings. However, in a vacant lot a pile of branches lay waiting to be removed. In the tiny basement apartment where the Ramirez family lived, two small, front windows with curtains flapping in the wind allowed the only air to enter.

Miss Anacasta, the school social worker, had said to Mrs. Corea earlier that even among the small group of poor families at their school the Ramirez children lived in a most desperate situation. Roaches and mice ran about freely in the old building and sometimes the girls' clothing had a roach on the sleeve of a coat or sweater. In the cold winter weather the girls often wore clothing that was too small and inappropriately flimsy. It was no wonder that they were often sick. The tiny apartment of three rooms had no bedroom for the girls. Their bed was placed in the small foyer at the front door, which could be very cold when the temperature dropped well below freezing. Nevertheless, Mrs. Ramirez worked hard to keep the place neat and even decorated for the holidays.

The school's multidisciplinary team was finally meeting today to consider Mrs. Corea's referral. It had been difficult to get at least one of Maria's parents to attend any meeting, and everyone was relieved to see Mrs. Ramirez. Mr. Ramirez, as usual, was looking for work, interviewing whenever and wherever possible, and could not attend the meeting. Mrs. Ramirez, on the other hand, had a job at a private school laundry where she had to report at 6:30 A.M. and was not allowed to take time off without losing pay. Thus, she was never home early enough to attend school meetings. However, Miss Anacasta had convinced her of the importance of today's meeting, and Mrs. Ramirez would lose the day's pay.

In addition to Mrs. Corea, the multidisciplinary team included the chairperson, Miss Burns; the school psychologist, Mr. Bowen; Mrs. Ramirez; Miss Houghton, the district's translator; and Miss Anacasta, the social worker. They met in a large conference room at a rectangular table. Miss Burns sat at one end and other members of the team sat together on one side. Mrs. Ramirez and Miss Anacasta sat together on the other side, facing the other committee members. The facial expressions of the committee reflected the serious nature of the meeting,

As the meeting began, Miss Burns welcomed everyone and explained, "We will deviate a little from our usual procedure in order to allow Mrs. Ramirez to share her view of Maria's problems. This is the very first time that Mrs. Corea and Mrs. Ramirez have met and had an opportunity to exchange information." She then turned to Mrs. Ramirez and asked her to describe what she believed to be her daughter's strengths and also what difficulties she thought Maria might be having.

Mrs. Ramirez spoke through the translator. "I am very worried about Maria. She doesn't like school and she wants to stay at home whenever possible. She never talks about school and doesn't seem to have much interest in it. She's having lots of trouble learning, and the school officials recently held a meeting that we were asked to attend, but I am not allowed to leave work early or I lose the pay and my husband had a job interview that day. When I arrived at the school everyone had left."

Miss Burns then asked, "What was school like for Maria before she came here?" Mrs. Ramirez replied, "Maria has had lots of problems since she started school. Although she was born in the United States, she attended kindergarten in Mexico and first grade in Texas. When she started school in New York, she began second grade, and because she did not learn to speak or read English, the teacher decided that Maria should repeat second grade here at Washington Elementary. Even now, in third grade, Maria's English isn't very good. I wish I could help her more, but I don't know English and my husband, Manuel, doesn't either. We speak only Spanish at home, so it's difficult to practice English. Recently, I started a night class to learn English so that I will be able to help Maria and the other children with their schoolwork."

"Tell us about how Maria gets along with other children," Miss Burns remarked. Mrs. Ramirez continued, "Maria is a sociable, friendly girl who has friends around her age with whom she gets along well. She likes to please people, is very affectionate, expressive, and sentimental. Like all other children, she's very active and energetic and she enjoys sharing her favorite activities—riding a bicycle, playing, and watching television. Maria doesn't have many chores at home; she's not asked to do much. She tries to clean up sometimes when she feels like it, but she doesn't do a good job. So she has lots of time for playing."

"What about Maria's medical history?" Miss Burns asked. "We know that she has recently had some problems."

Mrs. Ramirez responded, "Maria has sure been sickly. She weighed only 3 pounds when she was born and she needed oxygen because the cord was wrapped around her neck. She was in an oxygen machine for 24 hours. Maybe that's why she's always sick now. She always has colds and sore throats, and now she has urinary infections, too. I know the school nurse is very concerned about these infections, but sometimes our old car won't run and many times we have no money for the medicine. I wish that Maria could get an ultrasound test to find the cause of the urinary infections."

As Mrs. Corea tried hard to maintain her attention, she thought how difficult it was to wait for the translation of whatever Mrs. Ramirez had to say. Nevertheless, she was impressed by the problems that Mrs. Ramirez had described. She then turned to Maria's mother and said, "Is there anything else that might help us to understand Maria's problems in school?"

Mrs. Ramirez answered with obvious sadness in her voice, as Miss Houghton translated, "It has been almost 4 years since we came to America to find a better life and we have had many troubles. We have five girls, ages 16, 12, 10, 9, and 8, and I worry about all of them. I am now 38 years old and Manuel, my husband, is 48. I know that we have not been stable parents for the girls. We've moved a lot and it has been hard to find work. There have been times when either my husband or I had to work far away from home and could see the children only one weekend every other month or two. Maria always asks me, "Do you love me?" She doesn't believe that we love her as much as we love her sisters. Now, with my job at the laundry and my night class, I am away from home until 9:30 many evenings, but I want to learn English so that I can help the girls with their schoolwork."

Mrs. Corea, thinking about the personal feelings shared by Mrs. Ramirez, turned to express appreciation to her, "Mrs. Ramirez I know that it must have been difficult to share that information. It really helps me to understand the circumstances in which Maria has lived that could have affected her educational progress. I would like to share my observations now and my experiences with Maria as her teacher."

"At the beginning of the school year Maria's second grade teacher told me that Maria's strength was in mathematics and that she would need help with work habits, completing her work, and organizational skills. But, in my opinion, Maria's areas of excellence are her manners and respect for authority. She did learn some sight words in second grade because she received daily help in the ESL class."

After the translation, Mrs. Corea continued, "Maria doesn't seem to have a clue about what's going on in the classroom. She often wastes time and is limited in all academic areas, as well as in oral expression. Even when I modify work for her, she only occasionally completes it. Maria is at the preprimer level in reading according to the Botel Reading Test that I recently gave her. I believe that she has a disability and needs a special education program. I would really like to see her needs addressed so that she can begin to make some progress in school."

Miss Burns smiled and inquired, "How would you describe Maria's social development, Mrs. Corea?"

The teacher responded, "I must say that Maria is basically well behaved, but recently she has been periodically nasty, hits other students, and sometimes cries in class. Nevertheless, her behavior continues to be manageable since she does respond to authority. Then, too, she seems to like being here and she blends easily into the room. But, I really think that Maria needs special education."

The chairperson nodded and said, "Thank you, Mrs. Corea, it seems that you and Mrs. Ramirez agree on the fact that Maria needs help now, and I hope that we can help her. Perhaps Miss Anacasta can also shed some light on Maria's difficulties."

Miss Anacasta, the school's social worker, had been to the Ramirez home several times to try to help the family obtain winter clothing, food, and transportation. She had also sought answers to questions concerning the girls' health problems. She began her comments with a heavy sigh, "Well, I certainly don't think that Maria should be placed in special education. When I talk to her in Spanish, she seems really intelligent. My experience with Maria has been very positive. She has a very pleasant and friendly manner and she smiles and laughs a lot. When I tutor her sometimes, she tries hard to complete the tasks involved. She appears to want to learn and to succeed in her schoolwork."

Miss Anacasta continued, after the translation, "The Ramirez family is very close and supportive, which helps Maria and the other children. However, it is difficult for the parents to help their children with schoolwork because neither speaks English. In addition, Mr. Ramirez only completed ninth grade in Mexico, and Mrs. Ramirez completed eighth grade there. When you consider, also, the long hours that Mrs. Ramirez works and the difficulties with employment for Mr. Ramirez, it is obvious that assistance for the children is not often possible. Nevertheless, Mr. Ramirez insists that the girls go to the library more often so that they will improve in reading.

"When I first met the family at home, only Mrs. Ramirez seemed friendly. Mr. Ramirez was not very enthusiastic about my visit and asked several times why I had come. He appeared to be very authoritative and to make all the family decisions. For example, he decided that the girls must do the laundry every Saturday and they must walk with the laundry to the nearest laundromat, which is far from the home. In fact, the entire day is occupied in this way on Saturday. Mr. Ramirez is currently doing factory work off and on; his employment has been unstable for the past 8 months, and the family has had difficulties obtaining food, clothing, and transportation. They have a very old car that runs far less than it's running. I must say, however, that gradually Mr. Ramirez has become friendlier and now, in hesitant English, he likes to talk with me about the difficulty in learning a second language.

"The family's only place for community involvement and socialization is their church, which does give them such assistance as Thanksgiving and Christmas food baskets. However, the children continue to have many needs that are unmet, primarily health—vision and hearing tests, for example. While Maria's difficulties are most critical, all the children have problems. Some of their health needs have been met through collaboration of the school and community health center. However, the most recent problem faced by the family involves an investigation of child neglect and abuse by the State's Child Protective Services. This was prompted by a series of problems observed by the school: Maria's recurring urinary infections; the fact that often she receives no medication because the family has no money or transportation; the inappropriate clothing worn by the children—flimsy and too small during the winter; and the frequent crying in school by some of the girls.

"In my opinion, Mr. and Mrs. Ramirez appear to be sincerely concerned about their children; however, the dire poverty in which they live, in addition to their limited English proficiency, interferes with their best intentions. The family needs decent housing and the opportunity to earn adequate income. Perhaps the poverty contributes to the children's' difficulties with their peers. Sometimes the girls have reported to me that children on the bus have turned up their noses when they sit beside them, as if the Ramirez children smell bad. They have also been called negative names by their classmates on the bus."

Miss Anacasta turned to Mrs. Ramirez to say, "I know that you would certainly like to live in a better place." On hearing the translation, Mrs. Ramirez smiled and nodded her head in agreement.

Miss Burns thanked the social worker and turned to Mr. Bowen, the school psychologist. "What have you determined to be Maria's major problems, Mr. Bowen, and what did your testing show?"

Mr. Bowen responded. "I believe that Maria's health problems are interfering with her ability to learn. Even now, she needs testing for lead. Her eye exam was finally completed a few days ago after a long delay and now we know that she cannot function without glasses. This means that her earlier test scores are probably unreliable. On testing she showed problems in memory and information processing in both Spanish and English. Her expressive vocabulary is very limited in both languages. Maria has a considerable delay in reading, but is on grade level in mathematics. She scored in the slow learner range on the intelligence test, but we must consider that her language, vision, and physical problems probably interfered. Socioeconomic difficulties and culture could also influence the test results.

"I did observe Maria in the classroom several times during the language arts period. The 28 students sat in a random pattern; however, Maria sat behind a bookshelf, like a room divider, which did not allow for good visibility of Maria from the teacher's desk. On one occasion, students were completing a worksheet. Maria was able to follow directions and volunteered the correct answers to several questions. Sometimes she seemed distracted, talking to a student nearby or tying her shoe. Eventually, Mrs. Corea directed Maria to move her desk where it could be seen.

"The class was then told to write a paragraph with at least six words in each sentence and Maria appeared puzzled. The teacher then directed them to finish the paragraph for homework and read it to someone at home. I think that Maria probably wasted a little time during the lesson, but she was involved."

"Yes," interjected Miss Burns, "your observations are helpful. The test results are somewhat unreliable since Maria did not have her glasses." The chairperson then began to summarize all the evaluation data that had been collected. She continued, "The following tests were completed: physical examination, reading assessment, language assessment, intelligence testing, and home visits. The team is ready to make a decision and recommendation. However, Maria does not fit any of the 13 disability categories. She is not eligible for a learning disability classification due to her IQ test score, and since she has 20/40 vision with glasses, she cannot be considered visually impaired. We are unable to verify a specific disability. Another point to consider is that Maria cannot be retained another year. Furthermore, there is really no resource room program that will help her."

"Perhaps a bilingual program or one-to-one tutoring would help," suggested Miss Anacasta.

The team did not recommend any of the suggestions. As the meeting ended, they all felt as if they had gone around in circles. "What's next," Mrs. Corea sadly reflected as she left the room, angry and disappointed. "What in the world will happen to Maria? Is there anything I can really do to help her? How will I manage?"

DISCUSSION QUESTIONS

1. How can research and expert opinion help in our search for alternatives?
2. To what extent does Mrs. Corea's ignorance of Maria's culture and language contribute to Maria's lack of progress?
3. How would you explain Maria's ineligibility for special education?
4. Identify the options now available to Maria and her family that could improve Maria's academic achievement.
5. Describe the change in Mrs. Corea's attitude before and after the meeting.

THE CASE OF SARAH SCHULTZ

My Goals for the Future

I have a lot of goals for my future. To be able to reach these goals I have to learn in high school. One goal I have is to get really good grades to pass. I am going to be in regular classes and my worries about that is I will look or feel stupid. I want to be able to study so that I can remember things. But I have problems knowing how to study and remember what I'm doing. I also want my grades to be above 75. But I'm worried I'll be nervous or even scared. In school I want good grades, but my worries are that I'll be scared to answer a question in front of so many people because I get nervous. Like I know how to answer the question but I just cant say it. I want to graduate the high school and I'm good in some stuff like English but I'm worried that I wont do so good in social studies or science.

I want to have a career but I'm not sure of what I want. I used to want to become a singer but my worries are I have to be perfect in singing. I also have to be able to read music. That would be hard for me. In my life I want to become a psychologist but I always get nervous. I also want to become a preschool teacher but I have to go to collage for being a teacher. But my worries are I don't think I could come up with that much money. But I'll have to work hard. In my life I also want to work in a nursing home. But my worries are that I might do something wrong. In my life I want to go to collage. I always thought about going to collage but I have to do a lot of things myself. I also want to go to college so that I could learn a lot more and I could get a better job then most other person that has never went. I want to get a job so that I could make money to go to college.

In my life I want to make money for college but then I will need money for my own place. I want to live in a big city because there is a lot more better jobs and get a lot more money. As I get older I hope I do have a good life and be able to do most of the thing I had said.

by Sarah Schultz

Sarah's Mom, Vicky Schultz. I want Sarah to be able to graduate from high school and have a better life than I've had. My mom was never in my life and she died an alcoholic when I was 25. My dad worked all the time building houses or driving a truck, so I didn't see much of him when I was young. He had four other children, so he had to work. We got along, but he just wasn't around much. By the age of 2 I was in a foster home and my father got me back. That's why my last name is Schultz, not Rosetti. My foster parents were bad to me.

When I was in school, I played a lot of sports like softball and basketball. I even wanted to play football, but they wouldn't let me. I made it all the way to twelfth grade, but never graduated because I was short one and a half credits in Health and Social Studies. I never did drugs. Even when I was in high school, I worked after school. I kept working until I had Sarah at 21. Sarah's dad, Joe, was 12 years older than me and we never married. His mom didn't like me and didn't think he was the father. He was—I had a blood test to prove it.

Sarah says she wants to go to college, and I hope she will. But she's going to have a tough time graduating from high school, especially with that 69 grade she got in math on her last report card. Sarah says she wants to be a teacher or a "psychology person" or work with older people like I did for awhile in the nursing home. Her grandfather has a bank account with some money in it for college, but she can't use it for anything else. And that won't cover it. She's going to have to work to pay for college.

Right now, she won't even go get her working papers and get a job this summer. She spends all her time with her boyfriend. I don't want to become no grandmother. Sometimes we get along great and other times she has a mouth on her. It's like she has two personalities. I yell at her when she's doing stupid stuff because I don't want her to get into trouble. But I don't like anybody else being negative about my kids. That's for me to do.

Sarah has all these plans. She wants to go to college, get a job in the city, have a car and a house and nice furniture. I'd like her to have that stuff, too. But she's going to have to work hard in school and get a job if she wants things. I worked for 4 years at the same job, but I got carpal tunnel syndrome from all the lifting. The doctor operated on my arm and now I can't even hold things and I'm in pain a lot. Right now I don't even know if I'll have enough money to pay the rent next month and buy food now that I'm on disability. I'd do anything for my kids, but with three of them to feed and buy clothes for, it's tough. The boys are good athletes, so maybe they'll get money for college for playing football or basketball. But Sarah's just going to have to work hard.

Sarah's Mentor.   It's hard to believe that I've known Sarah for over 6 years now. I first met her when she was a second grader with a long, brown pony-tail and slightly scared gray eyes. The elementary school Sarah attended had a community mentor program, and I volunteered to meet with her once a week at school. I knew she was in a special education class and needed help with all academic areas, especially reading. It took awhile for Sarah to warm up to me, but now she says it's like she's known me all her life.

Because of my job, I couldn't meet with Sarah on Wednesday after-noons when most of the mentors came. Instead, I came before school started when Sarah and about 80 percent of the rest of the children in the school came in for breakfast. We would read books together, although I did most of the reading. It was hard for me to find books for her at first because she was virtually a nonreader. However, we kept at it, made flash cards of the words she didn't know, and wrote each week in a journal or on the computer.

As she got older, I tried to introduce her to new information and expe-riences. Sarah's world was geographically very small. To the best of my knowledge, before she met me, she had never been outside the two-county area, much less outside the state. I would take her out to restaurants for her birthday so she would know how to act and eat a variety of foods. She loved it! Once we went to the "Big City" on the train at Christmas time and visited all the major department stores. She was totally amazed by the size of the skyscrapers and the opulence in the stores. Her experience with shopping was the Family Dollar store. One summer, I took her on a family weekend to the beach. She had never seen the ocean and was overwhelmed by the big houses that lined the streets. It was hard to get her out of the water.

I also tried to get her to read more, but it was always a struggle. Once, when Sarah was in fifth grade, I began to read Sarah the book *Sounder* by William Armstrong. Knowing she likes animals, I thought she might enjoy the touching story revolving around a hunting dog. It mentioned that the family lived near the homes of Negro sharecroppers. I asked Sarah if she knew what the word Negro meant. She did not. I quickly tried to explain the use of the word in the context of slavery. I found myself galloping through the slave trade, cotton fields, the causes of the Civil War until I realized that I could not fill this void in 5 minutes. Yet the blank look on Sarah's face told me she was unaware of any of this history.

I kept meeting with Sarah until she graduated from fifth grade. Even after that I would stop by to see her on a regular basis to see how middle school was going. Sometimes she would come by with a friend or her brothers since she lives within walking distance of my home. Once in awhile she would ask for help with a school report, and we would do a search for information on the computer. Sarah loves to sing and has a lovely voice, so she's especially interested in popular musicians. Once she did a report on Charlie Parker for her music class, and she seemed to enjoy reading the things we found on the Internet.

She's certainly had her ups and downs academically. She's been in a self-contained special ed class as long as I've known her, and she's always wanted to be in regular classes. She talks about feeling dumb and says she wishes "she could put everything you have in your head in my head."

I don't think I intended to get involved with Sarah and her family as much as I have over the years, but it has been a very rewarding experience for me. It's certainly made me extremely thankful for my stable, middle-class family and my college education. I grew up in a fairly wealthy suburban area in another state and knew little of the poverty or near poverty many experience in this small city of about 20,000. Fifteen years ago a major technology company closed its plant here, and we lost many professionals who were making higher-end salaries. While the rest of the country has experienced an economic boom, we're still recovering. This is really the only city in the county, so many individuals in need of social services live in the city center. What was once a middle-class residential and business midtown section has become an uneven patchwork of historic homes, corner food stores, former single-family houses that are now run-down multiple family apartments, and a food pantry. The police have a strong presence given the amount of crime in the area.

Sarah is one of four children, although her sister died soon after birth when Sarah was 10. Over the years I've visited her apartment building many times and gotten to know the extended family. She has two half-brothers, William and Wallis, who are now in first and second grade. About every other month they come with Sarah to my house and love to play the piano or plant flowers in the garden. They especially love my husband's cooking. Every time I stop by their apartment, they want to know when they can come for dinner. William and Wallis are both handsome, athletic, biracial kids who have to play in the concrete parking lot behind their apartment house. There are always lots of kids around, but it's also a low-income building occupied primarily by people who are down on their luck or chemical abusers. Last month a 10-year-old child accidentally shot a 2-year-old in the head and, amazingly, the toddler lived through it. Over the years there have been knife fights and many drug-related arrests. Sadly, William and Wallis's father has been in and out of prison on drug charges for as long as I've known the family. Sarah's mom, Vicky, is adamantly against drug use and says repeatedly that she wishes that she could move to a safer neighborhood. The reality is that she is already paying $625 a month for this three-bedroom apartment and can't afford anything better.

The boys' father has a fairly extended family in the area, so Sarah and the boys often have cousins staying overnight or after school until their parents come home from work. When I first got to know Sarah, Vicky was on welfare, so she would often baby-sit for family and neighbors. After 10 years on welfare and unsuccessful attempts to pass her GED, she went to work at a job that demanded a fair amount of physical labor. Then she had to find someone to take care of the children while she worked four 12-hour days a week. She worked for 3 years at a physically demanding job, but seemed to feel good about the fact that she was getting a paycheck. Recently, however, she had surgery for carpal tunnel syndrome in her left hand and has been on disability. Vicky thinks the surgeon did a bad job since she's been going to physical therapy all that time and still can't grasp anything in that hand and often has pain up and down her arm. Right now the future is unclear since the payments for disability hardly cover the rent. I took Vicky to the welfare office once and I couldn't believe the runaround she got.

Vicky's dad has been a consistent figure in their lives over the years. When I first met him, he was driving a semi, but he's been on medical disability for his back for several years now. Sarah loves to visit her grandfather; however, he lives about 25 miles away and has to pick her up and take her back since Vicky doesn't have a car and bus transportation just doesn't connect to his small rural town. Yet he comes to see them at least once a month and often takes Sarah shopping each fall for new school clothes.

Sarah's father was never in the picture when I first mentored Sarah. I think he and Vicky split when she was very young, and Sarah had little good to say about him. It wasn't a good relationship and Sarah used to talk about when "mom and I were in the shelter." He didn't send any money to support Sarah and has since married and had a daughter. I guess that Sarah's curiosity about her heritage got the best of her last year, so she called him up from a friend's house and he arranged to pick her up. Since then, Sarah has visited him on weekends occasionally. Because he lives at least 30 miles away, transportation is an issue, and I think their visits are less frequent now. Sarah seems glad to have reunited with him, but I don't think he'll be a major factor in her life—certainly not financially.

Sarah and her mom have their ups and downs. One minute Vicky defends Sarah's actions and the next she complains that Sarah is mouthy, lazy, and disrespectful. I've heard Sarah be a lot more critical of her mom lately. I suppose that's part of adolescence. She's at that stage of telling her mom all the things Vicky's done wrong and how she won't be that kind of mother. Sometimes Vicky gives her hell, and other times she just rolls her eyes and says, "Yeah, just wait." Once, Sarah even left home for several days. Ultimately, I think they love each other very much, but these next few years could be tough.

When I try to imagine what will happen to Sarah in the future, I can only hope that she will make good decisions for her own future. Sometimes she gets herself in trouble. Once a kid at the bus stop broke her glasses with a snowball and she beat him up. Another time she was at the mall and a "rich kid" started calling Sarah and some friends nasty names for no apparent reason. In both cases the police were involved and Sarah had to appear before a judge. I can't say that I even blame Sarah for standing up for herself, but I know she has to learn better ways to defend herself. She lives in a tough neighborhood and probably has to be able to negotiate that environment for many years to come.

I also worry about the people that Sarah hangs out with. She calls them her "ghetto friends." Many of the girls have dropped out of school, had children very young, or have been involved with drugs. Sarah usually stops spending time with them once she realizes it's hurting her progress in school. Now she has a boyfriend who is 21. I've met him and he seems like a nice, quiet guy, but I worry about that relationship, too.

I know she has many plans for her future. She wants to own a car, go to college, and own her own house someday. I doubt that she has any idea how much these things cost. However, I'm glad she wants to graduate from high school, and I hope she doesn't get totally overwhelmed next year. Her mom really can't help her academically that much and, as much as I want to help Sarah, the reality is that my work schedule just doesn't allow me to see her that often.

Sarah has always been very respectful toward me and appreciative of the help that I've given her. She's a caring person and deserves a far better hand than she's been dealt. Although she can put on a tough exterior, at core she's very much afraid of going to high school. Unless her teachers go the extra mile, she could easily decide that dropping out is better than failure. To make it through the next 4 years, Sarah is going to need a lot more than good instruction.

Sarah's Teacher.   I have taught an eighth grade self-contained special education class for 7 years now. It's always gratifying to see the students getting their diplomas on graduation night. At the same time, I can't help but wonder whether they'll be there at graduation in another 4 years. I try to have great expectations for my students, but I know that the next 4 years for my students will be a real struggle. Their life circumstances are often so difficult that it's quite an accomplishment for them to have made it in school this far.

Take Sarah, for example. She's a great kid in many ways. Her attendance at school has been very good this year, and she's conscientious about getting her homework done. She has a strong sense of herself and is very social. She is always respectful to Ms. Lewis, my teaching assistant, and me, although she is fully capable of putting her peers in their place if she feels attacked. When one of the five boys in class tells Sarah her clothes are too tight, she tells them they don't have to look if it bothers them. I know she uses street language outside of class, but usually uses Standard English around me.

I teach Sarah all her academic classes. She writes fairly well and spelling is a strength. Recent assessments show that she is reading on a fourth grade level while her math scores are closer to fifth. Ms. Lewis and I try to use the regular curriculum, but some of the textbooks are ancient or on much too difficult a reading level, so I have to find materials written on an easier reading level or rely on auditory and visual presentations. This approach doesn't always help Sarah, since she really struggles when she has to process a lot of information auditorially. The other day we were about two-thirds of the way through watching the video of *The Diary of Anne Frank* and Sarah asked me why they were hiding. She just doesn't have the background knowledge that other students bring with them from home, life experiences, or their own reading. Her short- and long-term memory seems limited, but sometimes I think it's because there's just no established mental schema for her to attach new information to. When we practice data-based questions like the ones required on the new state tests, she has great difficulty getting the main idea and drawing inferences. There's so much that I have to catch Sarah up on and I just don't have that much time in class. Even with only 12 students, I feel like Ms. Lewis and I are always playing catch-up.

But school is not the only source of struggle for Sarah. It's obvious that her family's financial resources are limited. Sarah didn't go on the class trip to Great Adventure or the pool party this year. The family doesn't have a phone at home, so when I call her mom, I have to call her at work. Her dad lives in another town, although I know Sarah sees him on weekends sometimes. This fall Sarah was always squinting at the board. It was obvious that she needed glasses, but it took until Thanksgiving for her to get them. I think her grandfather finally paid for them. Sarah's grandfather is very important to her, and she's written that she likes spending time with him better than anything else in the whole world.

Sarah's physical and mental health are amazingly strong given some of her life experiences. Although Sarah rarely misses school, she seems tired on many mornings. Sometimes she says her little brother slept with her and kept kicking her all night. Other days she says her asthma is bothering her. I don't know much about Sarah's family situation, but I do know that she's been through real family stress. On one paper, she wrote the following:

"There was this man that was in my mom's life for many years. He used to always abuse her and hurt her in so many ways. And every time I look at my mom I always think of what he has done to my mom. It really hurt me. I was always scard that he would come and get her. But I got him out of her life and she has gotten so much better. She shows her love towards my brother's and me. So I could stop thinken about it, but thinken of how wonderful my mom is now. My energy goes to having fun now and being able to do things and not be scared."

It's hard to imagine that any child could concentrate in school, knowing that she would go home to an abusive environment. She has reason to be angry, fearful, and withdrawn, but she is actually quite the opposite. Unlike some of her classmates, Sarah seems to be able to negotiate socially with both adults and peers. I know she goes through many of the typical adolescent self-doubts about physical appearance, such as acne and her large size, but she clearly has respect for herself. Sarah has strong opinions on some topics and can be very outspoken.

I try to ask students to write about topics that affect their health and life-style. For example, Sarah has written about being vehemently against smoking. She's written about how crazy her friends are to smoke and how much money her mother throws away on "sigs" each year. She knows it's a bad example since her 8-year-old brother already talks about wanting to smoke. We've also had class discussions about pregnancy and abortion. All the students have friends and relatives who were parents at age 14 and have dropped out of school. Sarah, like all the girls in class, believes that having an abortion is wrong. I can only hope that they feel as strongly about avoiding sexual intercourse or using protection.

Sarah is a strong advocate for herself. Last fall, when I asked the students to write about their goals for the year, Sarah said she wanted to be in a regular class for social studies, science, and math. She said she knew it would involve getting her homework in and studying harder. Sarah received Bs and Cs in her academic classes with me this year, but I doubt that she would have done that well had she been in regular classes. This spring, when we had her IEP meeting, her mom wasn't able to come. However, Sarah seemed to know what she wanted. She asked to be in regular classes next year in high school, but she said she knew that she still needed support. The team decided that Sarah deserved to have a shot at general education, but I'm not quite sure how it will be structured. I know that, unlike this year, she'll have different teachers for each class.

In many ways, Sarah has done extremely well for herself. Yet she has goals that may exceed her family's financial and emotional capabilities. I'm not sure she understands what's involved in going to college, since no one in her family has preceded her. Our high school draws from the two middle schools in the district and Sarah will be in a class of over 600 students. It will be very hard for any other of Sarah's teachers to get to know her as well as I do, simply because they don't have the time with her that I do. I have 12 students and they have well over 100 each day.

Right now the state has mandated that all students pass competency tests in all major content areas in order to graduate. While there are exceptions for students with severe disabilities, Sarah is not one of those students. I believe in setting high standards, but sometimes I wonder if anyone on the state level has thought about what it will take for a kid like Sarah to graduate.

She's overcome some amazing hurdles so far, but I'm not sure how high we can raise that bar before she just stops trying.

DISCUSSION QUESTIONS

1. What barriers presently exist between Sarah's goals for herself and the realities of her present educational and economic situation?
2. What interpersonal and intrapersonal conflicts in values that are relevant to Sarah's future exist among the four voices in this case?
3. What goals should be initiated to promote a successful high school experience for Sarah?
4. What programs and support should the educational community provide for Sarah and other students like her?
5. Are there any limitations on what teachers and other education professionals can do to assist students like Sarah?

REFERENCES

Bahrampour (2001). Getting homework checked (and teeth as well). *New York Times,* Metro Section, p. B8.

Bauman, Z. (1998). *Work, consumerism, and the new poor.* Buckingham, PA: Philadelphia Open University.

Becker, E. (2001). Shift from food stamps to private aid widens. *New York Times,* Nov. 14, 2001, National Section, p. A14.

Bennett, N., Li, J., Song, Y., & Yang, K. (2001). Young children in poverty: A statistical update. National Center for Children in Poverty. New York: Columbia University. http://cpmcnet. Columbia.edu/dept/nccp/99uptext.html

Cheal, D. (1996). *New poverty: Families in postmodern society.* Westport, CN: Praeger.

Chinyavong, A., & Leonard, J. (1997). *Poverty matters: The cost of child poverty in America.* Washington, DC: Children's Defense Fund.

Darling-Hammond, L. (1995). Inequality and access to knowledge. In J. A. Banks & C. A. McGee Banks (Eds.), *Handbook of research on multicultural education* (pp. 465–483). New York: Macmillan.

Kagan, S. (1989). Early care and education: Beyond the school house doors. *Phi Delta Kappan, 71*(2), 107–112.

Kozol, J. (1991). *Savage inequalities.* New York: Crown.

Macroff, G. (1998). Altered destinies: Making life better for school children in need. *Phi Delta Kappan 79*(6), 425–432.

National Center for Children in Poverty (2001). *Low income children in the United States: A brief demographic profile.* Child Poverty Fact Sheet, June 2001. Retrieved January 10, 2002, from http://www.cpmcnet.columbia.edu/dept/ncep/ycpf-01

National Law Center on Homelessness and Poverty. (2001, November 28). *What you need to know about the education of homeless children* [on-line]. Available: http://www.nlchp.org/rights.htm

Ohlson, C. (1998). Welfare reform: Implications for young children with disabilities, their families, and service providers. *Journal of Early Intervention, 21*(3), 191–206.

Payne, R. K. (1998). *A framework for understanding poverty.* Highlands, TX: RFT Publishing.

Report: U.S. poverty temporary (1998, August 10). *Poughkeepsie Journal,* p. B4.

Rothenberg, D. (1998). *With these hands: The hidden world of migrant farmworkers today.* New York: Harcourt Brace.

Salend, S. (1998). *Effective mainstreaming: Creating inclusive classrooms.* Upper Saddle River, NJ: Merrill/Prentice Hall.

Shore, R. (1997). *Rethinking the brain. New insights into early development.* New York: The National Health/Education Consortium Report. pp. 4–5.

Witt, R. (2001). Advocacy day. Rural and migrant ministry. Personal communication.

■ ■ ■ ■ ■

CHAPTER 10

GENDER AND SEXUALITY

ISSUES IN GENDER

Diversity exists both between and within genders in the United States. Inequalities in salaries, family and societal expectations for career choices and social and sexual behaviors, and gender-based teacher attitudes and behavior toward students are only some of the significant issues associated with gender. For example, Sadker and Sadker (1994) have noted:

> For more than four decades, researchers have been asking students to "Draw a scientist." In the 1950s high school students uniformly saw a scientist as a middle-aged or older man wearing glasses and a white coat and working alone in a lab. Forty years later, in the 1990s, little had changed. In the most recent "draw a scientist" study, 100 percent of the boys and 84 percent of the girls were still drawing men. However, students also attributed characteristics such as weird, sinister, crazy, and nerdy to the scientist—the very images adolescent girls, who are worried about appearance and popularity, want to avoid at all costs. (Sadker & Sadker, 1994, p. 123).

Other researchers have commented that if students today were asked to draw a mathematician the chances are that they would also draw a man. In the words of Muller (1998), "The study of mathematics in the United States is stereotypically regarded as the domain of boys and a field in which girls have difficulty" (p. 336). Deborah Haimo (1997) supports Muller's position in the following comment: "Up until the past two or so decades, whereas males who indicated an interest and proficiency in mathematics were taken seriously and encouraged to continue in the field, women with like bent were not considered creditable and were largely ignored. . . . Indeed, the image of a mathematician prevalent throughout the world, has been that of man" (p. 7).

Obviously, gender may strongly influence our perception of many careers and professions as well as other important aspects of life. However, in this chapter we are concerned mainly with (1) the issues surrounding gender and the field of mathematics, primarily with respect to African American females, and (2) issues involving sexual orientation and gender. The issues involved in these two important areas are most directly related to the case studies that follow. Thus, the chapter is organized in two major sections, followed by two illustrative case studies. First, issues involved in the study of mathematics by females from diverse cultural groups, particularly African Americans, are discussed followed by issues involving sexual orientation.

A review of the research literature on African American females and mathematics from 1991 to 2001 reveals a negligible number of studies. In fact, the result of the search raises the question of whether the small number of studies is a reflection of the actual scarcity of African American females in mathematics or a reflection of the claim by Haimo (1997) that females, in general who have shown interest and proficiency in mathematics have not been taken seriously and have been largely ignored.

However, a body of research findings is available on females and mathematics and also on minority students in mathematics. Thus, for the purpose of providing background information on the case of Cassie, an African American female with interest and proficiency in mathematics, in this chapter, we will review first, research on females and mathematics; followed by the academic experience of minority students as a group in mathematics; and finally, the small body of specific studies available on African American females and mathematics.

FEMALES AND MATHEMATICS

It is reasonable to propose that images of the scientist and mathematicians as men that are held by so many students will not change until female mathematicians are widely recognized and respected as serious scholars. However, intervention programs designed to increase female participation in mathematics/science/technology careers have become a recent phenomenon (Clewell, Anderson & Thorpe, 1992). In fact, The Association for Women in Mathematics (AWM) was launched only in 1971. From the beginning they have worked to increase the participation and improve the position of women in mathematics (Blum, 1997). Blum (1997) has pointed out that while very few mathematicians in the 1970s were concerned with programs to increase the number of women in mathematics, a variety of intervention programs have now been established, especially at colleges and universities across the country, to increase the participation of women. In fact, the shift in focus in some programs from entry level students who might not have thought of going into mathematics to programs for students who have already shown talent in undergraduate mathematics has resulted in serious debate (Blum, 1997). While some mathematicians believe that programs should continue to focus on increasing the number of women in the field, others argue that the focus must shift to students who need encouragement and nurturing to continue at the graduate level.

Nevertheless, gender differences persist in the participation of females in mathematics (Leder, 1990), although differences in achievement are rapidly disappearing. For example, fewer females than males enroll in advanced mathematics courses such as trigonometry, precalculus and calculus (Leder, 1990). Earlier studies were inconsistent regarding male and female performance in mathematics (Leder, 1990). Some studies have shown females performing better while others show better performance by males. In addition, consistent differences in performance have not been found at the primary school level while from the beginning of secondary school, males frequently outperformed females (Leder, 1990). However, more recent research has shown that the achievement gap between males and females in mathematics was only three or four points in 2000 (Phillips, 2001).

Interestingly, Kleinfeld (1999) presents a somewhat different point of view based upon the notion of male and female "areas of strength." She notes that in high school science and mathematics, females simply do not do as well as males although they are catching up. On the other hand, males do not do as well in literature or languages which are female areas of strength (Kleinfeld, 1999). However, Kleinfeld is most concerned about refuting much of the recent research on girls, especially the American Association of University Report, "How Schools Shortchange Girls," which created such a stir when it was published in 1992 because the schools' treatment of girls had not been previously publicized in that manner. With emphasis on the fact that the gender gap in mathematics is closing, Kleinfeld does note that, in her view, the main group of students that schools are truly failing are African American males—not females.

Nevertheless, among the possible influential variables considered by Leder (1990) at the beginning of the 1990s were school variables, teachers, peers, and learner characteristics. In fact, studies published during the 1980s and early 1990s focused on affective variables (Boswell, 1985; Clarkson & Leder, 1984; Fennema & Leder, 1990; Fennema & Sherman, 1977, 1978; Gittelson, Petersen, & Tobin-Richards, 1982) and peer influence (Leder, 1990).

Although 12 years have passed since the publication of Leder's work, the variables she identified continue to be investigated. Current studies have examined factors such as socialization practices (Clewell, Anderson & Thorpe, 1992; Sadker & Sadker, 1994); teacher attitudes, beliefs, and behaviors

(Evans, 1996; Grossman & Grossman, 1994; Singh, 1998; Tauber, 1998); peer influence (Ogbu, 1995); students' attitude toward mathematics (Ma, 1999); and parental involvement (Ma, 1999).

Socialization Practices.   The family as a gendered institution that socializes its young to embrace gender roles is one of the factors identified earlier by researchers to explain the idea of male and female areas of study, careers, and professions (Chodorow, 1978; Clewell, Anderson & Thorpe, 1992; Sadker & Sadker, 1994). Sadker & Sadker (1994), have pointed out that "even the most well-meaning adults can inadvertently let sexist expectations slip into their own behavior" (p. 251). As noted earlier, some studies have shown that boys and girls are given different toys: boys' rooms are filled with sports equipment, toy vehicles, and building kits while girls have lots of dolls and kitchen utensils as their playthings (Sadker & Sadker, 1994). Thus, sex-typed play is encouraged and girls are encouraged in nurturing and interpersonal skills while boys are developing spatial skills among others (Sadker & Sadker, 1994). These early experiences may then contribute to female versus male areas of study and careers. One can see these gender-based expectations in the toy displays and commercials during the holidays.

Teacher Attitudes, Beliefs, and Behaviors.   In the view of other social scientists, the gendered images may be due to the differential treatment by teachers who respond differently to boys and girls during mathematics instruction in the classroom (Tauber, 1998) or to teachers who believe that differences in gender are rooted in purely biological factors and that they should prepare girls to fulfill different roles (Singh, 1998). Increasing quantities of research literature suggest that gender issues underlie many classroom activities (Singh, 1998). For example, teachers' beliefs about the dominance or subordination of particular genders may determine whose ideas are heard or ignored in student discussions (Evans, 1996).

Teachers differ in their views of how they should address gender in the classroom (Singh, 1998). The different views are reflected in the work of Grossman & Grossman (1994), who have outlined four positions about the roles that educators think that teachers should play:

1. Since there are underlying biological differences between the sexes, teachers should prepare the genders to fulfill different roles.
2. Students should be prepared for gender-neutral or androgynous roles.
3. Teachers should help students to decide for themselves whether they want to conform to a particular gender role, since gender role socialization is mainly a function of the home.

4. Since some teachers may be uncomfortable dealing with gender issues, educators should decide if they want to prepare students for different gender roles or not.

The first position is often criticized because it limits individual freedom to make choices, while those who promote the second position believe that educators and schools should help to make the society less sexist (Singh, 1998). Among educators who believe that teachers should deal with gender issues, the question of gender equity or equality arises (Singh, 1996). Gender equality proponents believe that all students should receive the same opportunities to access resources and opportunities for learning, while equity proponents strive for having the same outcomes for all students. This means that students considered at-risk or less advantaged would receive unequal support to assure the same levels at the end of the class or course (Streitmatter, 1994)

Since African American and Hispanic students in particular are in the position of lagging in achievement in mathematics (National Assessment of Educational Progress, 1999), the question of equity or excellence may confront many teachers in diverse school populations or schools where these students are disproportionately represented. In view of the small numbers of African American and Hispanic persons represented in those careers that require advanced mathematics, the question is critical.

Teachers' expectations for gender differences can also interact with racial and ethnic differences, thus creating a self-fulfilling prophecy (Tauber, 1998). When teachers encounter African American female students in a mathematics class, expectations for achievement and gender role may interact and influence the teachers' behavior in the classroom. Research reveals that teachers form expectations of and assign labels to students based on such characteristics as body build, gender, race, ethnicity, given name and/or surname, attractiveness, dialect, and socioeconomic level (Good, 1987). Furthermore, studies show that teacher expectations can predict changes in student achievement and behavior beyond the effects of prior achievement and motivation (Jussim & Eccles, 1992). Thus, teachers who hold low expectations for African American students and also believe in specific gender roles may refuse to take an African American female's interest and proficiency in mathematics seriously, thus discouraging students through negative attitudes and behaviors. Peer influence and students' attitudes toward math will be discussed later.

Affective Variables.   In the view of Fennema and Leder (1990), affective variables within the learner also influence participation and performance in mathematics. For example, in older studies, males in grades 6 through 12 consistently showed greater confidence than females in their ability to learn mathematics (Fennema & Sherman, 1977, 1978). Studies on the "fear of success" suggested that the lower performance of females in mathematics was due more to the internalization of and conforming to the expectations of others than to ability in and of itself (Boswell, 1985; Clarkson & Leder, 1984; Leder, 1982).

With respect to attributions of success and failure in earlier studies, females tend to attribute success to effort, while males tend to attribute it to ability. On the other hand, males tend to attribute failure to effort, while females attribute it to ability (Fennema, 1985; Gittelson, Petersen, & Tobin-Richards, 1982; Leder, 1984). In the words of Sadker & Sadker (1994),

> When children internalize success and externalize failure (the male approach), they are able to tackle new and challenging tasks with a mastery orientation, one that perseveres in the face of difficulty and leads to future achievement. Children who attribute success to effort and failure to lack of ability (the female approach) exhibit learned helplessness. When confronted with difficult academic material, they do not persist. (p. 97)

Furthermore, affective variables in the learner can also influence the course-taking patterns of females. Girls at the high school level are particularly concerned with being popular, and being bright is thought of as in conflict with being popular (Sadker & Sadker, 1994). Girls may even fake mediocrity in an effort to camouflage their abilities (Sadker & Sadker, 1994). The cost can be considerable, as noted more recently by Hofstetter (personal communication, 2000): "The aversion of many females to mathematics limits their career choices and results in limited understanding of and skills in a basic component of daily functioning."

Closely related to the student's attitude toward mathematics and mathematics self-concept is the pattern for dropping out of mathematics. A recent investigation of individual variables most strongly related to individuals dropping out of mathematics in grades 8 to 12 showed that, after taking account of SES, prior achievement, and prior attitude, females were 1.08 times as likely as males to participate in grades 8 to 11; however, in transitioning from grade 11 to 12, females were only 0.74 times as likely as males to participate, resulting in a considerable gender gap (Ma, 1999). That author also found that the effect of prior achievement in mathematics was much stronger than SES, particularly in the earlier high school grades. Later, it was the student's attitude toward mathematics that appeared to be most important. According to Ma, the significantly less positive attitude of females in grade 11 explained the gender difference in participation in grade 12.

Parental Involvement.   Parental involvement has been associated with mathematics achievement (Sharp, Sharp, & Metzner, 1995). In fact, parental or family involvement is viewed as a "key mediator between family background and cognitive and affective outcomes of schooling" (Ma, 1999). Although the particular components of family involvement that affects outcomes of schooling are presently unclear, researchers have identified four dimensions of involvement: home discussion, school communication, home supervision, and school participation (Ma, 1999). Home discussion about school activities, as well as helping students to plan their programs, was found to have the strongest relationship to academic achievement in a study conducted by Ho and Williams (1996). Other researchers have indicated positive effects of parental expectations and home supervision.

Interestingly, Ma (1999) found that students whose parents volunteered at school were more than nine times as likely to enroll in advanced mathematics as those whose parents did not. However, there was some variation across grade levels. Researchers have also found differences in parent and family involvement based on gender (Muller, 1998). Some studies have found that parents are more likely to be involved with girls in home activities, for example, while they are more likely to be involved with boys in school activities. However, parents' involvement with boys was more likely to decrease as boys grow older (Muller, 1998). In a study more specifically related to the gender achievement gap in mathematics, Muller (1998) used a database that included the base year for eighth grade students and follow-up in grades 10 and 12. The results showed that girls talked more with their parents about school than boys, more frequently with their mothers than fathers. However, boys talked more with their fathers about their high school program than the girls did. Muller also found that parents restricted girls' out-of-school activities more than boys'; and parents intervened in their sons' lives more than their daughters', because boys enjoyed more freedom to get into difficulties. Interestingly, boys' test scores were higher in each grade in which the exam was administered, but girls' grades were higher, which raises questions about how teachers grade the male versus female student. The girls had higher educational expectations than the boys; however, the boys were more likely to "report being in all kinds of mathematics sequences, including advanced mathematics, algebra, remedial mathematics, and higher level course work in grade 10" (Muller, 1998). The boys also had higher mathematics self-concepts that were closely associated with test scores. Muller's interpretation of the results included the facts that (1) parental involvement may mask some of the gender differences in grade 8 students' performance; (2) parental involvement was associated with test performance both positively and negatively; (3) talking with parents about school was positively associated with performance; (4) higher test scores were associated with parents' restriction of eighth grade students' activities; and (5) the strongest positive predictor of grade 10 mathematics scores was parental restriction of activities. Thus, while the higher scores of students in grade 8 were associated with talking with parents about school activities, in grade 10 it was restriction of activities with friends and of weekday television watching (Muller, 1998).

Minority Females and Mathematics

Clewell, Anderson, and Thorpe (1992) have investigated barriers to minority as well as to female students' participation and performance in mathematics, science, and engineering. They identified important factors such as (1) negative attitudes and perceptions; (2) poor academic performance or achievement; (3) insufficient course and extracurricular preparation; and (4) limited knowledge of mathematics and science careers. It is important to note, however, that Clewell et al. did not consider poor teaching and other factors outside the students' control. Although the work of Clewell et al. did not directly focus on African American females, it did include minority students of both genders and is relevant to the issues of African American females in mathematics. A review of the barriers identified by Clewell et al. can be useful in our understanding of the issues.

Negative Attitudes and Perceptions.   Research suggests that the positive attitudes of females and minorities toward mathematics and science begin to decline as they reach the level of junior high school (Ma, 1999). The change in attitudes has been attributed to a poor math self-concept, a negative perception of the usefulness of mathematics and science in real life, the stereotyping of mathematics and science as white male activities, and the influence of parents, teachers, and peers in discouraging participation (Oakes, 1990). Females may also respond to society's message that mathematics and science are unfeminine activities, thereby creating a conflict between their interest in the subjects and the desire to be popular (Bossert, 1981).

The stereotyping of mathematics and science as white male activities is related to Ogbu's (1995) work on cultural diversity and learning. Ogbu makes the important point that "the meaning and value students associate with school learning and achievement play a very significant role in determining their efforts toward learning and performance" (p. 584). Based on his theory that minorities may be subdivided into autonomous, voluntary, and involuntary minorities, he proceeds to explain the development of secondary cultural characteristics in opposition to the dominant group in control. Thus, involuntary (or castelike) minorities, those brought here against their will through the phenomenon that Ogbu labels "cultural inversion," regard certain forms of behavior, events, symbols, and meanings as inappropriate for them because these are characteristics of white Americans. In his words, "among involuntary minorities, school learning tends to be equated with the learning of the culture and language of White Americans, that is, learning of the cultural and language frames of reference of their 'enemy' or oppressors' " (p. 587). Most importantly, Ogbu points out that "unlike voluntary minorities, involuntary minorities do not seem to be able or willing to separate attitudes and behaviors that result in academic success from those that may result in linear acculturation or replacement of their cultural identity with White American cultural identity" (p. 588). It is important to point out that this is an abbreviated discussion of Ogbu's position, and it is essential to read a more extensive discussion of his work as cited in the references. Nevertheless, the implications are that some minority students may reject learning mathematics due to the attitude that it is a white activity.

Ogbu's discussion of variability in minority school performance (1993) also underscores his point that some minorities are successful in school "even though they face barriers in culture, language, and post school opportunities." (p. 88). Based on his comparative studies as an anthropologist, he notes that

> By comparing different minorities, it appears that the primary problem in the academic performance of minority children does not lie in the mere fact that children possess a different language, dialect, or communication style; it is not that they possess a different cognitive style or a different style of interaction; it is not even that the children face barriers in future adult opportunity structure. . . . The main factor differentiating the more successful from the less successful minorities appears to be the nature of the history, subordination, and exploitation of the minorities and the nature of the minorities own instrumental and expressive responses to their treatment, which enter into the process of their schooling. School performance is not due only to what is done to or for minorities; it is also due to the fact that the nature of the minorities' interpretations and responses makes them more or less accomplices to their own school success or failure. (p. 88)

Poor Academic Performance.   Clewell, Anderson, and Thorpe (1992) attribute the underachievement of minority students to the negative attitudes described earlier; however, other factors may also explain the poor progress. For example, the instructional approaches and materials used may not be appropriate for the learning styles of many females and minority students, and poor schools and poorly trained teachers may also contribute to underachievement. In fact, the majority of mathematics teachers have not majored in mathematics in college. These important factors were discussed in Chapter 2.

Insufficient Course and Extracurricular Preparation.   As noted by Clewell et al. "Differential patterns of course taking have been related to gender and ethnic differences in mathematics and science achievement. A review of the research literature has revealed that course-taking in high school mathematics can differ according to ethnicity (Davenport, C., et al., 1998). Traditionally, these groups (except Asian Americans) have enrolled in fewer optional or advanced courses than White male students" (p. 9). However, the lack of availability of advanced courses in mathematics and science at the high school level for many minority students must be considered. In schools such as the one attended by Cassie in the case study to follow, few advanced placement courses are available.

Limited Knowledge of Mathematics and Science Professions.   Minority students and their families may have insufficient knowledge of mathematics and related professions when making career choices. Career counseling is especially valuable for (females) minority students who may not be exposed to role models in careers involving mathematics and related fields. However, counselors will need an awareness of their own bias. Stereotypes and myths may result in low expectations and inappropriate advising. In addition, the use of inappropriate assessment instruments for diverse students can also lead to erroneous advice and guidance (Kerka, 1998).

In some cases, underfunded schools may be unable to provide adequate career counseling (Kozol, 1991). For example, one counselor in Cassie's high school described his situation in this way: "I have an overwhelming case load of 300 students. How can I possibly help every one of these kids? I would love to do home visits, but when do I have time to?" (Ramirez, personal communication, 2001). Parents and families who lack information on careers in science and mathematics or who wish their daughters to enter more service-oriented, female careers might also influence the choice.

Peer Influence.   Peers also provide influence and may become another important variable in the performance of females in mathematics. In the words of Leder (1990), "It [peer influence] acts as an important reference for childhood and adolescent socialization and further perpetuates sex-role differentiation through gender-typed leisure activities, friendship patterns, subject preference, and career intentions" (p. 17). As noted earlier, peer pressure from those who view mathematics as a "white" activity can also

TABLE 10.1   Common Themes in Successful Programs for Increasing Minorities in Mathematics

1. Mathematics is related to students' daily lives, especially in early grades.
2. Cooperative learning is emphasized.
3. Intervention begins early.
4. The image of mathematics as a subject for "nerds" must be changed to "mathematics is for everyone."
5. Students learn about mathematicians who are minorities.
6. Teachers concentrate on successful learning of less material, rather than more content with less success.
7. Concrete examples are used to introduce abstract concepts.
8. Teachers are comfortable with mathematics.
9. Summer programs are used to help students to bridge the move between junior and senior high school.
10. At the college level, students are encouraged to study together in small groups.

Source: Selvin, P. (1992). Math education: Multiplying the meager numbers. *Science, 258*(5085) p. 1200(2).

result in negative attitudes toward mathematics (Ogbu, 1993, 1995). However, successful programs around the country are increasing the numbers of minorities in math and science (see Table 10.1). At each transition in the educational pipeline, minority students may drop out of mathematics without intervention. Programs like those designed by Robert Moses (the Algebra Project) and Uri Treisman can increase the numbers of minority mathematicians and scientists.

AFRICAN AMERICAN FEMALES AND MATHEMATICS

Research on African American females in mathematics is extremely scarce. Furthermore, the published studies that do involve African American females in particular are only indirectly related to our interests. A brief review of current research includes studies that are concerned with various aspects of adult education, teaching, and career and vocational preparation. Adenika-Morrow (1996) points out that where race and gender come together in the area of mathematics and science African American girls have been more excluded than any other group. She underscores that statement as she notes that "Studies of women generally overlook women of color, and studies of students of color de-emphasize gender differences" (p. 80). This situation may also explain, at least in part, the scarcity of research specifically focused on African American females in mathematics.

Interestingly, Adenika-Morrow (1996) identifies two reasons for the situation: (1) African American women's lack of tools to negotiate the racism and sexism that damage the belief that they can succeed, and (2) the African American community's world view that "stresses the pragmatism of obtaining immediate employment. African American girls must go to work early and be practical in a career selection" (p. 80). The author provides descriptions of two schools that target African American high school girls. One school offers a program that places the girls with science, mathematics, and engineering students at colleges and universities in Southern California. The girls also took science and mathematics courses that prepared them for college work. To elicit parents' support and understanding, students and parents completed a science project together. According to Adenika-Morrow (1996), the program helped the girls to realize that, with commitment and persistence, they could have careers in the sciences.

In another program, African American girls were extensively exposed to African American role models. Parent participation, guest speakers, and mentors were also included. Both programs involved high expectations and positive support from parents, teachers, counselors, principals, and peers, which gave the participants a solid foundation for the pursuit of a career in the sciences.

With respect to problems faced by those who do choose a career in mathematics as teachers, Brown, Cervero, and Johnson-Bailey (2000) conducted interviews of seven African American teachers of mathematics to investigate how their position in society affected their experience of teaching mathematics to adults in postsecondary institutions. Their findings also included reports of secondary school experiences by the women. Sadly, the women had all experienced marginality, isolation, discouragement, and devaluation as students in their mathematics classes. They reported feeling dumb and like an outsider. However, most of their observations related to experiences as undergraduate students, and it was difficult to separate the high school and college level experiences. Later, in teaching adults at the community college level, the women's *positionality,* a term used to denote status in the society, raised issues of credibility due to their race and gender and directly affected their classroom interactions and teaching strategies and philosophy. For example, because the women had experienced marginality in the society, they were especially sensitive to students who might feel this way. One of the interviewees stated that, since white males usually did most of the talking and questioning in the mathematics classroom, she called on females more often than males.

The authors concluded that these teachers had to draw on their own resources to develop teaching practices since they were influenced by their experiences of race and gender. They did not use universal teaching practices. Since the race and gender of the teachers influenced the students' perceptions of the teachers' credibility, it was necessary to find approaches to deal with these challenges. The findings agree with the view that teaching is not a neutral activity. It is permeated with values about individuality, knowledge, and society that reflect larger issues. In the words of Brown, Cervero, and Johnson-Bailey (2000), "There are no universal teachers but there are teachers whose experiences are affected by their race and gender" (p. 286).

In summary, African American females who have interest and proficiency in mathematics will need teachers who have the knowledge, skills, and attitudes required to not only teach them effectively, but also to encourage, support, and expose them to career opportunities in mathematics or related fields in science and technology. African American female students are likely to face barriers such as peer pressure, family influence, limited availability of role models and mentors, and various affective factors. The availability of special intervention programs, advanced placement courses, and appropriate guidance and counseling can be most valuable for talented African American females who deserve every chance to realize their potential. In view of the disproportionately small number of African American females with recognition in mathematics, we cannot afford to do otherwise.

ISSUES OF SEXUAL ORIENTATION

The issue of sexual orientation is undoubtedly one of the most controversial topics in American society today. The horrendous killing of Matthew Shepard, a gay college student, in 1998 brought to national attention the glaring fact that the number of hate crimes committed against gay men and lesbians is increasing in the United States (Human Rights Campaign, 2001). While virtually all Americans stand in opposition to such unconscionable acts, the degree to which they are willing to allow homosexuals the same rights and privileges granted to heterosexuals is still a hotly contested issue in the public dialogue. The public schools represent a microcosm of this debate. In fact, an argument can be made that the discrimination faced by teens who are not heterosexual is more intense than that which gay adults face.

> In virtually every way, lesbian, gay, and bisexual adolescents are *worse off* than their adult counterparts. While forces in the larger adult society might hint at political correctness, acceptance, and accommodation, the high school—the center of most adolescent life and culture—stands staunchly aloof and rigidly re-

sistant to even a suggestion that any of its faculty or student body might be homosexual or that homosexuals deserve anything but derision and scorn within its walls. High schools may be the most homophobic institutions in American society, and woe be to anyone who would challenge the heterosexist premises on which they operate. (Unks, 1995, p. 5)

To understand Unks's statement and discuss the issues relating to sexual orientation in the public schools, it is useful to understand the terminology used in the discourse. *Homophobia* has been defined as "prejudice, discrimination, harassment, or acts of violence against sexual minorities, including lesbians, gay men, bisexual, and transgendered persons, evidenced in a deep-seated fear or hatred of those who love and sexually desire those of the same sex" (Sears, 1997, p. 16). The fears, misunderstandings, and discriminatory behavior of heterosexuals directed toward gay, lesbian, bisexual, and transgendered (GLBT) individuals are well documented (Pharr, 1988; GLSEN, 1999). The intensity of these negative feelings and behaviors is correlated with a variety of personal, geographic, religious, and educational factors (Sears, 1997). *Heterosexism* is "a belief in the superiority of heterosexuals or heterosexuality evidenced in the exclusion, by omission or design, of nonheterosexual persons in policies, procedures, events, or activities" (Sears, 1997, p. 16). This is the pervading view in school and society and, despite an increased awareness of the injustice of such a view, the majority of school personnel are often inactive in changing behaviors that place GLBT students at risk daily.

Risk Factors for GLBT Students

The overriding risk factor for all teens is the lack of communication or support from one or more of their multiple worlds: family, school, religious institution, community, and peers. Many GLBT students experience significant stress knowing that there is little if any support in any of these circles for a nonheterosexual orientation. *Sexual orientation* is a term used to describe the attraction one feels toward either or both sexes, since individuals may be homosexual, heterosexual, or bisexual (GLSEN, 1999). Just as is the case with heterosexuals, adults who are nonheterosexual report that they have little control over their sexual orientation (Pharr, 1988). Sexual behavior involves the sexual activities in which individuals engage. While the median age for recognizing one's sexual orientation is 13, sexual behavior may or may not accompany this awareness. *Sexual identity* is a broader concept than sexual orientation involving a multitude of issues related to gender. Unlike most individuals struggling with their racial identity, youth forming their sexual identity can be recognized by others as having a different sexual identity than the one that the individual eventually determines. Others generally assume heterosexuality until a person "comes out" as gay or bisexual.

The consequences for coming out can be severe, ranging from verbal harassment and social ostracism to physical abuse (Remafedi, 1994). Being the recipient of verbal abuse is almost guaranteed, with 97 percent of youth reporting that they hear homophobic epithets in school (GLSEN, 1999). The low self-esteem and feelings of isolation and depression that GLBT youth experience are tied to any number of risky behaviors, including school absenteeism, dropping out, homelessness, substance abuse, risky sexual behavior that can lead to HIV infection, and suicide (GLSEN, 1999; Harbeck, 1997; Hunter, 1996; Remafedi, 1994).

The high rates of suicide attempts and actual suicide among GLBT teens have been highly publicized, with as many as 30 percent of the 5,000 suicides committed by adolescents and young adults (ages 15 to 24) annually attributed to distress over sexual orientation (O'Conor, 1995; Remafedi, 1994). A recent study by the Massachusetts Department of Public Health reported that 10 percent of Massachusetts high school students attempted suicide, according to a survey of about 4,000 students in 1997 (Healy, 2001). Of those, 40 percent of gay and bisexual students attempted suicide, compared to about 10 percent of their heterosexual peers. While some are concerned about the inflation of these statistics due to sampling problems (Unks, 1995), perhaps the most important message is that higher rates of attempted suicide and actual suicide among homosexual teens are not due to an inherent mental instability, but to a predictable reaction to a hostile environment.

Although most school staff are aware that GLBT youth are present in the schools, many teachers are uninformed about the population. Their views are based on a variety of societal beliefs and myths that have little empirical support.

Characteristics of GLBT Youth

Estimates of the number of GLBT adolescents in the United States varies from 1 to 30 percent, although a range of 5 to 10 percent is most commonly reported (Ginsberg, 1999; Harbeck, 1997). There is even a controversy over whether the actual figure is over- or underestimated (Harbeck, 1997; Sears, 1997). It is difficult to study the population due to the obvious threats involved in self-identification. On the other hand, many samples involve individuals associated with therapeutic settings. Much of the information accumulated comes retrospectively from adults (Anderson, 1995). As mentioned previously, gay teens usually report being aware of being more attracted to persons of their own sex between ages 12 and 14, although individual reports vary widely (Anderson 1995; Ginsberg 1999; Sears, 1991). Most homosexuals recall a period of intense anxiety when they realize that they belong to a stigmatized group and often go through a period of trying to change their orientation. They may begin or continue heterosexual activity despite an awareness of their orientation. Again, it is important to point out that sexual orientation is distinct from sexual behavior and that, despite the presumption of promiscuity that colors much of the public debate about homosexuality, studies have shown that GLBT students' sexual experiences are similar to those of their heterosexual peers (Ginsberg, 1999).

For many GLBT teens, coming out is an all-consuming issue that is rooted in a strong need for emotional support and often takes precedence over the many curricular and extracurricular activities that are associated with success in high school (Ginsberg, 1999). Students most frequently come out to trusted GLBT peers first, then close heterosexual peers or family members, although some may rely on a teacher, counselor, or coach (GLSEN,1999). Coming out to a sibling or parent can be very threatening, depending on the family members' beliefs and expectations. Parental responses can range from confusion or denial to threats of disowning the child or physical violence if the child does not "change" (Ginsberg, 1999).

Some of the negative response that parents display is rooted in the belief that a child can change his or her sexual orientation. To some extent, this belief is tied to the controversy over the factors that determine sexual orientation. There continues to be debate over the biological basis for sexual orientation (Jones, 1999; Lipkin, 1996). Some studies suggest that when one identical twin is gay there is a higher likelihood that the other twin is gay than with fraternal twins, suggesting a biological link. Furthermore, the sexual orientation of adopted children is unrelated to the orientation of the parents, suggesting that the trait is not socially rooted. Nevertheless, there is no foolproof way to identify sexual orientation, despite an array of theories based on genetic makeup, hormonal levels, socialization, and environment (Pharr, 1988). However, both heterosexual and homosexual adults report having little control over their sexual orientation.

One group that faces even greater risk is students who are both gay and people of color. They are more vulnerable to antigay harassment and face a more complex set of issues in coming out (Sears, 1995, 1997; Uribe, 1995). Although there are individual reports that the black community is less accepting of homosexuality than the white community, there is little empirical support for this belief. Nevertheless, these youth often feel extreme isolation in trying to keep separate the three worlds in which they reside: the homosexual community, their racial community, and the society at large.

Rationale for a School and Community Response

There are a variety of strong educational, psychological, legal, and ethical reasons for supporting students who are GLBT in the schools. Obviously, these are students who are at risk, and their existence is often denied by the school culture and curriculum (Unks, 1995). The public school culture—the newspaper gossip columns, the school yearbook signings, class ring exchanges, Valentine's celebrations, the prom—is based on a heterosexist view. Furthermore, like other diverse groups, the lives, literature, art, and music of GLBT individuals is either absent from the pages of elementary and secondary texts or not identified as such.

Many national educational, medical, and mental health organizations have written policy statements supportive of the rights of GLBT students and educators. For example, the National Association of State Boards of Education, representing the 50 state boards of education voted that "State boards should provide leadership in eliminating the stereotypes and discrimination on the basis of sex, age, disability, race, religion, sexual orientation, ethnic background or national origin in curriculum materials, counseling methods and other education processes" (Harbeck, 1997, p. 18). Similarly, since 1974 the National Education Association has issued strong statements opposing employment discrimination on the basis of sexual orientation.

The position statement of the National Association of School Psychologists (1999) supports sexual minority youth in public and private schools by endorsing (1) education of students and staff, (2) direct counseling, (3) advocacy, (4) research, and (5) programs for HIV prevention directed toward GLBT youth.

Those who view homosexuality as abnormal or immoral can exacerbate the psychological stress that may accompany coming out. The psychological implications of reparative therapy present another issue that has caused professional organizations to respond. *Reparative therapy* refers to psychotherapy aimed at eliminating homosexual desires and the belief that homosexuality is a mental disorder (GLSEN, 1999). *Transformational ministry* is an approach used by some Christian groups to attempt to eliminate homosexual desires. The American Psychiatric Association declassified homosexuality as a mental disorder in 1973; all major health professional organizations have supported this. Furthermore, 10 national education, health, and counseling organizations have supported a statement in opposition to reparative therapy and transformational ministry, saying that its promotion is likely to exacerbate the risk of harassment, harm, and fear.

Although there is considerable case law regarding homosexual students and teachers, the Nabozny case stands out. In 1995 Jamie Nabozny, a gay former student, sued the Ashland School District in Wisconsin for not protecting him against harassment (Jones, 1999). Jamie was mock-raped in a classroom, urinated upon in a bathroom, and kicked so badly that he required surgery to stop the internal bleeding. In this landmark case, the Seventh U.S. Circuit Court of Appeals ruled that the district pay Jamie Nabozny $900,000 in damages for violation of the Fourteenth Amendment Equal Protection Clause.

Although no federal law protects students simply on the basis of their sexual orientation, Title IX applies to cases of sexual discrimination in which sexual orientation issues may be present. The Office of Civil Rights has issued extensive guidance for school districts that outlines a school's responsibilities under Title IX, including grievance procedures and prevention (Office for Civil Rights, 2001). Massachusetts was the first state to ban discrimination on the basis of sexual orientation in public schools (Commonwealth of Massachusetts Governor's Commission on Gay and Lesbian Youth, 1993; Jennings, 1996). Similarly, case law has supported the rights of gay and lesbian teachers whose districts have attempted to terminate their employment on the basis of sexual orientation, although questions remain regarding a possible line between public and private behavior (Zirkel, 1999).

The ethical dimensions of the homosexual controversy in U.S. society are extremely complex, especially given the plurality of religious beliefs. However, there are issues on which many faith organizations can agree, especially the right of individuals not be discriminated against on the basis of sexual orientation in areas such as safety and employment (Interfaith Alliance Foundation, n.d.). Furthermore, it is not true that all religious organizations are opposed to homosexual orientation and behavior. Some organizations have openly supported homosexuality as healthy and acceptable (Parents, Families, and Friends of Lesbians and Gays, 2001), whereas in other major denominations there are groups within the denomination that are openly accepting of gay and lesbian individuals regardless of official church doctrine (Crew, 1997; Nugent, 1997). Nevertheless, it is clear that many conservative Christian denominations view homosexuality as sinful. However, the debate over the biblical view of homosexuality is far from resolved in most major Protestant denominations.

A final rationale for addressing sexual difference in schools is that all students benefit from gaining factual information. Homophobia hinders all students by confining people in rigid gender roles and inhibiting close personal relationships with members of the same sex (Blumenfeld, 1992). All students, whether gay or straight, are vulnerable to homophobic slurs, regardless of their sexual orientation (Sattel, Keyes, & Tupper, 1997). Although the issue is constantly appearing in the media in ways that may or may not be helpful or accurate, many community groups avoid the topic due to its controversial dimensions. Unless public schools respond to the void of information available, students will continue to rely on hearsay.

Staff Training and Resources

Although most teachers and support staff are aware that there are GLBT youth in their classrooms, they admit that they do not meet these students needs due to their lack of professional training, their own homophobic feelings, or their fear that colleagues will think that they were gay or lesbian, thus potentially compromising their reputation or employment (Sears, 1992). These responses indicate that, like their students, teachers and other school staff are in need of information about GLBT youth, as well as strategies for working with these students.

It is not reasonable to expect gay and lesbian teachers to become the standard bearers for change. The Employment Non-Discrimination Act, prohibiting employment discrimination on the basis of sexual orientation, was introduced and strongly supported during the Clinton administration, but it has not been passed (Harbeck, 1997). Therefore, it is up to state law whether sexual orientation is a protected category. Although case law has supported gay teachers, as stated previously, there are still fuzzy areas of the law. Many gay and lesbian teachers have come out in the last decade and made significant contributions (Anderson, 1996; Jennings, 1996; Prince, 1996). However, both gay and straight staff must be involved in the process to enact change.

It is important that both preservice and in-service teachers receive relevant information. In 1994 Massachusetts became the first state to establish an Advisory Commission on Gay and Lesbian Youth that must ensure that all teacher certification programs include information about serving GLBT youth (Harbeck, 1997). Workshops that address homophobia will certainly help many in-service educators to feel more comfortable about addressing these issues with students. In addition, many resources, such as speakers, brochures and books, policy statements, and videos, are available through organizations such as Parents, Families, and Friends of Lesbian and Gays (PFLAG, n.d.) and Gay, Lesbian, and Straight Education Network (Jennings, 1996; GLSEN, 2001) (see Table 10.2). At minimum, staff must understand the federal and state laws that govern their behavior toward students and follow accompanying procedures established by the school district. Although guidance counselors, social workers, health teachers, and coaches may have a higher likelihood of coping with students who are victims of harassment, school staff can encounter antihomosexual epithets from students and peers and must deal with them appropriately.

Curriculum Issues

While school staff are generally aware of the need to enforce antidiscrimination policies in the public schools, the process of including information about homosexuality and the histories, literature, art, and music of GLBT individuals in the curriculum continues to be a source of controversy across the coun-

TABLE 10.2 Organizations That Support Gay, Lesbian, Bisexual, and Transgendered Youth

Gay, Lesbian, and Straight Education Network 212-727-0135 www.glsen.org	Parents, Families, and Friends of Lesbians and Gays 202-467-8180 www.pflag.org
Hetrick Martin Institute 212-674-2400 www.hmi.org	Project 10 626-577-4553 www.project10.org
National Advocacy Coalition on Youth and Sexual Orientation 202-347-5700 www.advocatesforyouth.org	The Family Pride Coalition 619-296-0199 www.familypride.org
National Gay and Lesbian Task Force 202-332-6483 www.ngltf.org	

try. However, individual teachers and school districts have implemented curriculum change in a number of ways. For example, the Minnesota State Board of Education requires every school to submit a plan for including multicultural, gender-fair, disability-sensitive material and resources throughout the curriculum. Some districts include sexual orientation as part of the gender fairness concept (Sattel, Keyes, & Tupper, 1997). Districts include this content within courses or units on justice, equity, and prejudice reduction; health; and the history or psychology of sport. Sexual orientation can be appropriately discussed in social studies and English classrooms as well (Lipkin, 2000; Roy, 1997). Most recently, educators are exploring the need for addressing these issues on the elementary level (Boyd, 1999; Letts & Sears, 1999). An increasing body of information is available for districts seeking to make their curriculum more inclusive and is available through many of the organizations mentioned above (Lipkin, 2000; Schniedewind & Davidson, 1997).

School and Community Support Groups and Programs

Today there are over 700 support groups for GLBT youth (GLSEN, 2001). Known by a variety of names (e.g., Gay–Straight Alliance, BIGAYLA, Allies), many of these groups have grown out of GLSEN because the organization emphasizes education, action, and the inclusion of people of all sexual orientations (Jennings, 1996). Each group or chapter sets its policies and procedures; however, a universal policy is that youth are not required to declare their sexual orientation. Often groups meet on campus after school, but other groups are sponsored by a variety of service organizations and may meet in community buildings.

Another organization that is helpful to youth and their families is PFLAG. Its mission is to support the needs of parents and friends of lesbians and gay men, to educate them and others, and to advocate equality for their gay and lesbian children (Durgin-Cinchard, 1997). In addition to sponsoring 450 affiliates, PFLAG provides newsletters, help lines, programs, brochures, and advocacy activities (PFLAG, 2001).

There are two organizations that work to provide education and support. Two fairly comprehensive district programs that have been created to address the needs of GLBT teens are Project 10 at Fairfax High School in the Los Angeles Unified School District and the Harvey Milk School in New York City.

Project 10 began in 1984 to address the needs of GLBT youth by focusing on "education, reduction of verbal and physical abuse, suicide prevention, and dissemination of accurate AIDS information" (Uribe, 1995). The centerpiece of the model is a weekly support group averaging 10 to 12 students for students who are suffering the effects of stigmatization and discrimination based on sexual orientation. The adult cofacilitators (usually a male and a female) are trained through workshops and must be nonjudgmental with regard to sexual orientation. When appropriate, students are referred to community agencies for additional services. Project 10 also includes a district resource center, a paid coordinator, ongoing workshops for school staff, school support teams, lists of books for school librarians, enforcement of nondiscrimination policies, and advocacy for gay and lesbian student rights through the school system and community. This program has been successful partially due to its collaboration with social service agencies in Los Angeles that offer discussion groups, a youth hotline, emergency shelter for homeless gay youth, and group homes and foster placements for teens rejected by their families (Gover, 1996).

The Harvey Milk School, opened in 1985, grew out of the same concerns for gay and lesbian youth that spawned Project 10 (Gover, 1996; Hunter, 1996). It is a small alternative school in Manhattan that, in addition to a traditional curriculum, offers substantial social services, including a family counseling program. Serving students primarily between the ages of 15 and 17, Harvey Milk is a transitional school that encourages students to return to traditional schools when ready.

Conclusion

Many other issues relating to gender and education could be discussed in this chapter: stereotyping of gender roles, sexism, sexual harassment, the representation of women and men in the curriculum, and the implications of Title IX. While the following cases do not directly address all these issues, we believe that grappling with both cases will help you to consider many of the important issues related to gender that caring and responsive educators must be prepared to address.

THE CASE OF CASSIE BROWN

As she left the office of her mathematics teacher, Mr. Tempe, tears ran down Cassie's cheeks. In fact, she began to cry before Mr. Tempe had finished his advice to her. She had gone to him the second time for help with a difficult calculus problem, using logarithmic functions: $1.7(2.1)^{3x} = 2(4.5)^x$ after working on it for days.

Mr. Tempe reminded her, "Cassie, you told me earlier that you wanted to major in mathematics in college." Cassie turned to face him and he continued. "Are you really sure that you want to continue to study mathematics?" he queried. "There are not many minorities in this field and you are also female and African American. Are you sure that you don't want to reconsider your goal?"

Cassie responded firmly, "No, I'm going to study mathematics" and quietly left his office. Although she was shocked by his words and had wanted to say so, as a very shy person who had been reared to respect all adults, especially teachers, she simply took his advice as an honest opinion of her ability to succeed. Mathematics had been Cassie's favorite subject since she was in middle school.

Yet it was true that despite her usual persistence, which almost always paid off, she simply could not solve the problem and had become very frustrated. As she rode the bus home from school, she began to talk to herself silently, wondering what she should do now. She loved mathematics and computers more than anything and always thought of mathematics as her strongest subject. She did not want to give up. However, she just could not get it, even after Mr. Tempe explained the process twice.

As the older bus bumped along, she cried quietly as she thought, "Here I am in October of my senior year in high school, a student who has an average of 85, a member of the National Honor Society, and with 1,300 on my SATs. I've received good grades in all my mathematics classes until now in precalculus, and Mr. Tempe is suggesting that I give up."

When she arrived home, Cassie was comforted by her parents, who encouraged her to stick to her plan to become a mathematics teacher. After all, they knew that Cassie had always loved school and wanted to be a teacher. Now, inspired mainly by her mathematics teachers in the middle school, she had chosen to study it after high school. Furthermore, since neither parent had been blessed with opportunities to go to college, they wanted all their children to accomplish that goal. But, perhaps she could not pass the class with Mr. Tempe!

After deciding that she must find someone to give her advice, Cassie chose to share her problem with the new minister of their church after the Sunday service. The family attended church together every Sunday without fail. Perhaps he could help her decide what to do. Although the new minister, Mr. Horton, had just arrived last week, Cassie was accustomed to going to the former minister with her problems. She hoped that Mr. Horton would understand.

As she shook hands with the minister on Sunday, she smiled and said, "Remember, Mr. Horton, I met you last week with my parents. They were telling you about our family. Well, I'm feeling very upset about something that happened at school last week and I would appreciate your advice." After hearing a bit of Cassie's story, the minister encouraged her to arrange a meeting with the counselor at school and to ask if he could also attend the meeting.

On the following Wednesday morning, Mr. Horton drove to the high school counselor's office. As he drove through the fringes of the city, there were some attractive, middle-class homes and townhouse developments, which bordered on communities of surrounding suburbs. However, the closer he got to the center of the city, the more the buildings deteriorated. The main street of the inner city could be imagined as a "war zone" where, Mr. Horton had heard, drugs were bought and sold, homeless people regularly pushed their belongings in shopping carts, most businesses were boarded up, and young men who appeared to be without jobs hung out on corners. The high school was located on a street of small, neatly maintained older homes, which was not too far from the decaying, inner core of the city.

When he arrived at Jefferson High School, Miss Jensen introduced herself to Mr. Horton and greeted Cassie warmly. She then said to Mr. Horton, "I need about 15 minutes to handle a special problem. While you are waiting, would you like to read today's newspaper? There's an article about our district." Mr. Horton responded, "Yes, of course, thank you."

As Mr. Horton read, he discovered that the Jefferson School District in this community faced all the problems associated with urban schools, but on a smaller scale. Although the percentages for the city's population are 52.8 white, 35.7 black, 0.4 American Indian, 1.6 Asian, 10.6 Hispanic, and 5.3 other, the public school population is predominately black. According to the most recent demographics, the percentages for the students are approximately 64 black, 6 Hispanic, 29 white, and 1 other. Seventy-five percent of the students in the district are eligible for free lunch and 2.0 percent of the students are English language learners. The most recent high school dropout rate is an encouraging 4.4 percent; however, the suspension rate is 17.2 percent. Although the total spending per student for 1999 was $11,542, all the school buildings are very old, overcrowded, and in need of repairs. No computers are available for students at any level. The administration does plan to present a bond proposal soon to fund a new elementary school.

The data for mathematics and science achievement from a recent "report card" published by the state's education department were included in the newspaper article. On the grade 4 math assessment the percentage of students at all district elementary schools who performed on grade level ranged from 1.35 in one elementary school to 21.3 at the top school. On the fourth grade science assessment, the percent passing ranged from the lowest score of 42.86 to 71.56 in the highest school.

In the grade 8 mathematics assessment, 15.19 percent of the students at the middle school met the standards. Twenty-nine percent of the students at the high school passed the state biology exam, the lowest in the county, and 35 percent of the students passed the physics exam, again the lowest score in the county. Sixty-four percent of the students at the high school passed the chemistry exam and 40 percent passed the exam for Math I and 50 percent for Math III.

As Mr. Horton looked up from the paper, Miss Jensen came out of her office. "Thank you so much for your patience," she smiled to both Mr. Horton and Cassie. Miss Jensen invited them into her office and, as soon as they were seated, told Mr. Horton that Cassie was one of the best students at Jefferson High School, one who never had problems.

Miss Jensen turned to Mr. Horton. "How well do you know Cassie?"

When Mr. Horton replied, "Not very well," Miss Jensen proceeded to share the following information with him.

"I am so proud of Cassie. I encouraged her to participate in a special program, the Science, Technology Entry Program, which is provided by a cluster of state colleges in the Northeast. These programs have been very successful in recruiting, retaining, and encouraging minority and low-income students to pursue careers in mathematics, science, and technology" (Box 10.1).

Miss Jensen then turned to Cassie. "I was surprised when you came to ask for an appointment, Cassie, since I know that your program is set for your senior year and your decisions about college have been made. Please tell us about the problem."

Cassie began: "Up until last week, I was totally convinced I wanted to be a math major in college. Then Mr. Tempe questioned my abilities and now I'm beginning to doubt everything I've believed about my abilities until now.

"If you remember, I was born in Jamaica, where I attended school until 7 years ago. I began school there in kindergarten and continued through sixth grade. I came here in the middle of seventh grade. Teachers in Jamaica were very strict, yet motivating and encouraging. Punishment worked very well! The teachers there were very good, and I'm sure that if I had remained there I could have learned just as well. After all, when I came here I was immediately placed in eighth grade mathematics! However, I would have had a real problem when it was time for high school in Jamaica, because you must pay for both tuition and books. In fact, kindergarten also requires tuition, but grades one through six are free.

"When my family moved here, I entered the Jefferson Middle School in seventh grade. I was immediately moved up to eighth grade mathematics and I continue to love mathematics. My grades have been good in all my mathematics classes, even though our high school teachers in mathematics have

■ ■ ■ ■ ■

BOX 10.1

THE SCIENCE AND TECHNOLOGY ENTRY PROGRAM

The Science and Technology Entry Program (STEP) is in its thirteenth year. It is funded by the State Education Department and has as its mission the enhancement of the mathematics, science, and technology skills of diverse and low-income students. Ultimately, the goal is to encourage the participating students to continue their education after high school in the fields of mathematics, science, and technology.

Participants must belong to a minority ethnic group or meet low-income requirements to apply. Students must also be enrolled in a grade-level course in mathematics at their school, have an interest in technology (computers), science, or mathematics, and have the approval of a parent or guardian. STEP students receive instruction over a period of six Saturdays during the academic year.

Program components include large-group speaker presentations, a Saturday Academy comprising enrichment modules in science and math content, motivation, college preparation, academic tutoring and counseling, field trips, internship opportunities, and student monitoring and evaluation. It is expected that the program will foster student matriculation in college with a designated major leading toward a scientific, health, or health-related profession.

The accomplishments of the program to date have been due, in part, to altered instructional strategies as teachers have become more "hands-on," interdisciplinary, and inquiry based. They have also adopted or developed new curricular materials that are more engaging and transparently related to real-world issues and concerns. Secondary and postsecondary educators who deliver instruction, academic enrichment, and tutoring to the STEP students have critically examined their own biases, assumptions, and expectations of minority and low-income students as they witness such students excelling in programs that demand and expect excellence of them and provide them with the support that they need.

been very traditional; there is no such thing as 'hands-on.' Even so, my middle school mathematics teachers and several here at the high school have really inspired me to continue to study it and think about a career in mathematics. Although Mr. Tempe seems to doubt my ability now, I was in the top track in middle school and also now in high school."

Miss Jensen turned to Mr. Horton. "Mr. Horton, the tracking system separates students into those pursuing a regular or honors diploma."

Cassie continued, "I would like to have taken advanced placement courses, but we have very little advanced placement or AP courses available. Apparently, not many other girls want AP math classes. I have only one friend who has continued mathematics with me in twelfth grade. Although the numbers of males and females in my mathematics classes were almost even before grade 11, at that point we began to have more boys in class. Now, in my twelfth grade mathematics class in precalculus, only five in fifteen students are females.

"I believed that my persistence, open-mindedness and willingness to help others had paid off in my progress in mathematics. That is, until I reached Mr. Tempe's class. There have been times when I have persisted in solving a difficult problem for several days until I found the answer or solution! Open-mindedness has helped me to accept a different method in problem solving from a teacher after I have already learned another approach. When the teacher says, 'You learned an incorrect way to solve that kind of problem,' I am able to say, 'O.K.' "

"I know you're a very responsive student and a well-rounded student," Miss Jensen interjected. "Cassie, tell Mr. Horton about some of your extracurricular activities."

Cassie responded, "My main extracurricular activity in high school is the National Honor Society and, as a member, I sometimes do volunteer tutoring. Outside school, my social activities are connected with church. Sometimes, I have invited friends to church, but I usually see them only at school. I never did hang out, so peer pressure hasn't been a problem for me. In fact, my parents always taught us with the question, 'If you see someone jump off a bridge, would you jump?' "

"And what about the STEP program?" Miss Jensen asked.

"I enjoyed the program. For me, the most valuable thing that the program offered was the guest speakers. Although I liked the program, my personal opinion is that such a program is not the most critical factor in increasing diverse students' interest in mathematics. I think more encouragement from teachers, college recruitment beginning in high school (because that's when students drop out), more hands-on learning in mathematics, and parent involvement could make a difference. My parents did not spend a lot of time at the school, but they were very interested at home and we always had to finish homework before we could watch television."

Mr. Horton commented, "It seems that church has had a strong influence on you, Cassie. Are there other things that have helped you to succeed in school?"

"Yes," Cassie smiled, "Although teachers may not think of persistence when they think of the characteristics of successful students in mathematics, I believe that it is a very important trait. However, I can think of other characteristics, too. I would add, also, some type of religious involvement. As my grandfather says, 'What's wrong with all these children now is that they need Jesus.'

"Church has been a major focus in my family and we have had to go every Sunday. There are also social activities at church in which we participate. For example, we have had an award ceremony at church at which all children who passed or have good report cards or have graduated are recognized with an award. Sometimes, even during regular church service, our old minister would mention someone's grades or even someone's difficulties in school with which they need help.

"My parents have continued to encourage and support all three of us. My sister is now in college, and my brother, who is the youngest, is beginning high school. My brother says that he hates mathematics, so he calls on me for help with his homework. My sister is majoring in business. So, it looks like I'm the only one who has planned to major in mathematics.

"That is, until Mr. Tempe spoke to me on Friday. I went to him for help with several examples of a problem I just couldn't do. After he tried to explain what I was doing wrong, which I still don't understand, he discouraged me from continuing to study mathematics. He said that there are not many minorities in the field of mathematics and besides, I am also female and African American. Then, he asked me if I wanted to reconsider my plans for the future. He even pointed out that to become a mathematics teacher I'll need to take many more difficult courses. He obviously doesn't think that I have the ability.

"After I cried all weekend, my parents encouraged me to stick to my goals for the future. But, what do I do about this class? This teacher?"

Mr. Horton replied, "You have a difficult situation to deal with and I understand why you are so upset."

Miss Jensen interjected, "I wonder if he was simply trying to be helpful if he saw that you were upset. Of course, I'm not sure. We need to meet with him."

Cassie replied solemnly, "I don't see how a meeting will help me with the grade in his class and the decision I must make, although an apology would be considerate. Mr. Tempe may hold a stereotyped view of African Americans and their mathematical abilities."

Mr. Horton then interjected, "We should arrange a meeting with him and hear his point of view."

Miss Jensen agreed to arrange the meeting within the following week so that Cassie could resolve the issue before she lost too much time for planning. Mr. Horton thanked the counselor again for her interest and assistance.

Cassie left the meeting still saddened by the situation at this point in her high school experience and wondered how they could get Mr. Tempe to understand that he was wrong and should apologize.

DISCUSSION QUESTIONS
1. What are the facts in Cassie's case?
2. What is Mr. Tempe's perception of Cassie as a student?
3. How does Mr. Tempe's perspective on Casssie's future differ from Cassie's perspective at this time?
4. What is Mr. Tempe's responsibility as Cassie's teacher in view of her difficulty with the math problem?
5. In deciding on an action plan, what are several major goals to help Cassie at this point? Can the goals be prioritized?
6. How would you describe Mr. Tempe's response to Cassie's difficulty? His comment?
7. What does research offer as a guide to understanding the issues in this case?

THE CASE OF RENEE FISCHER

As a social worker I've always been concerned about the need to support students who are struggling with sexual identity, especially those who think that they may be gay, lesbian, bisexual, or transgendered. However, it wasn't until last spring that a real opportunity to reach some of these kids presented itself.

I got an announcement of a conference to be held at Abington University for high school students in a four-county area encompassing about 20 schools. It was sponsored by a state-funded agency for safe schools and Kevin Jennings, the director of GLSEN, was the keynote speaker. To be honest, I didn't know much more about the conference than that, but I saw it as a way to get kids to identify themselves as interested in these issues. I wasn't asking them to declare their sexual orientation; that was up to them. I was just providing them with an opportunity to gain information in a supportive atmosphere.

I talked to George Foster, our principal, about advertising the conference and he didn't hesitate at all. He didn't hold a faculty meeting to explain his rationale or consult with the superintendent. George lives by the motto, "It's easier to ask for forgiveness than permission."

He simply said, "This looks like a way to identify those students who we know are out there, Renee. Since it's off campus, they may feel safe enough to come to you and find out the details. Get some fliers up right away, and we'll see what happens."

I had enough neon pink fliers printed to cover every bulletin board in every hall in the high school. There was no way that anyone—students, teachers, administrators, or staff—could say that they hadn't heard. I was somewhat apprehensive, but excited. I guess that's why I'm still a school social worker, despite the stress of the job; I believe that it's possible to make an impact on the lives of adolescents that can have long-term positive outcomes. O.K., I admit it. Challenges like these take me back to my 1960s activist days when marchers sang "We shall overcome" and believed it. But this decision wasn't about me—it was about supporting kids who deserved a place where they could talk freely and be taken seriously without threat of harassment.

I came in at 7:00 that morning before any students and most faculty and staff were in the building. Even if you were still asleep, these fliers would wake you up:

CONFERENCE ON
MAKING SCHOOLS SAFE FOR GAY, LESBIAN,
BISEXUAL, AND TRANSGENDERED KIDS

MAY 5
ABINGTON STATE UNIVERSITY

SEE MS. FISCHER FOR MORE INFORMATION

That's all the fliers said, but it was enough to get the basic information across and let students who were interested contact me without having to take a major risk. Sure, they'd have to let me know they wanted to go, but I would keep it confidential.

George and I had been talking about the need to support GLBT students for 5 years—as long as we've worked together. Our major goal has always been to provide a safe educational environment for students. We were concerned about safety and violence prevention long before people were talking about it on the state and national level. Our high school is an urban school and the student population is diverse: 80 percent African American or Caribbean American, 7 percent Mexican American, 10 percent European American, and 3 percent "United Nations." Racial conflict in our school is minimal because we constantly work to prevent it from erupting. For example, when the Rodney King beatings occurred, we stopped school for two days and held forums so that kids could talk about racial issues and the violence they saw repeatedly on TV.

I've heard George state his philosophy to teachers and community groups so many times now I can give it myself.

> In order to provide a safe environment in this high school, we have to open up as many communication channels as we possibly can. The students who have difficulties here are students that don't have a place where they feel they belong. They are alienated from peers, counselors, teachers, administrators, and parents. They feel alone and misunderstood. It's our job to identify the risk factors that break down communication and create new ways for students to let us know that they need support. We can't ignore the facts; our job is to keep kids in school and learning.

That's not to say it's been easy for George to back an initiative to support GLBT students. He's honest about having to deal with his own homophobia. There's plenty of pressure for a high school principal in an urban school to present a tough persona and George is aware of that. But George is tough in the right way. He's assertive and willing to make hard decisions that he believes are right and then take the flack that inevitably follows.

So plastering the halls with these neon fliers was the culmination of a lot of events in this building that most students and teachers hadn't really had on their radar screens. I suppose it became more apparent to us that we had an issue in the school after we initiated the pizza lunches for students. The purpose of these lunches was to keep communication lines open. Every Wednesday we would have a free pizza lunch for a different homeroom group. During lunch we would open the discussion up to the students, and they could talk about whatever concerns they had. All students were given the chance to come over the course of the school year. The discussion would range from no soap in the bathrooms to climate in the building, sexual harassment, bullying, cafeteria food, pass time between classes, and locker room stink. The topic of GLBT kids came up once in awhile. I remember one lunch at which kids were making some fairly homophobic comments like, "Can you imagine two girls doing it? How disgusting!"

Later, George had the idea that we should start an Adopt-a-Clergy Program. It was part of his goal to increase communication with the community and provide students with another means of support. The purpose was to introduce priests, pastors, rabbis, and ministers to students so that they could get to know each other. The clergy would come to the pizza lunches and help to facilitate the discussions. Then, if the students wanted to talk to the clergy further on any issues, they could call their "clergy of choice" on their own. Phone numbers were available, but it was up to the kids. It became a type of mentoring program.

People were a little suspicious of having clergy talking with students at first. They wanted to know about the First Amendment and the separation of church and state. But George got the clergy to sign a memorandum of agreement pledging to participate in the program without proselytizing. There were ground rules that they had to adhere to. The clergy involved were part of the Interfaith Clergy Council, so we had all faiths involved.

The Adopt-a-Clergy Program was another step toward assisting students with a broad range of needs, but we still didn't have any way to give students the opportunity to discuss issues around sexual orientation. As far as we knew, the only one on the faculty who was talking about homosexuality in the classroom was the health teacher. In fact, it seemed to be a topic that everyone else avoided. We knew from the educational literature that as many as 10 percent of our students could be dealing with questions about being gay, lesbian, bisexual, or transgendered. However, we didn't know who these students were and, if the discussion was taking place, we hadn't heard about it. These students were invisible to us and the rest of the school.

That's why the conference seemed like a logical next step. After putting up the fliers, I headed to my office in the guidance department. I had a busy day. There were about six students to see and a mile-long list of phone calls to return. Somewhere around 11:00 while classes were in session, I finally emerged from my office to take a break and headed down the hall toward the main office. In every direction I saw neon fliers that had been ripped up, stepped on, and mutilated all over the floor. I turned the corner toward the cafeteria and the scene was identical. On every floor and hallway I checked neon confetti littered the hallway.

I hurried back to George's office and, as usual, there was a line waiting to see him. I asked Mona, his secretary, if there was a chance I could get in to see him.

"I don't know. I'll ask him as soon as he's done with Mr. Ritter. He's had a lot of unscheduled meetings this morning."

As I turned to go back to my office, George opened the door and Harold Ritter, one of the senior history faculty, was emerging. Neither one of them looked happy.

Before Mona could get a word in, George said, "Ms. Fischer, do you have a minute?"

I entered the office and sat down at the long conference table that extended down from George's desk. As always it was piled with stacks of proposals, state laws and regulations, and reports. His phone was ringing and several lines were blinking. Today the room felt like more of a war room than a principal's office.

"Have you seen the hallways?" he asked.

"That's why I'm here."

"I've had a few visitors. Harold Ritter wanted to know why we wanted kids to go to a conference on homosexuality. He wanted to know what our goals were. When I said we wanted to set up a support system for students who were gay, lesbian, and bisexual, he said he didn't have any of those kids in his classes. He wants to know if this is something particular kids have been asking for or just our attempt to be politically correct. Harold says we don't have any problems with gays and lesbians in the school now and this could easily incite something. 'Those fliers on the floor are just the beginning of your problems, George,' he says to me. 'The students are trying to tell you something and you better listen to them. We've got enough fire kegs in this building ready to explode over racial issues. We don't need to start our own fire.' "

"Did you tell him that there ARE gay kids in this school? There are gay kids in every school in the U.S.!"

"Sure, I did. But I can't honestly say that they've come to us and asked for this, can I? I told him it was just like trying to reduce heart disease. We know what you do to reduce the risk of a heart attack: stop smoking, get exercise, and watch your diet. We also know that kids who are struggling with their sexual orientation are at risk for dropping out of school, drug abuse, suicide, and a lot of other things. So we have to figure out what we can do to reduce the risk that they'll choose those options. We need to help them get answers to their questions in a safe environment where peers and staff won't harass them."

"Harold doesn't like conflict. He doesn't understand the issues and thinks they'll go away if we ignore them."

"Harold was mild compared to our most conservative teacher, John Askew. John asked me how I could possibly endorse the idea of the high school supporting attendance at a conference on sexual immorality. He says, 'You might not think so, George, but there are still a lot of people in this community, including me, that believe that homosexuality is an abomination. You're going to raise a lot of hackles if you try to promote a life-style that many people in this community view as immoral. You can put your foot down and squash this right now.' I realized he was here to deliver his opinion and wasn't about to listen. I tried to talk with him but his is the last mind I'm going to change."

"Have you had any students down here complaining?" I asked.

"Not yet. Have you heard from any students who want to go?"

"No, but I'm not surprised. Given the condition of those fliers, I'm sure any kids who thought about wanting to go are having second thoughts."

"Seems like we have to just wait it out. I've only heard from a few teachers. I'm expecting phone calls from parents once the kids go home. Just let me know if you hear kids talking. And let me know right away if anyone wants to go."

"George, I have an idea. Tomorrow is the pizza lunch and three clergy members are planning on attending. Why don't I ask the students what they think about starting an Allies group to discuss GLBT issues?"

"I'm sure the topic will come up whether you initiate it or not, so you might as well structure it to see what the students are thinking. It might be a chance to educate a few kids about the needs."

"Makes sense. I'll prepare some questions that allow them to talk but also help them to consider the value of such a group. I'll also call the clergy so they know what the topic will be and have a chance to think about it ahead of time."

I thought I had better see if George and I were on the same page for the long run.

"Of course, if there are kids that want to go to this conference, they are going to hear about other schools that have started Gay–Straight Alliances. Other schools have been able to enlist faculty or staff who will act as sponsors for the group. At minimum, they have to be willing to provide a safe room for the kids to meet after school. And that's just a minimum. An advisor should help moderate the discussions and assist with activities the kids may want to be involved in," I reminded him.

"Well, I don't have an answer to that. Can you do it, Renee?"

"George, I'm already running four support groups in this school. I can't be seen as the only person who deals with identity issues."

"O.K. Who would be an advisor?

"Right now we don't have any teachers in this school who have identified themselves publicly as gay or lesbian. I know they exist, but it could be too threatening for them to be seen as promoting a particular orientation. Besides, it's not necessarily good to expect gay or lesbian teachers to be the standard bearers for these things. But I don't know of any straight teachers who are willing or able to stick their necks out. The teachers who might support this idea are already involved in one or more extracurricular activities and they're feeling overwhelmed. The rest are afraid that they'll be suspected of being gay themselves. We may need to use community resources."

"As far as I'm concerned, the more we work with community agencies, the better. But I have to know that students want this first."

At the pizza luncheon the next day, clergy from Jewish, Lutheran, and Unitarian traditions attended. I prepared a series of questions that I thought would ground the discussion. The clergy and I primarily facilitated the meeting and listened to student response, although we all asked thought-provoking questions when it seemed appropriate. First, I explained that some high schools across the country had established Allies groups for students who were interested in discussing GLBT issues and asked if they thought we should start such a group. The students didn't need much prompting; their responses followed each other in rapid fire.

"I think we should have a group like this. Everybody should be open in our school."

"What? You are looking to start trouble. What if students are against this group?"

"Yeah, the administration won't let us have a KKK group, so why have a homosexuality group?"

"We can't have a hate group on campus, so why is it O.K. to have an Allies group? What if someone wanted to start an Anti-Allies group?"

Then I asked what the reasons might be for having such a group.

"For one thing, high school prepares you for college where you are exposed to all kinds of people."

"True, and what about right now? Where else do kids who want to know about homosexuality have to gather and meet?"

"I think it would be more negative than positive. There are some things I don't need to know. What about being in the locker room changing? I'd be very uncomfortable knowing someone was gay."

I asked them what they were fearful of.

"I think we shouldn't be afraid. It's worse to be ignorant regarding sexual matters."

"But if we're not comfortable, why *force* us to accept it?"

"No one was comfortable when women and blacks started fighting for their rights!"

"Those are two different things."

"Are they? What about the fact that the largest number of adolescent suicides is among young people with gender diversity?"

I asked them if it would be worthwhile to have an Allies club in school if it saved a life.

"Of course!"

"That's what they have psychiatrists for. School is calm now. It will start problems if 'they' are here."

" 'They' are the same people you know now."

"No one is trying to push homosexuality on anyone else. It's about keeping people from being alone and isolated."

Finally, I asked them what the goals of such a group should be if we were to establish it.

"Well, first, it shouldn't be an administrative decision. It should be up to a student vote."

"The goal is to provide a safe environment for everyone."

"Yeah, it's about getting educated so we won't be uncomfortable."

"Besides, if any group disrupts the education process, they will be asked to leave."

"This is the same discussion they had when they desegregated schools in Kansas and when we talk about gays in the military."

"I used to be uncomfortable around gays. I had strong negative feelings about seeing guys holding hands and kissing. *I* had to learn, too."

Although the clergy didn't have much of a chance to speak, they did occasionally share their experiences. It was clear that at least two of the clergy had dealt with the issue within their respective congregations. They talked about family members who weren't straight or mentioned that they were PFLAG members. I appreciated their input. It would have been a lot harder being the only adult in the discussion. There was no doubt that student opinions were all over the map. While some may have thought twice about their beliefs, it was obvious that many held the same position coming out of the session as they did coming in.

After that discussion, a few of the students had regular contact with the clergy who were sensitive to GLBT issues. The clergy were open to these discussions and, although we didn't know who the kids were or what their interests or concerns were, we knew that they were contacting the clergy about gender diversity.

On Thursday I typed up my notes from the meeting and shared them with George. I was surprised to hear that he hadn't gotten any complaints from parents. Maybe kids weren't about to talk about this with their parents. However, I still hadn't heard from any students who wanted to go to the conference.

During last period our secretary, Helen, buzzed me and said that Stacey Whitman wanted to talk with me but wouldn't say what she wanted. I thought she might have heard that she was admitted to one of the highly selective colleges she had applied to.

Stacey stopped by after school. She came into the office and simply said, "Ms. Fischer, I want to go to the conference and so does Alisha Hammond."

By the next day there were two other female students who wanted to go. I gave them each information about the conference that was to be held the following Friday at Abington State University. Although transportation was left up to the students, they were excused from classes for the day.

The Monday morning after the conference the four girls were in my office.

"Ms. Fischer, that conference was fantastic!" they chimed.

"Yeah, there were kids from high schools and colleges all over this area. Did you know they already have an Allies group at Plainsville High School? And there's a BIGALA at Matthew College that meets on campus every month. We could even walk there!"

"It was so exciting to hear Kevin Jennings talk about his experience as a high school teacher and then what's happening all over the United States!"

"Ms. Fischer, we want to start an Allies group here. We're not the only ones who think this is important."

Later that morning I got in to see Mr. Foster.

"George, there are four students who want to start an Allies group. But I'm concerned that it's not safe yet for these students to meet on campus, even if it's after school."

"I tend to agree. I'm not sure I should approve of a group meeting here on campus until I have a better sense of whether I have some faculty support. It's almost the end of the school year. How about drumming up some of that community support you spoke about when we discussed this earlier?"

So I contacted the advisor for the BIGALA group at Matthew College. She and many of their students had been at the conference. They had met some of our students and were willing to invite them to the Matthew meetings. Stacey and the other girls seemed happy with that alternative and attended their meetings for the rest of the spring. In the fall, Alisha Hammond and several others continued attending, even though Stacey had graduated and was away at college. They occasionally stopped by my office to tell me what they were learning and their excitement level had not subsided.

Just before Thanksgiving, Alisha and the other girls asked to speak to me.

"Ms. Fischer, it's been great to go to the BIGALA at Matthew, but I think we've gotten about as much from that as we can. We really want to have a presence in our own high school. More kids would be able to come, and we could plan activities that WE think are important. What do we have to do?"

"O.K. I'll talk to Mr. Foster. Stop by my office after Thanksgiving vacation and I'll let you know what he says."

My apprehension level spiked back up again. I knew it was important to the students to be able to meet at the high school, but I was concerned about their safety. How could I ensure that they wouldn't be heckled or even physically assaulted? Who would be willing to provide adult supervision and guidance?

I was planning to meet with Mr. Foster that afternoon, so I decided the issue could wait until then.

"Before we get started, George, I wanted to let you know that the students who have been meeting with Matthew's BIGALA group asked me this morning if they could start meeting here. Now what?"

DISCUSSION QUESTIONS

1. What is the impetus for starting a group for students who want to discuss issues around gender diversity?
2. What are the attitudes of teachers, students, and administration toward the establishment of a BIGALA group?
3. What do we know from research about adolescents and sexual identity that would support or dispute the establishment of a BIGALA group?
4. What responsibilities do teachers (both gay and straight) have with regard to students who have questions about sexual identity?
5. What can be done in schools and in the community to promote a greater understanding of the issues related to gender diversity and the implications for our society?
6. How can the public schools work in a constructive manner with parents, community groups, and religious organizations that disagree with a homosexual life-style on a moral basis?

REFERENCES

Adenika-Morrow, T. J. (1996). Lifeline to science careers for African American females. *Educational Leadership, 53*(8), 80–83.

Anderson, D. A. (1995). Lesbian and gay adolescents: Social and developmental considerations. In G. Unks (Ed.), *The gay teenager* (pp. 17–28). New York: Routledge.

Anderson, J. D. (1996). Out as a professional educator. In D. R. Walling (Ed.), *Open lives, safe schools* (pp. 17–28). Bloomington, IN: Phi Delta Kappa.

Blum, L. (1997). Women in mathematics: Scaling the heights and beyond. In D. Nolan (Ed), *Women in mathematics: Scaling the heights* (pp. 2–6). Washington, DC: Mathematical Association of America.

Blumenfeld, W. J. (1992). *Homophobia: How we all pay the price.* Boston: Beacon.

Bossert, S. T. (1981). Understanding sex differences in children's classroom experiences. *Elementary School Journal, 81,* 254–266.

Boswell, S. L. (1985). The influence of sex-role stereotyping on women's attitudes and achievement in mathematics. In S. F. Chipman, R. L. Brush, & D. M. Wilson (Eds.), *Women and mathematics: Balancing the equation* (pp. 175–198). Hillsdale, NJ: Erlbaum.

Boyd, B. F. (1999). Should gay and lesbian issues be discussed in elementary school? *Childhood Education, 76*(1), 40.

Brown, A., Cervero, R., & Johnson-Bailey, J. (2000). Making the invisible visible: Race, gender, and teaching in adult education. *Educational Quarterly, 50*(4), 273–288.

Chodorow, N. (1978). *Reproduction of mothering: Psychoanalysis and the sociology of gender.* Berkeley: University of California Press.

Clarkson, P., & Leder, G. C. (1984). Causal attributions for success and failure in mathematics: A cross-cultural perspective. *Educational Studies in Mathematics, 15,* 413–422.

Clewell, B., Anderson, B., & Thorpe, M. (1992). *Breaking the barriers: Helping female and minority students succeed in mathematics and science.* San Francisco: Jossey-Bass.

Commonwealth of Massachusetts Governor's Commission on Gay and Lesbian Youth. (1993). Making schools safe for gay and lesbian youth: Breaking the silence in schools and in families. Boston: Author. In G. Remafedi (Ed.), *Death by denial: Studies of suicide in gay and lesbian teenagers.* Boston: Alyson Publications.

Crew, L. (1997). Changing the church: Lessons learned in the struggle to reduce institutional heterosexism in the Episcopal Church. In J. T. Sears & W. L. Williams, (Eds.), *Overcoming heterosexism and homophobia: Strategies that work* (pp. 341–353). New York: Columbia University Press.

Croker, D. L. Putting it on the table: A mini-course on gender differences. *English Journal, 88*(3), 65–70.

Davenport, E., Davison, M., Kuang, H., Ding, S., Kirn, S., & Kwak, N. (1998). High school mathematics course-taking by gender and ethnicity. *American Educational Journal, 35*(3), 497–514.

Durgin-Clinchard, E. (1997). A three-legged stool: PFLAGs support, education and advocacy. In J. T. Sears & W. L. Williams (Eds). *Overcoming heterosexism and homophobia: Strategies that work* (pp. 141–147). New York: Columbia University Press.

Evans, K. (1996). Creating spaces for equity? The role of positioning in peer led literature discussions. *Language Arts, 73*(3), 194–202.

Fennema, E., & Leder, G. (1990). *Mathematics and gender.* New York: Teachers College, Columbia University.

Fennema, E., & Sherman, J. A. (1977). Sex-related differences in mathematics achievement, spatial visualization and affective factors. *American Educational Research Journal 14,* 51–71.

Fennema, E., & Sherman, J. A. (1978). Sex-related differences in mathematics achievement, spatial visualization and related factors: A further study. *Journal for Research in Mathematics Education 9,* 189–203.

GLSEN (Gay, Lesbian, and Straight Education Network). (1999, January 1). *Homophobia 101: Teaching respect for all.* Retrieved March 18, 2001, from http://www.glsen.org

GLSEN (Gay, Lesbian, and Straight Education Network). (2001, January 2). How to start a GLSEN chapter. Retrieved July 11, 2002, from http://www.glsen.org/templates/chapters/record3.html?section=38&record=5000.

Gay, Lesbian, and Straight Teachers Network. (1999). *Just the facts about sexual orientation & youth: A primer for principals, educators and school personnel.* New York: Author (ERIC Document Reproduction Service No. ED 436 619).

Ginsberg, R. W. (1999). In the triangle/out of the circle: Gay and lesbian students facing the heterosexual paradigm. *Educational Forum, 64,* Fall, 46–56.

Gittelson, I. B., Petersen, A. C., & Tobin-Richards, M. H. (1982). Adolescents' expectancies of success, self-evaluations, and attributions about performance on spatial and verbal tasks. *Sex Roles, 8,* 411–420.

Good, T. L. (1987). Two decades of research on teacher expectations: Findings and future directions. *Journal of Teacher Education, 38*(4), 32–47.

Gover, J. (1996). Gay youth in the family. In D. R. Walling (Ed.), *Open lives, safe schools* (pp. 173–182). Bloomington, IN: Phi Delta Kappa.

Greenbaum, V. (1996). Bringing gay and lesbian literature out of the closet. In D. R. Walling (Ed.), *Open lives, safe schools* (pp. 81–92). Bloomington, IN: Phi Delta Kappa.

Grossman, H. & Grossman, S. H. (1994). *Gender issues in education.* Needham Heights, MA: Allyn & Bacon.

Haimo, D. (1997). Excellence in mathematics. In D. Nolan (Ed.), *Women in mathematics: Scaling the heights* (pp. 7–12). Washington, DC: Mathematical Association of America.

Harbeck, K. M. (1997). *Gay and lesbian educators: Personal freedoms, public constraints.* Malden, MA: Amethyst Press.

Healy, P. (2001, February 28). Suicides in state top homicides. *Boston Globe.* Retrieved March 8, 2001, from http://www.boston.com

Ho, S. E., & Wiliams, J. D. (1996). The effects of parental involvement on eighth grade achievement. *Sociology of Education, 69,* 126–141.

Human Rights Campaign. (2001, February 13). HRC calls on Congress to pass comprehensive hate crimes legislation as FBI releases final report detailing problem. Retrieved March 18, 2001, from http://hrc.org/hrc/hrcnews/2001/010213FBIreport.asp.

Hunter, J. (1996). New directions for lesbian, gay, and bisexual youth: Reflections on the Harvey Milk School. In L. M. Bullock, R. A. Gable, & Ridky, J. R. (Eds.), *Understandings individual differences: Highlights from the National Symposium on What Educators Should Know about Adolescents Who Are Gay, Lesbian, or Bisexual* (pp. 24–27). New York: Council for Exceptional Children.

Interfaith Alliance Foundation. (n.d.). Discrimination against gays and lesbians in housing, employment, and education. Retrieved July 11, 2002, from http://www.interfaithalliance.org

Jennings, K. (1996). "Together for a change": Lessons from organizing the Gay, Lesbian, and Straight Teachers Network. In D. R. Walling (Ed.), *Open lives, safe schools* (pp. 251–260). Bloomington, IN: Phi Delta Kappa.

Jones, R. (1999). "I don't feel safe here anymore." *American School Board Journal, 186,* 26–31.

Jussim, L., & Eccles, J. (1992). Teacher expectations: II. Construction and reflection of student achievement. *Journal of Personality and Social Psychology 63*(3) 947–961.

Kerka, S. (1998). Career development and gender, race and class. (ERIC Digest No. 199 ERIC Document Reproduction No. ED421641).

Kleinfeld, J. (1999). Student performance: Males versus females. *Public Interest, 134,* 3–20.

Kozol, J. (1991). *Savage inequalities.* New York: Crown.

Leder, G. (1982). Mathematics achievement and fear of success. *Journal for Research in Mathematics Education, 13,* 124–135.

Leder, G. (1984). Sex differences in attributions of success and failure. *Psychological Reports, 54,* 57–58.

Leder, G. (1990). Gender differences in mathematics: An overview. In E. Fennema & G. Leder (Eds.), *Mathematics and gender* (pp. 10–26). New York: Teachers College Press.

Letts, W. J., & Sears, J. T. (1999). *Queering elementary education: Advancing the dialogue about sexualities and school.* Lanham, MD: Rowan and Littlefield.

Lipkin, A. (1996). The case for a gay and lesbian curriculum. In D. R. Walling (Ed.), *Open lives, safe schools* (pp. 47–69). Bloomington, IN: Phi Delta Kappa.

Lipkin, A. (2000). *Understanding homosexuality, changing schools.* Boulder, CO: Westview Press.

Ma, X. (1999). Dropping out of advanced mathematics: The effects of parental involvement. *Teachers College Record, 101*(1), 60–81.

Muller, C. (1998). Gender differences in parental involvement and adolescents' mathematics achievement. *Sociology of Education, 71,* 336–356.

National Association of School Psychologists. (1999). Position statement: Gay, lesbian, and bisexual youth. Bethesda, MD: Author (ERIC Document Reproduction Service No. ED 431 983).

Nichols, S. L. (1999). Gay, lesbian, and bisexual youth: Understanding diversity and promoting tolerance in schools. *Elementary School Journal, 99,* 505–519.

Nugent, R. (1997). Homophobia and the U.S. Roman Catholic clergy. In J. T. Sears & W. L. Williams (Eds.), *Overcoming heterosexism and homophobia: Strategies that work* (pp. 354–370). New York: Columbia University Press.

Oakes, J. (1990). *Multiplying inequalities: The effects of race, social class, and tracking on opportunities to learn mathematics and science.* Washington, DC: National Science Foundation.

O'Conor, A. (1995). Breaking the silence: Writing about gay, lesbian, and bisexual teenagers. In G. Unks (Ed.), *The gay teenager* (pp. 13–17). New York: Routledge.

Office for Civil Rights. (2001, January). *Revised sexual harassment guidance: Harassment of students by school employees, other students, or third parties.* Washington, DC: Department of Education. Retrieved March 18, 2001, from http://www.ed.gov/offices/OCR

Ogbu, J. (1993). Differences in cultural frame of reference. *International Journal of Behavioral Development 6*(3), 483–506.

Ogbu, J. (1995). Understanding cultural diversity and learning. In J. A. Banks & C. A. McGee Banks (Eds.), *Handbook of research on multicultural education* (pp. 582–596). New York: Macmillan.

Ogbu, J. (1996). Variability in minority school performance: A problem in search of an explanation. In E. Jacob & C. Jordan (Eds.), *Minority education: Anthropological perspectives* (pp. 83–111). Norwood, NJ: Ablex.

PFLAG (Parents, Families, and Friends of Lesbians and Gays). (n.d.). Is homosexuality a sin? Retrieved March 10, 2002, from http://www.pflag.org/store/resources/isitasin.html.

PFLAG (Parents, Families, and Friends of Lesbians and Gays). (n.d.). PFLAG reaches milestone: 450 affiliates. Retrieved March 10, 2002, from http://www.pflag.org/press/releases/010202.htm.

Pharr, S. (1988). *Homophobia: A weapon of sexism.* Little Rock, AR: Women's Project, Chardon Press.

Prince, T. (1996). The power of openness and inclusion in countering homophobia in schools. In D. R. Walling (Ed.), *Open lives, safe schools* (pp. 29–34). Bloomington, IN: Phi Delta Kappa.

Remafedi, G. (Ed.) (1994). *Death by denial: Studies of suicide in gay and lesbian teenagers.* Boston: Alyson Publications.

Roy, A. (1997). Language in the classroom: Opening conversations about lesbian and gay issues in senior high English. In J. T. Sears & W. L. Williams (Eds.), *Overcoming heterosexism and homophobia: Strategies that work* (pp. 209–217). New York: Columbia University Press.

Sadker, M., & Sadker, D. (1994). *Failing at fairness: How America's schools cheat girls.* New York: Charles Scribner's Sons.

Sattel, S., Keyes, M., & Tupper, P. (1997). Sexual harrassment and sexual orientation: The coaches' corner. In J. T. Sears & W. L. Williams (Eds). *Overcoming heterosexism and homophobia: Strategies that work* (pp. 233–246). New York: Columbia University Press.

Schniedewind, N., & Davidson, E. (1997). *Open minds to equality: A sourcebook of learning activities to affirm diversity and promote equity* (2nd ed.). Boston: Allyn and Bacon.

Sears, J. T. (1991). *Growing up gay in the South.* New York: Haworth.

Sears J. T. (1992). Educators, homosexuality, and homosexual students: Are personal feelings related to professional beliefs? In K. M. Harbeck (Ed.), *Coming out of the closet: Gay and lesbian students, teacher, and curricula* (pp. 29–79). New York: Haworth.

Sears, J. T. (1995). Black–gay or gay–black? Choosing identities or identifying choices. In G. Unks (Ed.), *The gay teenager* (pp. 135–158). New York: Routledge.

Sears, J. T. (1997). Thinking critically/intervening effectively about homophobia and heterosexism. In J. T. Sears, & W. L. Williams, (Eds.). *Overcoming heterosexism and homophobia: Strategies that work.* (pp. 13–48), New York: Columbia University Press.

Sharp, R. M., Sharp, V. F., & Metzner, S. (1995). *Scribble scrabble: Ready in a minute math game.* Blue Ridge Summit, PA: TAB Books.

Singh, M. (1998). Gender issues in the language arts classroom. (ERIC Digest. ERIC Document Reproduction number ED 426409).

Streitmatter, J. (1994). *Toward gender equity in the classroom: Everyday teachers' beliefs and practices*. Albany, NY: State University of New York.

Tauber, R. (1998). Good or bad: What teachers expect from students they generally get. ERIC Digest. (ERIC Document Reproduction number ED426985).

Unks, G. (1995). Thinking about the gay teen. In G. Unks (Ed.), *The gay teenager* (pp. 3–12). New York: Routledge.

Uribe, V. (1995). Project 10: A school-based outreach to gay and lesbian youth. In G. Unks (Ed.), *The gay teenager* (pp. 203–210). New York: Routledge.

Zirkel, P. A. (1999). Are you gay? *Phi Delta Kappan, 81*(4), 332–333.

CHAPTER 11

RELIGION

Just as ethnic, linguistic, and cultural diversity in the United States is expanding, so is America's religious landscape. Some would argue that no other nation on Earth has experienced such wholesale changes in its religious composition as has the United States. This assertion is based primarily on the numbers of individuals reporting allegiance to various religious groups since colonial times (Ostling, 1999). Others suggest that diversity of religious affiliation has always been a hallmark of the United States, especially in the last century, but the shifting content of beliefs within and between the various denominations and religions constitutes the most significant changes on the religious landscape (Williams, 2000). Whether change is viewed in terms of numbers or content of belief, we agree with Sewall (1999) that religion is not simply a cultural artifact. It is a separate entity in the kaleidoscope of diversity that warrants considerable attention from educators. In using the term religion we do not reject the idea of spirituality, which is increasingly under discussion as an important component of the education process. Rather, we are recognize that religious affiliation with a particular group, no matter how tenuous, is an important marker that distinguishes individuals from those who report having no religion. However, spirituality may be present or absent, regardless of religious affiliation.

RELIGIOUS DIVERSITY IN THE UNITED STATES

One primary reason that Europeans came to the United States was to escape religious persecution. A 1776 survey of American religious congregations found British groups dominant. Congregationalists, Presbyterian, Baptist, Episcopalians, and Quakers constituted almost 80 percent of America's congregations (Ostling, 1999). Catholics had 65 congregations and Jews had 5 synagogues. By 1890, Catholics claimed first place with 7.3 million, a place that they have kept ever since due to the diversity of Protestant denominations. A ranking of the number of congregations of various denominations is displayed in Table 11.1. Americans today report a high degree of religiosity,

252

TABLE 11.1   Number of Congregations in Religious Denominations in the United States

DENOMINATION	NUMBER OF CONGREGATIONS
Southern Baptist Convention	40,565
United Methodist Church	36,361
National Baptist Convention, USA, Inc.	33,000
Roman Catholic Church	22,728
Church of God in Christ	15,300
Churches of Christ	14,000
Assemblies of God	11,884
Presbyterian Church USA	11,328
C.o.J.C.o. Latter-day Saints	11,000
Evangelical Lutheran Church in America	10,396
Jehovah's Witnesses	10,671
African Methodist Episcopal Church	8,000
Episcopal Church	7,415
United Church of Christ	6,110
Lutheran Church—Missouri Synod	6,099
Church of God (Tennessee)	6,060
American Baptist Churches	5,839
Independent Christian Churches	5,579
Church of the Nazarene	5,135
Seventh Day Adventist Church	4,363
Christian Church (Disciples of Christ)	3,840
United Pentecostal Church	3,790
Baptist Bible Fellowship	3,600
Jewish congregations (all denominations)	3,416

Source: Ostling, R. N. (1999). America's ever-changing religious landscape [Electronic version]. *Brookings Review, 17*(2), p. 10(1).

with anywhere between 60 and 90 percent of individuals reporting affiliation with some religion, depending on how the question is posed (Goldhaber, 1996; Ostling, 1999).

Non-Christian religions also are part of our diversity. The Jewish community constitutes about 3 percent of the population, although younger American Jews marrying Gentiles are now a majority for the first time in history (Ostling, 1999; Williams, 2000). Estimates indicate that there are at least 6 million Muslims, 401,000 Buddhists, and almost 80,00 Hindus in the United States (Ostling, 1999; Wisenfeld, 2000), although publicists for these groups give much greater estimates. This is often because these groups have comparatively little organizational infrastructure. For example, not until

■ ■ ■ ■ ■

BOX 11.1

ISLAMIC WOMEN AND GIRLS
IN THE UNITED STATES

At her wedding four years ago, Amanny Khattab wore an Islamic veil under her translucent lace tulle one. She remembers the "living hell" of her freshman year at Farmingdale High School on New York's Long Island. "The week before school started, I bought all the cool stuff—Reebok sneakers, Guess! Jeans," recalls Khattab. "I wanted to look just like everybody else, but with the scarf." It didn't work. But enduring all the cracks—"towel-head," "rag-head"—made her tough. "Non-Muslim women think I'm oppressed because I wear too much?" says Khattab. "Well, I think they're oppressed because they wear too little."

In Pakistan, tradition dictates that women pray at home rather than at the mosque. In America, women not only go to the mosque—they're on the mosque's board of directors. Saudi Arabian clerics have ruled that it's un-Islamic for women to drive. But try telling a 16-year-old from Toledo, Ohio, who's just gotten her driver's license that the Koran prohibits her from hitting the road. She'll probably retort that the Prophet's favorite wife, Aisha, once directed troops in battle from the back of a camel.

Power, C. (1998, March 16). The new Islam. *Newsweek*, p. 36.

1996 did Muslims establish a school for training clergy at the graduate level to parallel the Jewish and Christian seminaries.

A growing number of Americans define themselves as "spiritual" but not "religious" (Ostling, 1999). More than any previous generation, Americans age 18 and under do not accept traditional Christian concepts, such as the idea of moral absolutes or the belief that the Bible is God's word. In fact, this trend is evident in several religions, as some Jewish children of mixed marriages receive little or no religious education. Similarly, the tenets of Islam are being reexamined by Muslim youth, who are maintaining some traditions while rejecting others (see Box 11.1).

While Judeo-Christian beliefs have traditionally been the underlying value structure in public education, an increasing number of students hold different beliefs. These beliefs cannot be left at the schoolhouse door.

WHY RELIGION IS AN ISSUE
IN PUBLIC SCHOOLS

Many scholars interested in public education and the law are convinced that new models for understanding the relationship of religion and education, or church and state, must be developed. Charles Haynes, a senior scholar with the Freedom Forum First Amendment Center, has emphasized this concern by stating, "If we are going to sustain the American experiment—E Pluribus Unum—then we can't afford culture wars in our schools that rend apart the fabric of our communities and undermine the education of our children. We need a fresh, bold approach to the conflicts—an approach that enables us to live with even our deepest differences" (Haynes, 1999, p. 7).

This need for a new approach is apparent in many arenas. This is especially apparent when considering the acrimony that has grown up between public educators and the Religious Right (Kaplan, 1994; Sewall 1999). Conservative Christian groups have been viewed by many educators as irrelevant and by others as sinister. Nevertheless, there has been a resurgence of conservative religion in the United States. Conservative churches such as Southern Baptists, Assemblies of God, Seventh-Day Adventists, and Church of the Nazarene have experienced significant increases in membership while more liberal churches such as the Methodist, Presbyterian, Lutheran Church of America, Episcopal, Disciples of Christ, and United Church of Christ have lost members steadily (Nord, 1995). There is little doubt that a conservative Christian agenda continues to have broad-based support in the United States. In addition, public school personnel often view the beliefs and customs of adherents to Islam as conservative and intrusive.

The fear and prejudice resulting from terrorist attacks by Muslim extremists around the world and, most recently, here in the United States have cast a spotlight on the growing Muslim population in the United States. While unsettling reports of anti-Muslim or anti-Arab hate crimes have been reported (Warikoo, Capeloto, Askari, & Kresnak, 2001), many political and religious leaders and communities have rallied to support their Muslim, Middle Eastern, and Arab neighbors (Southern Poverty Law Center, 2001). Many Americans are motivated like never before to gain a better understanding of the tenents of Islam. Nevertheless, many Muslims feel that some Americans act in prejudicial ways toward them simply due to their religious affiliation, country of origin, or physical appearance (see Box 11.2).

Failed Models of Religion in the Public School

To evaluate models that describe the relationship of religion to public education, one must have knowledge of constitutional law. The Constitution does not speak about religion, apart from a statement that no religious test be required for public office, because the framers believed that the federal government had no power to infringe on religious liberty (Nord, 1995). However, the states did not agree that religious liberty was assured by the Constitution, and therefore the First Congress added the Bill of Rights, including the first amendment, which states that: "Congress shall make no laws respecting an establishment of religion, or prohibiting the free exercise

■ ■ ■ ■ ■

BOX 11.2

HIDING IN BROOKLYN: AFGHAN AMERICAN
FEARS FOR SAFETY
September 12, 2001

I'm hiding in my house in the heart of an Arab neighborhood in Brooklyn, four miles from the terror that struck Manhattan. As an Afghan American, I fear the retaliation in the aftermath of the tragedy. If this "act of war" is like Pearl Harbor, will Arabs and Afghans living in America become targets of hate as Japanese Americans did during World War II?

From the roof of my brownstone home, I watch the billowing smoke darken the sky above the World Trade Center. I heard the sirens, the screams of victims falling to their death, and the rage that New Yorkers expressed afterward. Americans are angry—rightly so—and want someone to blame and attack. But I shudder thinking of the innocent Muslims who could be the victims of this fury.

On New York radio stations, callers shouted slurs against Afghans and Arabs, demanded they be killed and called for war against Afghanistan, whose rulers are suspected perpetrators of the attack. I turned off the radio and in a daze walked to the Promenade where people stood looking at the disaster across the East River. Some held any extra fabric over their mouths to block the fumes and stench of burning steel. A man appearing to be in his twenties said to a friend, "These damn Islamic people in this country should be under surveillance. They're getting away with too much." In bars where patrons crowded to watch TV, men and women clapped as President Bush swore to seek revenge.

I paced back home with my two Muslim friends, locked the door and sat still in shock. I hoped no one on our street knew that Muslims live in the house. Ever since the Taliban seized my birthplace, Afghanistan and Afghans have become the butt of slurs, jokes, and ridicule. But stereotyping and verbal attacks are not my fear anymore. The magnitude of this tragedy may provoke violence against Muslim and especially Afghan communities in this country. Few listen to the warnings by the media that Americans should not convict any group without proof.

Source: Nawa, F. (2001, September 12). Hiding in Brooklyn: Afghan American fears for safety. *Alternet.* Retrieved September 13, 2001 from http://www.alternet.org/story.html?Story ID=11482.

thereof." The first part of the amendment has come to be called the establishment clause and the second part the free exercise clause.

Given these legal principles, it becomes easier to understand why two models of schooling have failed (Haynes, 1999). The *sacred public school* was one in which one religion, that of the dominant culture, dictated school policy. While this model was prevalent in the early history of the United States, it has been determined unconstitutional and decried as unjust today. More recently, the *naked public school* model has been espoused. This model promotes a strict interpretation of the idea of separation of church and state and, therefore, declares schools to be religion-free zones. While the intention of this model was to eliminate conflict based on a determination that the state must be neutral on issues of religion, some have charged that this approach is equally as unjust as the sacred school and possibly unconstitutional. Critics of the naked public school model point out that eliminating religion from the curriculum is, in fact, a violation of neutrality in that secularism becomes the de facto curriculum (Nord, 1995). Few educators would deny that concepts of history such as nationalism, imperialism, slavery, and capitalism have important religious aspects (Sewall, 1999). Furthermore, difficult issues such as anti-Semitism or evolution must be discussed rather than avoided in the context of their religious dimensions. In fact, critics of the naked school argue that schools have a responsibility to teach values and the religions that have established the moral foundations of our civilization. Because they do not, silence on issues of religion is equally as discriminatory as silence on issues of gender, race, and culture.

The Civil Public School

The *civil public school* is a model that holds promise for fair application of First Amendment principles in public education. This model avoids inculcation of religious views while promoting respect for religious belief or unbelief. Furthermore, the civil public school recognizes the importance of study about religion as part of a good education. Remarkably, 24 religious and educational groups have issued a joint statement entitled "Religious Liberty, Public Education and the Future of American Democracy: A Statement of Principles" (Haynes, 1999) that outlines the commitments of the civil public school. Organizations as disparate as People for the American Way, the Christian Coalition, and the Council on Islamic Education have endorsed this statement.

CURRENT RELIGIOUS ISSUES IN THE PUBLIC SCHOOLS

Many issues related to religion have caused tremendous controversy in public schools. Some of these issues, such as student prayer and religious discussion, religious activity in schools, religion in the curriculum, religious holidays, released time for religious observance and instruction, and student dress, have been either challenged in the courts or addressed by presidential directives and appear to have resolution (American Jewish Congress, n.d.). Of course, challenges to these resolutions continue, but adequate consensus from legal and educational sources exists to guide the development and implementation of good policy on these issues. Other thorny issues such as the teaching of evolution or sex education continue to reappear in the national news and on school board agendas. While guidance regarding these issues may be available, the results have not been adequate to satisfy many parents, teachers, students, and religious leaders. Furthermore, issues are emerging that relate to minority religions in the United States, such as Islam, that have only begun to surface nationally.

Legal guidance on any number of issues regarding religion and the schools is available from a variety of sources. In addition to the "Statement of Principles" just mentioned, another document entitled "Religion in the Public Schools: A Joint Statement of Current Law" (American Jewish Congress, n.d.) was endorsed by 35 religious organizations (see Box 11.3). This state-

■ ■ ■ ■ ■

BOX 11.3

EXCERPT FROM "RELIGION IN THE PUBLIC SCHOOLS: A JOINT STATEMENT OF CURRENT LAW"

The Constitution permits much private religious activity in and about the public schools. Unfortunately, this aspect of constitutional law is not as well known as it should be. Some say that the Supreme Court has declared the public schools "religion-free zones" or that the law is so murky that school officials cannot know what is legally permissible. The former claim is simply wrong. And as to the latter, while there are some difficult issues, much has been settled. It is also unfortunately true that public school officials, due to their busy schedules, may not be as fully aware of this body of law as they could be. As a result, in some school districts some of these rights are not being observed.

We offer this statement of consensus on current law as an aid to parents, educators and students. . . .

STUDENT PRAYERS
Students have the right to pray individually or in groups or to discuss their religious views with their peers so long as they are not disruptive. Because the Establishment Clause does not apply to purely private speech, students enjoy the right to read their Bibles or other scriptures, say grace before meals, pray before tests, and discuss religion with other willing student listeners. In the classroom students have the right to pray quietly except when required to be actively engaged in school activities (e.g., students may not decide to pray just as a teacher calls on them). In informal settings, such as the cafeteria or in the halls, students may pray either audibly or silently, subject to the same rules of order as apply to other speech in these locations. However, the right to engage in voluntary prayer does not include,

ment addresses what is and is not permissible under the First Amendment. In a 1995 speech on religious liberty, President William Clinton stated that "The First Amendment does not . . . convert our schools into religion-free zones. . . . There are those who do believe our schools should be value neutral and that religion has no place inside the schools. But I think that wrongly interprets the idea of the wall between church and state. They are not the walls of the school" (Jurinski, 1998). Clinton directed the U.S. secretary of education, Richard Riley, to issue guidelines regarding religious expression in public schools that reflected the Joint Statement (Riley, 1998). The purpose of these guidelines is to encourage the development of school district policy regarding religious expression and to inform teachers, students, and parents of their responsibilities. Many school districts have undertaken such policy

for example, the right to have a captive audience listen or to compel other students to participate.

TEACHING ABOUT RELIGION

Students may be taught about religion, but public schools may not teach religion. As the U.S. Supreme Court has repeatedly said, "[i]t might well be said that one's education is not complete without a study of comparative religion, or the history of religion, and its relationship to the advancement of civilization." It would be difficult to teach art, music, literature and most social studies without considering religious influences. The history of religion, comparative religion, the Bible (or other scripture) as literature (either as a separate course or within some other existing course), are all permissible public school subjects. . . .

These same rules apply to the recurring controversy surrounding theories of evolution. Schools may teach about explanations of life on Earth, including religious ones (such as "creationism"), in comparative religion or social studies classes. In science class, however, they may present only genuinely scientific critiques of, or evidence for, any explanation of life on Earth, but not religious critiques (beliefs unverifiable by scientific methodology). Schools may not refuse to teach evolutionary theory in order to avoid giving offense to religion nor may they circumvent these rules by labeling as science an article of religious faith. Public schools must not teach as scientific fact or theory any religious doctrine, including "creationism," although any genuinely scientific evidence for or against any explanation of life may be taught. Just as they may neither advance nor inhibit any religious doctrine, teachers should not ridicule, for example, a student's religious explanation for life on Earth.

Source: American Jewish Congress, n.d.

development, and their efforts are instructive (Lane Education Service District, 1996; Haynes, 1999).

Consensus Issues

While nothing can preclude further challenges to any issues regarding the place of religion in schools, school districts that establish reasonable policies that involve all stakeholders are less likely to face ongoing disputes. For example, there are definite parameters under which student prayer and religious discussion can occur in public schools. Students may pray in a nondisruptive manner individually or in a group when not engaged in school activities or instruction. In fact, the Supreme Court recently rejected an appeal claiming that Virginia's morning minute of silence is unconstitutional (Gearan, 2001). Students may also speak to their peers about religious topics as long as this speech does not constitute harassment of others. Students may participate in before- or afterschool events with religious content, but school officials may neither discourage nor encourage participation in such an event. The Equal Access Act gives student religious activities, including prayer and worship, the same access to public school facilities as are given to student secular activities. Furthermore, school officials may not mandate or organize prayer at graduation nor organize religious baccalaureate ceremonies. They must remain neutral regarding all religious activity.

In regard to the curriculum, public schools may not provide religious instruction, although they may dismiss students to off-premises religious instruction. Teachers may teach *about* religion, including the Bible and other scripture. Therefore, teachers may teach the history of religion or the role of religion in history. Similarly, they may discuss the influence of religion on art, music, and literature. Although schools must be neutral with respect to religion, they may teach civic values and virtue and the moral code that holds a community together. Furthermore, students may express their beliefs about religion in their assignments, and these products must be judged by ordinary academic standards. In regard to clothing, schools can adopt policies relating to student dress, but cannot prohibit religious attire. In addition, students may display religious messages on items of clothing to the same extent that they are permitted to display comparable secular messages.

Controversial and Emerging Religious Issues in the Public Schools

Clearly, there has been tremendous progress in our understanding of the delicate relationship of religion and public education. While some would argue that the wall of separation is too high and others too low, the courts have produced enough case law on some issues to assist us in at least knowing where the wall stands. However, contentious issues remain. Often this is because the issues involved get to the core of religious belief for some, and they are unwilling to let the state make statements that they view as either immoral or false.

The teaching of evolution is one such issue that reappears over and over again, despite legal battles. Americans are divided on this issue. In one survey of religious belief in the United States, 39 percent of respondents agreed with the statement "Evolution is the best possible explanation of human existence," while 46 percent disagreed (Goldhaber, 1996). Individuals who consider themselves religiously liberal or who have graduate or professional degrees are more likely to agree with this statement than those who consider themselves to be religiously conservative and have a high school diploma or less. Consequently, it is important for teachers to understand the legal, educational, and philosophical factors affecting this debate.

The Teaching of Evolution.   In 1925 the famous "monkey law" trial took place in which John Scopes was convicted and fined for teaching evolution when Tennessee law made it a crime to teach anything but the biblical version of creation. Then in 1987 the Supreme Court in *Edward* v. *Aguillard* barred Louisiana from requiring the teaching of "creation science" alongside evolution theory (Nord, 1995). Creation science teaches that Earth and most life forms came into existence suddenly about 6,000 years ago. More recently, the Tagipahoa Parish Board of Education in Louisiana voted 5 to 4 to reject a proposal to teach creation science in its school (Associated Press, 2000). Subsequently, they crafted a disclaimer to be read by teachers in the district to students about to study the theory of evolution. The disclaimer read in part that the theory of evolution was "presented to inform students of the scientific concept and not intended to influence or dissuade the biblical version of creation or any other concept" (Associated Press, 2000). The fifth Circuit Court of Appeals ruled that this disclaimer must be struck down because it had the effect of promoting religion. The Supreme Court refused to hear the case, although Justice Scalia, writing for the three dissenting judges, criticized the court for not allowing a school district to even suggest to students that other theories besides evolution are worthy of consideration.

Another battleground was established when the ten-member Kansas Board of Education voted to adopt new science standards that de-emphasize evolution in science classes and permit school boards to allow the teaching of theories of macroevolution, such as creation science or intelligent design (Haynes, 1999; Learning, 1999). The American Civil Liberties Union responded by warning that they would take legal action if teaching macroevolution theories was permitted. Subsequently, Kansas voters removed conservative members of the state Board of Education, thereby eliminating the state support for teaching macroevolution (Belluck, 2000). Allies such as the National Council of Science, the National Association of Biology Teachers, and the American Civil Liberties Union oppose the Creation Science Association, which holds that there is a vast amount of scientific evidence that supports the biblical creation account (Matsumura, 1999). Interestingly, a recent national survey released by People for the American Way Foundation reported that 83% of Americans generally support the teaching of evolution in public schools, but 79 percent think creationism has a place in the public school curriculum (Glanz, 2000). Respondents often said the topic should be discussed as a belief rather than a competing scientific theory.

Positions on the Relationship between Religion and Science.   These conflicts arise from the very disparate positions regarding the relationship between science and religion that various groups and individuals espouse (Nord, 1999). One view is that when conflicts arise religion trumps science since only religion provides reliable knowledge. This is the view of creation scientists. A second is that only science can offer reliable knowledge since it is through the scientific method that we discover truths about nature. A third view is that science and religion are independent of each other, because the scientific method is used to uncover knowledge in the field of science and narrative and faith are the basis of the study of religion. Because science and religion ask different questions and utilize different methods, the fields can be compartmentalized. This is the view of the National Academy of Sciences and the National Association of Biology Teachers (National Academy of Sciences, 1998; National Association of Biology Teachers, 1997). Another position that seems to be gaining more adherents is that science and religion make claims about the same world and, therefore, there is a need to attempt to integrate the knowledge that both fields provide. This view may be growing due to developments in science regarding quantum mechanics, cosmology, chaos theory, and ecology that do not fit the models of classical science and developments in theology that view religious claims as testable (Nord, 1999).

One's position on the relationship between religion and science will inform his or her opinion about the teaching of the theory of evolution in the public schools. We believe that both legal precedent and the models presented here will assist your discussion of the following case regarding evolution. In addition, the Public Broadcasting System has produced an excellent series on evolution that discusses many of these issues in the schools and provides teachers with additional thought-provoking material (Public Broadcasting System, 2001).

Although the principles set forth by case law assist teachers in making informed decisions regarding this issue, there will undoubtedly be legal challenges in the future. The Supreme Court has refused to review recent cases, but a change in the composition of the justices could easily open the door to reversals of lower-court rulings that now stand. Furthermore, the shifting of positions regarding the relationship of science and religion in the academy and the general public may further activate this national discussion.

Emerging Issues in the Public Schools.   There are many emerging issues regarding religion in the schools. Certainly, the changing demographics of religious belief in the United States will prompt new discussions regarding the appropriate role of religion in the public schools. For example, the prediction that the number of adherents to Islam will surpass those to Judaism in the United States by 2010 and make it the second-largest faith in the United States (Power, 1998) has implications for teachers and programs across the country. The religious practices of Islam are not always accommodated in today's public schools.

Another emerging issue is that of character or values education (Sizer & Sizer, 1999). A primary educational concern of many American families is school safety. One suggested remedy for the incivility displayed by some students is character education. However, there is an ongoing debate about the appropriateness and content of moral education in the public schools. It appears to be the case that schools may teach civic virtues (e.g., honesty, good citizenship, courage, respect for others, moral conviction, tolerance), but may not teach them as religious tenets. The fact that most religions also teach these values does not make it unlawful for schools to teach them (American Jewish Congress, n.d.).

Still another topic appearing in the educational consciousness is the nature of spirituality in the schools. While educators such as Palmer (1998–1999) and Scherer (1998–1999) reject the imposition of any religion in public education, they encourage the exploration of the spiritual dimensions of teaching and learning. Of course, a clear definition of what constitutes spiritual content and how it might overlap or conflict with values education is yet to be fully determined. The list of emerging issues could go on. As one example of emerging issues of religion in the schools, we have chosen to present a case about a middle school student who is struggling to bridge the multiple worlds of his family's Muslim faith, recent immigration from Pakistan, and his new American school.

Muslims in the Schools.   Islam is one of the major world religions with over 1 billion adherents worldwide (Wisenfeld, 2000). In the United States, it is estimated that Muslims constitute 1.4 percent of the population, and they are concentrated in the states of California, New Jersey, New York, Ohio, Michigan, and Illinois (Power, 1998; Curtiss, Alamoudi, Johnson, & Reda, 1999). Furthermore, Islam is the fastest-growing religion in the United States (Curtiss, et al., 1999). Of the estimated 6 million Muslims in the United States, about 42 percent are African American, 25 percent are South Asian, and 12 percent are Arab. There have been black Muslims in the United States for over 100 years, but the movements within that group have changed political and religious commitments over time (Gollnick & Chinn, 1997). South Asian Muslims come from countries such as Pakistan and India. Arab Americans represent more than 20 countries in the Middle East and Northern Africa. This diversity of national origins among adherents to Islam in the United States presents many dilemmas to those trying to forge an identity.

Muslim families are facing new challenges as they attempt to follow the tenets of their faith in a country that practices religious pluralism. While many Muslim youths in America are questioning the strict rules of the Qur'an (or Koran), they also are proud of their faith and the moral stance that it upholds. The place of women in Muslim society is certainly changing. Women who would have prayed at home rather than at the mosque in their country of origin now go to the mosque to pray and are on the board of directors (Power, 1998). Teen-agers question the rationale for arranged marriages. Although it is not yet clear how second- and third-generation Muslims will acculturate, it is certain that teachers and administrators will need to address the challenges that Muslim students bring to the public schools. While there are now over 200 Islamic schools in the United States (Sachs, 1998), the majority of American Muslims will attend public schools.

Muslims believe that there is one god, Allah, and that Islam was the faith of all God's prophets from Adam to the last prophet, Muhammad (Breuilly, O'Brien, & Palmer, 1997). Muhammed revealed God's final words to mankind in the Qur'an. The only authorized version of the Qur'an is in Arabic and translations are never used in worship. Learning to read and recite the Qur'an is an important part of a child's education. Because Muhammed is believed to have interpreted the word of God in his actions, the stories and sayings of Muhammed are collected in the Hadith, which is also a source of guidance.

The five pillars, or basic beliefs, of Islam must be practiced by all Muslims (Breuilly et al., 1997). The first is the *shahada* or affirmation that there is no god but Allah and Muhammad is his prophet. So, like Christianity and Judaism, Islam holds to monotheism. The second is *salah*, five daily prayers that each individual is obliged to offer unless one is ill or traveling. Prayers are said communally at the mosque each Friday afternoon. Fasting, or *sawm*, is performed during the ninth Muslim month known as Ramadan. During this month an adult Muslim refrains from eating, drinking, smoking, and conjugal relations from dawn to sunset. Children under the age of puberty are exempt, but may partake in a limited fast. The Eid ul-Fitr celebrates the end of this fast, and special prayers, foods, and festivals accompany this holiday. The fourth pillar is *zakat*, a welfare tax for the needy. It is believed that the Muslim community has the right to surplus wealth, which is calculated as a minimum of 2.5 percent of the annual family income. Finally, once in a lifetime a *Hajj* or pilgrimage to the holy city of Makkan (Mecca) is expected of all Muslims who are able to travel and can afford to go without risking the family's well-being.

There are two major sects within Islam: Sunni Muslims and Shiite Muslims (Gollnick & Chinn, 1997). Sunni Muslims constitute the largest group, whereas Shiite Muslims are smaller, but highly visible. This is due, in part, to their belief that the state should adhere to Islamic law. It was a radical group of Shiite Muslims, followers of the Ayatollah Komeni, who overthrew the shah of Iran and later seized American hostages. Subsequent terrorist attacks against western countries have led to ongoing political mistrust. Unfortunately, this situation has led to negative reactions from some Americans against individuals with Arab backgrounds (Noor Al-Deen, 1991; Schwartz, 1999).

Certain rituals separate Muslims from non-Muslims (Weiss, 1995). Muslims do not eat pork or drink alcoholic beverages. They require that animals be slaughtered in a ritual manner. Another practice is that their sons should be circumcised. Traditionally, boys and girls are educated separately, and girls are required to wear modest clothing, including a hijab, or head covering. However, cultural and religious norms are not necessarily identical. While Islam does not require a woman or girl to cover her head, apart from during religious worship, some cultural groups do require it. Therefore, it is important to try to determine the cultural norms that particular families adhere to.

School leaders must be aware of the personal and religious rights of Islamic students. There is certainly a need to counteract possible harassment of Arab American students by including the Arab culture and Muslim religion fairly and accurately in the curriculum (Schwartz, 1999). Similarly, educators should accommodate Islamic practices such as fasting, prayer, and dress. Students should be allowed access to a room other than the cafeteria if they are fasting, and pork products in the cafeteria should be labeled. Just as student prayer is allowed for other religious groups, Muslims should be able to pray. Girls should not be harassed for wearing head coverings or traditional dress. In some places where there is a concentrated population of Muslims, schools offer separate physical education classes for girls. Some would argue that if such classes cannot be provided then Muslim children should not be required to participate in physical education, since taking group showers and wearing typical gym clothes may violate the Muslim tradition of modesty.

The religious beliefs of students have a significant effect on their behavior both in and out of school. It is critical that teachers understand and respect their students' beliefs and include information about religion in the curriculum when appropriate. Educators must be aware of the bias against Arabs that is portrayed in some textbooks and children's literature (Barlow, 1994) and promote the acquisition of accurate materials. Such resources are available through the American Forum for Global Education (Kelahan & Penn, 1996); the Arab World and Islamic Resources and School Services (Shabbas, 1998), and the American-Arab Anti-Discrimination Committee (1993). Finally, school staff must approach religious issues that arise in their schools in a legal and inclusive manner. As former President William Clinton has said, religion can't be left at the schoolhouse door.

THE CASE OF JON HITCHCOCK

Jon walked down the hallway, headed for his eighth grade team meeting. He was still excited about the museum that the students on his team had created in the library and the great job that they had done the day before when they displayed their projects to the rest of the school. Yesterday the library had been transformed into the Woodburn Middle School Museum of Natural Science and History. There were models of Greek temples, a life-sized papier maché giant panda, and posters about famous scientists. He was particularly proud of the time line poster that one of the groups in his anthropology class had created that started with a common ancestor of apes and man and then showed representations of the Neanderthals and Cro-Magnon men at the times of their approximate appearance. He looked up to take another look at it on the way out. Instead he saw only a strip of blank wall. Where was it? Everything else was still there. Jon picked up his pace and all but ran to the team meeting.

"Hey, where's the time line?" he barked as he entered the door.

The other three members of the team were already sitting in a circle, discussing the successes of the museum tour.

"Which time line?" asked Margaret, the team leader and math teacher.

"The history of man time line. It's gone. Did one of the kids in that group come in after school and ask to take it home? I told them we were going to leave the museum up until the end of the week."

"No. No one asked me," said Jennifer Larsen, the science teacher. "They know that the projects don't belong to just one person."

"Are you sure it didn't just fall off the wall overnight?" asked Bethany. "I looked in there before I left last night and everything was there. But we did move some projects my class built for the mythology course off the tables so Alice could have classes in there today."

"I'm sure," Jon replied forcefully. "I put that poster up myself and there's no way it was going to come down until someone took it down."

"Well, Superintendent McAlister sent us an announcement saying there would be a board of education meeting in there last night," said Margaret slowly.

"Do you think someone took it down so the board members or parents wouldn't see it?" gasped Bethany.

"What do you mean?" Jon shot back. "I went through hell to get approval to teach that course during activity period. First I had to get approval from our beloved principal, Elaine Prentice. She wouldn't sign off on it until I gave my spiel to McAlister. Then McAlister made me get written permission from every parent whose kids took that module."

"Yes, but it never went to the board of ed and someone probably decided it wasn't worth raising any hackles when they didn't have to. The major agenda item was presenting the new technology proposal and they probably didn't want to get off track," said Jennifer.

"What?" fumed Jon. "I'm going down to Prentice's office right now to find out what she knows about this. Principals should stand up for their teachers. This is outrageous!"

Margaret jumped to her feet and grabbed Jon as he headed out the door.

"Now just sit down and talk about this a minute, Jon," she insisted. "You're too upset to talk to Mrs. Prentice now and you'll only get yourself in trouble without solving anything."

"I know she took it down. She never wanted me to teach that unit in the first place. Either that or McAlister removed it. She was against it from the start, too. She was afraid she'd bump heads with the board of ed," he stormed.

"You may be right, Jon. But you have to remember that we don't have tenure," chimed in Bethany. "You're already on shaky ground with the administration."

"I don't care. This is wrong. They made me go through that whole approval process. I sent out detailed letters to each kid's family explaining what the mini-course on anthropology would be about and got approvals from each family. The two kids whose parents didn't approve were allowed to pick one of your courses. Now they're afraid to let the board of ed know. The administration needs to support the teachers when they are doing new, innovative things, not hide them."

"Let's talk about this," said Jennifer. "We really don't know what happened to that poster. Mrs. Prentice just got done reprimanding you up for wearing jeans last week. The last thing you need is another altercation with her."

"That jeans incident was totally unfair, and you know it. I had on a tie and a jacket with those jeans. It was a planning day and I never met with students. That whole incident is irrelevant. She's just looking for ways to criticize me because I'm an innovative teacher and that scares her."

"There's no doubt that the kids have a great time in your class, Jon," said Margaret, trying to calm him down. "I know how much they got into researching their topics for the anthropology mini-course. But always pushing the envelope may not get you the results you want and may even make things worse. Evolution is a controversial topic and you took it on in middle school. They let you teach that module on anthropology, in spite of the fact that you had to jump through a lot of hoops to do it. Fifteen years ago, when I joined this faculty, no one would even have let you talk about the theory of evolution in middle school, much less the evolution of man. If you go down there now, you might say some things you'll regret later and, more importantly, lose the opportunity to ever teach that mini-course again."

"That's true, Jon," said Jennifer. "You know, the state curriculum only includes evolution in the biology curriculum. They stress that it's a theory that seems to be supported by the scientific community. Even most high school textbooks avoid talking about the evolution of man. It's just too controversial. It's one thing to talk about homologous structures in frogs and birds and another to have a poster on the wall with apelike pictures of prehistoric man that point to a common ancestor with the apes."

"People have to learn the truth," insisted Jon. "The scientific record supports everything that I taught them. I had to bring in my college textbooks and *National Geographic* and other scientific journals and textbooks because this library just doesn't have much information. I never said they came from apes. I was showing them bones and geologic records and artist's conceptions of what early man looked like. I taught them the scientific facts; that's it."

"That may be true, but you know how some of the other kids reacted when they toured the museum yesterday," Margaret responded. "When they wrote down their reactions to that time line some of them just wrote 'I didn't come from an ape.' That kind of response may be because they weren't in your class and didn't have the opportunity to study the scientific findings, but it's still a reaction we have to expect from some students and their families. Any discussion of evolution is going to step on the toes of those who believe that God created man in his own image and God couldn't look like an ape."

"Look, you know that I'm not religious. I can't imagine that any well-informed person could believe that Earth was formed in seven days and that Adam and Eve were real beings who were supernaturally created out of clay. But I never put down anyone's belief in God. I simply showed them the books that point to the likelihood of a common ancestor."

"I'm not particularly religious either, Jon, and I don't understand why people feel so threatened by scientific facts," said Jennifer. "But I can tell you one thing. If I get the chance to teach high school biology someday, I'm going to spend about two days on evolution. They'll learn about Darwin's *theory* of evolution, and information on fossil dating, comparative embryonic development and anatomy, and geographic isolation. That's it. I'm not even going to talk about the evolution of man to any extent. It's just too controversial."

"But kids want to know about this stuff! They love it. Why should we skip over information that is so central to their existence—the origin of man? If I have to avoid controversy, then I'd rather not be a teacher."

"Well, if you walk down to Mrs. Prentice's office and say what you are saying now, you may not be a teacher in this district much longer," insisted Bethany.

"There's something else to think about, too, Jon," said Margaret. "This is the first year we've been given permission to have these mini-courses. In fact, each of you was hired last year to work on the team with me to develop these special topics that are totally based on teacher and student interest. We've never had this much choice for either students or teachers before. We can have the courses last 5 to 8 weeks and we have flexibility with scheduling. We can teach topics that are technically outside our certification areas. We have joint planning time each day. True, they didn't give us any resources to buy new teaching materials, but there are still teachers who would love to be involved in such an innovative program. Is it really such a big deal that the administration might not want to cause waves with the board of ed?"

"I think it is a big deal. It's censorship. There was nothing on that time line that scientific fact doesn't support," Jon insisted.

"Jon, you know that the vast majority of parents in this district would agree with you. But this is a rural district with a fair number of people whose families go back many generations. Their ancestors lived off the land and went to church on Sunday. Many people in this community still do the same things today. They have a right to tell their children what they believe the Bible says, even if it's literal," replied Margaret.

"Yeah, but some of those Baptists, they are really conservative—and outspoken," said Jennifer. "Even the state syllabus says that 'scientific creationism' is not accepted as science by the majority of experts."

"They still have the right to keep their children from hearing things they believe are antithetical to their religious beliefs," replied Margaret.

"I know, I know," agreed Jennifer. "But we have a responsibility to give them an education. Shouldn't an educated person know about the theory of evolution?"

"And I have the right to let my students display scientific findings and not have them taken down just because the board of education or community members might see them," said Jon. He turned and stormed down the hall in the direction of Elaine Prentice's office.

"Boy, I hope he changes his mind before he gets down there," said Bethany. "If he says the same things to Mrs. Prentice that he said to us, there's no way he'll get tenure next year."

"I don't think he's thinking very clearly. He's a risk taker; there's no doubt about that. He never would have chosen the topic of anthropology in the first place it he weren't," said Margaret.

"And he's a good teacher. The kids love him. He's a great soccer coach, too. I know he likes this job. We all work hard and have lots of creative ideas. We have a great time on this team. He's not mad at us," added Jennifer.

"I know. I think he bit off more than he could chew. There are plenty of controversial books I could have the kids read in language arts. I'm waiting until I get tenure to suggest them to the English faculty. His certification is in history, not science. I wonder if he knows enough about evolution to teach that mini-course? We don't know what he actually said since we're all teaching different topics at the same time," said Bethany.

"He took a course in anthropology in college," said Jennifer. "I didn't. He probably knows more about the evolution of man than I do."

"All I know is I'd hate to see the opportunity to offer mini-courses denied over this. Did you see how excited those kids were when the rest of the school came by to see the Roman Coliseum that my group produced for the mythology course? They got lots of great written and verbal feedback," interjected Bethany.

"The museum idea is wonderful. The kids in my group did wonderful displays on endangered species and the other classes loved it," replied Jennifer.

"Even the projects on famous mathematicians got some kid's interest. It made an abstract concept more real," agreed Margaret. "It would be a shame not to have mini-courses or to have the topics limited. It would be even worse to lose Jon as a teacher on our team."

"Maybe we should run after him and stop him before he says too much to Mrs. Prentice," said Jennifer.

"That might work, at least temporarily," agreed Margaret, "but Jon isn't the kind of person to avoid controversy when he thinks he's right."

"You may be right, Margaret," responded Jennifer. "But he's making a decision that will ultimately affect all of us. I don't want to lose Jon and I don't want to lose the momentum and camaraderie our team has developed. If we can just avoid this controversy, we can keep implementing the innovative curriculum ideas we've all talked about."

"Well, while I run to get him, you and Jennifer think about what we can say to Jon to work this out," said Jennifer as she ran for the door.

DISCUSSION QUESTIONS

1. What conflicts between and among teachers, administrators, students, and community members are apparent with regard to disagreement over issues related to the separation of church and state?

2. What additional issues between and among the case constituencies result from differences in expectations and actual events?
3. What values and beliefs do various individuals and groups hold regarding the teaching of evolution in public schools?
4. What can we learn from the first amendment of the U.S. Constitution and recent court cases involving the teaching of evolution that affect this case?
5. What goals regarding the teaching of evolution might be established to address the conflicts among constituencies in this case?
6. What resources should be available and what approaches could be implemented to assist the district in determining an equitable policy regarding the teaching of evolution?
7. What other resources, activities, or strategies might be brought to bear to address other issues apparent in the case?

THE CASE OF FOME QURESHI

September 6

A new school year, a new teaching position, a new group of students and curriculum, two new school faculties, a new beginning. Not everyone gets to experience this much "newness" in mid-life! After 18 years of teaching study skills to underprepared community college students and 3 years of teaching ESL to adults, teaching in the public schools is a welcome but challenging change.

I'm glad that my master's is behind me and I have a teaching position in ESL to show for it, even if I am traveling back and forth between the elementary school in the morning and the middle school in the afternoon each day. The district has chosen to bus all LEP students to Lincoln Elementary and Henderson Middle, rather than ask us to travel to eight different elementary schools and two middle schools. We only have an ESL program since none of the grade levels have enough speakers of any one language to warrant bilingual instruction.

Teaching elementary students is quite a contrast to teaching middle school students! Working with middle schoolers is like taking a roller-coaster ride every day. I have the additional challenge of having students whose primary languages include Spanish, Arabic, Chinese, Gujarati, and Urdu. Half of the teachers in this school have never heard of Urdu, so I have to continually say, "That's what they speak in Pakistan." Fome Qureshi is the first student I've worked with who speaks Urdu, so I want to try to keep a log of his activities.

He's a handsome young man with thick black hair, respectful behavior toward his teachers, and an eagerness to learn. He's only been in the United States since May of last year and, after a month in New York City, his parents and two younger sisters came to Riverton. He dresses like all the other boys, so you wouldn't necessarily know his cultural background without asking. It's clear that the Qureshis are concerned parents since they immediately brought Fome to school and he was given the Language Acquisition Survey (LAS) last June. Fome's oral level was low and he was on level 1 for reading, which is equivalent to being a nonreader. He has quite a way to go to reach level 3 to be out of ESL, but right now I just want to help him to acclimate to sixth grade in the United States.

September 13

I've had a chance to review the records that Fome's parents gave June Adams, his guidance counselor, when they enrolled him last spring. June said the Qureshis arrived with the district supervisor for ESL and Mrs. Mukherjee, a 15-year resident of Riverton who grew up in India and speaks Urdu. She wasn't sure how much they understood of what she said. June believes that Mr. Qureshi understands fairly well because he responds with some English phrases, but Mrs. Qureshi says little in English beyond greetings.

June also said that the Qureshis asked that Fome not take physical education with girls. I guess they would prefer that he not be exposed to girls who are "part dressed." Come to think of it, I took P.E. separately from boys in junior high, but that changed years ago. June says she's going to ask Mrs. Mukherjee, a community member, to speak to the Qureshis. I wonder what the administration will do if they insist? It's time for me to arrange a meeting with Fome's parents, but it's not a simple task to get everyone together. Without a translator, we might as well not meet.

September 23

I'm anxious to meet Fome's parents. I'm concerned about his vision. Fome's big, dark eyes are usually watery, and he often tells me that he must go put drops in them. I hope he's been to a doctor.

His transcript from his last school in Rawalpindi is difficult to interpret; they don't use letter grades and I can only guess at what the numbers mean. I can easily see that he took math, science, Pakistani history, and Urdu. It looks like he took Islamiat (sounds like religion) and scouting. He also had English, but often the study of English in another country is very different from what he'd learn in the United States. What I didn't realize until now is that Fome was born in Libya and actually lived in Tripoli until he was 8 years old.

This year guidance has agreed that Fome should be in science, reading, math, English, physical education, and a quarter each of health, music, and art. However, in order to fit him into the limited times ESL is offered, they're exempting him from social studies. His ESL class includes all emerging readers: two students from Mexico, a student from Saudi Arabia, and one from Puerto Rico. He won't be receiving report card grades this quarter since they would all be failing if he were compared (unfairly) to his classmates. Instead, he receives a comment such as "ESL: No grade assigned. Satisfactory effort." However, I think some of his teachers do show him what his grades are on papers and tests and, naturally, they are low.

September 27

Mrs. Mukherjee spoke with Fome's mother and told her that he has to take physical education with girls because that's how it is in America. I guess she sounded fairly convincing since I haven't heard any more about it. Mrs. Mukherjee says that Fome has always gone to schools where Islam is taught and practiced and, at this age, he would be attending an all-boys school. I know that his younger sister refuses to work with boys in her fourth grade class. This kind of separation just doesn't exist in the public schools in America, at least not in a city of 25,000 in which there is only a small mosque on a main street and there are probably fewer than 70 families that are Islamic.

October 13

Natalie Vaughn, his science teacher, says that Fome is very quiet in class and doesn't usually know the answer when she asks him a question. I know she tries to use hands-on experiments when she can, but he's still on the Basic Interpersonal Communication Skills (BICS) level and most of what they are talking about involves Cognitive–Academic Language Proficiency (CALP). Besides, who knows how much science background he got in Pakistan?

On the other hand, Fome is starting to talk quite a bit in ESL. We're reading a simplified version of *Oliver Twist*, and I've been having them act it out as they read. The students seem to really enjoy this, and it helps us talk through the new vocabulary. Of course, allowing students to act also opens the door for all kinds of interaction, both positive and negative. Fome and Omar aren't friends, and sometimes I have to separate them or they get into a verbal altercation. Omar has a reputation for getting into trouble. Last year he pulled the fire alarm. He's been in the United States for several years and has made little progress academically. I think Fome is actually a little afraid of Omar, but so are a lot of students. Unfortunately, he's going to have to learn to deal with it.

November 5

Linda DeNunzio showed me a story Fome wrote for English class. I guess she asked them to write about a friend. She wondered if I knew why he lines his words up in columns like this.

My	friend	name	is	Michel.
He	was	bron	at	St. Mary
hospital	in	Riverton,	On	14, Oct.86
He	was	named after	a	person
in	a	movie.	He	has lived
in	Riverton	and	Columbia.	
He	has	two	brothers	and
three	sisters.	He	had	a
pet.	His	pet	name	
is	pitbull.	He	likes	
his	dog.	His	easy	subject
is	Math.	His	best	year
is	97	because	He	
like	the	homework.	He	always
do	one	work	in	his
roller	skiting.	His	favorite	station
is	Rap.	His	favorite	sport
team	is	49	ners.	

I know that Urdu is written from right to left, but I'm not sure how that would relate to this. Fome knows how to use simple sentences and his spelling is respectable even if his vocabulary is still limited. He's still confused by verb tenses and the use of possessives. I wonder what he means by "one work" in the sentence about roller "skiting" (skating)? Linda told him he would get a C for content and D for mechanics on this assignment if she were giving him a grade.

Apparently, Fome doesn't let that kind of news bother him. He wrote another paragraph about how much he likes his teachers at Henderson Middle School. I'll have to find out more about what school in Libya and Pakistan is like.

December 2

We just got back from Thanksgiving vacation and Linda asked the students to write something of their own choice for their portfolio. This is what Fome contributed:

> I like thanksgiving but I forget to check and burn my turkey. I am going to tell my mom. They turkey was ready. Come down and check it. Before my mom

came down the cat come frist. And then me and the cat try to put the turkey in the oven. Then my friend coming out. And I go play outside to play two hour later I smell burning. And I tell my friend my friend I burned my turkey. And they make fun on me.

I thought he did a nice job of telling the story (although we certainly still need to work on verb tense and not starting sentences with "And"). However, I'd be surprised if he had turkey for Thanksgiving!

Mr. and Mrs. Qureshi didn't come for parent–teacher conferences (a miscommunication). I want them to know that Fome is trying hard, and I have many questions to ask them. Things are too hectic now, but after winter break, I'm going to ask June to call them in so we can talk using Mrs. Mukherjee as the translator.

Natalie Vaughn says that Fome is trying, but he says that she is talking too fast for him to understand. She doesn't feel that she really talks too fast. In fact, she tries to restate things frequently to Fome and others in the class. He is doing his homework and he continues to be respectful and well behaved. He's willing to work in groups (even with girls), but hasn't seemed to develop that many friendships outside the boys he knows in ESL.

January 10

Finally! The Qureshis met with June, Natalie, Linda, Mrs. G, and me today. They were a little late because they had to take a taxi. Mr. Qureshi has a job at a service station but had off this morning. Mrs. Qureshi had on a beautiful green kameez (shirt) and salwar (pants) and covered her head with a dupatta. He did most of the talking and then Mrs. Mukherjee translated. Sometimes Mrs. Qureshi would add things, especially about Fome's school experience.

We started by asking how they like Riverton. They seemed most pleased that it is not crowded and that the children like school. They were glad to hear that Fome is trying hard in school, but were concerned that he doesn't study more at home. They want him to go to college. We assured them that he is doing most of his homework. We encouraged them to get him a library card so that he can take out books at the public library.

I asked about his eyes, which seem better but are still red. Apparently, Rawalpindi is a huge city and he lived in the commercial section where there are few plants. He has developed asthma and severe allergies here, which are aggravated by the sun. He was riding his bike all over, but they had to take it away from him. Fome, while not overweight, looks like he's gained 20 pounds since he arrived. Perhaps he's not getting enough exercise—or perhaps he's enjoying having food so readily accessible in the United States!

I asked about Fome's school experience in Pakistan. In fifth grade, Fome had 38 students in his class. Pakistan's educational system is essentially the

British system, which bases promotion to the next grade on yearly exams. There are both public and private schools, and there is a great difference in the quality of education between the two. The Qureshis have always paid for Fome and his two sisters to go to a private school. He has been taking English for several years. The books are in English, but the teachers often speak in Urdu. Islamiat is an explanation of the holy book Qur'an in Urdu. Boys and girls take this class separately. It's still not clear to me how much Fome was required to write and speak in English before coming here.

When the Qureshis were in Tripoli, Mr. Qureshi worked for an Italian oil company. The children went to a Pakistani school that included children who spoke Arabic, Chinese, English, and Filipino. I can't imagine being an ESL teacher there!

I wondered why the Qureshis came to the United States since they don't have relatives here at all. Apparently, they submitted their names to an emigration lottery. Within 6 months, their names were called. They answered questions, filled out forms, and they were on their way to the United States. Mr. Qureshi is working double-shifts 6 days a week and Mrs. Qureshi manages the household.

Another important piece of this lengthy conversation was about Islam. The Qureshis explained that Fome must pray five times a day since this is one of the five pillars of their faith. He must go home and "make up" the afternoon prayer that he didn't offer in school. One of the evening prayers takes about 25 minutes before he goes to bed. Soon he will be fasting for Ramadan. He is not to eat pork, and red meat must be "halal," which is something like kosher from what I could gather. Fome has been to Mecca with his father. These are things I didn't realize, since Fome does not speak of them in school.

I really was pleased to have Mrs. Mukherjee there as our conversation would have been minimal otherwise. The Qureshis seem like very concerned parents. They say that they like U.S. schools because their children like the teachers and parents can be more involved than in Pakistan. However, they seem to be concerned that their children are not able to learn about religion in school, so they must teach that at home.

P.S. The Qureshis said they did *not* have turkey for Thanksgiving since they didn't know about these traditions.

January 27

I decided to sit in on one of Linda's English classes so that I could see how Fome and the other ESL students in that class respond. She's right—they are quiet in the regular classroom! The period started with sustained silent reading. Fome has listed about 12 books that he has read since September, including *The Matchlock Gun, Super Hoops, Dragons Don't Cook Pizza,* and two

Nancy Drew stories. Fome got up from his seat to ask Linda what the word "grave" meant (the burial place). After 10 minutes, Linda asked the students to take out their language arts book and reminded them they were reviewing nouns, verbs, adjectives, and adverbs. The definition of each of these terms was on the board and they discussed them. Then they went over the homework, which was on forming comparative and superlative adjectives. Here are some of the types of errors Fome made on fill in the blank items:

early	earlyer	earlyest
bravely	more braverlyer	most bravelyest

On the sentences, these are samples of his responses:

Of these two, I like pea soup *well*. (Then he corrected it to "best.")

Joe drives *more recklessly* of all the race car drivers.

He did get some right, but I'm not sure that he wasn't just benefiting from the law of averages. It's obvious that Fome doesn't understand all the rules that are operating here, and it's not easy to teach them all when he still is working on a basic understanding of vocabulary. It would also help if English didn't have so many exceptions. I guess I'll try to work on some of this in ESL. Forty-two minutes just aren't enough. Fortunately, he often stays after school for extra help (and also to socialize). Linda does make an extra effort to look over Fome's shoulder as he's working and to help him when he asks.

At the end of class, Linda asked them to write a response to one of the following two writing prompts in the book for homework:

1. A wizard has just cast a spell. You and your best friend will be fish for the next 24 hours. You will be a shark and your friend will be a goldfish. Write a brief paragraph telling who has the better time and why. Use several adverbs in the comparative form in your paragraph.
2. In old television westerns, the good cowboys wore white hats and rode white horses. The bad cowboys wore black hats and rode black horses. In movies about King Arthur and Sir Lancelot, good knights wore white armor and bad knights wore black armor. Write a short story about the cowboys or the knights. Compare the good guys and the bad guys. Use both adjectives and adverbs.

This should be interesting!

February 3

Today Linda showed me the story that Fome wrote for that homework assignment. He said he didn't want to write on the topics assigned, and Linda said that was fine. This is what he produced:

Fome Qureshi   English

2/28/98   Period 1

Life is hard without school & collage

Without school and Collage the life

is bad. You cannot do nothing. You don't go

school then you have to work in Pizza hut, Plaza

Pizza e.t.c. You do robbery and said bad word to

other people. If you want to go to school. You don't do your home. Its not

teacher responsibility Example you have 5 subject homework. You just do 1. If

she told you to stay 9th you don't stay. You don't go school. then you pay.

I guess that's why Fome always stays for ninth period to get extra help. He doesn't want to work at Pizza Hut! I think the only adjective he used correctly is "bad." However, I would love it if I could transfer this work ethic to several other students.

It's clear that Fome has heard admonitions like these at home. Mrs. Mukherjee told me that the Qureshis came here primarily because they want their children to get a good education. Yet it seems like they have left so much behind—culture, language, and family. I believe that the Qureshis used to live with almost their whole family. Mrs. Mukherjee said they had a three-story house where Mr. Qureshi's four brothers and their families live. They shared one kitchen and ate together, watched TV together, and shared the household work. There were 12 children in the house, so they never needed to find playmates. They could even play tennis on the large roof of the house, so they didn't go out of the house that frequently.

I also got the impression that it must be hard for them to be religious educators for their children, although they clearly feel it is important. It is not easy to encourage children to pray five times a day, especially a teen-age boy who doesn't see his peers doing the same. It sounds like at least two of the prayers can be rather long. I wonder if Fome ever questions these traditions?

One day we did talk about fasting during Ramadan, and he said he had to refuse some snacks because they might have pork products in them. Because there are a few other Muslim students in school, I suppose that fasting is not seen as quite as extraordinary as if he were the only one.

February 24

June came in this afternoon to tell me that Fome and his family may be leaving to go back to Pakistan for awhile! Apparently, Mr. Qureshi's father is quite ill and they are concerned about him. The family feels that they should all return to Pakistan.

It seems so pointless to take the children out of school after just 6 months and then possibly return 6 months later. I checked with the guidance office and, apparently, on the middle school level there's no minimum number of days that he must complete to move to the next grade. However, academics are certainly adversely affected by poor attendance. Right now, Fome seems to be making real progress. I doubt that he wants to leave. June says his sisters want to stay, too.

What should I do? In some ways I can't do anything. The Qureshis might not appreciate my interfering in family affairs. I'm not sure how well I would be able to communicate my feelings to them. Perhaps I should call Mrs. Mukherjee, explain some of the problems, and suggest that they stay if possible. Would he be able to enroll immediately in Pakistan or would he miss time there as well? Just when it seems Fome is getting used to American schools and culture, he's going to have to go through reverse culture shock in Pakistan. If only I could at least convince them to stay until June. Maybe by then things would seem more hopeful and the Qureshis would see the benefits of staying in America.

DISCUSSION QUESTIONS

1. What problems does Fome face in gaining an education in the United States?
2. What beliefs do Fome's parents have regarding education and religion that conflict with the teacher's beliefs?
3. As Fome tries to acculturate, what conflicts does he face in school and at home?
4. What are Fome's rights in school in terms of his religion?
5. What goals for educating Fome will Fome, his parents, and school be able to agree on?
6. To what degree and on what issues should the teacher try to influence Fome and his parents?

REFERENCES

American-Arab Anti-Discrimination Committee. (1993). *Teachers' resources on the Middle East.* Washington, DC: Author (ERIC Document Reproduction Service No. ED 363 531).

American Jewish Congress. (n.d.). Religion in the public schools: A joint statement of current law. Retrieved October 21, 2001 from http://ajcongress.org/clsa/clsarips.htm

Associated Press. (2000, June 19). Supreme Court refuses to review evolution-disclaimer case. Retrieved November 7, 2000, from http://www.freedomforum.org/news/2000/06/2000-06-19-10.asp.

Barlow, E. (Ed.). (1994). Evaluation of secondary-level textbooks for coverage of the Middle East and North Africa (3rd ed). Ann Arbor, MI/Tucson, AZ: Middle East Studies Association/Middle East Outreach Council.

Belluck, P. (2000, August 3). Evaluation foes dealt a defeat in Kansas vote. *New York Times,* P. A1.

Breuilly, E., O'Brien, J., & Palmer, M. (1997). *Religions of the world: The illustrated guide to origins, beliefs, tradition, and festivals.* New York: Facts on File.

Curtiss, R. H., Alamoudi, A., Johnson, J. W., & Reda, H. (1999). Symposium: American Muslims and U.S. foreign policy. *Middle East Policy, 7*(1), 1.

Gearan, A. (2001, October 30). High court favors silence rule. *Kingston Freeman,* p. D5.

Glanz, J. (2000, March 11). Survey finds support is strong for teaching 2 origin theories. *New York Times,* p. A1.

Goldhaber, G. (1996). Religious belief in America: A new poll. *Free Inquiry, 16*(3), 34–41.

Gollnick, D. M., & Chinn, P. C. (1997). *Multicultural education in a pluralistic society* (5th ed.). Englewood Cliffs, NJ: Prentice-Hall.

Haynes, C. C. (1999). Religion in the public schools. *School Administrator, 56*(1), 6–10.

Jurinski, J. J. (1998). *Religion in the schools: A reference handbook.* Santa Barbara, CA: ABC-CLIO.

Kaplan, G. R. (1994). Shotgun wedding: Notes on public education's encounter with the new Christian Right. *Phi Delta Kappan, 75*(9), K1–K12.

Kelahan, B., & Penn, M. (Eds.). (1996). Spotlight on the Muslim Middle East—Crossroads. A student reader and teacher's guide. New York: American Forum for Global Education (ERIC Document Reproduction Service No. ED 415 144).

Lane Education Service District. (1996). An educator's handbook for teaching about religion in public schools. Eugene, OR: Lane Education Service District (ERIC Document Reproduction Service No. ED 401 638).

Learning, J. (1999, August 19). Education, civil rights groups mount efforts to save evolution science. *The Freedom Forum Online.* Retrieved November 11, 2000, from http://www.freedomforum.org/religion/1999/8/19ksevolution.asp.

Matsumura, M. (1999). A new tactic for getting creation science into classrooms? *Reports of the National Center for Science Education, 19*(3), 24–26.

National Academy of Sciences. (1998). *Teaching about evolution and the nature of science.* Washington, DC: National Academy Press.

National Association of Biology Teachers. (1997). Statement on teaching evolution. Retrieved November 15, 2000, from http://www.nabt.org/evolution.html.

National Center for Science Education Recommended Policy Statement on Science and Education. (1999). *Reports of the National Center for Science Education, 19*(2), 23.

Nawa, F. (2001, September 12). Hiding in Brooklyn: Afghan American fears for safety. *AlterNet.* Retrieved September 13, 2001, from http://www.alternet.org/story.html?StoryID=11482.

Noor Al-Deen, H. S. (1991). Arab-Americans and the Gulf crisis. Paper presented at the Annual Meeting of the Southern Communication Association, Tampa, FL (ERIC Document Reproduction Service No. ED342 025).

Nord, W. A. (1995). *Religion and American education: Rethinking a national dilemma.* Chapel Hill: University of North Carolina Press.

Nord, W. A. (1999). Science, religion, and education. *Phi Delta Kappan, 81*(1), 28–33.

Ostling, R. N. (1999). America's ever-changing religious landscape [Electronic version]. *Brookings Review, 17*(2), 10(1).

Palmer, P. J. (1998–1999). Evoking the spirit in public education. *Educational Leadership, 56*(4), 6–11.

Power, C. (1998, March 16). The new Islam. *Newsweek,* 35–37.

Public Broadcasting System (2001). Evolution: A journey into where we're from and where we're going. Retrieved October 21, 2001, from http://www.pbs.org/wgbh/evolution.

Riley, R. W. (1998). *Secretary's statement on religious expression.* Retrieved November 7, 2000, from http://ed.gov/Speeches/08–1995/religion.html.

Sachs, S. (1998, November 10). Muslim schools in U.S. a voice for identity. *New York Times,* pp. A1, B10.

Scherer, M. M. (Ed.). (1998–1999). The spirit of education. *Educational Leadership, 56*(4).

Schwartz, W. (1999). *Arab American students in public schools* (ERIC Digest, No. 142). New York: ERIC Clearinghouse on Urban Education (ERIC Document Reproduction Service No. ED 429 144).

Sewall, G. T. (1999). Religion comes to school. *Phi Delta Kappan, 81,* 10–26.

Shabbas, A. (Ed.). (1998). *Arab world studies notebook.* Berkeley, CA: Arab World and Islamic Resources and School Services.

Sizer, T. R., & Sizer N. F. (1999). Grappling. *Phi Delta Kappan, 81,* 184–190.

Southern Poverty Law Center. (2001). Tolerance in the news: Americans vs. Americans. Retrieved October 19, 2001, from http://tolerance.org/news/article_tol.jsp?id=275.

Warikoo, N., Capeloto, A., Askari, E., & Kresnak, J. (2001, September 14). Anxiety in Michigan: Arabs and those who look like them face hate. *Detroit Free Press.* Retrieved October 19, 2001, from http://freep.com/news/nw/terror2001/arab14_20010914.htm.

Weiss, A. M. (1995). The society and its environment. In P. R. Blood (Ed.), *Pakistan: A country study* (pp. 75–146). Washington, DC: Library of Congress.

Williams, P. W. (2000). Plus ca change: Has American religion changed during the past century? *Cross Currents, 50*(1–2), 264–276.

Wisenfeld, L. P. (Ed.). (2000). *The world almanac.* Mahway, NJ: World Almanac Books.

INDEX

Ability grouping, 23–24
Absenteeism among homeless children, 191
Academic achievement. *See also* Educational progress of diverse learners
  of females in mathematics, 214
  levels of diverse learners, 21–22
  meaning and value associated with, 219–20
  poverty and, 193, 220–21
  of students with disabilities, inclusion and, 160
Acceleration, academic, 164, 169
Access to services, 55
Accommodation, 7
Accountability in plan of action, 76
Acculturation, 7–8
  of Hmong, 137
Achievement, academic. *See* Academic achievement
Action approach to integrating ethnic content, 30
Adaptability, family, 54
Additive approach to integrating ethnic content, 30
Additive bilingualism, 130
AD/HD. *See* Attention-deficit/hyperactivity disorder (AD/HD)
Administrators
  demographics of, 14
  principals, xxiii, 14
Adolescence, racial identity in, 106
Adolescence stage in family life cycle, 56
Adulthood stage in family life cycle, 56
Advanced placement courses
  availability of, 221
  enrollment of diverse students in, 22
Advisory Commission on Gay and Lesbian Youth, 230
Affective variables, females in mathematics and, 216–17
Afghan Americans, 256
African Americans
  black Muslims, 264
  gay, 227
  migration to the South, 10
  racial identity development in, 106
  use of term, xxiv
African American students
  books for or about, 34
  classroom discourse patterns with, 39
  communication style with, 131
  demographic changes and, 8–9

equity issues for, 216
female, in mathematics, 213, 222–24
  case involving, 233–38
  problems faced by, 223–24
  programs to encourage, 223
in gifted programs
  family involvement and, 164
  underrepresentation of, 163
high school completion rate of, 24
math scores of, 20
reading scores of, 18–19
science scores of, 21
in special education, disproportionate representation in, 111, 157, 158
teacher expectations of, 216
writing scores of, 19
Age, poverty rate by, 189–90
Aid to Families with Dependent Children (AFDC), 194
Algebra Project, 35
Alternatives, search for, 73, 74–76
  in migrant student case, 92–94
American-Arab Anti-Discrimination Committee, 266
American Association of University Women Report, 214
American Civil Liberties Union, 261, 262
American Forum for Global Education, 266
American Indian, use of term, xxv
American Indian and Alaska Native, use of term, xxiv. *See also* Native Americans
American Psychiatric Association, 228
American sign language (ASL), 126
Anthropology, educational, 28, 29
Arab Americans, Muslim, 264
  counteracting possible harassment of, 265–66
  hate crimes against, 255
Arab World and Islamic Resources and School Services, 266
"Areas of strength," notion of male and female, 214
Asian, use of term, xxiv
Asian Americans, 134–39
  cultural patterns shared by, 136
  Hmong culture, 136–39
    case involving, 150–53
  model minority myth and, 135–36
  overrepresentation in gifted programs, 163
  subgroups, 134–35
Asian-Pacific Islanders
  high school completion rate of, 24

model minority myth and, 135–36
overrepresentation in gifted programs,
163
subgroups, 134–35
dominant culture in U.S., 125
implications for education, 129–31
bilingual education, 24–25, 34–35, 93,
99, 130
communication style, 130–31
language, defined, 125–27
Native American mascots, 131–34
case involving, 139–50
orientations toward differences, 127–29
deficiency orientation, 127–28
difference orientation, 128
political orientation, 128–29
Culture of poverty, 188
Curriculum, xxii
inappropriate, as barrier to learning, 26–27
integrating multiple worlds, 26, 27
modifications for gifted students, 165
multicultural education and
approaches to curriculum reform, 29–32
infused in curriculum, 97
sexual orientation issues and, 230–31

Deafness, 126
Decision making. *See* Case Decision-Making
Scaffold
Deculturalization, 133
Deficiency orientation toward cultural and
linguistic differences, 127–28
Deficit perspective on parental involvement,
50
Demographic changes
immigration patterns and, 8–14
in central cities, 8–10
in schools, 8–9, 11–14
religious belief in U.S. and, 263
Dental health, 195
Desegregation, 118
Developmental milestones, cultural
differences in, 58
Dewey, John, 23
Dialects, 126
Difference orientation toward cultural and
linguistic diversity, 128
Disabilities, individuals with, xxv
creating inclusive schools for, 161–62
IDEA and, 156–57, 159, 167
SSI benefits for, 194
students in special education by disability,
157, 158
Discipline practices, cultural differences in,
58
Discourse patterns. *See also* Communication
classroom, 38–39
differences in, 131

Discrimination
family experience of, 51
against GLBT youth, 224–25
placement in special education as form of,
157
racism and, 110
Discussion of cases
ground rules for, 79
methods of, 77–79
value of, 70–72
District task force to examine resources and
programs, establishing, 97
Diversity. *See also* Culture and language,
issues of; Race and ethnicity
meaning of, xx–xxi
as norm in inclusive schools, 161–62
terminology related to, xxiii–xxv
Diversity class of admissions in IMMACT, 5–6
Dropout rate, high school, 24
poverty and, 193
Dropping out of mathematics, gender pattern
for, 217
Drug Enforcement Administration, 167
Dysconscious racism, 133

Early childhood stage in family life cycle, 56
Economic disparities among countries,
international migration and, 3
"Ecosystem for youth," 55, 56
Educational anthropology, 28, 29
Educational attainment of parents, poverty
and, 190
Educational progress of diverse learners,
17–25
achievement levels, 21–22
bilingual education and, 24–25
in high-poverty schools, 22–23
high school completion, 24
in mathematics, 19–20
in reading, 18–19
in science, 21
tracking and, 23–24
in writing, 19
Edward v. *Aguillard*, 261
Effort, gender and attribution of
success/failure to, 217
Elementary school years stage in family life
cycle, 56
Emotional resources, poverty and, 187
Emotions, framing stage of decision making
and, 74
Employment, poverty and, 190
Employment Non-Discrimination Act, 230
English
comparison of Spanish language and, 129
fluency in, xx
proficiency in, of parents, 59–60
Standard, 126